"The wisdom of Dr. Riley can help ... fy your ... life without purpose is a life waste.."

—SIR JOHN M. TEMPLETON, founder,
Templeton group of mutual funds

"For both personal and professional growth, read this book!"

—PAUL "KINKO" ORFALEA,
founder/chairperson, Kinko's, Inc.

"Building on the heritage of a highly responsible family business, the author distills and accents the common sense of three prime personal principles whose application (a) casts each of us by self-initiative as a leader whose (b) achievement will abound from uncompromising trustworthiness while (c) emphasizing 'the positive.' "

—ROBERT W. GALVIN, chairman of the
Executive Committee, Motorola, Inc.

"A commonsense approach to career and job management with a creative twist. . . . A new slant on some of the buzzwords we've all come to take for granted—contribution, goals, empowerment—and reminds us of their relevance to success in a fresh light.

. . . also touch[es] on many of the everyday roadblocks to motivation and productivity, and while stressing the importance of leadership and example-setting in removing or lessening those roadblocks, the message is also one that emphasizes the responsibility to oneself in determining and reaching goals."

—JOHN G. SPERLING, founder and CEO of the
Apollo Group and the University of Phoenix

continued . . .

"I've been using Mary's Three Rules ever since I heard them from her about ten years ago. They are profound in the way they cut through matters to get to the heart of things. Furthermore, Mary's alignment process (the Personal Growth Plan) is a most amazing process. I have used it extensively now for most of the last ten years, and it always produces good results. The process guides people to the promised land of strengthened relationships and heightened productivity. It truly works!"

—JOHN DIETZ, CAO, Miller Valentine Group

"Mary Riley has done it again! Her latest book, *Leadership Begins With You*, should be read by every serious businessperson. Mary understands corporate structure and she knows exactly what it takes to change a job into a career. Her sound principles unite with her profound respect for workers at all levels to produce a work that has the potential to change the face of business—and to change your life."

—MARY MANIN MORRISSEY, senior minister and
author of *Building Your Field of Dreams*

"We have been applying the tools that Mary introduced to us twelve years ago, and we can't say enough about the enthusiasm from both management and staff. They have helped define relationships as well as making all of us more productive. We've grown from 100 million to 760 million in assets during that time."

—TOM SARGENT, CEO, First Technology Credit Union

"*Leadership Begins With You* is the result of impressive effort, research, and knowledge devoted to the subject of leadership. It provides valuable insights that will benefit mid-managers who wish to assume meaningful positions of leadership in their respective organizations.

Leadership Begins With You can be a highly useful source of information for those individuals who are serious about their personal leadership development."

—STANLEY C. GAULT, retired chairman and CEO,
of Goodyear Tire and Rubber Company and of Rubbermaid, Inc.

Most Perigee Books are available at special quantity discounts for bulk purchases for sales promotions, premiums, fund-raising, or educational use. Special books, or book excerpts, can also be created to fit specific needs.

For details, write: Special Markets, The Berkley Publishing Group, 375 Hudson Street, New York, New York 10014.

Leadership Begins With You

3 Rules to Transform Your Job Into a Career

MARY MORGAN RILEY, PH.D.

A Perigee Book

A Perigee Book
Published by The Berkley Publishing Group
A division of Penguin Putnam Inc.
375 Hudson Street
New York, New York 10014

Copyright © 2001 by Mary Riley, Ph.D.
Cover design by Dawn Velez Le'Bron
Text design by Tiffany Kukec

First edition: April 2001

Published simultaneously in Canada.

The Penguin Putnam Inc. World Wide Web site address is
http://www.penguinputnam.com

Library of Congress Cataloging-in-Publication Data

Riley, Mary, 1946–
    Leadership begins with you : 3 rules to transform your job into a career / Mary Riley.
        p.   cm.
    Includes index.
    ISBN 0-399-52653-6
    1. Leadership.   2. Organizational behavior.   3. Career development.   I. Title.
HD57.7 .R55   2001
650.1—dc21   00-061145

Printed in the United States of America

10 9 8 7 6 5 4 3 2 1

Dedication

To

- My mother, *Margaret Clark Morgan,* for quietly and gently living the 3 Rules every day without even knowing it.

- My father, *Burton Morgan,* for showing me that building a profitable business can be fun.

- My three children, for still applying the 3 Rules in our family life after all these years:

  Mark, with respectful humor
  Keith, with everpresent integrity
  Brooke, with loving strength

- *Captain Steve,* for his contagious clear thinking

- *Jo-Anne Kennedy,* for her miraculous typing of this book and her cheerful professionalism

- *Peter Drucker,* for his empowering advisorship on my Ph.D. committee.

- . . . to all the clients, students, business partners, associates, and friends who have also been sources for this book:

Jo, Robyn, Eileen, Jack, Wang, Ron, Bill, Gil, Tom, David, Hal, Rich, Allejandro, Judy, Tina, Omid, Elham, Dorothy, John, Theresa, Steve, Andy, Sam, Raul, Trieu, Lap, Phil, Tommy, Kay, Mike, Tim, Pat, Karen, Sharon, Mary, Frank, Mary Ellen, Chris, Don, Debi (my editor) and Sheila (my publisher)

Contents

Introduction: Origin of the Rules   ix

1. Take Charge! You Are the
   CEO of Your Own Career   1

2. Why Companies Need the Three Rules   16

3. Rule 1: Everyone Contributes   31

4. What a Contribution Is—and Isn't   50

5. Achieving Mutual Contribution   67

6. Rule 2: No Put-downs   95

7. The Power of No Put-downs   115

8. Transforming Put-downs into
   Responsible Communication   129

9. Rule 3: Keep Agreements   151

10. The Power of Keeping Your Agreements   169

11. Creating Agreements That Work   181

12. Successfully Introducing the
    Three Rules to Your Workgroup   203

13. Generating Buy-in to the Rules   222

14. Jump-starting the Rules with a
    Three Rules Performance Appraisal System:
    The "Professional Growth Plan"   237

15. Second Opinion: A Tool for Inner Wisdom   254

16. Why Mid-Managers and Employees Need
    the Rules Now and in the Future   274

Appendix of Tools   295
Notes   337
Bibliography   343
Index   349

Introduction:

Origin of the Rules
HOW & WHY the Rules came about

W HOEVER hates rules the most has to design them. That would be me.

What qualified me as the rule designer was not that I was good at follow-ing rules; it was that I had been a lifelong rebel against rules. On reflection, I realized it was not the rules I was rebelling against, it was the abuse of power that repulsed me. Since some rules came from dominators, I reacted defiantly to all rules until I learned to distinguish between helpful and abu-sive ones.

My gentle and kind mother could attest to this. While she acted as leader of my Girl Scout troop, I led the rebellious crowd in the back of the room. We strongly disagreed with every Girl Scout rule and were fearless in expressing our dislikes. By eighth grade, I had recruited one of my best friends Tina, to accompany me on private cigarette breaks behind the bushes. Together we were labeled by the adults in authority as the group rebels. My parents tried grounding me, but nothing convinced me to stick to the rules. The worst, though, was the abuse I dished out to substitute teachers, whose presence seemed to ignite my passion for pranks.

Throughout my adolescence, I burned with the urge to break the rules, particularly when it came to parking. I called it my loading zone routine, and it was one of my favorites. I would drive up to the entrance of a down-town restaurant, park in the loading zone, and open the trunk of the car. Then I would walk inside and enjoy a leisurely meal. Finally, feeling satisfied with the wonderful meal and the delicious deviation from the rules, I would walk out, close the trunk, and drive away. Fortunately, I never had anything stolen.

Second only to my loading zone prank was my frequent failure to abide by the stop sign rule. After all, why stop when there are no other cars in sight, right? I've got to admit, the police didn't see things quite the same way and rightly so. Rule breaking can be dangerous. Eventually, these two activities plus speeding and illegal U-turns qualified me as a regular at traffic school.

By the sixth traffic school I attended, the whole thing became a joke. I even enrolled in the "comedy traffic school" course. Two-thirds of the way into the eight-hour session, I persuaded the instructor to show us how to avoid getting a ticket for failure to make a complete stop at a stop sign. All we had to do was make it look like we stopped when we didn't.

"No problem," the instructor said with a grin. "As you approach the stop sign, slow down, bob your head forward, and then suddenly jerk it back. This will make it look like you came to a complete stop even though you didn't."

At first, I sat there practicing over and over again the jerky head bob, guaranteed, I thought, to give the impression that a moving car had stopped. The whole exercise bordered on the ridiculous, and before long I started to laugh uncontrollably. It finally occurred to me: Mary, how about just stopping at the stop sign instead of practicing all this head bobbing? The pleasure of rebellion just wasn't worth all the bother.

Laughing at this childish act of self-sabotage was a long-overdue breakthrough for me. I realized that drivers had a subtle, unwritten agreement to follow the driving rules. The idea that rules could be for *everyone's* best interest was intoxicating to me. Every time cars pulled to the right side of the road to allow a passing ambulance to proceed, I was touched by our connection as synergistic drivers. Soon, what was learned in my personal experiences spilled over into my business endeavors. The door of opportunity had been opened wide, and I was about to discover the beauty of implementing universally empowering rules in the workplace.

When and Where the Rules Came About

I discovered the 3 Rules first through fear, then through a consistent pattern of group synergy. The 3 Rules were formulated about twenty years ago when I was puzzling over how to handle a tough teaching assignment. I was a fresh Peter Drucker–taught Ph.D., hired as an instructor at the University of Southern California. As I was preparing for my first master's-level teaching job, I worried that I was in over my head. The master's program was filled with police officers, and many faculty members were intimidated by the officers' uniforms and guns.

I wanted to replace my fears and anxieties with a positive image, so a few nights before class I mentally pictured the class just the way I hoped it would be. When this mythical class seemed to be running at optimum performance, I wrote a description of what was happening. Three issues stood out in my mind: (1) everyone was contributing; (2) there were no put-downs; and

(3) all of the students were following instructions. It was then that I decided to try out these positive activities as ground rules for the class. To support these 3 rules, I would base 25 percent of the students' grades on their adherence to the Three Rules while in class.

On the first day of class, I passed out a syllabus stating the ground rules and asked for a show of hands: How many students would be willing to abide by these three rules during the course? All but one of the students raised their hands. I asked the "rebel" why he had not raised his hand, and he explained that he would not be willing to follow instructions blindly. I explained the nature of the instructions again to make sure he understood, but he still refused.

Fortunately, there was an evening class in the same building, so I withdrew him from my class and helped him enroll in one more suited to his needs. It wasn't an angry or resentful withdrawal. Instead, we immediately established that he deserved to work under agreements he could keep and I deserved to start out with agreements everyone in class would be willing to adhere to. I decided to practice the Three Rules myself. It was important to me not to criticize him or put him down for his refusal, or to act as if he were wrong. So there were no snide comments or raised eyebrows—just a transfer.

The rest of the class meetings were exciting and productive. Strangely enough, I attributed this positive outcome to the uplifting atmosphere at USC and the enthusiasm of the law enforcement officers attending the class. It simply didn't occur to me that the Three Rules had much to do with our success that year.

In addition to teaching, I became director of training operations for Xerox Learning Systems, charged with developing curriculum and conducting seminars on leadership, team building, and performance review. Again, I incorporated my three ground rules, and the classes went exceedingly well. During the first course we presented at a steel-refining plant, the man-hours per ton decreased from 113 to 101—the kind of significant improvement that very quickly shows up on a balance sheet. As before, I assumed these results were attributable to the Xerox curriculum not the Three Rules.

In 1982 Xerox closed our division. Shortly afterward, I acquired the rights to the Xerox research and expanded Xerox's performance review into what became the professional Growth Plan™ Program. For seven years my colleagues and I taught the materials to hundreds of groups, wrote articles, continued our research and answered requests from all over the country for information about our system. During this process, Rule 3, which was "follow instructions," evolved into "keep agreements."

We'd come a long way in just a few short years. By 1990 I began my speech at a Total Quality Management Conference with the 3 Rules. The session was synergistic and productive, surpassing my highest expectations. In 1992 I was one of the keynote speakers at the American Society for Quality Control's (ASQC) national conference. Much to my surprise, I was voted best overall speaker. I believed other speakers were more technologically oriented and certainly better known than I, so why did I get the award?

Then the light went on. It was because of the rules. When all five hundred people at the session agreed to contribute, not to put anyone down, and to keep all agreements, they became synergized. They were 100 percent present, connected, and alive. I may not have felt like the best speaker that day, but the Three Rules were a way for the audience to be the best audience. It was then I realized that for twenty years the Three Rules had been what made the difference in my personal and professional environment.

By 1999 I was using the Three Rules with every client, meeting less resistance and more immediate acceptance. A culture developed in high-tech, "new economy" companies that seemed hungry for the Three Rules. As managers were asking for simpler ways to manage chaos, we developed the Mid-managers Toolbox to implement the Three Rules (see the appendix).

Finally, by the year 2000, I was assigned to teach two M.B.A. technology courses. Since I was no technology whiz, I agreed to be the class facilitator, not the expert. Half of the students in the classes were from the United States and half from outside the United States, but they were all recognized experts in their fields. Approximately the same percentage—half—represented high-tech companies like Cisco Systems, Agilent Technologies, GTE Mobilnet, Cellular One, Advanced Fiber Communications, Motorola, Apple Computer, and JDS Uniphase. The others were from "old economy" companies—Pacific Lumber, State Farm Insurance, General Electric, Charles Schwab, and various public agencies. It was a perfect testing ground. As I had done for twenty years, I based one-quarter of their grade on their ability to adhere to the Three Rules during class.

The group was profoundly synergistic. They were doing original research to discover how to manage effectively in the global culture spawned by the Internet Revolution. Since the textbooks were already outdated and we needed some common assignments, the students asked to implement the Three Rules in their workplaces and report back. What they reported is woven throughout this book. Examples include using the Three Rules to handle workplace violence, bargaining for huge raises and stock options, and finding ways to contribute existing talents. Students said it cleared the path for them to develop emotionally intelligent leadership skills during this technological explosion known as the Internet era. That's when I realized it was time to write a book and pass these new leadership skills on to you.

Take Charge! You Are the CEO of Your Own Career

When you rule your mind, you rule the world.

—JOHN TEMPLETON

As more and more organizations become technology- and information-based, they are transforming themselves into responsibility-based organizations in which every member must act as a responsible decision-making leader. All members have to see themselves as executives.

—PETER F. DRUCKER

WHETHER we like it or not, the twenty-first century has brought us to what John Chambers, CEO of Cisco Systems, calls "the Internet Revolution." Much like the Industrial Revolution two hundred years ago, the Internet Revolution is dramatically changing the workplace, the work, and the global economy. The new revolution began very quietly. Most people thought the Internet would be delivered to homes via television, but that commercial direction was almost totally bypassed, for in 1994 Netscape came on the scene. The Internet Revolution that quickly followed escaped the notice of many of high tech's most prominent leaders—including Microsoft and Hewlett-Packard. Peter Drucker reminds us "Your first and foremost job as a leader is to take charge of your own energy."[1]

According to Dr. Patricia Wiklund in *Taking Charge When You're Not in Control,* taking charge means doing what you can do now rather than waiting for the situation to change. No use expecting the other person to act or a white knight to come to the rescue. Taking charge means taking action—finding a purpose in life, creating a mission, setting goals, and reaching those goals regardless of whether or not there is an Internet Revolution.[2]

Theresa, a project manager at Motorola, represents the Internet Revolution mid-manager. She lives in Arizona while coordinating her workgroup in Illinois. She has not met most of her workgroup and may never do so. Both Theresa and each member of the workgroup must manage themselves to investigate and recommend possible mergers and acquisitions that will be successful for Motorola. They communicate daily and hourly via a wireless "Barbie computer" that acts as pager, phone, computer, and E-mail all in one. They send and receive data in minutes. "Much faster," says Theresa, "than days of leaving paperwork in someone's in-basket and waiting until they got around to responding."

Who it is that Theresa is working with and what she is working on are not actually visible. She and each member of her project team have become what Peter Drucker has coined as "responsibility-based leaders."[3] Whatever your work involves, you are going to find yourself in need of new management skills: skills that will ensure your success in the Internet Revolution. We can no longer assume that high tech's prominent leaders will lead us; we must lead ourselves.

In order to make the most of these times—to capitalize on them rather than just cope with them—each person needs to realize that he or she is an integral part of the success or failure of the organization. Yours is not "just a job." Regardless of your job title, you are the CEO of your own franchise: your life. To be a success at the end of the day, you must take responsibility for exploring opportunities and implementing guidelines that will create and foster both personal and professional satisfaction.

Defining CEO

To be your own CEO is to be a Creative, Entrepreneurial Opportunist. Unfortunately, in our culture, the term "opportunist" has come to connote something negative: someone who takes advantage of others' weaknesses or shortcomings. What Drucker says, and I concur, is that in today's competitive environment, we must all be opportunists for our own career growth and happiness. Whether you currently manage a staff of many or are an employee aspiring to a managerial position, you have the personal freedom to be responsible for the job satisfaction you feel at the end of the day. Your satisfaction can ensure your financial success, but achieving job satisfaction requires you to be both creative and entrepreneurial.

This is not the first time a century started out with the need for you to be your own CEO. In John D. Rockefeller's memoir a hundred years ago, he offered this creative, opportunistic entrepreneurial advice:

> The fundamental thing in all [successful careers] is . . . if people can be educated to help themselves, we strike at the root of many of the evils of the world. This is the fundamental thing, and it is worth saying. If I were to give advice to a young man starting out in life, I should say to him: If you aim for a large, broad-gauged success, do not begin your business career, whether you sell, you labor or are an independent producer, with the idea of getting from the world by hook or crook all you can.
>
> In the choice of your business employment, let your first thought be: Where can I fit in so that I may be most effective in the work of the world? Where can I lend a hand in a way most effectively to advance the general interest? Choose your vocation in that way and you have taken the first step on the highest road to a large success.
>
> THE MAN WILL BE MOST SUCCESSFUL WHO CONFERS THE GREATEST SERVICE ON THE WORLD.
>
> The penalty of a selfish attempt to make the world confer a living without contributing to the progress or happiness of mankind is generally a failure to the individual.
>
> The pity is that when he goes down, he *instills* heartache and misery also on others who are in no way responsible.[4]

It's easy to be told, "contribute to the workplace," but how do we know what contributes in the midst of the Internet Revolution? How do we successfully ride the roller-coaster economy and revamp an ever-changing corporate environment in which NASDAQ may plummet one trillion dollars in a month? One step at a time—that's how. First, let's target the workplace.

Achieving Contribution in Today's Workplace

Contribution is achieved through clean management. Every problem within an organization must have a clean, simple, agreed-upon way to be managed. "Clean" means without strings, games, favoritism, or politics.

While today's corporate wisdom is often "lean and mean"—and this can be an advantage in the marketplace—today's companies also need internal strength and harmony to create cutting-edge performance. Thus, lean, mean, and *clean* reflects a solid corporate culture that has great staying power in a crisis.

What I have found in my work with hundreds of corporations is that a successful business—a successful manager—balances financial health with mental health. This concept of balance is something that cannot be factored in on a profit-and-loss statement, but it does exist. When a number of seemingly intangible factors are present, a firm will be profitable. Those factors may not show up in a columned spreadsheet, but they substantially contribute to the overall success of the individual *and* the company.

How can these intangibles be measured? When both manager and employee are able to articulate what constitutes quality of product and quality of life; when you have an agreement, you have balance—and a highly successful organization.

Beyond the Bottom Line

Intangibles not only affect attitude, they also have everything to do with dollars and cents. Corporations seeking to improve their bottom line have the most to gain by consciously implementing these intangibles. As a culture, we understand "better, faster, cheaper"; it's the mantra of hundreds of businesses. What we have difficulty with is accessing what will motivate us to achieve those goals. I have found that motivation soars when the following seven factors are part of a "lean, mean, and clean" management machine.

1. Everyone contributes to the measurable success of the company.

2. The company adds value to some part of the general public.

3. Everyone treats others with respect and integrity, particularly in times of crisis.

4. Learning is valued and regularly emphasized—a key source of motivation.

5. Goals for quality and productivity are clearly stated, and a system is in place to ensure that they are met.

6. Stress occurs, but it can always be resolved cleanly and clearly through agreed-upon tools.

7. Each member of the organization keeps agreements with coworkers, customers, and vendors.

In such an environment, each person takes both personal and private responsibility for his or her negative emotions and sabotaging behavior. Managers and employees treat the workplace with respect, even when experiencing turmoil themselves. Keeping conflict out of the work environment allows employees to bring work problems to their managers' attention and allows managers the confidence to make specific and frequent requests of their employees. There is minimal gossip or placing blame if mistakes are made; instead, there is confidence about problem solving and positive communication. Degrading or derogatory remarks are not acceptable, and those who focus on what's wrong with people rather than what's wrong with the procedures are out of place. Mutual respect ensures that, at every level, people are rewarded for their contribution to the bottom line. Synergy is a common occurrence. Learning is fun.

The Three Rules for a Financially and Emotionally Healthy Workplace

Most business owners, executives, managers, and employees would like to be part of such a business. However, honing your workgroup or organization into a state where quality, productivity, and joy are the rule rather than the exception can seem an elusive goal. Even if everyone starts out on the right foot and has the best intentions, many things can—and do—go wrong. An ongoing, focused effort is needed to maintain high-level functioning. That's where the Three Rules for profit and integrity come in. Like modern business, the Three Rules for the mental and financial health of an organization are lean and clean:

Rule 1: Everyone Contributes

Rule 2: No Put-downs

Rule 3: Keep Agreements

At first glance these rules may appear simplistic, yet while some behaviors initially appear easy to change, lasting behavioral change is difficult to achieve. In the same way a diet seems easy the first day—or even the first week—making and keeping substantive lifestyle/eating changes is extremely difficult to accomplish. So, while "No Put-downs" may seem simple in the abstract and may even be easy to adhere to for a day or so, will it really be as simple when your manager garbles your figures in the next meeting? Will it be as effortless when your assistant accidentally cuts off your next important phone call?

Frankly, announcing rules is one thing; adhering to them is another.

Reading them on the page, on the bulletin board, or on the computer screen has a limited effect on lasting behavioral change. The *Leadership Begins With You* goal, then, is to adopt and internalize these rules until they become second nature. You will be addressing the "intangibles" and ensuring that they become an inherent part of your corporate culture. You will encounter exercises that will challenge the way you problem-solve with superiors and subordinates. You will learn strategies for refining and altering these tactics so that you can begin to function as your own CEO as well. When you are finished, you will be ready to take charge.

Simple, Powerful—and Definitely Not Easy

These Three Rules seem simple because they are simple. They are also extremely powerful; so powerful they can make profound changes in both the complex web of business organizations and the day-to-day functioning and happiness of every member of an organization. They have been tried and tested in scores of companies over a twenty-year period, from day-to-day corporate operations to training sessions, management courses, quality programs, executive retreats, and performance review systems. They have a positive effect on the success of any undertaking.

Though simple and powerful, the rules are not easy. In order to effect lasting change, we need not only to look at our company's goals or our employees' areas for growth, we also need to look long and hard at ourselves—something far easier said than done.

This important, introspective step is a crucial element to the success of the Three Rules because the Three Rules are not imposed from above. In addition, there is not a separate list of rules for executives. The Three Rules, like Robert's Rules of Order, require the cooperation of every person present, from the CEO to the mailroom attendant. They are effective because they level the playing field. Every person is required to follow these rules, even when it is uncomfortable. So, while they may seem somewhat understated and simple, they require a strong personal commitment from everyone involved in order to achieve success.

Rule 1 in Action: Everyone Contributes

The rule Everyone Contributes means just that—*everyone*. If one person does not contribute, it hurts the entire group. Some people pretend to contribute but don't. Others believe they are *not* contributing when they are—like Tony at Water Flo.

A water meter manufacturer, we'll call Water Flo, had sales of about $10 million. The three owners decided to grow the business, and they set a goal to more than triple its size. They were excited about their decision and called my firm for a supervisors' training class to teach leadership skills to their existing managers and growing numbers of management potentials. There I met Tony, who had been with the company for about twenty years. He was a capable supervisor but, in truth, he had given up on the idea that he could advance to a managerial position. His reasoning? "He wasn't the management type." Tony was often heard saying that he didn't want to be a leader. He tried once and it didn't work, so he had given up on the idea. Tony was a very capable supervisor and an intelligent man, but his negative attitude had caused him to view his work as "just a job."

We began the class by explaining the company's new ground rules—Everyone Contributes, No Put-downs, Keep Agreements—and applying them to seminar activities. When we used an exercise that defined each person's strength, Tony discovered he was "contributing, motivating, and powerful." At first he dismissed this as silly flattery. When he saw that everyone else's strengths had been accurately pinpointed, however, Tony had a breakthrough. He had never seen himself this way before. Not only was he an important cog in the wheel, but he had the ability to motivate and lead others to achieve their personal best as well.

"For twenty years, I just punched my time card. Then we had this class, where learning was actually fun. We set goals and I realized just how much I actually *do* contribute here. Now I want to go back to college and get a management degree." That's exactly what Tony did, and it changed his "just a job" attitude to one of "lead or get out of the way."

Realizing that his performance had the ability to triple the firm's financial goals made a big difference to Tony, and his contribution grew. Tony would probably get a salary increase as the firm expanded, but he never mentioned it as a motivating factor. His excitement came from transforming his job into a career. Like most people, Tony wasn't satisfied with a "punch in and punch out" type of job. He really wanted to contribute to what he now considered a worthwhile leadership career.

Sound familiar? Many of us have developed a resigned attitude toward our jobs and our potential to contribute to our workplace. Perhaps we tried to contribute and got burned, so now while we're working we are merely going through the motions. "Better to keep a low profile, do my job and head for the weekend. I'll be my real self outside of work." What we don't realize is that when we listen to this voice, we are not protecting ourselves. Rather, we are denying a fundamental part of ourselves: our self-respect. We are saying we can't possibly make a contribution here. But who knows our job better than we do? If we can't make a contribution here, who can?

In some cases this attitude may have been warranted. We may have made suggestions that were ignored or had run-ins with other personnel who were set in their ways. If this has been the case for you, don't despair. In situations where employees are apathetic or management's attitude appears disrespectful, there are often other coping strategies that you can adopt instead of giving up your dream of becoming an outstanding leader.

Rule 2 in Action: No Put-downs

"Put-down" has been defined by George Zimmer, president of Men's Warehouse, as "criticism without hope."[5] We all know the discouraging effect of a put-down directed at our self-esteem. It is also important to recognize the effect that put-downs have on morale when they are directed at those around us. Seemingly innocuous put-downs rob us and others of the information necessary to define contribution and ensure continuous improvement.

For instance, a well-established, ninety-person accounting firm had been in business for seventy-five years when it unexpectedly experienced a decline in business. It was a mystery as to why this should be happening. After all, the company had an outstanding reputation, a beautiful new building, the best accountants in the area, and branch offices in four rapidly growing nearby communities. Naturally, the people in the firm expected to be thriving in this environment, but instead business was falling off.

As in many established businesses, stagnation had set in. Resentments of one sort or another had built up and spread. Gossip and negative thinking were the order of the day. The firm's atmosphere had become so unpleasant that some of the best people, including its long-term partners, had quit. The remaining partners realized they had to improve quickly or die, and that was when they decided to call in the experts. They hired one consultant to conduct an all-day motivational seminar about positive thinking. Immediately following the seminar, everybody experienced a high for several days, but they had no tools with which to achieve lasting change. After a few days, everyone reverted to the old, unspoken ground rules of the firm:

1. Look for the negative in others.

2. Gossip whenever you can.

3. Never tell others what you want—let them guess. If their guess is incorrect, punish them.

Next, our firm was called in to present a six-week seminar called "Grow Your Practice." We began by telling the group the seminar would be conducted according to the Three Rules. Some of the people in the group were not too happy with the Three Rules—after all, they were experts in their field. What did the Three Rules have to do with them? They had no idea how enmeshed they were in their old modus operandi and how destructive it was, not only to the company but to themselves as well. During our six weeks together, it became obvious how difficult the No Put-downs rule was for them. Accountants, like many other professionals, are taught to look for mistakes and problems—both in the work of others and in their own. So when it came to dealing with colleagues and employees, professionals who were skilled at finding problems needed to be retrained to increase their contribution by recommending a solution for the problem. Otherwise, the situation just became another opportunity for put-downs.

A striking example of this occurred when a supervisor became aware of the negative impact of her fault-finding ways. She set a double goal for herself—if she liked what a coworker did, she was to compliment it. If she didn't, she was to privately write down what she would like to be changed and bring it to class. After two weeks of failure, she realized with chagrin that she didn't know how to begin. What also became evident was that her inability to compliment others or to make requests for change was severely hindering her own performance, since many people in her department had begun to thwart her power both overtly and covertly, though still in fear of her negative feedback. In our seminars, we began working with her and the others on ways to communicate what was working well and to offer specific suggestions for tasks and activities that desperately needed improvement. This was something very different from the usual criticism or put-downs for every perceived mistake.

You see; the reason for the No Put-downs rule is not a moral consideration. I believe that beneath 98 percent of all put-downs is a creative solution that can energize the employee and, if used correctly, grow the business. I have spent ten years collecting converted put-downs. I'd like to share with you how amazing it is to see what put-downs look like when they are converted to positive requests. Take a look at the following chart of converted put-downs:

Conversion from Most Common Put-downs of Middle Managers to . . .

Most Common Employee Requests of Middle Managers
Rule 2: No Put-downs, i.e., Convert All Put-downs into Complaints

Original Put-Down of the Middle Manager	What Do You Want Your Supervisor to Do for You?	What Will Your Supervisor Do?	What Would Be Different?	When Should It Happen?
He's a control freak.	Delegate more responsibility.	A. Put me in charge of the data area. B. Let me call for repairs. C. Let me train the new person.	Errors would drop below two per week.	By August 11
She makes me nervous every time she comes by.	Allow more independence.	A. Tell me the goal you want. B. Trust me to do it my way. C. Let me come to you if I need help.	I'd get the orders out by 5:30 each day.	By February 5
He's obsessed with the negative.	Give me more recognition.	A. Tell me when I have done a good job handling a customer complaint. B. Let me know when customers say they are pleased with my service. C. Include my name on reports I write.	I'd know the standard and thus satisfy customers sooner. You'll get no more than one complaint monthly.	By September 1
She has zero tact or communication skills.	Maintain better communications with me.	A. Meet with me in your office every Wednesday from 9:00 to 9:15 A.M. B. Discuss the items on my agenda. C. Let me know how I'm doing.	We'd get ISO 9000 certification by December 31.	By August 5
He expects people to just do the job with no training.	Supply me with more training.	A. Teach me more about our new rental equipment. B. Send me to the course at the local college. C. Get an extra manual for me.	I'd be more efficient with the equipment and more able to explain its use to others without calling you.	By March 21
She's so paranoid she doesn't trust anyone's opinion but her own.	Let me have more input on goals.	A. Include me when you write out biannual goals for my department. B. Ask me what timeline I see as realistic. C. Let me review goals before publishing.	I'd reach all my goals we agree to.	By April 26
He's a loose cannon with no respect for boundaries.	Go through the chain of command.	A. Talk to me before you discuss problems or requests with my group. B. If one of my employees comes to you with a problem, send him or her to me. C. Advise me of agreements you make with someone from my group.	I'd measure progress on an ongoing basis with my knowledge of activity by project members. We could get the product out under budget and on time.	By May 15
She is secretive about what is going on.	Keep me informed.	A. Keep me better informed about division and company-wide business. B. Let me attend the monthly meetings. C. Give me memos about issues that affect my department.	I'd meet my deadlines.	By June 6

Surprisingly, the entrepreneurial spirit lives beneath put-downs, and it is consistently and endlessly incredible to see the difference once put-downs are converted to requests.

Seem too good to be true? Perhaps. But consider the following: Imagine you have just attended a meeting where you didn't have all the facts you needed at your fingertips, but you managed to get a halfhearted response with your limited presentation. During the meeting your boss turned to the others and sarcastically commented, "I believe he's been partying too late on the weeknights." In that moment, you were once again the kid in trouble, the teenager who took the car without asking.

Even if the boss's sarcasm rang true, there was no need to publicly emphasize the poor performance. Most people know when they have bungled something. It's an effective leader who can find a way to talk about one's mistakes without degrading the employee. Imagine your reaction if he had privately said, "I admire your ability to think on your feet, but next time could you bring the client's file to the meeting so you have the information on hand?" Focusing on a solution, rather than on the poor performance, creates an environment more conducive to problem solving. While this may not always seem feasible—we'll always have those types of people who push us to our limits—developing the skills you need to help you to stay focused on the positive and facilitate solutions will keep everyone's self-respect intact.

Rule 3 in Action: Keep Agreements

A local hardware company had two stores. The original store was doing well, but the new store was having some problems. The problems seemed to center around the employees. Some of them had exhibited erratic behavior: one or two were known to be drinking in the store, and petty theft was becoming a common occurrence. Behavior and morale among the others were affected by having to work in an atmosphere of distrust and cover-up for the unreliable coworkers.

We began our seminar by explaining the Three Rules. One attendee named Larry was disruptive and unwilling to follow instructions. When I asked each participant to keep the three agreements, he said, "I'm not following no instructions."

"Think of baseball, Larry," I replied. "I know you realize you have to touch second base on the run around the bases—otherwise it's not baseball, right? We all need to follow the Three Rules at the seminar, otherwise we can't play ball and nothing gets accomplished."

However, Larry still refused to comply with the Three Rules of our session, so I asked him to leave the seminar. Because Larry was not able or willing to comply with the class's agreements or follow the rules, he could not benefit from the required training. Consequently, the store management was within their rights to discharge him without getting into a confrontation regarding his possible alcohol usage. (Drug and alcohol issues are often best resolved by focusing on a person's ability to follow instructions and perform the job rather than on suspected substance abuse.)

Many of us have found ourselves confronted with a "Larry" situation—or an instance of an underperforming colleague. Although we identify the problem, we often hesitate to take overt action. Instead, we begin to perform at less than 100 percent ourselves, justifying our behavior with such thoughts as, "Well, look at so-and-so. Coming in half an hour late isn't half as bad as drinking beer in the storeroom."

Having your coworkers adhere to Rule 3, Keep Agreements, can seem to be an impossible task. It's difficult to rouse a sense of personal responsibility in people whose morale has consistently been undermined by coworkers, particularly when the problem has been compounded by a "code of silence." In this environment, make yourself do the difficult—put yourself on the line and say, "I'm as guilty as the next guy of not performing at one hundred percent. I'm going to try. I'd like you to do the same." Nobody wants to be the first to point the finger at others' behavior or to jump headfirst into the deep end.

When we respond by keeping our agreements, as hard as it is to do sometimes, doing nothing is infinitely worse. When we do nothing, we damage our own morale as well as the morale of those around us. We want to be perceived as competent, professional, and motivated? But when we behave in a way that undermines that perception, we undermine our self-esteem as well as our job performance. In this era of global competition and ever-changing, fast-paced business, if we are not acting in emotionally intelligent ways as well as financially intelligent ways, we will be left behind.

Personal motivation is the key in Rule 3. It's impossible to talk to others about keeping agreements if you don't. Just by making a commitment to Rule 3, you are taking charge by choosing this rule: Keep Agreements. Recognizing that this begins with you is a fundamental first step. The next step is remaining motivated yourself and working to motivate others to strive to keep their word too. Transformational change begins one person at a time. You first. You are the CEO of your career.

Putting It All Together

The companies discussed above provide insight into the clarity and effectiveness of the 3 Rules and the importance of their application. They provide a template for everyone in a firm, from top executives to hourly wage earners. This template helps to achieve continuous improvement in the financial and mental health of the business.

The real bottom line in business is this: we are all our own managers and our own employees. If we are not constantly checking in with ourselves to ensure job contributions and fulfillment, if we are not continually looking for ways to enhance that fulfillment, then we are not leading. Results? We will be led elsewhere. In order to impress those around us with our ability to lead and to manage others, we need to increase our awareness of, commitment to, and passion for our role as CEO.

Implementing the Three Rules

The 3 Rules are flexible, dynamic, and designed to help individuals deal with the inner attitudes that prevent them from achieving peak performance. The rules can be used by companies to help everyone move in a positive, profitable direction. Although they are great team-building tools, the Three Rules can help individuals to stay on track with personal, departmental, and company goals as well. They will also help people to exercise strong self-discipline, convert complaints into positive requests, and make and keep agreements.

As a group leader, you can use the Three Rules to establish and communicate the goals of the company and the contributions you need from employees to meet those goals. The Three Rules will provide and support alternatives to put-downs and create well-balanced agreements between supervisors and employees, team members, vendors, and customers. Bottom line—the Three Rules drive out fear and liberate you to operate at your personal best, to affect your workplace and your career in a positive way, and to significantly enhance your professional growth.

A Template for Tomorrow

A good CEO (whether you are running a company or your own career) exemplifies the attributes of both an effective manager and a productive employee. Before focusing on our individual situations for being creative, entrepreneurial, and opportunistic, let's lay the groundwork.

While it is vitally necessary that you formulate your own definition of what constitutes an effective manager and a productive employee, the following list, based on my interactions with hundreds of employees of both large and small companies, may help you get started.

A good employee:

- contributes every day to the profit and quality of the company by supporting his/her supervisor's goals and requests

- refrains from put-downs; instead, makes requests and suggestions for improvement in ways that give others their dignity, give himself or herself job satisfaction, and give the company greater success

- keeps all agreements with his/her customers, coworkers, vendors, self, and the manager.

A good manager:

- contributes daily to the profit and quality of the company and respectfully listens to and acts upon the employees' requests while supporting the boss's goals

- refrains from put-downs; instead, makes requests and suggestions for improvement in ways that do not rob others of their dignity or diminish his or her own job satisfaction. He or she constantly engenders the company's greater success.

- keeps all agreements with customers, coworkers, vendors, himself or herself, **employees**, and the manager.

Employees and managers:

- contribute to the success of their organization and their careers

- take responsibility for their own resentments and hostilities

- convert put-downs into requests

- set personal goals to support the mission

- write down a personal mission statement

- keep agreements with others and themselves

- learn to manage themselves.

According to Peter Drucker in *Management Challenges for the Twenty-first Century*, the urgent call to action for 2000 and beyond is Managing oneself: "More and more people in the workforce—and most knowledge workers—will have to manage themselves. They will have to place themselves where they can make the greatest contribution; they will have to learn to develop themselves. They will have to learn to stay young and mentally alive during a fifty-year working life. They will have to learn how and when to change what they do, how they do it and when they do it."[6] His book offers ways to remedy bad habits and poor manners so as to get on with building strengths. The Three Rules and the tools you will find in this book are the vehicle to do what Drucker calls "manage oneself" and we call "lead oneself."

Taking Up the Gauntlet

As you continue to read *Leadership Begins with You*, think not only of the most creative, entrepreneurial, opportunistic ways to incorporate these rules into your life today, but also of how they will apply a year from now, five years, ten years, or even twenty years from now. Keep notes on what you have learned and consider how these tools can be used in many situations as you move up the corporate ladder. Rest assured, once you have made the commitment to yourself and your career, you will be on your way to fulfilling all the personal and professional goals you have set for yourself.

Why Companies Need the Three Rules

Wisdom is knowing what to do. Virtue is doing it.

—DAVID JORDAN, *Forbes* magazine

THE reason companies need the Three Rules can be explained by a scientific law of nature: the law of entropy. Entropy—the second law of thermodynamics in physics—states that "All things in the universe—animate and inanimate—lose energy over time." A more simplified definition is: all matter in the universe is always running down or all matter is always moving toward disorder.[1] Take a piece of land, for example. If you do nothing with it, it will usually fill with weeds—disorder. If you want the land to produce something, you follow simple rules: plant, fertilize, weed, and water. If you want it to keep producing, you plant, fertilize, weed, and water some more. Companies without rules are like bare, cleared land. Both are invitations to the law of entropy—to run down, to be taken over by weeds, erosion, or other undesirable intrusions.

Workplace people-entropy is a natural law of the universe, too. If you do nothing to prevent it, it will happen. Subtle workplace entropy could take the form of too many coffee breaks or procrastinating a little here or a lot there. Extreme workplace entropy is evidenced by violent, run-down, hopeless employees who eventually get fired, only to return to the office to shoot those they blame for their misfortune.

Rule 1—Everyone Contributes—can help to counter the law of entropy. Just marking time or hanging out does not contribute; it invites entropy. Since entropy is a universal law, action must be taken to reverse it. Growth of a company requires consistent, focused, contributing energy.

According to Peter Senge, author of *The Fifth Discipline: The Art and Practice of the Learning Organization*, "The purpose of all scientific laws is not the accumulation of knowledge, it's the creation of mental maps that bring constant participation between nature [entropy] and consciousness [business success]."[2]

Having rules like: (1) plant, (2) fertilize, (3) water gives a game plan or map of how to grow a successful garden. Having Three Rules like (1) Everyone Contributes, (2) No Put-downs, and (3) Keep Agreements provides leaders with a map of how to create a successful company.

The Three Rules Provide a Business Plan

A company is an association of persons carrying on a business. Companies are usually made up of people creating or collecting a product or performing a service. Business conducted by these companies is an activity that takes the majority of the time, attention, and effort of a person or group. Companies need the Three Rules because they need to structure the time, attention, and effort of their people and give them a map to follow that leads to profitability. If people wander around undirected, doing whatever they want, the chances that the company will make a profit are very slim. Mapped guidelines will ensure that the time, attention, and effort that each person contributes in add up to more than what is being taken out.

LESSONS FROM BEES

Bees automatically gather nectar, distribute pollen, create more bees, and make a new queen if one dies. No one has to tell the bees how to do this. A business apiarist, however, does have to provide a setting conducive to a healthy hive—good water, sturdy frames, a sizable opening to come and go, and blooming plants and flowers nearby. In short, the apiarist needs to provide the ideal environment for the bees to perform at their best so that the results (honey) will be of high quality and quantity.

Ten families joint-ventured a bee business on a tropical island in 1988. Given the projections of what 10,000 hives could produce, ten people invested $10,000 each, and a young manager, who was a relative of one of the investors, was hired. After three years the business had declined to 750 hives. The board assumed that the relative of the young manager was guiding him; the relative assumed that the young manager could lead himself. The time, attention, and effort of the new manager were not focused in a profitable direction, and thus the business failed.

The board, made up of family and friends, hesitated to interfere and hold the manager accountable to document, record, work every day, and run the apiary like a profitable business. The rules were unclear and everyone was trying to be polite. By the time three of the board members voluntarily stepped in and tried to institute objectives and weekly communication, entropy had already set in. As a result, the board got nothing for their investment. The manager felt he got nothing for his work and effort. Put-downs ensued, and soon the agreements faded, along with the business. By 1995 the company was defunct.

Five years later, a major hurricane went right through the exact place where the 100 remaining hives were located. I was there on the same tropical island after the hurricane and saw that the hives were full of bees and nectar, brood and honey. The hurricane was not as devastating for this company as the law of business entropy. The lack of a map or contribution agreements in a company can be worse than the force of nature. The bees were producing honey without having a business plan or the Three Rules to follow, but the company sure wasn't functioning.

Usually, when a company first starts, a significant amount of energy is spent to ensure its success. As companies grow, machines wear out, supplies rust, buildings age, products become obsolete, crops contract diseases, hurricanes and floods destroy. Good business plans factor in techniques for coping with these problems.

Peoples' energy and attention within companies can also disintegrate, and without some system or infrastructure that promotes growth, entropy will take over. The Three Rules are a structure that, if applied regularly by a company, can reduce the law of entropy and increase the productive focus. Because the middle manager is usually faced with the most constant chaos, it is he or she who can best use the Three Rules as a map to direct employees' attention, time, and effort toward the company goals. Having the Three Rules as a map will save managers a tremendous amount of wasted emotional energy.

The Three Rules Prevent Sabotage

Workplace entropy usually manifests in the form of sabotage. When six or more people work together for two or more years, sabotage usually sets in. Sabotage is a natural process in which groups start to engage in activities that keep them from achieving the very thing they wish to be working toward. They are often not consciously aware of their behavior. And most of the time they are unaware to what extent their behavior is sabotaging the company.

SABOTAGE DEFINED

Sabotage comes from the French term *sabot,* which means "wooden shoe." During the Industrial Revolution, people often felt frustrated by the automation and dehumanization of their jobs. In moments of exasperation they would throw a wooden shoe into a work area or assembly line to "botch it up." Webster defines "sabotage" as "the action by discontented workers to make it difficult for others to work." The Internet Revolution one century later seems to be bringing on the same discontented worker reaction. According to Los Angeles's *Knight-Ridder Newspaper*, January 2000, "Conflict is a growing ugly problem at the office—gossip, snide comments, icy silences— it's another miserable day at the office."

SUBTLE SABOTAGE 2000

Sabotage among a knowledge- and technology-based workforce is sometimes more likely to be subconscious than conscious, and it is much more difficult to identify. Department managers may harbor jealousies, team leaders may be loaded down with resentments, men may hold grudges when women have authority over them, and vice versa. Though the people involved believe they are fully and openly participating in achieving the company's goals, there are endless scenarios that can lead to sabotage. Human resources consultants say managers spend 20 percent of their time resolving employee battles. When deadlines are missed and work is shoddy, a company's bottom line can be negatively affected in the extreme.

Subconscious resistance to change often afflicts the officers or principals of a business. It's especially hard to deal with sabotage when it starts at the top, because managers are increasingly reluctant to confront their bosses. In one firm, problem-solving sessions regularly deteriorated into harangues from the owner whenever he came to the table. Rather than confronting him with the fact that he was sabotaging the firm, employees met on their own and made their own decisions. The owner never saw that he was wasting everyone's time and causing people to circumvent him to complete their work.

There are more overt forms of sabotage. For example, a police department required all officers, old and new, to learn to use new computers. As you might expect, some of the veteran officers resisted. They spilled coffee into the laptops, developed carpal tunnel syndrome, and missed training sessions. They were acting out the definition of sabotage: "action by discontented workers to make it difficult for others to work." As an expression of their discontent with modernization, they even started a group that refused croissants and café lattes and ate only donuts with strong black coffee.

SELF-SABOTAGE

The rules can overcome sabotage even when it is self-sabotage. The case of an East Coast manufacturer and distributor of health produces that expanded rapidly and needed a new building illustrates this point. As the structure neared completion, department heads wondered why the owner of the company had become distant and unresponsive to their needs. "He goes over and looks at the woodwork all day," one supervisor grumbled. "He seems to have lost all interest in the business. All he cares about is the building." The owner, obviously overwhelmed by the rapid change, was unable to keep his unspoken agreement to lead his company. He never recovered from the stress of rapid expansion, and, as the business began to lose money, his managers had to find other jobs. Their careers had been sabotaged, but the owner never realized the origin of the problem.

In this case, the business owner was facing some problem within his own mind, heart, or spirit that manifested itself as self-sabotage. He procrastinated until he could not recover his balance; he withheld his best efforts from his organization and did not face his hidden negative tendencies. He became so stressed out that he couldn't see what was happening to him or identify the cause of his discomfort. Worst of all, he was apparently unwilling to seek the help that he needed to get back on track. He lost his company and, most likely, his self-respect as well.

Middle managers need to be on the alert for an owner or general manager who no longer follows the Three Rules. Owners have been known to sabotage themselves and hence their companies, and it's guaranteed that the employees will feel the "trickle-down" effects of their owner's behavior.

The 3 Rules are an excellent *barometer* of sabotage. If this health products business owner had had them in place, he could have realized that he was neither contributing nor keeping his agreements. Perhaps he might have decided that the business had grown too big for his expertise and that he should hire a general manager to oversee its operation. When growth became too much for Thomas Watson Sr. of IBM, he recognized it through his inability to keep agreements. Fortunately, paying attention to this barometer gave him the wisdom to step aside and hand the business over to his son, Thomas Watson Jr. IBM taught us by example the result of courageous, conscious awareness of self-sabotage and how one man saw that he could either change or pass on the responsibility to one who could keep agreements.

MANAGING SELF-SABOTAGE

It is often said, "We are what we repeatedly do." If we repeatedly con-tribute to the most important goal, we replace the urge to put others down with a respectful request, and we are a person of our word. In doing so, we *are* the leaders of our careers. Can you imagine someone in your workplace repeatedly contributing with respectful integrity and not becoming a leader?

As the leader of your career, you can choose how to act and how to respond each moment of each day. Are you willing to quietly begin today to keep all of the Three Rules in your own world? This means constantly check-ing on the most important ways to contribute and then taking action. It means making positive, respectful requests and always keeping your word even when you feel highly resentful of another. Remember what Victor Frankel, the Auschwitz survivor and famous author, advised: "No one can know your attitude or take your attitude away from you."[3] They can and will try, but like any leader, you will have the tools necessary to overcome any obstacle.

Remember, though, the biggest obstacle to most careers is ourselves, our own personal entropy. Once we are conscious of the behaviors that sabotage our own careers, we will be able to overcome our personal entropy.

THE EIGHT MOST COMMON TYPES OF WORKPLACE SABOTAGE

1. Blaming

Blaming, according to Webster, means "finding fault with." When some-thing goes wrong, many people's first instinct is to scan the environment and discover what went wrong, then point a finger at others, blaming them for our distress. A blamer holds someone else responsible for whatever goes wrong. He or she may shame or humiliate his target in front of their peers, causing embarrassment followed by resentment. To rationalize the condem-nation of others, he or she might think, "I'm the only one who really knows what is going on and who can do anything effective. There are so many dum-mies out there. I'm doing all the work." Unless the employees who are the targets of a blamer are very strong, they may actually begin to believe that they are guilty for mishaps and failures—though nothing could be further from the truth. Confidence diminishes and, like a self-fulfilling prophecy, a cycle of failure begins to wreak havoc.

Middle managers are an extremely easy target for blamers. Blame can hin-der creativity, entrepreneurial spirit, and opportunities for growth. Blamers may get a temporary high by venting stored-up frustration and experiencing the resulting feelings of power. In short order, however, they'll discover that power gained at the expense of someone else's self-respect is not real power and contributes nothing to the organization or to one's career. Finger-pointing goes in all directions in companies, from the top down, from the bottom up, and laterally from peer to peer. Usually blamers are secretly resented and disliked. In *Big Business,* John D. Rockefeller points out that "People who do not contribute, generally fail. The pity is that when he goes down he inflicts heartache and misery also on others who are in no way responsible."[4]

2. Gossiping

Gossip in the workplace exhibits two main characteristics: (1) talking to someone about a situation that the gossiper does not have authority to resolve, and (2) talking about a person who is not there to defend herself or himself. Conversing with others can make one feel included and connected, but when workplace conversation is habitual, nonproductive chatter, it may have a negative impact on all concerned. Gossip starts when uninformed employees wonder what is going on. If management withholds information, rumors start to fly. Gossip becomes an information highway of sorts, but the information is usually distorted. Talk may start innocuously enough with a statement of fact: "We're getting a new manager in production." By the end of the day it may become, "We are all going to lose our jobs when the new manager arrives." The day a rumor like that takes hold is probably not a very productive day. You might say, the day has been effectively sabotaged.

Many people form cliques and gossip about coworkers, who then wonder what's being said behind their backs. At the very least, gossip creates an uncomfortable atmosphere. It also distorts reality. When I was a consultant with Xerox Learning Systems, one of my clients was Certified Alloy Products in Long Beach, California. Our work there went very well, and the vice president of Certified Alloy sent my boss a commendation letter touting the great job I had done. I was very pleasantly surprised when I saw my copy of the letter. The letter went to a Xerox supervisor who was the scheduler, but not to our direct boss. The supervisor told my boss I had asked Certified Alloy Products to write it. I didn't know she'd said this, and I wondered for months why my boss never mentioned the commendation. I finally found out, several months later, from the client that the scheduler had called and asked if I had requested the letter. Even though they said no, the scheduler still chose to spread the rumor.

Gossip makes it difficult for people to work together harmoniously. People may indulge in gossip to get that temporary ego high, to mask their own feelings of inadequacy, or to get agreement that their own discontent is justified. No matter what form gossip takes, sooner or later it will have a detrimental effect on the workers and the company at large.

3. Procrastinating

Procrastination is the temptation and/or *urge* to put off projects until the last minute. Often it involves living in a state of denial that time is passing and there are things that demand and deserve your immediate attention and best efforts. Laziness may be a component of procrastination, or it may be an avoidance pattern to escape unpleasant tasks. When we procrastinate, we actually feel held back by some inner or outer force. Some procrastinators have admitted to feeling rebellious about completing a particular assignment.

Deadlines put off are often missed, and completed work may be shoddy because it is rushed in order to meet the agreed-upon time specifications. Though it is widely believed that depression causes procrastination, it may well be that procrastination is a causal factor of depression.

A procrastinator may get a temporary high from the adrenaline produced while rushing. Then, in a dramatic deadline rush, he may turn around and congratulate himself for getting the job done fast. Unfortunately, doing things quickly may not result in the best work. Inherent in procrastination, however, is the perfect excuse for poor performance—there wasn't not enough time to do it well. Procrastination wastes both individual and corporate time.

4. Creating Chaos

There are many ways to create chaos in the workplace. Employees might lose things and involve others in finding them, cause arguments and fights, create factions, or mentally or sexually harass others. In an extreme, a worker may intentionally open an E-mail that he knows will cause the computer system to shut down. Attention is diverted from the task at hand and disorder ensues. Productivity decreases and time is wasted. The most extreme chaos-causing events are workplace shootings, which happen in an attempt to create havoc as well as to blame.

Some of those who create chaos are seeking the limelight. Even if it is negative attention, they bask in their moment of glory. For some people, being recognized as a troublemaker may seem preferable to receiving no recognition at all—to being an invisible person. An atmosphere in which employees are not praised for a job well done or do not receive adequate training is a spawning ground for chaos and dissension.

Managers may also inadvertently create chaos by their decisions. Employees often feel undermined when the manager frequently changes his or her mind about procedures and goals. A chef at a fine dinner house, for example, spent hours preparing sauces for the dishes scheduled that night, only to suffer the frustration of having the owner make last-minute changes in the menu that made the sauces unnecessary. Hard feelings resulted and loud arguments followed. As a result of the owner's throwing the kitchen into chaos, the chef quit. It turned out that the next day the *New York Times* ran a good review of that newly discovered restaurant and hundreds of new patrons showed up to enjoy the chef's special dish that the food critic had praised. The dish wasn't even on the menu, and the restaurant got no second chance with its potential customers.

Chaos can also be intentional. At Agilent Technologies, a robot was put in place to stop the line when certain parts were missing or out of place. Waving one's arms in front of the robot would also cause the line to stop. Workers could not resist that urge to wave and see the robot stop the line. This went on day after day, making the middle manager furious and significantly reducing productivity. Sometimes chaos is created by not thinking through decisions that affect people or by an urge to get attention or make a point. Whatever the cause, creating chaos stops the flow of work.

5. Stealing

According to U.S. Justice Department estimates, workers steal an annual $100 billion in goods and money from their employers. If stolen time was included, and hours paid for but not worked, that amount would probably triple. People who steal rationalize their actions by telling themselves they are worth more to the firm than they are receiving, so they are owed a little something extra. Stealing is also a form of revenge, a chance to get back at the employer for real or imagined slights. A high number of employees pilfer small amounts, like petty cash or postage, but the bills add up. No matter what the amount, the perpetrator is guilty and the employer is violated. Doubt and dishonesty sabotage the atmosphere of trust and optimism. In perhaps more subtle ways, owners and managers also steal from employees. Many companies expect their people to work overtime or weekends without compensation. For years we've heard stories of pension funds that have been misappropriated, or even of the United States Government losing Social Security money.

After working for nineteen years for the same company, Elmer was fired. Because he didn't make twenty years, he was ineligible for his retirement pension. His pension was literally stolen from him by the company, and years later, Elmer's family still suffers this injustice. When companies practice this form of stealing from employees, other employees will worry that it could happen to them. Eventually it sabotages the organization.

Embezzlers engage in a more blatant form of theft from companies. They often justify their illegal actions by saying that they deserve the money as compensation for their contribution to the company.

When dealing with clients who have caught employees or managers stealing or scheming, I find that the employees often do not admit their culpability, saying, "That's your perception that I was stealing." Their way to deal with the problem is to discount the accusation and then blame the one who has the "misperception" regarding the theft. I believe most people cannot rationally fathom that they are thieves, so they justify and/or blame. Theft is theft, however, and adopting such behaviors and/or beliefs causes irreparable damage to individuals and their companies.

6. Abusing Substances

Mood-altering substances affect one's ability to solve problems or to produce consistently. They cost untold millions each year in the form of lost time in the workplace. The abuser destroys his or her chance to have a natural high and to feel real enthusiasm on the job. While drugs and other mood-altering substances may alleviate boredom and pain, it is a fool's game, which provides only temporary relief. Excessive drug use often creates a blame-and-shame cycle and is damaging for everyone concerned. Users may destroy their health and create losses, or at least embarrassment, for the employer. When there are drug or alcohol users in a company, other employees may cover for them, and then resentment brings the entire workforce into the sabotage cycle.

Substance abuse can also lead to abusive behavior. At a catalog sales organization on the east coast, Angie, a supervisor, came to work each morning with a nagging hangover. Irritable during the course of the day, Angie would yell at the operators. Between calls she would tell them they were bumbling idiots, and next she would threaten to tell the department head that they were making errors in entering orders into the computer system. Several of the women were afraid of her and felt so nervous that they began to get flustered and actually did make more mistakes. As their stress levels soared, they became so petrified that they were afraid to report Angie's abusive behavior, and it escalated for months before someone got up the nerve to tell the department manager.

A 2000 HMO study reported that workplace substance abuse costs employers more than $145 billion a year. And it's not just illegal substances: more than 50,000 scientific studies have reported the adverse health consequences of smoking. One published study, used by Kaiser Permanente, estimates a total annual financial burden carried by the organization of $4,500 per year per smoker as the result of costs associated with medical care, disability, and absenteeism.[5]

7. Building Empires

Within an organization, fiefdoms may develop, usually around an en-trenched or ambitious manager or employee. While most good employees develop on the job, sometimes an employee or manager may choose to direct the resources of the organization toward his or her own private agenda. He or she places self-interest ahead of company welfare. Perhaps this person is an old-timer who feels entitled because of seniority or position. The manager may believe him/herself to be indispensable and to know better than the boss or anyone else in the organization. Empire builders may have controlling personalities and be unwilling and unable to delegate or to develop the skills of their direct reports. Often the "empire" doesn't contribute to the com-pany's mission.

At a small publishing company, a new circulation manager pumped up circulation figures by taking the magazine out onto newsstand, totally disre-garding the editor's concerns that it was a trade magazine and needed a com-plete editorial overhaul if it was to interest the general public. With impressive computer printouts, the circulation manager dazzled the pub-lisher into thinking that all they had to do was publish and the magazine would sell. Resources were allocated for hiring additional staff, and the cir-culation department grew rapidly, but the editorial staff and budget were not increased. Tons of paper and untold hours of press time were purchased, and large numbers of copies were distributed. The magazine failed to sell on the newsstand, and copies were returned by the tens of thousands. As the pub-lisher struggled to recover from the loss, the manager used the pumped-up circulation figures to get herself a better job with a larger publisher.

Empire builders often leave wreckage in their wake. Their activities may squander company resources and divert it from its goals. In extreme cases, the employer may be destroyed as the empire builder goes on to bigger and better things. This kind of sabotage is hard to spot, for empire builders seem full of promise. They look like up-and-comers with big ideas, the kind of people that owners of firms find attractive. Unfortunately, many have decided that they are smarter and more powerful than the employer and have adopted their own values, mission, goals, and objectives, which oppose those of the company. Trying to get ahead by empire building will usually sabo-tage both the firm and your career. If you are a manager who has empire builders working below you, it is best to redirect their efforts. Keep in mind that it is many times more difficult to change the course of an empire builder who is entrenched above you than that of a subordinate whom you may still have the ability to teach or fire.

8. Withholding Useful Information

In some companies there are secrets that everyone knows but nobody talks about. Speaking to the right people about these situations would have a healthy effect on the firm. However, no one wants to bring the issues up because it could "hurt" others. Or they may fear reprisals, so they keep their mouths shut. One type of unspoken truth that needs to be revealed, but rarely is, may be that whenever the boss is at the meeting, nothing gets done. A tacit agreement may develop among employees who want to move forward with a plan or resolve an issue: "Don't bring it up at the meeting." Like the emperor who had no clothes, the boss never hears the truth and so plows forward with self-defeating behavior.

In a Virginia law firm, one of the partners conducted an ongoing affair with a decreasingly competent receptionist. The woman was paid an extraordinary salary and was viewed by the others as a nail polisher. When the affair was over, the receptionist threatened to sue for sexual harassment, and the firm settled with her by paying her from profits that rightly belonged to all of the partners. This withheld piece of information—that they were really financing an adulterous relationship for one partner—financially and morally hurt everyone in the firm. Partners were afraid to confront the offender and discuss possible and probable ramifications of his behavior. Consequently, the partners each took the loss and said nothing, but they were ultimately sabotaged by their silence.

Withholding might mean keeping back information that someone else needs or not discussing feelings that make others uncomfortable. But withholding positive feelings can also have a detrimental effect.

Joyce worked in the home office of a dry cleaning establishment consisting of a cleaning plant and five retail stores owned by Harry. She turned in her resignation and left her job of ten years because she believed Harry disliked her. Harry was shocked. He relied on Joyce, appreciated her work, and had always known he would leave Joyce in charge upon his impending retirement. The problem was, he had never been able to express his delight with Joyce's work. As a result of withholding praise and appreciation, Harry lost the best person he'd ever had in the business, and it was impossible to fill her shoes. He sabotaged his own efforts to retire early and leave the business in the hands of someone he had trusted implicitly and relied upon for years. Harry was a smart businessperson who had been effective in detecting sabotage among his workers, but he had a blind spot when it came to seeing his own withholding of positive information in that light. According to the U.S. Dept. of Labor—46 percent of people leave their job because they feel unappreciated."[6]

An incredible amount of energy toward productive goals is lost in the midst of any form of sabotage. Fortunately, holding to the Three Rules can counter all eight forms of sabotage. It stands to reason, if people are not looking to contribute and work toward company goals, they are more likely to build empires, gossip, create chaos, or abuse substances. If your people cannot stop the put-downs, you know they may be involved in blame and gossip. If they are incapable of keeping agreements, they may be procrastinating, withholding information, or having a substance abuse problem. Companies need a few key anchors (rules) to help their leaders stay focused on their future rather than spending 50 percent of their time dealing with the darker side of managing their people.

The Simplicity of the Three Rules

The Ten Commandments have been in existence for centuries. Today we are still hard-pressed to find anyone who keeps all Ten Commandments all of the time. Because I grew up in the Presbyterian Church, I didn't memorize the Ten Commandments, but I was aware of them. When my daughter attended a Catholic school, I was surprised that her Catholic classmates also didn't know all the Ten Commandments.

One company's mid-managers had read *The Seven Habits of Highly Effective People* along with a seven-week supervisory class. Every week he would add one new habit and review the rest. At graduation, everyone knew all seven, but at our follow-up sixty days later, almost no one still remembered all seven habits. Memory plays havoc with the best of plans. For eighteen years, all three of my children and I have been in the 4-H program. When I tested them this year, none knew all four of the H's—each remembered three. Rotary International has a 4-Way Test I like a lot—but few Rotarians recall more than three.

Deming's "Fourteen Points[7]" for Quality are very effective and were popular for many years. I used them both with client companies and with M.B.A. students. But they soon became too cumbersome and managers repeatedly followed just a few.

The best-seller *Don't Sweat the Small Stuff at Work*[8] lists 100 ways to minimize conflict and bring out the best in others. All are good ideas, but those great ideas are rarely acted upon except to find their way to the bookshelf. Dale Carnegie's *The Leader in You: How to Win Friends and Influence People* lays out nine basic principles.[9] Graduates of the course usually recall three. Groups of three rules seem to be easier to remember. We all know "stop, look, and listen". "Go, fight, win." "ABC." Although many people confuse "participate" with "contribute," most do remember all of the Three Rules.

A real test of the Three Rules occurred when I was a junior high youth group leader at a local church and we sponsored dances for junior high children from all over town. The secret to the dances was the Three Rules and everybody's willingness to adhere to them: Everyone Contributes, No Putdowns, Keep Agreements. These teens knew they had to decorate, clean up, and bring food or music to contribute. They also could be confident that during the dances they would not be put down too badly and that they all had a no-drinking agreement to keep. Fifteen years later at a wedding of one of these young men, the groom instantly recalled the Three Rules. Two of the ushers then each cited the Three Rules they had to follow in the junior high youth group.

The Three Rules represent a simplified system, designed particularly for the Internet Revolution middle manager who has information overload from people above and below.[10] They will assist the manager in guiding others to bring contribution, respect, and integrity to the workplace.

The Three Rules are substantive enough to create systemic change; simple enough to remember; powerful enough to counter entropy; consistent enough to last through changes in leadership, and deep enough to transform jobs into careers. If the Three Rules are not put into place, other less effective or even damaging rules may come into play.

PRICEWATERHOUSECOOPERS—COST-BENEFIT ANALYSIS

PricewaterhouseCoopers (PwC) had few behavioral rules to follow but many financial and legal ones. When Price Waterhouse and Coopers and Lybrand merged, they spent a great deal of money to make the transition. After the merger, the partners decided to increase their salaries by 12 percent, which required a cut in overhead achieved by laying off administrative staff. One executive assistant outlined the unspoken "rule" at the newly formed PwC: (1) Focus only on numbers; (2) To increase profit, cut staff without plans to increase revenue; (3) Treat laid-off employees like potential gunmen. By not outlining positive whole-systems-oriented rules, management allowed these negative, unproductive rules to take over.

The rules of accounting are usually not the complete list of rules for growing a business. One executive assistant did a cost-benefit analysis of replacing the PwC rules with the Three Rules. By using Rule 2 and converting her complaint ("quit being so anal") to a request of the president, she devised the following:

#1 REQUEST: Lead the way to increase **business** by 12 percent.
How Achieved: a. **Hire** six more executive assistants.
                  b. **Redefine** job descriptions of executive assistants to add business growth items.
                  c. **Involve** executive assistants by having them select one client file each week and identify one new area of additional accounting from which this client could benefit. Then give the suggestion to the partner in charge. (Average new billing would be $5,000.)

Result: Partners could gain 12 percent salary, no layoffs would occur, six new executive assistants would be hired, and EA's could receive a 6 percent increase @ $5,000 per new area per executive assistant per week: $52 \times \$5,000 \times 10$ EA's = $2.6 million.

Two days before her cost-benefit analysis was finalized, this executive assistant was abruptly laid off and escorted to her car as if to keep her from harming the firm.

Accounting firms are great at documenting contribution; unfortunately, they often do not know how to encourage, create, or motivate contribution. Two days after this employee was terminated, PwC got national visibility for its huge administrative layoffs. Lack of conscious rules to empower people left this accounting firm written up in the *Wall Street Journal* as "hard, cold, number crunchers."

Companies need the Three Rules to battle entropy, create a map so employees can work together as a system, decrease sabotage, and provide consistency through changing management trends and globalization. They need these Three Rules to be short enough to remember, deep enough to be effective, and to ensure that negative, unproductive rules do not gain a foothold and potentially sabotage the company.

3

Rule 1: Everyone Contributes

Our mission is to meaningfully contribute to local, national, and international communities in which we trade, by adopting a code of conduct which ensures care, honesty, fairness, and respect.

—ANITA RODDICK, founder of the Body Shop

Are You Making a Contribution?

"Do you want to know if you are on track to make it to the top? Ask yourself this question: "Am I making a contribution?" This is the challenge Bob Galvin, chairman of the executive board of Motorola, presented to managers at a recent U.S. Leadership Conference. It was amazing to the attendees how one simple question, a seemingly innocent question, could create such a stir. The initial reaction to Galvin's question was this: "Of course we're contributing! Isn't it a given that any manager worth his or her salt contributes to the well being of the company?" What is certainly true in theory can become clouded in practice, so let's look closer into this issue about contribution. In order to address the idea and examine the importance of "contribution," it may be necessary to first clarify its meaning.[1]

Effective Contribution

To contribute means to add value to—to move forward—to support, advance, promote, provide, bestow, furnish, give or donate. Recognizing the importance of contribution carries with it a responsibility to effectively communicate well-stated goals and to align those goals with commonly desired outcomes. Just showing up for work and taking up space doesn't necessarily mean you are contributing. Being a hard worker and a responsible employee doesn't necessarily mean you are contributing, either. Instead, effective contribution requires all of the above and agreement on a desired result that you are working toward. Sometimes it takes a great deal of courage to discover whether your activities actually support or inhibit the desired result, but you won't know that if you cannot identify the desired result.

Contribution requires knowing your position in the company just like athletes on a sports team know their positions. If the center kicks the ball, the game can't move forward. Each of us in a company must contribute first and foremost to our designated position. A president who keeps tinkering in engineering and does not tend to his executive responsibilities does not contribute nearly as much of what the company needs. If you are an executive, an owner, or both, below the following guiding principles are for you. If you are a middle manager, make sure your boss follows these principles so you can tend to your job.

Guiding Principles for Executive Contribution

In order of priority, make sure these are in place:

- **Values**—What you stand for as an individual and as a company
- **Mission Statement**—Reason for being in business
- **Goals**—Long-term activities that describe where the company wants to be in the future
- **Objectives**—Short-term activities with specific time period
- **Alignments**—Two-way agreement, boss and employee, on most important objectives for both
- **Tactics**—Detailed plans for specific allocation of energy, financial resources, and personnel
- **Budgets**—Allocation of financial resources to business units
- **Monitor**—Set up controls to follow up and accomplish goals

Participation Is Not Necessarily Contribution

It is important to distinguish contribution from participation, for the two are quite different in nature. More than half the employees and managers in the companies I work with mistakenly interchange these terms. I have made it a practice to do a two-week follow-up after we have begun just to see if the attendees remember the Three Rules. Most remember Rules 2 and 3 but what many say for Rule 1 is "Everyone Participate." No! It's "Everyone CONTRIBUTES."

Participation is to partake, to take part in or have a share in. Participation does not necessarily add value or move the group toward success. In school we are taught to raise our hand and say something, and that helps our "participation" grade. In business, however, participation is not enough.

To contribute, as we saw earlier, is to "have a part in bringing about a desired result." Contribution reinforces company values, helps to enact mission statements and goals, creates mutual objectives, supports fiscal responsibility, and helps to put check and balances in place.

By definition, participation can include very negative behaviors like blaming, gossiping, empire building, abusing substances, creating unnecessary chaos, and so on. Most companies have a high percentage of negative participation. You can participate through demanding, whining, and gossiping, but these behaviors do not contribute to your career or company goals.

Contributions, on the other hand, can be powerful, action-packed, total involvement. It is important to our very souls, our entrepreneurial spirits, and our careers to continually contribute. It is essential to our vitality and success to make meaningful contributions and to learn how to ask others to do the same. The question is, "How do we do that when our past setbacks stand in the way of future positive contributions?"

What Contribution Is Not

There is a fine line between contribution and participation. Only a complete awareness of your individual mandate and alignment of that mandate with the company's mission can lead to the most effective contribution.

THE DOOR SLAMMER

Sometimes we may think we are contributing, but negative behaviors may cancel out our initial perceived contribution. Take Lois, for example: Lois mistakenly imagined herself to be contributing to the commonly desired outcomes of a nonprofit organization. Her agenda—what she considered to be contributing—was not in alignment with the organization's desired result. She wanted authority and leadership; they wanted assistance and support. What began as a difficult situation simply continued to go downhill. Lois was asked to fill a position in the organization after the untimely death of its well-liked administrative manager. Because of the urgency of the situation, Lois was not appropriately screened, and proper communication of expectations and company objectives did not take place.

Starting off under these stressful conditions was bad enough, but Lois had a way of always looking busy and acting "unnaturally" cheerful, which made everyone around her very uncomfortable. When peers or supervisors gave direction or gently brought mistakes to her attention, it was Lois's practice to become defensive, adopting the "shoot-the-messenger" mentality. She would say, "Fine!" and walk away, slamming doors behind her. Logical, healthy people found themselves tiptoeing around Lois. The chasm developing between what the organization expected and what Lois was capable of delivering grew more and more impossible to bridge.

In Lois's mind she was doing everything possible to make the transition easier—and to maintain a positive attitude—no matter how much it killed her to do so. To her friends she said, "No one appreciates my efficient, cheerful nature." Her perception of the situation was, "I'm being wronged, but I am strong; I can take it, and I won't give up." To her coworkers and associates, Lois's disposition, along with such behaviors as the door slamming, was destructive and was damaging to the unity of the organization. No one could communicate with her. In fact, good employees were beginning to leave the organization because they could not endure her inability to communicate. When one of the service club members called to try to discuss the group's concerns, Lois promptly hung up the phone. Unfortunately, the group quietly dissolved, and no one could really explain why.

THE PENNY COUNTER

An accounting firm had a staff accountant, whom we'll call Frank, who loved to find the last penny in the accounts of his clients. For some clients this was terrific. They wanted to know where the last penny went and were glad for Frank's work. But Frank's largest client was running short on cash flow and could not afford the luxury of paying to find where the last penny went.

The client was complaining about the bill, saying the company was happy with a number that was plus or minus $50 and did not want to pay for the extra time taken to totally reconcile their accounts. Frank, however, just couldn't live with stopping at plus or minus $50. He became almost obsessed and wanted to put in his own time to find the last penny. As far as the client was concerned, this behavior did not contribute to the organization. According to Peter Drucker, "Quality in a service or product is not what you put into it. It is what the client or customer gets out of it." If contribution is measured by the same criterion as quality—judged by what the organization or customer gets out of it—then Frank and Lois were not contributing.

NOT ALL CONTRIBUTION IS VISIBLE

Differing views about measuring and rewarding contribution are the main sources of conflict in management teams and partnerships. In one large CPA firm, some of the partners were concerned about not getting higher bonuses, so they ranked partners by billable hours. The managing partner, Dan, was the glue that held everyone together. He resolved complaints, kept communication going, created fun events, and kept an upbeat tone, all while maintaining records and appeasing clients.

When Dan was on vacation, an angry partners' meeting got out of control, and they decided to fire Dan. He was fired because he was not a CPA, and the partners could not measure his contribution in billable hours as they did their own. Thus, his contribution was invisible to them.

Once Dan left, conflicts arose. The best partners left and formed competing firms. The morale and cohesiveness of the remaining partners disintegrated. They almost never shared work with one another, and one of their branches soon closed. While measuring billable hours to show contribution can work in one area, it was not the correct measure of Dan's contribution.

DISTORTED CONTRIBUTION

A Texas management consulting firm had five "equal" partners (four of whom were formerly middle managers), twenty-eight consultants, and more than 450 large clients. The five partners often had conflicts because of what they perceived to be their contribution. Linda was the creator of most of the copyrighted material and holder of the excellent Dun and Bradstreet history around which the corporation was formed. Pete was a super salesperson who brought in most of the business and trained new salespeople. Shari was the source of endless manuals, books, tapes and other tools for general information that enhanced each assignment. Mark, the best and lead consultant in the group, was a great role model for new consultants. With a little help from Linda and Pete, Mark trained the twenty-eight consultants.

Bruce was the systems and financial person who coordinated people, tools, and talents into one business. As the business grew, spats occurred about contribution: Pete, in sales, wanted to be paid more. Linda, Mark, and Shari felt they were so critical to the success of the company that they should be paid more, too. And Bruce maintained his arrogant attitude throughout all the discussions. Ultimately, it was decided that the five owners would all be paid equally. This seemed to temporarily resolve the arguments over who was worth more.

A sixth person, an entrepreneur from the Midwest, saw the system in

Texas and wanted to invest in its proposed national expansion. He was a silent partner who wanted equal ownership. After he reviewed the company's five-year expansion plan, his cash was in the business in November. Given a $5,000 limit and a cosigner for the checks, all seemed safe.

Bruce was CFO and president, and he was to lead the plan. However, by December the long term accountant left and a new cosigner was needed for the checks. Bruce agreed to interview prospective new accountants. The only one he liked, however, was a friend. Two of the other partners objected to Bruce's hiring a friend, so he interviewed a few more people. But each week he would claim that he didn't like any of them.

December became January, and Linda and Mark began insisting on an inside and an outside accountant. Shari and Pete, on the other hand, agreed with Bruce's hiring his friend. The vote was three to two, and the friend became the accountant. Linda and Mark, the two dissenters, then privately met with Bruce on January 7 and asked if he would be willing to rotate the president position. He was not pleased, and he walked out of the meeting.

On January 8, Bruce began regularly writing himself checks for just under his $5,000 limit—$4,999, $4,987, $4,989. He cashed them at different bank branches to avoid suspicion. He was clearly a pro. He documented the checks he wrote to himself as "past earnings" that he had not yet taken, and itemized additional amounts supposedly owed him, thus ensuring that he would be covered legally. The additional amounts were part of the package. "Sweat equity" was Bruce's term for what the other partners contributed to his self-generated rewards. In Bruce's mind, he saw his own unpaid contribution as billable. His check writing continued daily until March 1, when over the weekend Mark and Linda discovered a hidden letter Bruce had prepared listing all the amounts and indicating some new amount owed to him. He planned to resign on March 3. By March 2, the police were contacted and all of Bruce's items were removed from the building. The locks were changed, and a termination letter was prepared and given to him Monday morning.

As soon as Bruce received the termination letter, he immediately obtained a restraining order preventing the rest of the group from mentioning the word "embezzlement." This was done suspiciously quickly and smoothly—as if he was following a pattern. Unfortunately for the business, because of Bruce's activities, the money for expansion was gone, the consultants quit, and the IRS, the State Tax Board, and many vendors were demanding to be paid. A three-year legal battle ensued.

During the lawsuit it was discovered that Bruce had "compensated for his contributions" many times before. In fact, the County Recorder had nine pages of judgments recorded against him. This meant many other businesses had taken Bruce to court and won. But Bruce had set himself up to be "judgment-proof." He had most of his money in a Swiss bank account, and he had a rented apartment and a rented car. After spending huge sums of money on attorneys, detectives, and accountants, Mark and Linda conceded that there was no way the company could ever recover the money from this judgment-proof professional embezzler.

Bruce calmly continued to go to an office with a sign out front reading, CONSULTING SERVICES. He acted as if nothing had happened, and the sudden disappearance of all the consultants was "their problem" and their accusation of theft was "their perception."

The IRS began going after Linda because she was the original owner of the business. They demanded all past taxes and threatened to put a lien on Linda's home, so she reluctantly set up an appointment with the IRS. Surprisingly, when she showed the agent the boxes of deposition papers and the attorneys' bill and explained the story, the IRS agent recognized Bruce and said they had been trying to complete a case on him for years. Linda was thrilled to have some help. In exchange for all the legal information, the agent gave her immunity from all IRS liens on her personal property. He then became a silent partner in helping Linda develop the case against Bruce.

Just before the case was to go to trial, Linda's attorney warned her that Bruce was a pro at this and she would pay for the trial that he could easily win. Linda asked Bruce to meet and to try to settle the case out of court. Because it had been drawn out for three years, Linda thought that a reasonable conversation was possible. Nervous and fearful, she called Bruce, and he agreed to meet. Linda stated to Bruce, without assigning blame, "You and I are responsible for these investors and vendors. What do you think we should do?"

"Well, that is why you have a corporation," Bruce replied. "Then you don't owe anything to these investors and vendors."

Linda responded, "But they all contributed to our business, and they deserve some of the money that is gone."

"Oh, no," Bruce said. "That's the corporate game—it's a risk and we are protected."

Linda then asked, "Well, what about the other partners? There is no corporate veil between us six, and we feel we contributed as much as you to the business. Since you have the money, we want you to pay the vendors and us their portion from the last investment."

With an artificial laugh, Bruce replied, "That's just your perception—that you all deserve the money. I am the one who built this. If it hadn't been for me, we would never have gotten the business off the ground. I came in at five o'clock every morning; they didn't come in until nine; I built these systems."

Linda, trying to be calm, said, "Bruce, we all contributed. Pete sold; I created; Mike trained. We think we contributed as much as you." Bruce gave another nervous laugh.

Linda said in an amazingly calm way, "Bruce, we also have these nine pages of judgments here from the County Recorders Office listing other businesses that took you to court and won. They also think you took their money. I'm not saying you did or didn't, and maybe our five partners and twenty-eight consultants and these nine pages of other businesses are wrong, but it *is* as you say, 'their perception' and the perception of the court and of these businesses."

Bruce's eyes glistened, and he said to Linda, "Well, no one ever appreciates my contribution. Especially my mother. She always negated my contribution," etc., etc.

As his defense continued, Linda counted to ten in her mind and told herself to breathe. She then asked, "Bruce, when Mark and I asked you to step down as president on January 7, did you feel as though you had better get what was owed to you right then? Did you experience that same old feeling from your mother and these other business over and over? To avoid someone 'negating' your contribution, did you feel like you were going to take what was yours?" He responded affirmatively and went on with his defense.

After she spent three years and $35,000, Linda could finally see his distorted perception of the value of his contribution versus that of others. His misperception that he could justify compensation taken secretly was also evident. A psychiatrist suggested that Bruce has a borderline personality disorder, in which a double standard is the norm. A double standard here meant "I deserve—you don't." His hostility may have stemmed from his relationship with his mother, which is how he justified all his embezzling. That carefully masked hostility made others see him as calm and competent. Many of the people on the nine pages of judgments said they felt like *they* were crazy.

The case finally went to court, and Linda won the judgment, but she was never able to collect all the money. One more case of distorted contribution to add to the nine pages at the County Recorders office. If contribution is clearly defined up front and restated regularly, someone like Bruce cannot distort it for long.

Middle managers, beware. If you get too absorbed in the daily work you may not see your contribution. Be sure you still have time to know what you and others are contributing and how those contributions are measured. Make sure you and others are being rewarded regularly and appropriately. There are many professional con artists like Bruce who feed on the hard work of the middle manager. This is why automatic checks and balances are necessary. If the procedures had required a second signer for the checks, this distorted contribution could have been remedied much earlier.

Middle Managers Juggle Two-Way Contributions

It is important for the middle manager to contribute to his/her manager's primary goal so that the time spent at work will be both valuable to the boss and meaningful to the mid-manager. At the same time, mid-managers must extract real contribution from their employees so the employee can meet the mid-manager's goals. To simplify how to work both sides of contribution, let me condense, in one simple sentence, what I learned from thousands and thousands of top managers about what they want from their mid-managers. "Support me and my goals." More specifically, what top managers want is some version of *"more, better, bigger, faster."*

For mid-managers in their employee role, their number-one requests of their bosses are generally in the areas of *"recognition, respect, or freedom."* While not always stated in these exact words, recognition, respect, and freedom are what employees want from their managers to help them do their jobs. Examples of employee requests appear below. Note that these requests follow the same clarity as those of managers.

Mid-managers have two different roles to play. Contribution varies depending on your role; in your manager role, you contribute by giving your employees recognition, respect, or freedom. In your employee role, you contribute by supporting your boss (more, better, bigger, faster).

Following is a chart that illustrates what most top managers want from their staffs. Note that the burden is on the manager to be clear about what she wants, why she wants it, and when it should be completed.

Typical Top Manager Requests

What Do You Want?	What Will Your Employee Do?	What Would Be Different?	When Should It Happen?
Motivate and develop your staff.	A. Set clear goals. B. Find out what is needed from you to reach goals. C. Follow through—acknowledge and reward.	We would decrease turnover from 40% to 20%.	By February 1
Keep track of materials.	A. Inventory your materials every day. B. Request needed materials at least three days before. C. Lock your materials cabinet when you leave the office.	We would be able to support the needs of the managers to get the product out the door 24 hours before deadline.	By February 15
Socialize only during your lunch hour.	A. Remain at workstation during business hours. B. Talk only business on the phone. C. Be a role model.	We would complete 25% more transactions weekly.	By January 15
Clean up your station before you leave at night.	A. Put floormat in place. B. Wipe down work area. C. Put tools in toolbox.	We would be ready to begin working by 7:00 A.M.	By January 22
Let me know about problems before they become crises.	A. Give me a weekly report on any problems you see in your work area. B. Give me recommendations to solve your problems. C. Follow through on solutions to problems.	There would be no union grievances.	By January 31
Prioritize your tasks.	A. Meet with me once a week, Mondays at 8:00 A.M. B. Give me weekly accomplishments each Friday. C. Ask me if you get confused.	Inventory would have a 24-hour turnaround.	By January 15
Take responsibility for your hostility in the workplace.	A. If you feel hostile, take a walk; go outside. B. Before criticizing, count to ten, rephrase. C. Focus on your part in the problem.	People would come to you for help each day.	By June 1

Most Common Employee Requests of Middle Managers

What Do You Want?	What Will Your Supervisor Do?	What Would Be Different?	When Should It Happen?
More responsibility	A. Put me in charge of the data processing input section. B. Let me call for repairs. C. Let me train the new person.	Errors would drop below two per week.	By August 11
More independence	A. Tell me the goal you want, then trust me to do it my way. B. Trust me to do it my way. C. Let me come to you if I need help.	I'd get the production out on time.	By February 5
More recognition	A. Tell me when I have done a good job handling a customer complaint. B. Let me know when customers express being pleased with my service. C. Include my name on reports I write.	I'd know the standard and thus satisfy customers sooner. You'd get no more than one complaint monthly.	By September 1
Better communications with me	A. Meet with me in my office every Wednesday from 9:00 to 9:15 A.M. B. Discuss my job with me. C. Let me know how I'm doing.	I'd get work done sooner and have time to work on the emergency plan.	By August 5
More training	A. Teach me more about our new rental equipment. B. Send me to the course at the local college. C. Get an extra manual for me.	I'd be more efficient with the equipment and more able to explain its use to others.	By March 21
More input on goals	A. Include me when you write out biannual goals for my department. B. Ask me what timeline I see as realistic. C. Let me review goals before publishing.	I would reach all my goals.	By April 26
Go through the chain of command.	A. Talk to me before discussing problems or requests with my group. B. If one of my employees comes to you with a problem, send him or her to me. C. Advise me of agreements you make with someone from my group.	I could measure progress on an ongoing basis with my knowledge of activity by project members. We could get the product out under budget and on time.	By May 15
Keep me informed.	A. Keep me better informed about division and company-wide business. B. Let me attend the monthly meetings. C. Give me copies of memos that affect my department.	I'd meet my deadlines.	By June 6

If managers and employees contribute, they will build a career, and see great, positive results.

JOSÉ IN SHIPPING

In order to contribute effectively, employees must know to which company goal they are contributing. José shows us an example of how an employee's personal goals and the company's goals do not always match. Notice how the middle manager masterfully both supported his manager's goals and managed José's contribution.

José worked in the shipping department of a well-known winery, which was famous for shipping bottles with customized labels. The management team of this company spent a full weekend two years in a row outlining their mission, values, and goals. One of their advertised goals was to have 100 percent accuracy on labels. During their two off-site sessions, they saw that the biggest loss to their company was errors in labels—they had to pay double in shipping, plus customers became enraged when labels were wrong. If they were to continue to advertise their accurate-label business, they needed to make label accuracy a reality. The finance, production, sales, human resources, and customer service departments as well as the winemaker all agreed on this as the priority—100 percent accuracy in labels. It had slipped to 84 percent, which was intolerable.

José had worked for this company for ten years, and his personal goal was to get the product out the door by 5:00 P.M. each day. On days when he didn't achieve that goal, he became irritable and could not sleep well. On days when he got it all out the door by 5:00 P.M., he felt fulfilled and slept well.

José's manager explained to him the new priority goal. The manager asked José to check all the labels before shipping them and to make sure they matched the order form. José agreed, and he checked the label against the order form. But every once in a while, when it got close to his personal 5:00 P.M. deadline, he would rush the last few cases through to the truck and go home with a good feeling from having made what he thought was a good contribution.

In time, labels were showing up with errors. It turned out the graphics were right, the labels were correct, but the address it was shipped to was the problem. Thus, shipping (José) needed to make the final check to see that the correct label went to the proper client. Because the recipient was sometimes not on the label and the buyer might not be the recipient, it took more help to verify each order.

José was asked to have two managers initial all orders before they were shipped. He did this for a while. A day came, however, when both managers were out, so José initialed the two lines himself in order to ship by 5:00 P.M. Having again met his personal goal, he went home with that sense of accomplishment and had a good night's sleep. One week later, all hell broke loose. The labels were wrong, two customers were irate, and the winery took a huge financial loss on the order.

The manager was red-faced and on his way to fire José, but the human resources manager took him aside and diffused the anger. "It's not that José is stupid, as you called him. He just has a different goal. Don't put him down. Ask him for a solution." The manager waited a day to cool off, then respectfully informed José of the continuing label problem. José basically said that his personal contribution to this company is to ship every order by 5:00 P.M., and it was just not as important to him for the label to be accurate as it was to ship every order on time. "I have always appreciated this about you, José," said his manager. "You have done miracles to get orders out on time, and it has helped so many times. But our company's goals are different this year. Our new number one goal is 100 percent accuracy on labels, and I am held accountable for the new goals. How can we work this out so you can still have that sense of accomplishment while maintaining 100 percent accurate labels?"

José was asked to think about it and make some suggestions. He realized that if shipping by 5:00 P.M. did not always contribute to the company, it had less meaning to him. He came up with three suggestions: (1) Divide shipping into customized and noncustomized; then he would only work on noncustomized orders; (2) Have a wall chart tracking label accuracy, so he could see how he was doing each day and each week; (3) Get a job in a different winery where they didn't have customized labels.

His manager picked the second option. It took a while to get it in place, but it finally worked after a few months. José could again measure his contribution—even if it was in a different way, and the company's label accuracy went from 84 percent to 93 percent in the first quarter. Both parties won. The winery eventually got to 97 percent accuracy, and José found a new way to contribute to the company's goals while his own needs were also met.

Contribution was important for José; it gave him security, meaning, challenge, and a sense of accomplishment. Contribution was important to the company too. Since management clarified what *does* contribute to the company, the employee could respond. When contribution is clearly explained, it is not necessary for one person to personally attack another. In this situation, the temptation would be to put down José and make him the problem. When, however, the contribution a person makes does not fit the goals of a company, professional and respectful changes should be made to satisfy both the needs of the individual and the company. By realigning contribution, the financial health of the company and the emotional well-being of the employee are enhanced.

CONTRIBUTION CAN TRANSFORM JOBS INTO CAREERS

It is important to ask people to contribute, and it is important for people to know they are contributing. I have been amazed at the career change that occurs when employees truly understand the importance of their work. Such was the case with both Medtronics and the Body Shop.

Medtronics is a company that makes heart catheters and stents. These balloonlike devices are used to clear arteries and prolong the quality of life. Recently, Medtronics was listed as one of the one hundred most desirable companies to work for in America. Why? It not only pays well and has clear goals, but it also found a way to show employees how they contribute to the customer.

At least once a week an E-mail is sent to all employees from recipients of the stent procedure that saved and/or changed their lives. And, on a regular basis, these happy recipients are brought in to meet with assemblers, product specialists, and shippers to tell the story of how their lives were enhanced by the stent. One such visitor said that because of his clogged arteries and high blood pressure, he was given only six months to live. His daughter was newly pregnant and he thought he would never see the baby. The man opted for the stent, and two years later he brought his year-old granddaughter to the office.

During his talk with the employees of Medtronics, the grandfather's glistening eyes and beaming face empowered them—they now could see firsthand what an important contribution they had made to his life. Later that week I heard someone ask an assembler what her job was. She said, "Adding meaningful years to people's lives." Her job had become a career.

CONTRIBUTION CAN CHANGE A COMPANY INTO A GLOBAL CONTRIBUTING PROFIT CENTER

As I travel around the world I see the Body Shop in every airport and major mall. When Anita Roddick began the Body Shop, she had a passion and a mission to contribute to local, national, and international communities. Her mission statement electrified employees and customers worldwide.

THE BODY SHOP—MISSION STATEMENT
OUR REASON FOR BEING

To dedicate our business to the pursuit of social and environmental change.

To creatively balance the financial and human needs of our stakeholders, employees, customers, franchisees, suppliers and shareholders.

To courageously ensure that our business is ecologically sustainable, meeting the needs of the present without compromising the future.

To meaningfully contribute to local, national and international communities in which we trade by adopting a code of conduct which ensures care, honesty, fairness and respect.

To passionately campaign for the protection of the environment, human and civil rights, and against animal testing within the cosmetics and toiletries industry.

To tirelessly work to narrow the gap between principle and practice whilst making fun, passion and care part of our daily lives.

Contribution and Disabled Employees

John Naisbitt in *High Tech High Touch* takes a strong stand on the downside of technology: "While expanding information and choices, technology is starving our soul." Naisbitt would argue that today's workers are hungry for high touch: inner peace, human connection, and enthusiasm. As a result of technology overload, Naisbitt asserts, many employees and employers are emotionally unable to cope with the information overload and, consequently, they become emotionally disabled.[2]

I recently returned from a meeting of business leaders. It was their "50th Annual Leadership Award" to promote the employment of people with disabilities. Workplace disabilities in 2000 have three categories—now emotionally disabled has been added to the categories of physical and mental disabilities.

The first employee award was to Vincent Majerowicz, who is employed by Rod Dole, auditor controller for Sonoma County, the new fast-growing wine county in Northern California. Rod manages seventy employees and has always displayed a profound awareness of the two-way boss/employee contribution that makes workplace relationships successful.

It was no surprise when the employee award went to Vincent for becoming an excellent clerical helper. Rod explained that the coaching was two-way and so was the training. Rod said Vincent had contributed just as much to the staff as they had to him.

Rod had this to say about Vincent: "Vincent gives it all, in spite of all his disabilities. This is inspiring to watch in an office. This was our chance to help someone else do good work and watch him become independent. Vincent is so excited about being part of our world that it makes us realize how good it really is here."

This is the real goal for successful disabilities programs. Not to patronize employees and act like employers are doing a favor, but to let both contribute in their diverse ways. The "disabled" Vincent gave the Auditor Controller's Office a consistent and contagious daily burst of enthusiasm, which we all need. He gave them high touch to balance their high tech.

In *High Tech High Touch*, Dr. Andrew Weil, well-known physician and author, says that if you test any group of people today, most will have a sympathetic system overload.[3] He says we are all operating in a state of chronic emergency—heightened stress—and it has perpetually overloaded our sympathetic system. This is a form of emotional disability.

What to do about the stress? One solution came from Scott, a teller at a grocery chain in the Sebastopol, California, branch of Wells Fargo Bank. Scott was in a wheelchair on the inside of a desk-level teller window. The customer would sit down on the outside of the desk/window to do the transaction across from Scott. Scott's physical disability was also slightly in his hands, but he was still able to count money, initial forms, and handle necessary transactions. As months went by, I found a nice few moments of relaxation when I could sit and do my banking at Scott's window, as he slowly and carefully went through the procedures. He knew how to be very present and peaceful as he did his task. Each time I dealt with Scott, I felt relaxed and centered afterward. When I sold some property, I decided to put the cash in his bank's CD.

When the nominations for Employers Who Hire Persons with Disabilities Award came up, I thought about Scott. The very next time I went to his window I discovered he had left the company. I called the branch manager to find out why, and she said, "He didn't think he was fast enough." I regretted not having told him just how much he contributed and in what capacity he contributed. Although I entered his name for the award, his manager received the award because she hired him. But, I really wanted Scott to know that *he* contributed. His disability helped slow down the pace for all of us. He contributed to me by relieving my day's stress, even if just for five minutes a week. It wasn't just a favor he did for the bank. It was a favor to the customers.

According to Mary Farrell, a managing director for PaineWebber and regular analyst on *Wall Street Week* with Louis Rukeyser, the population today has the highest level of stress *ever*, because of the information and choice overload. Farrell's statistics indicate more stress in the population now than during wartime. Contribution in the twenty-first century can often lie in providing human connections, enthusiasm, or peace in a highly technical and frantic workplace. Naisbit's, Weil's, and Farrell's argument that we are becoming uncontrollably stressed because of our lack of "touch" was evident when the workplace disabilities began to include the emotionally disabled category.

EVERYONE CONTRIBUTES IN THE FAMILY

When my sons, Mark and Keith, were seven and two years old, my husband and I were working full-time. To compensate for our absences, we got in the habit of trying to do everything for our children, leaving few opportunities for them to contribute. Day after day, we rushed them home, cooked dinner, did dishes and laundry, and then put them to bed.

One day we were having some of my husband's prospective architecture clients to dinner, so I guiltily left work early, whisked up the boys from day care, and rushed home to clean the house and prepare a fancy dinner. I hadn't thought much about the boys, but they were underfoot as I cooked and cleaned. I automatically revacuumed where they were playing, but after listening to the sounds of them fighting over a loud, irritating tape, I yelled at the top of my lungs, "QUIT SUCKING FROM THE SPACE!" I'd never said that before and wasn't much of a yeller, so we all stopped in silence. Finally, Mark, with his "Dennis the Menace" face on, said, "We don't know what that means." I wasn't sure I did, either, not to mention what it meant to two-year-old Keith.

I started complaining about the noises and the crumbs and the fighting, but then I stopped and recalled what I would have done in the workplace. I would never treat my employees this way. We always tell them how and when and where to contribute. I froze and then made a promise to myself:

"Whenever I want to yell, 'Quit sucking from the space,' I'll stop, count to ten, and ask in a nice way for them to help with a specific task." So we started that day.

Mark vacuumed, Keith set the table, and at the dinner, they were acknowledged in front of the guest for their contributions. The guest enjoyed the family atmosphere, and my husband got a new client that night. Seeing a professional architect as a family person was helpful. What a difference. My family still teases me about that phrase, "Quit sucking from the space," but we use it to describe the opposite of contribution.

Everyone Contributes became a house rule that year. As time went on, "contribute" came to mean that both boys cooked one night a week, and once a week they had to present a family activity or a dinner topic for discussion. We started checking in with one another regarding contribution, and every six months we would reveal things we appreciated about each other.

This is what led to our original family mission statement: We will all be productive, hardworking, and loving members of a family team. We added "No Put-downs" and "Keep Agreements" to the house rules. And, as we replaced "Quit sucking from the space" with "Everyone Contributes" it transformed our group of four people living together to a productive, loving team. That was in 1980, and for twenty years we have wrestled with the maintenance of the Three Rules.

When our daughter, Brooke, was two years old, the boys were 16 and 11; their new contribution was to do the grocery shopping each week. They bought the ingredients for their cook night, lunch items, three treats each, and worked their way down our long family grocery list. It was a wonderful contribution and helped us all tremendously. It wasn't long before people in the store took note of these two shopping boys and began to make comments.

Six months into this plan, Keith, who was in sixth grade, was given a social studies homework assignment about his home life. It asked questions like, How many doors are in the house? Where do people usually gather? What animals do you have? What is the most recent holiday you celebrated? Who was the latest guest? And so on. The key question was, When did your mother last get groceries? Keith wrote, "Six months ago." I was sure that a social worker would arrive at the house any day to rescue this poor, unfed child. Many people over the years gave subtle signs of disapproval, but we learned to live with it and keep our family mission and rules.

When you apply the Everyone Contributes Rule and the other two rules to your family, it will help you keep the Three Rules in your workplace. The Three Rules are simple enough and universal enough to be used for all ages and in all cultures—in both your home life and at your workplace.

What a Contribution Is—and Isn't

To live well is to work well.

—THOMAS AQUINAS

Mutual Contribution Helps to Get the Job Done

We can never be sure we are contributing to our work or even to our lives unless we have consistent goals to aim for and measure against, no matter how small they may be. Others cannot contribute to our goals if we don't clarify how. Goal setting for contribution must be specific, achievable, measurable, and, most important, mutual.

For example, a brick factory in a hot Southern town employed a large number of Korean workers, who were being tempted to join a union. The summer heat of ninety degrees, and the brick-making ovens made the factory a very unpleasant work environment. When the company asked for three more bricks per day per employee, the union drew up a contract covering collective bargaining, more breaks, and so on, assuming that what the workers wanted most required union membership.

Further exploration revealed that what the brickmakers really wanted to make it worth three more bricks per day was not just more breaks. They had a deeper issue. Their boss kept referring to them as "the Koreans." They wanted to be called by their real names. This was the respect they needed in exchange for supporting the company against the union. They developed balanced, mutual contribution goals: factory managers call employees by first name; employees support a non-union shop and pull three more bricks per day.

In keeping contributions mutual, it is important to let the employees set some goals of their own, because money is not always what they are after. (See page 41 for typical employee requests of management.) More than a hundred employees of a hardware company, for example, held a secret basement meeting with a union representative, who outlined pay and benefits, breaks, and so forth. When asked indirectly what they wanted, however, the hardware store employees spoke more about respect than raises:

- A career ladder—a chance to see how to get promoted
- One boss, not three
- "Correct me in private, not in public"
- Communication— "Tell me how I am doing"

When the hardware manager asked employees to support the store by getting inventory done one day sooner and when he listened to their "respect" list, they were able to agree on goals as well as on a timeline for meeting the goals.

Procedures for Implementing "Everyone Contributes"

1. Get agreement from the top executives of your organization as to what their number one goal is for your department.

2. Find out your boss's number one request for you to meet your department goal.

3. Set personal goals daily, weekly, monthly, and yearly that include your number one goal. Communicate your goal achievement progress to at least one other person in the office.

4. Give honest, positively stated acknowledgments of others' contributions to your goals by providing specific details.

5. Take responsibility for your own resentment, dislikes, or sabotage on a regular basis—in private.

6. Listen and take interest as others share their goals.

7. Take the responsibility to ask for and get the support you need to be successful.

8. Delegate in ways that empower your employees.

9. Once a month, bring in a current event, an article, a book, a tape, a flyer, a song, a saying, a piece of information, a success story, an exercise, etc. to share with the group at work.

10. Save money where possible.

11. Come to the staff meetings with an open heart and an open mind. Clear issues with people on a one-on-one basis before the staff meeting.

12. Always look for ways to improve.

Contribution Makes Careers Out of Jobs

Rule 1 Everyone Contributes, can be a bit tricky to apply because generally everyone believes that he or she is already contributing. The argument about what does and does not constitute a contribution can be resolved by keeping the goal of the company in mind. Contributions must support the firm's goals. It is middle management's job to make sure the efforts of each employee actually SUPPORT the company's ability to make a profit. It is also middle management's job to give employees the individual recognition and respect they need to keep their contributions alive and well.

In chapter 1, we introduced the water meter manufacturer who had sales of about $10 million and wanted to triple that figure. There we met Tony, who had been with Water Flo for twenty years. He was a capable supervisor, but, in truth, running his group was just a job to him. He had a chip on his shoulder; he resented management, and he did not want to be part of them.

We began the supervisory skills class by explaining the Three Rules: Everyone Contributes, No Put-downs, and Keep Agreements. We then applied those rules to what we were doing in the seminar. As we began to apply the rules in the class, Tony kept arguing that his job needed no contribution—just participation at the "clock in/clock out" level. He said he didn't want a pressured, goal-oriented job and the word "contribution," as opposed to "participation," was bugging him. So he agreed to contribute in the session, but he would participate on the job.

As the course went on and others measured their contributions, he began to measure his. For the first time in twenty years, Tony realized that doing his part day in and day out had contributed immensely to the company, even if he wasn't pushing himself. When he saw how he contributed to the goals of the company, his eyes fixed on the wall chart that outlined his part. I noticed him bite his lip and turn away; then he was quiet for what seemed like a long time. It was obvious to the rest of the group that he was a meaningful cog in the wheel, and we could all see how he could make a significant contribution to the new goal of tripling the business. Suddenly, contributing was looking like more fun than resenting and withholding. Finally, in the last session, Tony spoke:

"The first two months I was here I made several suggestions, but no one acknowledged or implemented them. The last time I said something, a coworker made a sarcastic remark about me being a 'kid,' so I decided then to never make another suggestion. For twenty years, I've just clocked in and out and quietly resented management. That's the old way. I am ready to let go of that old, worn-out resentment. I see you younger employees doing the same thing and getting the same attitude. Now I see the goal. We're here to triple our size. We're here to make money, so let's make money." He got excited about his work and went back to school in the evenings to get a degree in management.

Realizing that his performance contributed so much to the firm's goal, even if he was full of resentment, made a big difference for Tony. Once he became aware of his impact, his contribution to the firm grew even more. As the business expanded, Tony got a salary increase. He was excited about finally seeing his job as a career, realizing that he was a valued member of the organization and that his contribution counted for something. When he discovered he could grow his job three times bigger in six years, it ignited an unbeatable passion for his working toward even greater goals. Tony no longer really wanted to be the type of employee who just punched in and out forever.

After working with the Three Rules, Water Flo was on the road to becoming a functional business. The executive vice president of the firm reported that it achieved a 28 percent increase in revenue in the first six months.

Like Tony, many people withhold their contributions. Often this happens because of past hurts and resentments or in reaction to a hostile work environment. A strong supporter of Everybody Contributes can be witnessed in this Mother Teresa quote that the dean of the School of Business at the University of Portland E-mailed to all professors for Christmas:

> *People are often unreasonable, illogical, and self-centered:*
> *Forgive them anyway.*
> *If you are kind, people may accuse you of selfish, ulterior motives:*
> *Be kind anyway.*
> *If you are successful, you will win some false friends and some true enemies:*
> *Succeed anyway.*
> *If you are honest and frank, people may cheat you:*
> *Be honest and frank anyway.*
> *What you spend years building, someone could destroy overnight:*
> *Build anyway.*
> *If you find serenity and happiness, they may be jealous:*
> *Be happy anyway.*
> *The good you do today, people will often forget tomorrow:*

Do good anyway.
Give the world the best you have, and it may never be enough:
Give the world the best you've got anyway.
You see, in the final analysis, it is between you and God:
It was never between you and them anyway.

We can add: "Mid-managers can contribute immensely and get put down for it, contribute anyway."

Short-Term Contributions Are Valuable Too

The examples of contribution so far have involved long-term on-the-job or deep personal contribution. Contribution is also important in meetings, seminars, and other short-term, job-related interactions. The key to accomplishing this, however, is to set contribution as a goal for all involved.

Never consider starting meetings, off-site management retreats, or conflict negotiation sessions without the Three Rules. It is imperative to get a show of hands ahead of time by all participants that they will contribute to the goal (e.g., develop a mission statement, resolve a problem). If they are not asked to do otherwise, many people will complain, bring up problems, or get the group off track. Occasionally, someone will not agree to contribute. That person must then be asked not to participate in the group. It must be agreed ahead of time that at this meeting, for this time span, all participation will be directed toward resolution, creation, analysis, decision making or whatever the stated purpose. In Tony's case, for example, he finally agreed to contribute to the session even though he was still determined to just participate in his job.

You will love what happens at a convention or conference when you ask between 50 and 350 participants if they are willing to contribute to the session. Contribution is defined for them as "adding value to the others in the group." As soon as they agree, there will be an energy shift in the room. Instead of wondering if this session will be interesting enough to them, the participants begin to look for ways they can make the discussion more interesting to others. From this point on, the level of involvement goes from conscious awareness to synergistic exchanges. All that is needed is to muster up the courage at the beginning and ask people if they would be willing to contribute. They almost always say yes!

You Determine What Contributes to You

Usually the board of directors gives direction, and the president and executive staff set the plan and goals to get there. The middle manager is the one who takes the parts of each goal and makes sure he or she and the staff meet them.

Middle managers need business structures within which to work. In order for them to survive, some basic things must happen: sales and production deadlines are only two. Once a management team or president determines the goal, whether it is to triple business in six years or 100 percent accuracy on labels, every worker has an unspoken agreement to contribute to that goal. In Tony's case, resentment kept him from fully contributing (even though he was accidentally contributing anyway). In José's case, he was contributing to the day-to-day meaning in his work, but not to his career or to the company.

Who determines company contribution? One's boss and ultimately the president. Even though José's boss did not mind an occasional label error, the management team was adamant about 100 percent accuracy. Middle managers who move quickly in the company are those who always make sure they know their boss's number one goal and are contributing to it. Additionally, they also do what they can to make sure their employees are contributing to that goal.

Who Determines What Contributes to You? YOU!

Knowing how to delegate is critical. The following eight steps show how you can lead the contribution of your employees so that they will accurately and consistently meet your goals. It is very common for middle managers to get sidetracked with personal issues or employee conflicts. But by clearly delegating and setting up goals and expectations, you will empower your employees and motivate them to contribute to your career—and theirs as well. When they are focused, they will not create conflict.

HOW TO DELEGATE

1. Explain the purpose of the job that needs to be done, and why that job is important.

2. Explain what results are expected.

3. Define authority—parameters of the operation.

4. Get agreement on a deadline.

5. Ask for feedback—establish mutual understanding of what needs to be done.

6. Provide for controls—along the way, ensure that the job is being done right.

7. Provide for support—make sure it is the support your employee wants.

8. Acknowledge and give recognition to employees who have completed an assignment.

CONTRIBUTION CAN BE CONTAGIOUS

Fourteen-year-old Morgan had always been very close to her dad. For five years she and he did a sheep project together for the 4-H club. Both of her divorced parents, Bill and Melinda, separately volunteered with many fund-raisers for her club, but the club was losing members, so Morgan had to be switched to another club. Bill was remarrying and abruptly relinquishing joint custody to move out of state. The loss of both her familiar club and her father made raising sheep a very low priority for Morgan, and she wanted to give it up. Yet she had two sheep grazing at home, and her mother wanted her to finish the project she had started. Because she was missing her dad, Morgan was starting to display psychosomatic illness. Morgan's mother became more determined to get her daughter focused on something useful.

Larry, the 4-H club sheep leader, had welcomed Morgan to the club several months earlier, but he had some twenty children that he knew well, whose parents had contributed to their club for years and years. Neither Bill nor Melinda had managed to assist with any fund-raisers or projects in the short time with the new club. Two weeks before the county fair, Larry gathered all forty sheep at his ranch, and the twenty kids had duty every day from 6:00 A.M. to 1:00 P.M. and 1:00 P.M. to 8:00 P.M.

The first morning Melinda dragged a tearful, moody teen to the 6:00 A.M. session. Morgan protested all the way, claiming that she wanted to quit raising sheep. She missed her dad, and there was nothing Melinda could do. Melinda felt she couldn't ask Larry for any extra help with Morgan because she was new and she hadn't yet done her fair share. Morgan huffed out of the car and toward the barn, alone and weepy. Melinda wondered how Morgan was ever going to get through the next two weeks, plus the four days at the county fair.

All twenty kids were on time at Larry's ranch and ready to get their sheep in tiptop shape. Larry didn't waste a minute buying in to the lethargic attitude of the noncontributing new teen. He joked with her and got her right to work exercising, feeding, shearing, and practicing. He did all the eight steps on the delegation form without even knowing it.

That evening at eight o'clock, Melinda picked up a filthy but bright and happy teen. It turned out Larry had playfully joked with her, assigned little children to help her, encouraged her, and delegated like mad. When kids did well, they were cheered; when they did poorly, they had to hoe thistles in the pasture. The next day Melinda tried so hard to tell Larry what an amazing job he had done with Morgan and how it was so perfectly timed with her dad's abrupt distancing and Morgan's acting out, but she was all choked up with gratitude and couldn't speak.

The next morning Morgan was up and ready to go before six. She was dressed for the occasion and concerned about the time. On the first half of the trip to Larry's, she spoke of the four younger children whom she was in charge of motivating, teaching, and managing. Larry had delegated this responsibility to Morgan. The responsibility for their success as well as the goal and the timeline had taken Morgan completely outside of her own aches and pains and on to the bigger, better goal: Get selected for Group I, make $500 per lamb, and earn showmanship ribbons for herself and her younger 4-H'ers. Morgan spoke of shearing, sheep food, fun, discipline, structure, and Larry. "Larry is such a cool husband and dad." She described how his wife and two small boys were always nearby, and he never acted irritated, even with twenty kids and forty sheep. "How does he still have time to contribute so much to Morgan and the others?" Melinda wondered.

When Melinda dropped off Morgan on day two, she tried again to tell Larry how much he had contributed to Morgan and how he had turned a depressed, lethargic teen into one who was enthusiastically caring for sheep and helping the younger 4-H'ers. To her, this delegation and empowerment was a miracle. But again, when she tried to talk, the words got lost as she fought back grateful tears.

By days three and four, Morgan again got a little moody, but Larry snapped her right out of it when he restated the goals, gave specific feedback, and asked her opinion. More hours led to continued enthusiasm. Melinda had a very difficult time accepting this wonderful contribution from Larry. Melinda asked her good friend, "Why do I deserve Larry contributing so much to Morgan?" She got an important insight. Her friend reminded her that when she was a youth group leader for three years, she had helped other teens; now she was on the receiving end of that assistance. Contribution had come full circle.

The next day when she finally told Larry how much his leadership meant, she was able to finish her sentence with only a few tears. Larry said, "Oh, no, this isn't just a favor to you, Melinda. This has helped me. I have a twenty-two-year-old daughter from a former marriage who was taken from me at age six and is just now able to see me occasionally. I missed all her teenage years, and Morgan is filling that void for me."

Melinda was surprised that a moody, lethargic teenage daughter of two noncontributing 4-H club parents actually contributed to a sheep leader who already had twenty participating kids around him. At the fair Morgan received third place and top Group I. Lamb was selling for 57 cents per pound, and Morgan's top lamb was bid up to $10 per pound—more than $1,000 total—twice her $500-per-lamb goal. Her four young 4-H'ers also all got Group I.

Larry had a nice clear way to measure his contribution goal—the price per pound of lamb that his 4-H'ers received compared to the going rate. In the past, Morgan had never received more than $4 per pound and had never gotten above Group II. Having a clear goal in dollars and cents helped realize the goals of both parties.

Mutual contribution was the key in how Larry worked with his 4-H'ers. He contributed by setting clear goals and by holding children accountable (hoe thistles if you goof off). Second, Larry could contribute because he was free of his own resentment. By making sure he was fulfilling a need in himself, he could contribute to others and they to him. Morgan left the experience with more than achieving Group I and $10 per pound. When she started back to school that year, her first assignment was to write a paper about someone she had contributed to over the summer. Her paper was about how she contributed to Larry by being a teenager. She got an A.

MISALIGNED CONTRIBUTIONS CAN LEAD TO IMPASSE

John and Paul were both middle managers with very strong career goals. John attended West Point and went to work for a truck manufacturing company as a young engineer with an M.B.A. John was a general manager, reporting to the president, who was in another state. Paul was the chief engineer reporting to John.

A brilliant planner, John could see projects from contract to delivery and was able to outline every step it took to get there. He was so career-oriented that he lived down the street from the plant and worked six days a week. Because of his workaholism, his wife left him and moved their two children to a city 1,500 miles away. When his family left, he began working seven days a week from 6:00 A.M. to midnight. He was so work-driven that his health was failing and his regular but dreaded Monday memos sent to everyone in the company were losing credibility. John's response to his employees' lackluster attitudes was to yell and issue more memos. They saw his orders as obsessive and noncontributing. His staff began to sabotage his instructions, and meeting deadlines became a thing of the past. The work environment deteriorated so completely that several managers were fired on the spot during shouting matches, and the president wanted John to explain what was happening.

After reviewing the situation, the president pointed out that John's style was dictatorial and was contributing to the company's complete failure to meet any deadlines and their total disregard for on-time quality delivery. John was enraged and blamed Paul. Although Paul was also a family man with two children, he made it a habit to maintain a normal work schedule. He was quiet but firm, goal-oriented, and gentle. The engineers who worked for him liked him but knew he had no authority over them. Since John often criticized and undermined Paul's authority, Paul was not able to empower the engineers to meet their deadlines. He also could not convince them to stop sabotaging John. While John was obsessed with what he perceived to be his own incredible contribution, he did not recognize his sabotaging behavior, to both himself and his people.

It is important that middle managers be given a chance by their manager to contribute. Otherwise, they are hindered from getting results from their people. Having a strong goal from corporate was the only thing that pulled John and Paul out of their noncontributing impasse. The corporate office had a chance to sell specialized mining trucks to China. Their trucks met all the specifications of the Chinese company. However, having a record of missing all their deadlines was not acceptable. The president needed to have assurance that John's group could meet at least 90 percent of all the trucking deadlines for the Chinese contract.

John and Paul's company goal was to sell $17 million worth of trucks within six months, and reach $21 million by the ninth month. John knew exactly what it would take to produce those trucks to deadline, but no one would follow his lead. Paul knew how to get everyone to contribute to a goal, but he had no authority or control. This situation epitomized two misaligned contributions, one of which canceled out the other. The truth is, nothing positive would happen and company goals would not be met until John and Paul could come to a mutual agreement regarding contribution.

How to Get a Raise Every Time

As a consultant and an M.B.A. college instructor to both managers and employees for twenty years, I have worked with thousands of requests for raises. Most middle managers think that requesting a raise or listening to a request for a raise will have to do with cost of living, inflation, salary surveys for similar jobs, personal needs, or threats to leave. NO! If you want a job and not a career, you can base your request on these things. If, however, you are career-minded, you must address your creative entrepreneurial opportunity (CEO).

You can get by with an occasional inflation argument or a threat to leave, but if you really want to think career—meaningful career—here is the secret. Tell your boss what you plan to contribute to his or her goals in the next year, and keep your promise.

You are the CEO of your career. It is up to you to lead your boss to the raise. The number one thing your boss wants is support (more, better, faster). If you can outline the more, better, faster goals you intend to achieve, your boss will not only give you a raise but will do so without resentment. When you've achieved that level of communication and mutual contribution, there will be no guilt, no blame, and your boss will have pure belief in you and plenty of reason to empower you.

Asking for a raise is an emotionally difficult situation for both the person asking and the person being asked. The person asking has put his or her self-worth on the line. In her book *Breaking Free of the Shame Trap,* Christine Evans describes a bright, competent woman at Hewlett-Packard who was offered a raise and promotion, which she turned down because she felt unworthy. The "shame trap" was robbing her of a career that she deserved.[1]

It's not only the person asking who feels bad in most raise discussions. The person being asked can feel guilty, threatened, fearful, uncomfortable, and/or hostile or resentful. If you can break free of the shame trap, you will empower your boss to give you a raise enthusiastically and lead the way for both of you to support your career.

CLARIFY YOUR CONTRIBUTION

Allen was an excellent branch manager, but he had recently been terminated as the result of a bank merger. His self-esteem and career had taken a nosedive. In looking for a new job, Allen was feeling desperately insecure, and it showed.

The president of a large bank that was opening a branch in Allen's former hometown discussed the opening with him. At the end of the meeting, the president said, "Write me a proposal of how we might work together."

Allen's original proposal read: "Branch Manager of Bank X. Salary: $55,000; retirement, health plan, dental plan, annual conference fees and lunches paid for service club." Unfortunately this list did not reflect what Allen's contribution to the bank would be. His revised proposal read like this:

ALLEN JOHNSON

Dear Mr. Jones,

I appreciate the chance to talk with you regarding the possibility of my assisting you with the successful entry of Bank X in Town Z. I am extremely enthusiastic and excited about the possibility of returning to my favorite community and clients.

You asked me to outline an agreement of how we might work together. Below is a rough draft, which I invite you to add to, subtract from, change, etc. We can create this possibility together.

Branch Manager will:
1. Provide a full-service branch for Bank X.
2. Develop a substantial increase in deposits by building a strong client relationship.
3. Build on former contacts from my role as branch manager for Bank Y 1988–1996.
4. Establish and monitor an effective business development program to achieve/surpass established performance goals.
5. Develop local reputation for exceptional customer service for Bank X.
6. Build a strong support team with enthusiasm for sales and customer service.
7. Maintain exceptional customer service while growing the branch and increasing profitability.
8. Continue my love affair with the Z community.

Bank X will provide:
1. Corporate title: Vice President
2. Two-way communication, with clear definitions of responsibilities and authority
3. Mutually agreed-upon goals
4. Base annual salary of $75,000
5. Bonus incentive
6. Four weeks annual vacation

The result: Allen received an offer within twenty-four hours of this proposal, but he turned it down for an even better one. Once he was clear on his contribution, he was very clear on what salary he deserved.

Communicate Your Mission

Another very effective way to get a raise occurs without even mentioning money: Share your personal mission and your company vision with your boss.

Once I was asked to teach a five-week career development class for twenty-five working adults who were just beginning their bachelor's business degrees in evening classes. No more than any two worked in the same company. We had bank tellers, telecommunications assemblers, utilities technicians, trucking supervisors, grocery store supervisors, agricultural leaders, winery lab techs, brokerage firm administrative assistants, insurance underwriters, retail sales managers, health-care supervisors and law accounting firm executive assistants.

In week 1, I helped them clarify their personal mission. In week 2, we covered their company's and bosses' goals. In week 3, we used clarifying techniques to outline missions and goals in their personal lives.

In week 4, their assignment was to share their mission with their boss. Six of the twenty-five workshop attendees were offered a raise, which was not even anticipated. They were merely doing their homework to practice telling their boss their personal and business mission. But apparently it was so inspiring to the manager of each of these student/supervisors that their bosses were spontaneously moved to give a raise although none had been mentioned.

Several others reported a shift in their rapport with their boss, which could lead to a raise. This verified what Rockefeller told us a hundred years ago: Find out what needs to be done and do it. Don't try to make a living without contributing. Focus on your contribution, and communicate your future vision—and see if surprise raises come your way, too.

Balanced Contribution is Key

To whom do you contribute in your job? To whom might you not be contributing? Is there balance? Another banker I know is, above all else, completely focused on customer service. As I followed her through three branch manager positions, I saw her get red-faced over and over about how others treated customers. She was terminated in two jobs—one subtly and one abruptly. In two cases, the presidents said she was not a team player nor was she company-oriented. Her customers really liked her, but they got tired of changing banks.

On the flip side, Gordon Bethune, a new president of Continental Airlines, figured out how to escape the one-sided-contribution trap. Shortly after taking over, he burned the employee manual and set a new general goal: Do what is best for both the customer and the airline—not one or the other.[2] Employees were fully empowered by being asked to make that judgment call each day. The banker could have improved her contribution if she had done what was best for both the customer and the bank. What she failed to understand was that over-contributing to the customer and under-contributing to the bank hurt both the bank and the customer.

Identify and Clarify Goals

Let's take another look at the wonderful example provided by Continental's Gordon Bethune, a model business leader. It would help most of our careers tremendously to have a president who is clear about goals. But 90 percent of the time we do not have a leader like Gordon. This is why we must be the CEOs of our own careers—we must actually be our own leaders.

To navigate successfully through the chaos and uncertainty inherent in any position, as middle managers we must clearly identify our goals and get input from our supervisor that these are his or her number one goals. Even if we do not agree with them, we at least need to be able to identify and support them.

For a six-month period in 1979, I was employed by a leasing company named ITEL. ITEL decided to put more money and resources into sales than any other similar company. The company hired hundreds of salespeople from IBM and offered huge salaries, bonuses, unlimited expense accounts, and major sales support staff. The intention was obvious; the company wanted to make a visible and immediate splash in the market.

Much of the sales force was uncomfortable and thought it a waste to fly first class and travel long distances. Even though the president committed these resources to create a major impact on the market, the reluctant sales staff felt they were contributing more by traveling less, saving expenses, and setting their own appointments. So they ignored the president's directive and went the conservative route.

As a result, ITEL crashed so fast it was a news-breaking story. The salespeople did not carry out the number one request of the president because they thought they knew a better way. They forgot the first rule of contribution in career: Get agreement on the number one goal of your boss. Get it in writing and use three verbs and an outcome to define it (see p. 296); i.e., ask your boss what he or she wants from you. If it isn't illegal or immoral, just do it. Make sure the agreement is in writing and that he/she acknowledges this as the most important goal—then, just do it. If it isn't a "more, better, faster" goal, rephrase it until it is. Don't let it be a goal like "Quit _____" or "Don't _____." It should be positive and active.

When you have the company goal down pat, you can take the time to simultaneously include the enhancement of your job. Refer to the Most Common Employee Requests of Middle Managers chart (p. 297). Define your desire, align it with the company's, and watch your career begin.

My consulting business completely transformed when I started asking my clients to contribute to leadership programs I was conducting for them. For example, I would outline how I would guarantee an increased profit by three times what they paid me. A critical component of our success together, however, was their contribution to the success of the program too. What was expected of them was to:

- attend every session

- complete all assignments

- respond within forty-eight hours to any request for information from their employees participating in the course

- encourage others to complete the course

As CEO of your career, you need to be clear about both sides of contribution—what you contribute to your people and what you are asking them to contribute to you. You will be amazed at how willing and able all levels of coworkers are to respond to a specific contribution goal. Yet the number of times we guess at or assume contribution has exhausted many careers. You must be your own leader by finding out the big goal and doing your part to achieve its success. Don't be afraid to ask for what you want and need; write it down, clarify and revisit it.

How to Invite Contribution in Business—Systematically

An Oregon credit union branch manager wanted every employee who had any contact with the customers to offer at least one additional service to that customer. They called it the "Next Step Program." Employees were not that interested, but they did it occasionally. The branch manager was very upset that they didn't automatically want to sell more products to every customer, so the chairman of the board asked us to work with the branch manager to motivate the tellers to consistently sell "Next Step."

Upon hearing this, the branch manager said, "Why can't they up sell just because it's their job? We should fire them all and start over. I'm not here to motivate; I'm here to lead, and they won't follow."

Executives are usually surprised that some employees do not have the same goals as they do, and while they may think that usually firing those employees will change the situation, it won't. They have different number one goals and they always will. The best you can do is to find out their goals, agree to support them, then communicate your goals and get their agreement. Result—mutual agreement, mutual achievement.

To make a long story short, we worked with the employees to extract what nonmaterial requests they had that would make them want to increase their cross-selling. Each of the 7 had a unique request:

NONMATERIAL REWARDS
REQUESTED BY CREDIT UNION EMPLOYEES

1. Let me know the priorities each week.

2. Give me cross-training.

3. Let me have input on goals—ask my opinion.

4. Speak in a respectful tone of voice—especially in front of a customer.

5. Meet with me every Tuesday from 3:00 to 3:15 P.M. to discuss my job.

6. Have someone else do the mail once a week.

7. Give me board minutes 48 hours ahead of time.

IN EXCHANGE FOR PARTICIPATING IN "NEXT STEP" AND
OFFERING ANOTHER SERVICE TO CUSTOMER

The strategy was so successful that the general manager decided to try it with his executive staff, including the branch manager. The GM wanted the management team to increase the asset base by $50 million in one year. In exchange, the seven management team members had independent requests such as:

NONMATERIAL REWARDS REQUESTED BY CREDIT UNION EXECUTIVES
(FROM THEIR BOARD)

1. Treat me like a professional—trust my actions as long as results are on target.

2. Give me the authority to go with responsibility (e.g., if you require 6 percent dividend, don't blame me for decrease in income).

3. Follow chain of command. Deal with me—not my employees.

4. Sign the enclosed employment contract act.

5. Change my title from branch manager to general manager.

6. Accurately reflect active field of membership—not just original sponsor group.

7. Handle policy issues and long-range planning. Leave day-to-day problems to me.

IN EXCHANGE FOR AN INCREASE TO $50 MILLION IN ASSETS

As we middle managers sharpen our skills to request contribution from others as well as clarify the exact contribution we ourselves need to make, we are clearly in the leadership position of our own careers. It's invigorating and contagious.

5

Achieving Mutual Contribution

> Morale in an organization does not mean people get along; the test is performance, not conformance. Human relations not grounded in satisfaction of good performance results in a mean spirit.
>
> —PETER F. DRUCKER, *Management: Tasks, Responsibilities, and Practices*

Exploring the Company Mission

As a middle manager, you are not usually asked to decide if the company should go public or merge. But once the company has made policy and corporate-level decisions, you are asked to carry them out. This chapter will offer tools for you to clarify and get agreement on exactly how you can best contribute to the set mission and goals of the company.

Your leadership opportunity happens when you have, in writing, the mission goals and objectives and your boss has agreed that you are responsible for meeting these goals. Then it is up to you to decide how you and your employees or coworkers will achieve these "most important goals."

It is not up to you to determine or create the company mission, even though you may have the ability to do so. Remember the Serenity Prayer:

> *God, grant me the serenity to accept the things I cannot change,*
> *Courage to change the things I can,*
> *And wisdom to know the difference.*

Usually a middle manager has input into a mission or goal but cannot single-handedly set or determine it. What you can do is identify the goal. You and your coworkers and staff have the right to know the mission, values, and goals of the company in which you work. The following questions can help to clarify what a company strives to achieve.

Determining Company Mission

A. What business are we in?

_____

B. What is our mission?

_____

C. What are our company values?

_____

D. What are our company goals?

_____

E. Do we have a plan of how to get there? May I see it?

_____

F. How does our department contribute to the company goals?

_____

G. What is my manager's most heavily weighted goal for our department?

_____

H. What do I think I can do to contribute to the goals in "D" above?

_____

I. How does my manager think I can best contribute to "D" above?

_____

J. How would my manager or an outsider be able to verify that I significantly contributed to "D" above? (Will it be measurable? What will be the results?)

_____

For example, the founder of Revlon said that in the factory they make perfume, but in the store they sell hope. Knowing what business you are in—perfume or hope—makes a big difference in your planning.

Mission statements in this Internet era are influenced by the Internet itself, even if the companies do not use the technology. Let's take State Farm Insurance—its mission was to be "like a good neighbor." Agents were set up locally to be involved in community activities and to be neighborly. However, by not responding to the Internet, State Farm lost significant revenue.

Agents continued to be good neighbors as people were getting Internet access. The Internet offered buyers the opportunity to compare prices from all over the world as well as to purchase online policies. In 1998 State Farm's net income was $1.1 billion. In 1999 it shrank 26 percent, to $811.8 million. As the company hung on to its outdated mission, it lost market share to its more technology-minded competitors. According to John Chambers, CEO of Cisco, your company had better have a mission that reflects the Internet Revolution. If it doesn't, someone else will take your market share.

For the middle manager—again—you do not have to create or be responsible for the mission of your company. But you do have the right to know what the company's mission is so you can align your contribution with that goal. If you think the mission is outdated, you have the right to make a recommendation to update or revise it.

If you go to your manager and get answers to all these questions, you are probably in a good environment to lead your career. Should your manager get defensive, sarcastic, and/or avoid answering the questions, then prepare a mission and values and goals for your department or your area, and show it to your boss to get agreement or changes. If that fails, at least try to get the answers to the "Clarifying Contributions" questions that follow.

Clarifying Contribution

A. What is my company's business?

_____

_____

B. What are my company's goals?

_____

_____

C. How does my department contribute to company goals?

_____

_____

D. What is the most heavily weighted goal for my department?

_____

_____

E. What can I do to make sure the department goal in "D" (above) is reached?

_____

_____

F. How would I, my manager or an outsider be able to verify that we have accomplished the goal in "D" (above)? Will it be measurable? What will be the results?

_____

_____

G. What is my manager's #1 request of me regarding my part of the #1 goal?

_____

_____

H. Given A-G, my most important goal is: (make sure it is specific, measurable, attainable, realistic, and tangible)

_____

_____

In today's global high-tech revolution, more and more companies have mission, vision, and/or values in writing. It's up to you to find what and where they are. When you know the answers to the two sets of questions just presented, you are ready to answer Peter Drucker's famous 1999 Personal Contribution Analysis Question "How should I contribute?"

Personal Contribution Analysis

A. Who am I?

_____

B. What are my strengths? Am I concentrating on them?

_____

C. How do I work?

_____

D. How do I learn?

_____

E. What do I need to know?

_____

F. Where do I belong?

_____

G. What is my contribution? What should my contribution be?

_____

H. What habits of mine sabotage my career?

_____

I. How can I take better relationship responsibility?

_____

   1. How can I allow others to have their strengths?

   _____

   2. How can I take better responsibility for communications?

   _____

J. Where can I improve my manners?

_____

K. What is my plan for the second half of my life?

_____

Source: Adapted from Drucker's *Management Challenges for the 21st Century*, Final chapter, "Managing Oneself." 1999[1]

Michael Sullivan, Don Green and Tom Klein are three very well-liked presidents with whom I've worked. They live and breathe their mission and values. Michael Sullivan prepared Flex Products public, and Don Green took Advanced Fiber Communications public and Tom Klein grew a huge family-owned winery. All adhere to the Three Rules. It's been quite rewarding for me to see these three leaders put the Three Rules in action and to see the ongoing company benefits that they all experience because of their diligence and determination to practice them as well.

Examples of Company Mission and Values

ADVANCED FIBER COMMUNICATIONS:
- We will treat *all* individuals *fairly*, ethically, and with *respect*.
- We are a company built and sustained by people who are *customer-oriented*, empowered *risk-takers, team players,* and *results-driven.*
- We strive to be recognized as a leader in communication technology with products that improve the quality of life in our customer communities.
- We base our *decisions* on the critical *balance* of customer expectations, shareholder return, and the *well-being* of our people.
- We will continuously strive to improve the quality and efficiency of our business.
- **We will make it fun!**

FLEX PRODUCTS:
- The Golden Rule

- Personal Development
- Innovation
- Initiative and Recognition
- Standards of Excellence
- Teamwork
- Fulfillment and Balance

KLEIN FAMILY VINTNERS:
- We are committed to the pursuit of excellence.
- We take pride in our company, its people, and its products.
- We strive to achieve 100% customer satisfaction.
- We offer our employees a stable yet challenging workplace and treat all employees with dignity.
- We are committed to building an open, honest, and trusting work environment.
- We are dedicated to quickly identifying business problems and finding solutions.
- We consider the environmental impact of all our operations.
- We are committed to providing shareholders with a superior return and pride of ownership.
- Our goal is to be the best-managed company in the wine industry now and in the years ahead.

There are transformational missions, like Robert Mondavi's to "Change the Way Americans Think about Wine."[2]

There are also the fun missions, like Taco Bell's: "Be the largest distributor of food worldwide," or Disneyland's: "Put a smile on every face." Or Holiday Inn's: "A hotel at every crossing of two major highways."

Tool number one for contribution is to know exactly what it is you are contributing to and never give in to a defensive or sarcastic answer. You can't lead if you don't know where you are going. You can lead in a path that you determine, but it is better to get input from above.

In a worst-case scenario, you may get put down for asking questions with comments such as, "Duh!" "Hello!" or another form of "You should already have known, dummy." Rule 2, No Put-downs, will give you the tools you need to move right over this bump in the road.

Put-downs won't have lasting effects if you just remember that those who throw cold water in your direction are simply losing ground. Let me share with you one of my experiences with put-downs. I was on the board of directors for six years for a nonprofit performing arts center. My contribution was to assist in developing and updating their mission statement. As the months passed, whenever we were at a crossroads in decisions, I would always say, "Let's look at our mission statement to see if this fits." During six years, six different board chairs had various responses to that question: one detested my mentioning it, one ignored it, and four were grateful and always thanked me. The one who detested it mocked me and felt personally attacked when I brought it up. This ratio of response is typical in business—one in six don't like the topic and are offended, one in six don't pay much attention, but four in six, which is two-thirds, like the fact that you care and are asking the question.

Design Your Personal Mission Statement

"Where there is no vision, the people perish."

—PROVERBS 29:18

I have found a tool that in twenty minutes will guide you to a personal mission statement. With this personal mission statement in mind, you will be much better prepared to request something from your boss that will transform your job into a career. Don't ever be unprepared for that moment when your twenty-first-century manager asks for your number one request.

The tool is the Personal Mission Statement Worksheet,* and it was taken from Roger Merrill's book *Corrections* and used by Stephen Covey in his book, *The Seven Habits of Highly Effective People.* I have searched and searched but never found a better tool.[3]

Mission Statement Worksheet

MISSION STATEMENT EXERCISE

By following the suggested 4 steps in Process One below, you will begin writing a personal mission statement that will inspire you and will provide direction and guidance for your life. Remember that a personal mission statement is as much discovery as it is creation. Don't rush it or set rigid timetables for yourself; rather, go slowly through the process, ask yourself the right questions, and think deeply about your values and aspirations.

PROCESS ONE
The Creation of a Personal Mission Statement

A meaningful personal mission statement contains two basic elements. The first is what you want to be—what character strengths you want to have, what qualities you want to develop. The second is what you want to do—what you want to accomplish, what contributions you want to make. The third is what you want to have—what possessions, money, and so forth that you wish to have.

Note that it is relatively easy to identify the things we want to have; for many of us, that list will be the longest. It's important to keep in mind, however, that legitimate power and the highest levels of human happiness and fulfillment originate from the best.

Step 1 Identify an Influential Person

An effective way to focus on what you want to be and do is to identify a highly influential individual in your life and to think about how this individual has contributed to your life. This person may be a parent, work associate, friend, family member, or neighbor. Answer the following questions, keeping in mind your personal goals of what you want to be and do.

*Trademark of Franklin Covey Company. Used with permission. All rights reserved.

Who has been one of the most influential people in my life? _____
_____

Which qualitites do I most admire in that person? _____
_____
_____

What qualities have I gained (or desire to gain) from that person? _____
_____
_____

Step 2 Define What You Want to Be, and Do, and Have

What I'd like to be: _____
_____
_____
_____
_____

What I'd like to do: _____
_____
_____
_____
_____

What I'd like to have: _____
_____
_____
_____
_____

Step 3 Define Your Life Roles

You live your life in terms of roles—not in the sense of role-playing but in the sense of authentic parts you have chosen to fill. You may have roles in work, in the family, in the community, and in other areas of your life. These roles become a natural framework to give order to what you want to do and to be.

You may define your family role as simply "family member." Or, you may choose more specific roles, such as "wife" and "mother" or "husband" and "father." Some areas of your life, such as your profession, may involve several roles. For example, you may have one role in administration, one in marketing, one in personnel, and one in long-range planning.

Examples:

> *Wife/Mother, Manager—New Products, Manager—Research, Manager—Staff Development, United Way Chairperson, Friend.*

> *Husband/Father, Salesman—Prospects, Salesman—Financing/Administration, March of Dimes Regional Director, Friend.*

Define up to six life roles and then write these roles in the space provided. Next, project yourself forward in time and write a brief statement of how you would most like to be described in that particular role.

By identifying your life roles, you will gain perspective and balance. By writing these descriptive statements, you will begin to visualize your highest self. You will also identify the core principals and values you desire to live by.

Roles	**Statement**
_____	_____
	_____
	_____
_____	_____
	_____
	_____
_____	_____
	_____
	_____
_____	_____
	_____
	_____
_____	_____
	_____
	_____
_____	_____

Step 4 Write a Draft of Your Personal Mission Statement

Now that you have identified your life roles and defined what you want to be and do, you are prepared to begin working on your Personal Mission Statement.

In the space provided below, create a rough draft of your Mission Statement. Draw heavily upon the thinking you've done in the previous three steps. Carry this draft with you and make notes, additions, and deletions before you attempt another draft.

_____

_____

_____

_____

_____

_____

_____

_____

_____

_____

_____

_____

_____

_____

_____

_____

_____

_____

As soon as you have a personal mission statement, or if you already had one, run it through this five-way test developed by Mary Manin-Morrissey:[4]

1. Does this mission enliven me?

2. Does this mission align with my core values?

3. Do I need help from a higher source to make this mission come true?

4. Will this mission require me to be more of my true self?

5. Will this mission ultimately contribute to others?

Personal Missions Revealed

UNIVERSITY HOUSING MANAGER

A manager of a housing division at a Pacific Northwest university, whom we'll call Terry, met with me several years ago saying he felt a separation between his work and who he is as a person. He just did not know how to integrate the two parts of himself. At work he acted one way and at home he acted another way.

His first assignment was to complete the Personal Mission Statement Exercise and then test it with the above five-way test. This was his career mission:

"To integrate who I am with my work by expanding in these areas:

A. Expose my thoughts to others.

B. Initiate contact with staff; don't always react.

C. Do things I enjoy: take walks, read.

D. Observe the difference between enabling and empowering.

E. Create a budget in a positive manner.

F. Observe behaviors of others that are sabotaging.

G. Develop a daily spiritual dialogue.

Defining clearly who he was and what he wanted to do in his life enlivened him; it aligned with his core values; it required help from a higher source; it required him to be more of his true self.

EDWARD TELLER—NOBEL PEACE PRIZE WINNER

In 1976, I heard Ed Teller speak at my college about his obituary, which was written mistakenly about him after his brother had died. It said that Ed Teller had passed away "and will be remembered for designing the atomic bomb." Ed described the depressing sensation he had from having the only contribution he would be remembered for being something as deadly as the atomic bomb!

Because his obituary was done in error, it gave him the motivation to redirect the remainder of his life. Ed decided he needed to be more clear about his personal mission being peace, not war and death. The reason for the bomb, he said, was to keep others from bombing us. But in the obituary, he could see that it was not perceived as such.

Teller then developed a very clear personal mission statement for peace, and he was committed to it. The reward for this commitment was that he was awarded the Nobel Peace Prize some years later. A mission statement will help you restate and clarify your true mission, which helps drive you toward success.

Why is this tool so important? Because once you have your mission and give fuel to a meaningful and successful career, all other steps in your career will have a direction. Your mission and you will lead the way.

2000 OLYMPICS—VISUALIZATION OF A GOAL

The September 25 headlines during the Sydney 2000 Summer Olympics read "Broken Foot Proves No Obstacle for American Diver." An estimated three billion people were watching the Olympics, most of them no doubt expecting the favored Chinese divers to capture the gold medal, as they had for the past four Olympics. American diver Laura Wilkinson seemed an unlikely gold medal contender. A broken foot had kept her out of the water from March until August, one month before the games. Most prognosticators—including the television announcers—had her pegged for no better than eighth place.

But everyone who watched the competition unfold saw a shocking reversal of expectations. Wilkinson went from eighth place to first with a series of near perfect dives. How could someone who had not dived from March to August perform this well in September? Here is the answer: Wilkinson's coach did not stop with the news about her broken foot. Instead, he greatly intensified the visualization activities that have become a standard part of the repertoire among today's elite athletes. While Wilkinson continued to work on upper body exercises to maintain overall strength, her coach had her repeatedly hobble to the platform, rehearse her lead-in, then visualize the result: a perfect dive, done over and over and over. He had her breathe as she'd breathe during the dive, picture what she saw at every stage, how she'd feel—every moment burned into her brain as if it were really happening. The result spoke volumes about the power of visualization.

A similar process of visualization was written about in *Harvard Business Review* in the 1970s and is in Stephen Covey's *Seven Habits of Highly Effective People.* Covey's Habit Two is, "first set a goal and then get a mental creation of it."

The research on visualization is well-established. Wilkinson gave three billion people around the world a chance to view its effects firsthand. The one who visualized the perfect dive from March through September beat the ones who were literally practicing perfect dives March through September. Visualize your goal! Visualize your career!

"It is just as essential to know how to think correctly as it is to know how to act correctly."—Sir John Templeton

MARY—VISUALIZATION OF A CAREER

Twenty years ago, in January I attended a two-day career workshop in which I did a personal and career mission statement that changed my life. During the session, I surprised myself at the end by visualizing having my own business and living on a farm raising children and animals. In a skit we had to do, I was gathering eggs and running my own business. This was a long way from my current life as a middle manager for Xerox Corporation, living in a small condo with an ocean peek in Southern California. It was a fun weekend, but I put away the sheet and went back to my life working in the city.

In October of that year, Xerox Corporation suddenly announced that the company was closing the Southern California Systemix Division (we did research on employee motivation and designed performance review). Twenty-five of us were notified on October 25 that we had until January 1 to move to the East Coast or find other employment.

For me, the shock was short and not too painful because I had an option tucked away. I pulled out my career and personal mission from the career weekend and recalled the "own your own business" part of my mission statement. The next day I negotiated with Xerox and acquired the rights to the research and performance appraisal system we had developed. It was the first step to my entrepreneurial adventure. Then, to keep continuity with the current clients, I invited the seven best people to join me in a new company. Xerox agreed because they didn't know quite what to do with the current West Coast clients whom they could no longer service. It was a real win-win situation: Xerox was off the hook, and we had a ready-made business by January 1. We had all the rights to the research materials that became the Professional Growth Plan—our main product for the next twenty years.

By August of the next year, my husband and I had found a small farm in Northern California, where we have lived for fifteen years, raising our three children along with 4-H pigs, sheep, and chickens. The chickens weren't so great; the rooster attacked our daughter and the hens pecked their own eggs and made messes all over the place, but all the while I was learning. I learned how important it is to make sure that in your personal mission you really want what you picture! All five of us worked hard and enjoyed picking apples, planting gardens, and raising animals (except for the chickens, that is) Our family mission statement (covered in chapter 2) was to create a loving, hardworking, productive family.

My career mission for the first fifteen years I owned my business was to "increase productivity and morale simultaneously" in all client companies. Today my career mission is to "meaningfully contribute to the financial health and emotional intelligence of today's work place." This mission inspired me to write this book. I keep visualizing what that would be like if 5,000,000 mid-managers had rules and tools that could increase the dignity and meaning in their work. I'd hoped that these mid-managers could have the best possible tools available so whenever they choose to be the CEO of their own career, they could.

PERSONAL MISSION IN ACTION—
MARK, THE BARCLAY'S GLOBAL INVESTMENTS MID-MANAGER

My son Mark was a middle manager at a Barclay's global investment corporation. His personal mission was "to be part of a highly functioning work team that is lifted to a level higher than anyone can attain themselves—synergistic, fun, and effective." Mark's personal mission statement was tucked neatly away, and Mark went on with his job.

Ten months later he said his review was coming up that week. I asked him, "Will you tell your manager what she could do to help your group become a highly functioning work team?"

"Oh, we don't do those type of reviews. She will just check boxes and tell me how I'm doing."

"How about if just for fun we identify your number one request, just in case." Reluctantly, Mark got out the mission statement. He came up with a brilliant request that fit his mission statement: "Empower us to be a self-managed work team: (a) Tell us the result you want; (b) Give us timelines and a budget; (c) Let us contact you for check-in points. The result: We would have fewer turnovers and make more deadlines. We would also have fun in the process."

Two weeks later he called to say he had had his review, and guess what? *She asked what he wanted from her!* Mark scrambled to find the scratched-up sheet we had used. "She heard me and immediately started doing it. It's like she wanted to do it, but was waiting for me to ask for it. I told the truth to power, [which we'll explain further in the next section] and it worked. We are actually happy. It's fun because we are accomplishing something and people are listening."

One month later Mark's brother, Keith, reported on an Oakland Raiders game he had attended with Mark and his nine employees. Keith said, "They all had a lot of fun, but you could tell they all really respect Mark." Two weeks later Mark was promoted from supervisor to manager. Together, we saw his mission unfold—a synergistic, fun, effective team.

Telling the Truth to Power

Armed with the tool of your personal mission statement and your prepared number one request with three descriptions and an expected result, you will begin powerful leadership of your career. You will find yourself with a revitalized inner strength that opens the way to "tell the truth to power." Telling the truth to people in power has been identified as a twenty-first-century challenge for mid-managers.

Gaining power by telling the truth is not always easy. Bob Galvin, the Motorola CEO, can attest to that. At the same international leadership conference where he asked attendees to see if they are contributing, a theme that came up over and over in many different formats and groups was this: the number one problem that mid-managers face today is lack of courage. They are afraid to tell the truth to power.[6]

Once you know your personal mission and know how to ask "power" for the one thing that will help you get there and contribute to your manager's number one goal, you are in command. You are now the CEO of your career. These tools assist you in becoming creative, entrepreneurial, and opportunistic.

The Funnel and Alignment Tools Help Set the Stage for Success

As we've discussed, people often find it difficult to articulate what they need from one another in order to get a job done. The Funnel and Alignment process sets the stage for making contributions in an effective, professional manner and creating a safe environment in which it is acceptable to take risks and ask for what you want. It is a simple method that managers and employees can use to identify their number one contribution and their number one request. It then aligns these requests and contributions so they work together to achieve the overall goals of both individual and department.

Very often, when asked to list the things you wish your employees or managers were doing differently, you can think of a dozen things—large and small. The Funnel takes that swirl of ideas and helps you narrow them down. The funnel shape gives people the idea right away that the process is similar to using a funnel in the kitchen or garage. You need to narrow down your material, prioritize, separate the truly important from the (sometimes) petty and make your agreements for contribution pertinent to getting the job done well, as well as include some aspect of your personal mission.

At first, the resentment or frustration you have felt may cause negative requests, or those based on office minutiae. Statements like, "Could Fred be less lax about deadlines?" or "Could Jane stop combing her hair every ten minutes?" do not constitute a contribution from you, nor do they enable you to make progress toward your personal mission. The Funnel process allows people to transform negative thoughts into productive requests.

The first step is to consolidate into one positive statement the most important request you have for how your boss can contribute to you. Similarly, have your manager clarify for you the number one request he or she has of you that would most contribute to the bottom-line goals. Then each of you will clarify that number one request by adding three statements—always beginning with a verb as a catalyst for action.

Putting Funnel and Alignment Tools into Action

DANA'S COMPLAINT

Dana complained that her boss was a "control freak." In the Funnel process, she was asked, "What do you want from your boss?"

Dana wanted her boss to let her take more responsibility within the firm. With this in mind, she assessed her strengths and—based on her computer knowledge—formulated a positive request: "Delegate to me the responsibility of purchasing a new computer system." This was placed at the top of the Funnel. Then she came up with three active sentences that gave her boss an idea of the parameters for her new responsibility:

1. Announce to the staff that I'm in charge of computer purchases.

2. Tell me what the budget is for computers.

3. Trust me to come up with three choices from which you will decide.

Her next step was to provide a measuring stick for results: "How will I measure whether or not my boss is honoring my request? He will meet with me to discuss the details; there will be a memo with an announcement of the task assignment; and I will order the computer we agree upon. What will this contribute to the bottom line? We will save 52 man-hours per week."

Integral to this process was Dana's boss, who simultaneously formulated the number one contribution he wanted from her, based on his assessment of her job and the goals of the department. For instance, if he viewed her as someone who was intelligent but uncommitted, his request would be, "Take

Funnel

Your Name: Today's Date:

What is the Number One Thing the Other Person Can Do to Contribute to Your Career?

GOAL:
Stated in a positive way, the number one item I want from _____ is:

1.

SPECIFICALLY:
• What will this person do to meet your request?

• Use a verb to begin each of the three short descriptive sentences.

2a.

2b.

2c.

SPECIFICALLY:
• How will you know the request has been fulfilled?

• What will be different?

• How will the change be measured?

3.

a more active role in weekly departmental meetings." His three action sentences would include:

1. Meet with me the day before weekly meetings to compare notes and align goals.

2. Articulate your contribution to department heads during the meeting.

3. Write up a weekly memo detailing your suggestions and the department's response.

As before, a measuring stick for results must be provided: How will Dana know if she has met his requests? Complaints about wasted time in meetings will drop to zero. Meetings will be kept under thirty minutes and will cover all agenda items. What will this contribute to the bottom line? Our project on-time completion percentage will go from 65 percent to 80 percent.

As you can see, this process allows Dana and her boss to articulate potentially explosive changes, requests, and ideas to one another in a positive way. It is an equal-opportunity formula because both manager and employee can use it to channel a desire for change into a format that is nonconfrontational and consequently productive. Guidelines for responsibility and accountability are built in, and a "return on investment" is provided.

JOHN AND PAUL REVISITED—GETTING THROUGH AN IMPASSE

John, a technically very talented general manager, and Paul, a gentle engineer supervisor, were at a standstill in terms of achieving the goals of their company. The employees had entered a cycle of sabotage by "losing" important memos, E-mails, and faxes and maintaining a defeatist attitude toward John. This had put John and the entire company in a difficult position. The potential new Chinese customer expected at least a 70 percent performance in terms of getting the product out on time; but in a recent review, John and his department had scored an astonishing zero for on-time products. John's response to this was furious criticism, and his primary target had become Paul, a section manager whom he blamed for everything.

When we arrived at the firm, we started our work with John. It took most of our one-on-one, hour-long meeting to get John to say something that wasn't negative. He was extremely resistant to changing his thought processes, and Paul bore the brunt of his accusations.

It's critical to note that when formulating your own positive request, or managing a situation between coworkers, believe in the potential for success and avoid frustration with others if they are slow to break their cycle of negativity. This is the most important contribution you can make. If you are asked to help someone else funnel their needs, the following exchange demonstrates what you may encounter and offers pointers for the talking process leading to the Funnel:

"John, what is the number one thing you want Paul to do to help meet your deadlines?"

John swore like a sailor. "That *&%! He'll never change. He never takes the lead. He doesn't even know when a deadline's been missed. He's weak . . ." We took notes for fifteen minutes as John ranted and raved. As the facilitator, your duty is to bring the topic back to the question "What *do* you want?" even if it takes an hour to defuse the intensity of someone's feelings. It was quite difficult trying to keep my voice neutral and my expression alert and interested. My concern was not to badger but to be tenacious.

"John, what *do* you want from Paul?"

"To stop being so weak. He'll never be a good manager. He always backs down." (Ten more minutes of notes.)

When repeatedly asking this question, it sometimes helps to change the emphasis. In this situation, I asked again, "John, what *do* you want from Paul? Not what don't you like."

"I want him to quit." (Five more minutes of notes.)

We both knew this wasn't going to happen. Paul wasn't going to quit, and the turnover in John's department had become so high that corporate headquarters was taking note. I rephrased the question, "John, if Paul went to manager camp and came back as the perfect manager, what would he do differently?"

For the first time, John stopped to ponder, then his eyes opened wide with a "Hmm."

When you break the cycle of negative thinking and allow the possibility that circumstances can improve, hope enters into the exchange. Breaking through your own resistance, or that of others, creates a mind-set that allows change to occur which is a jump-start for No Put-downs.

I gave John plenty of time to think about it before I asked him again, "What do you want from Paul?"

"I want him to take a stand and be a leader," John said with clarity and conviction.

"Wow," I thought to myself. "He's made the jump." I wrote down this statement on the Funnel form as John's number one request of Paul. "Take a stand and lead." Then I asked, "John, what does Paul need to do to meet that request? How would he lead? What would he do?"

John was now enthusiastic, "Paul would build a model and make a video to show everyone else how to do it. Then, he should put together a schedule and get [the product] made. Then he'd set a schedule and hold them to it . . ."

We talked through his ideas and distilled them into the most elementary form we could. They were simple, declarative sentences beginning with verbs.

1. Build a model.

2. Make a video and show everyone.

3. Set a production schedule and hold them to it.

The next question on a Funnel sheet asks how the change will be measured. I asked John, "What would be different if Paul did these things?"

John didn't hesitate, "We'd meet ninety percent of our deadlines," and "We'd save ten percent in materials."

John filled out the bottom of his Funnel sheet with these statements. We shook hands and ended our meeting.

Next we met with Paul. He was reluctant to participate and initially claimed he had no requests of John. I explained that inactivity—nonparticipation—was like noncontribution. There is no way to do an Alignment with only one request—like aligning only one car tire. If he agreed to John's request but had no request in turn, the result would be minimal.

Once Paul accepted this, we began the process of filling out his form: What was his number one request of John? Specifically, how would John meet that request? And what would be the result if he did?

Paul's main concern was that he be allowed to participate in setting realistic goals and not be expected to reach goals set by John that were set with lack of information. He had been in the business for many years and had achieved a high level of expertise; he knew his opinions were valuable, but he couldn't understand why John had never solicited his help in planning.

In order for John to honor Paul's number one request: "Let me have input on goals," Paul felt John would have to:

1. Meet with him before giving deadlines.

2. Ask him whether deadlines were realistic.

3. Include him in goal-setting meetings with executive staff.

Like John, Paul believed that if his number one request was honored in this way, he could meet 90 percent of his deadlines.

Alignment Funnel

Your Name: **John**   Today's Date: **9/16/99**

GOAL:
Stated in a positive way, the number one item I want from _____**Paul**_____ is:

1. Take a stand and lead.

SPECIFICALLY:
• What will this person do to meet your request?

• Use a verb to begin each of the three short descriptive sentences.

2a. Build a model.

2b. Make a video and show everyone.

2c. Set a production schedule and hold them to it.

SPECIFICALLY:
• How will you know the request has been fulfilled?

• What will be different?

• How will the change be measured?

3. We'd make 90% of our deadlines.

We'd save 10% in materials.

Alignment Funnel

Your Name: **Paul**   Today's Date: **9/16/99**

GOAL:
Stated in a positive way, the number one item I want from _____**John**_____ is:

1. Let me have input on goals.

SPECIFICALLY:
- What will this person do to meet your request?
- Use a verb to begin each of the three short descriptive sentences.

2a. Meet with me before setting deadlines.

2b. Ask me when I think we can meet it.

2c. Include me in goal-setting meetings with executive staff.

SPECIFICALLY:
- How will you know the request has been fulfilled?
- What will be different?
- How will the change be measured?

3. We'd make 90% of our deadlines.

JOHN AND PAUL—THE ALIGNMENT MEETING

Once both Funnel sheets had been separately filled out, the next step was to set up an Alignment meeting. There, each party reviewed the other's number one request, discussed their Funnels, found a way to merge them, and came into alignment about what they would do and how they would do it.

In an Alignment meeting, the person of lesser rank always presents his or her request first so that he or she does not knuckle under and go along with the boss. In a situation where a tyrannical person like John is involved, the employee might actually fear for his job if he tells the truth. (Telling the truth to power is scary, but if it is a well prepared, positive, forward-moving request, it's much more effective.)

Alignment Agreement

Please Print

Organization: Today's Date:

Employee's Name: Employee's Job Title:

Reviewer's Name: Follow-Up Date:

INSTRUCTIONS: Before writing, Reviewer first hears the Employee's complete request, then it is discussed and agreed upon by both. Reviewer then clearly and concisely prints the Employee's request in full, and signs in agreement. Employee then hears the Reviewer's complete request, they come to agreement, Employee prints the request, and signs the form.

EMPLOYEE'S REQUEST (PRINTED BY REVIEWER)

1. The #1 item _____ wants from _____ is:
   _____
   Employee's Name   *Reviewer's Name*
   _____

2. Specifically what will the Reviewer do to meet your request?
   A. _____
   B. _____
   C. _____

3. How will you know the request has been fulfilled; how will you measure the change? _____
   _____

I agree to begin on _____ Signed _____
                        Date   *Reviewer's Signature*

REVIEWER'S REQUEST (PRINTED BY THE EMPLOYEE)

1. The #1 item _____ wants from _____ is:
                  Reviewer's Name   Employee's Name
   _____
   _____

2. Specifically what will the Reviewer do to meet your request?
   A. _____
   B. _____
   C. _____

3. How will you know the request has been fulfilled; how will you measure the change? _____
   _____

I agree to begin on _____ Signed _____
                                   Date   Employee's Signature

Alignment Agreement

Please Print

Organization: **Manufacturing Fortune 500**

Today's Date: **9/16**

Employee's Name: **Paul**

Employee's Job Title: **Manager of Engineering**

Reviewer's Name: **John**

Follow-Up Date: **11/1**

INSTRUCTIONS: Before writing, Reviewer first hears the Employee's complete request, then it is discussed and agreed upon by both. Reviewer then clearly and concisely prints the Employee's request in full, and signs in agreement. Employee then hears the Reviewer's complete request, they come to agreement, Employee prints the request, and signs the form.

EMPLOYEE'S REQUEST (PRINTED BY REVIEWER)

1. The #1 item _____**Paul**_____ wants from _____**John**_____ is:
                  Employee's Name   Reviewer's Name
   let me have input on goals.

2. Specifically what will the Reviewer do to meet your request?
   A. Meet with me before setting deadlines.
   B. Ask me when I think we can meet it.
   C. Include me in goal-setting meetings with executive staff.

3. How will you know the request has been fulfilled; how will you measure the change? <u>We'd make 90% of deadlines.</u>

_____

I agree to begin on ___<u>9/16</u>___ Signed _____
<small>Date</small> <small>Reviewer's Signature</small>

REVIEWER'S REQUEST (PRINTED BY THE EMPLOYEE)

1. The #1 item _____<u>John</u>_____ wants from _____<u>Paul</u>_____ is:
<small>Reviewer's Name</small>   <small>Employee's Name</small>

   <u>for Paul to take a stand and lead.</u>

2. Specifically what will the Reviewer do to meet your request?
   A. <u>Build a model.</u>
   B. <u>Make a video and show everyone.</u>
   C. <u>Set a schedule and hold them to it.</u>

3. How will you know the request has been fulfilled; how will you measure the change? <u>We'd make 90% of deadlines. We'd save 10% in material.</u>

_____

I agree to begin on ___<u>9/16</u>___ Signed _____
<small>Date</small> <small>Employee's Signature</small>

As the two men sat down, we gave John the blank Alignment Form and asked him to fill out the top half if he agreed as Paul spoke. I asked Paul to read his Funnel, beginning with his number one request.

"I want input on goals," Paul said, reading off the form so he wouldn't have to meet John's eyes.

"Impossible!" John said vehemently, "The goals are set in stone . . ."

I touched John's arm and said quietly, "John, you wanted Paul to stretch, take a stand and be a leader. Having input on goals is what he's asking in trade for your request." This reminder, that give-and-take is fundamental to the process and that Paul's contribution was integral to success, made John pause. After listening further, he filled in the Alignment Form, signed it, and handed the sheet to Paul. Now Paul had it in writing that his requests would be honored.

When it was John's turn, Paul looked somewhat worried. As John told him his number one request and what would be required to achieve it, Paul brightened considerably. He had been operating in a vacuum, not knowing what was expected of him. The items in the Funnel clarified his responsibilities and gave him the authority he was missing. He wrote down John's request and signed the Alignment Form without hesitation. The upshot? By our follow-up session sixty days later, the department was meeting 70 percent of its deadlines. The improvement was astonishing. Their struggle was all too familiar and was written up on the front page of the *New York Times* business section.[5]

This case clearly demonstrates the power of using the Funnel and Alignment system. It moved John and Paul out of the cycle of withholding contributions and into a place where they were able to work together to achieve the company's goals and feel better about their individual job performances.

Paul asked John for input on goals; John asked Paul to take a stand and be a leader. As in most cases, their requests were well matched and contributed not only to the other person but also to their ability to be successful together, which also contributed to the bottom line of the company.

How Can You Use These Tools?

The Funnel and Alignment Tool provides a one-sheet system for getting yourself focused on what you want and need to get your job done. It is a controlled process that encompasses designing and maintaining a structure for contributions, fact-finding, decision making and evaluating performance. It eases the translation of current skills into positive action and broadens the horizons of both participants.

You can use the Funnel and Alignment Tool as part of your ongoing, goal-setting process or you can keep it in your toolbox for those situations when a dispute appears impossible to resolve. Its potential for challenging conventions and reenergizing and renewing the thinking of all concerned is formidable, and its implementation is quite easy.

Completing a Funnel Form: The Employee's Perspective

WHAT DO YOU WANT? PHRASING REQUESTS FOR POSITIVE OUTCOMES

When I am working in a seminar situation, we have everyone participate in this exercise—from the newest entry-level employee to the president. The reason for this is twofold. First, even presidents are accountable to their boards and stockholders. Second, when upper management participates in this exercise in their humble role as an employee, they are able to "hear" what their employees are saying in a very different way. When people are wearing their "employer hats," they are generally making requests that have to do with more, better, faster. Those in "employee hats" most often make requests that deal with recognition, respect, and freedom. Unless management have participated in this exercise as employees, they tend to doubt their employees' requests—thinking they are hiding their true wants. Only after managers have participated and found themselves making requests of their boards regarding recognition, respect, and freedom, do they fully understand and accept the importance of these seemingly trivial changes in the professional and personal quality of life for their employees.

Working now from the employee's perspective, think of one nonmaterial request that you would like your supervisor to fulfill that would make your job better for you. If you have trouble sharing a request because you feel it's not okay to ask for what you want, think about your objective. It's not to complain; it's to make a difference for you, your employer, and your company. Then everyone can take a step toward getting needs met. If you are working to create alignment, it requires more than one person's needs and wants.

Remember to put your request in positive terms. Don't say what you *don't* want to have happen; say what you *do* want to happen. Avoid worrying about what happened in the past. This is your chance to get what you want in the future. If you are stuck, take a peek at Appendix B for possible ideas. More important, think of your personal mission:

Employee's Number One Request: _____
Then consider what this would look like. Remember to use three action verbs to describe this:

1. _____

2. _____

3. _____

What would be different?_____

How did it feel to make a positive request for change? Was it difficult because you were afraid of disturbing the status quo? Feeling selfish? Afraid you wouldn't get it? Don't feel alone. Many people have stated these responses.

Having collected thousands of employee funnels over the years, I have discovered several common threads in all of them. They have to do with responsibility, independence, and recognition—all things that will contribute to the company's success and the employee's satisfaction.

What starts out as a complaint and then becomes a seemingly selfish request almost always becomes a contribution. If you follow the rules and keep the requests nonmaterial and positive, you will be amazed at the results.

SIGNING AN ALIGNMENT AGREEMENT

Alignment meetings occur after employees and employers have separately completed their Funnel sheets. The Alignment Form is introduced by the reviewer. You will ask your employee his or her number one request, and write it in if you agree. Then he or she will write your number one request of management in the second half of the Alignment sheet. At that point, you will both sign and date the form, which becomes the tool for keeping agreements.

In Summary

The purpose of the Funnel and Alignment exercise is to help you identify and visualize potential contributions you may choose to make, enable you to view problems from different points of view and guide you to articulate what you want in ways that enhance your personal mission—all of which are abilities that are fundamental to being your own CEO.

Rule 2: No Put-downs

It's your job as leader of your career to create an atmosphere that transforms antagonism into creative energy.

—JOHN KAO, Harvard Business School

Put-downs Are Criticism Without Hope

Put-downs as defined by George Zimmer, president of the Men's Wearhouse, are "criticism without hope." In his remarks as the commencement speaker at the University of Phoenix in 1998, his advice to six hundred business and management graduates was this: "Never condone put-downs." Teasing someone in jest, when they get a laugh too, is not "criticism without hope." A put-down is measured by the recipient.

Put-downs are described by Kathleen Ryan and Daniel Oestreich in *Driving Fear Out of the Workplace*[1] in shades and scales.

LIGHT GRAY
1. Silence
2. Glaring eye contact: "the look"
3. Brevity or abruptness
4. Snubbing or ignoring people
5. Insults and put-downs
6. Blaming, discrediting, or discounting
7. An aggressive, controlling manner
8. Threats about the job
9. Yelling and shouting (including overuse of caps or exclamation marks on E-mail)
10. Angry outbursts or loss of control

DARK GRAY
11. Physical threats

No Put-downs means no one will say or do anything that will invalidate anyone else as a person. Although it's acceptable to disagree with their ideas, thoughts, or opinions, personal invalidation makes it unsafe for people to be creative or fully contribute. Put-downs can damage the energy in a workgroup and create an atmosphere of hostility and resentment. Constructive commentary, conversely, adds growth and life to individuals and their careers. The importance of No Put-downs is that if you can convert put-downs to suggestions or requests, you generate the juice that builds careers, businesses, and individuals.

The No Put-downs rule applies to customers, vendors, and peers as well as coworkers. I have noticed the dynamics change between vendor and customer when, in private, one has been putting down the other. At some level, people intuitively know when they are in the world of put-downs. Because this has been my line of work, I can tell you there is different eye contact and energy around a person who has been secretly putting another person down.

The difference between phrasing a concern as a put-down or as a request is dramatic. If Fred criticizes his boss to others for being a control freak, he is gossiping. By biting his tongue, gathering his courage, and rephrasing it as a suggestion for delegating more authority, he can enhance his career tremendously.

As the CEO of your own career, it is your job to transform the put-downs that fester in yourself and others into requests. Examples below will show how to do this privately at first. For some, it will be easy. For others, it will take effort and discipline.

The simple act of issuing a No Put-down rule doesn't eliminate the problem of put-downs, because the urge to put someone down turns inside and becomes resentment or hostility. The real goal of Rule 2 is not to suppress the put-down, but to release the resentment or hostility, pull out the constructive commentary, and then convert it into a request. A benefit of this is a deeper understanding of ourselves, which in turn will assist in leading our career direction.

A put-down is not inherently immoral or bad. Put-downs (the kind that are criticism without hope) rob us of knowing our own strengths, distort our strengths into self-sabotage, deprive us of leading our career in the direction we want, and cause depression to replace joy. In *The Argument Culture*, Deborah Tannen, author of *You Just Don't Understand Me*, has a section called "Why Does Criticism Speak Louder Than Praise?"[2] Tannen recalls the following: Admiral Boorda committed suicide after a group of attackers kept pointing out how one of his medals was unearned. He took it off and apologized, saying he had had no idea. One by one, not planning to be vicious, people kept talking about his unearned medal. Tannen says Boorda was trained for military invasion because he knew who his enemies were. In the gossip world things were different for Boorda. He did not know where or who the enemy was. Admiral Boorda could not find the enemy, so he took his own life in desperation. Let's let his life and his tragic death be a lesson for us to know that gossiping and putting down others can cause serious damage. "The culture of critique works stealthily, chipping away at the human spirit," Tannen said.

According to the Dalai Lama in *Ethics for the New Millennium*, "Whatever immediate advantage is gained at the expense of someone else is only temporary. In the long run causing others hurt causes us anxiety even if we can not tell at the time {Karma}. Whatever hardship it entails, disciplining our response to negative thoughts and emotions will cause us fewer problems in the long run than indulging in acts of selfishness."[3]

The No Put-downs Rule Allows for Exhilaration, Expansive Thinking, Productivity, and Joy

GEORGE—A STRUCTURAL ENGINEER

During some research I was doing on joy in the workplace, I interviewed George, a sixty-nine-year-old structural engineer. I asked him to recall a time when he felt the most joy in his work. Right away he said, "Back when I was working for Parsons Company in 1959, I was asked to come up with an economic and practical solution to radioactivity in hangaring atomic-powered aircraft, and I did."

Further research and interpretation showed that the U.S. Air Force was planning at the time to have atomic-powered aircraft. Because of the high level of radioactivity, there needed to be an improvement in storage facilities. They needed to find a way to build a hangar that was wide enough for wingspan yet able to contain all radioactive material. The problem was that concrete had to be used to contain radioactive material, but the wingspans of the planes required hangar widths that were unable to support so much concrete.

Parsons gave this assignment to a young engineer named George. George pondered it for several months. He did his normal tasks each day but always had the concrete hangar in the back of his mind. Eventually he came up with the idea of a concrete shell in a geometric shape called a hyperbolic paraboloid. This provided the long spans necessary for the wings as well as the strength to hold up the concrete.

When he presented it to his boss and staff, they recognized his brilliant solution and praised him for it. The U.S. Air Force eventually decided not to build the atomic-powered aircraft, but George's opportunity to solve this problem and the acknowledgment he received remained the peak experience in his work.

Later, George said the happiness he experienced was more from solving the problem than from the recognition. George bridged the gap between the Air Force's need for a building that could contain radioactive material and the laws of physics that govern the wide span of airplane wings and the heaviness of cement. In analyzing his joy, we found that his happiness was the result of coming to a creative solution when two sides of the problem seemed to be in opposition. It wasn't until forty years later that he understood the source of his joy.

Not knowing what caused his joy and not having ways to maintain it or stay conscious of it the next year, George fell into the common sabotage of the workplace—gossip and put-downs. Several of the engineers were discontented in their jobs, and rather than looking inward for change, they started to blame and gossip about the manager. To give credence to the gossip, it was important to them to get George to agree to the shortcomings of the manager. Little by little the engineers would point out the manager's mistakes, quirks, idiosyncrasies, even his unattractive ties until George was convinced and would join in.

In retrospect, George says this was the most depressing and negative time in his career. While the gossip was funny at the moment (putting down the boss), George had not realized until later the damage it did to himself. He lost enthusiasm for his work and even became depressed. He left Parsons Company the next year and never returned to work for a large company.

He now recalls that the "high" of the solution lasted for months and still lives in him today—forty years later. The "high" of the gossip lasted just a few minutes, and the damage marked a major low point in his working career.

During George's time at Parsons in the 1960s, there was little consciousness of what sabotage could do to work enthusiasm. People were not involved in self-development as we know it today and did not recognize its importance. Now, of course, we know better. We know we must change ourselves first and take responsibility for our own self-development. Put-downs do not contribute; they only sabotage.

Uncover the Pearls That Lie Beneath Put-downs

JOHN AND PAUL

John and Paul were in conflict over how to achieve the goals and deadlines set for them by management. They were at an impasse, but a put-down of John's revealed a pearl of a positive request for Paul. John began his private session (without Paul) with his angry put-down, "Paul will never be a manager. They walk all over him; he'll never change; he's too weak; his voice is like nothing." After an hour of complaints about Paul's ineptness, John took a new position when he answered truthfully the question, "What do you want from Paul?" John stopped, looked away and then suddenly his eyes opened wide. Then with a passionate rush, he said, "I want him to take a stand and be a leader . . . build a model; make a video; assign responsibilities; hold people accountable; take corrective action if necessary."

This was the pearl. Underneath his constant put-downs of Paul, John had a request that was just what Paul needed but had never been told. Because John was such a strong and powerful leader himself, he expected everyone else to be the same. When they weren't, he reverted to put-downs.

Paul and his fellow workers had been putting John down all along too. Not many people will tolerate constant put-downs without retaliating! So Paul and the staff gossiped that John was a mean, crazy, dictator-type person. Behind Paul's put-downs was his fear of telling the truth to power, and he was hesitant to be forthcoming in his individual meeting. His pearl underneath his complaint that "John is a dictator" was "Let me have input on goals." Because Paul always solicits input from others, it was hard for him to describe this request—it seemed too obvious.

You Can Remove Resentments That Are Holding Back Your Career

You are the CEO of your focus, attitude, direction, and resentments. If you can manage career inhibitors, you open new doors for your career. You will be amazed by the grace that permeates a group when they have been asked to avoid put-downs for a specified period of time. This is particularly important in conflict resolution. Like a cease-fire during a war, the No Put-downs rule aids in resolving conflict and rebuilding strong teams and partnerships. Whether you are working with subordinates, peers, or your boss, adhering to the Three Rules, particularly Rule 2, transforms the group.

A TELEVISION STATION IN CRISIS

A Midwest radio station was facing a problem with high turnover in the sales department. The top sales producers were leaving abruptly. I was commissioned to find out what the sales manager, Ted, was doing "wrong." As I interviewed various sales staff members, the criticism of the sales manager became more and more intense. But when it came time to convert each complaint or put-down into a request, it got very vague. Their suggested requests were along the lines of listen, lead, be consistent, motivate, and empower. Sara said, "Well, he does do that, but I guess not enough." Nothing concrete seemed to be defined. A thick feeling of contempt seemed to dominate the employees' dissatisfaction.

I then met with the sales manager, Ted. Ted told me how these salespeople were overly emotional, spoiled, distorting the facts, and demanding. He asked me what he was doing wrong and what he could do differently to keep his job. I gave him the following Eight-Step Checklist for Effective Listening and suggested that he use it.

Eight-Step Checklist for Effective Listening

#1 PAY ATTENTION; INTEND TO UNDERSTAND
- Focus attention on the person; do not interrupt.
- Maintain eye contact, sit forward, and lean toward the speaker.
- Take in the whole picture.
- Tell and demonstrate to the person that he or she has your full attention.

#2 SUMMARIZE WHAT YOU HAVE HEARD (USE *FEELINGS CHART*)
- Repeat back in your own words what you heard. "Let me see if I understand. You are feeling . . . because . . . Is that correct?"
- Use words that create pictures and feelings.

#3 ACKNOWLEDGE FEELINGS
- Ask how the person feels about the situation.
- Show empathy for the speaker: "I understand how you feel."
- Tell about a time when you had similar feelings or describe a similar situation.
- Suspend your own biases about the situation.

#4 ASK CLARIFYING QUESTIONS
- *Who* . . . is involved?
- *What* . . . have you said?
- *Where* . . . did you get that idea?
- *Why* . . . is this happening now?
- *How* . . . did you arrive at that conclusion/idea/agreement?

#5 ASK FOR THE OTHER PERSON'S SUGGESTIONS FOR RESOLUTION
- How would you recommend that this be handled?
- What would you like to see done?
- Ask for all relevant information.

#6 PRESENT YOUR POSITION
- If the suggestion above is suitable, tell the person: "That sounds like a good idea." Make sure the message is consistent; body language matches the verbal component.

- If the suggestion in #5 is not suitable, present your position: "I hear your suggestion and I have another point of view. What we might do is . . ."
- Collaborate: "Your suggestion works nicely in these areas. I'll support you. Can you support me in these areas?"

#7 DECIDE ON SPECIFIC COURSE OF ACTION AND FOLLOW-UP (USE *ALIGNMENT AGREEMENT*)
- "Now, let's see, I will . . . and you will . . . okay?"
- Ask: "Do you need additional support? How and in what form?"

#8 THANK THE PERSON
- Evaluate the conversation: Were you both heard and understood? Is the solution win-win?
- "I really appreciate your coming to me with your concerns."

We reviewed the eight steps, talked, and got more comfortable with each other. We decided to role-play with me as Sara (one of the staff) and him as himself. I began in the role of Sara, complaining. When it was time for him to summarize Sara's concerns (Step #2), he leaned over to me and whispered, "Mary, just between you and me, I don't feel compassion for her concerns."

I leaned toward him and said in the same whisper and with a friendly tone, "Ted, you don't have to feel compassion, just summarize what she said and ask questions." He hesitated—thinking that he had to feel a certain way immobilized him. Remember, "No Put-downs" doesn't mean you have to like everyone. It means to quit bitching, relieve your own contempt privately, and tell coworkers what you want. The freedom from having to "feel compassion" and "*like*" Sara was a huge relief for Ted. The workplace doesn't have to be filled with your best friends. You do not need to like every coworker. You do need each other to assist in career growth. Ted then filled out the Conscious Communication Form to relieve his resentment toward Sara. She privately did the same.

Conscious Communication

1. I make myself feel _____
   (use Feelings Chart)
   when _____
   (briefly describe situation)
   _____

2. I am concerned that what might happen is _____
   (what you want changed)
   _____
   _____

3. I would like you to _____

_____

_____

4. My goal is _____

_____

_____

5. It seems to me your goal is _____

_____

_____

6. Would you be willing to explore some alternatives to help us both achieve our goals? If "yes" finish with #7. If "no" finish process with thanking him/her for listening to you.

7. Some possibilities I have come up with that may be more effective or harmonious are:

1. _____

_____

2. _____

_____

3. _____

_____

Are any of these acceptable to you? Do you see other possibilities? Listen to response, possibly discuss and thank her/him for listening to you.

After Ted and Sara had *privately* expressed and released the worst of their hostility and resentment, they were asked to attend a meeting to resolve the disharmony between sales and management. Two officers of the television station, two salespeople, and one sales manager attended. Since Ted and Sara converted put-downs to requests ahead of time and then agreed to the No Put-downs rule during that meeting, the once prevalent contempt disappeared and a quiet opening of communication occurred.

The group diagnosed the disharmony between sales and management in a non-blaming way. Next they outlined fifteen possible solutions and then voted on four of them. Without put-downs they had become a problem-

Feelings Chart

Love	Hostility	Betrayed	Isolated
Hate	Confusion	Peaceful	Alone
Anger	Aggravated	Enthusiastic	Independent
Frustration	Protective	Empty	Trapped
Guilt	Possessive	Mad	Powerful
Anxiety	Happy	Sympathy	Needed
Worry	Sad	Embarrassed	Confident
Hurt	Excited	Shy	Wanted
Tired	Surprised	Terror	Secure
Confused	Shocked	Abused	Insecure
Curious	Afraid	Flexible	Cautious
Hopeless	Important	Misunderstood	Vulnerable
Hopeful	Rejected	Proud	Tender
Appreciative	Depressed	Pleased	Rage
Helpless	Nervous	Caring	Accepted
Overwhelmed	Grief	Carefree	Nurturing
Pressured	Inadequate	Fear	Weak
Sure	Disappointed	Mean	Deceived
Unsure	Lonely	Aggressive	Self-Defeating
Satisfied	Bored	Irritated	Disgusted
Relief	Blamed	Justified	Content
Joy	Self-Doubt	Defensive	
Scared	Deserted	Dependent	

solving think tank. One simple rule like No Put-downs and trying to convert put-downs to requests led this group to work effectively to resolve their conflict. No put-downs opened the way for the groups' pearls of wisdom and allowed them to work together, and achieve a state of synergy. Consistent synergy transforms jobs into careers.

A GERMAN PUBLIC UTILITY COMPANY AND THE SISTINE CHAPEL

Several years ago I was subcontracted by a public utility company in Germany to customize the Alignment tool for its use between all employees and their supervisors. It was actually a last-ditch attempt on their part to avoid a strike. It was a very difficult assignment with the language barrier and the threat of a strike, but I was excited by the challenge. My German counterpart consultant, Frank, commissioned me to work with his leadership program. I was to use the Funnel tool to show the managers how to include employee input; he would do the rest.

A few weeks before I was to leave on this assignment, my husband and I were beginning our divorce proceedings. It was a very difficult time, and I was constantly preoccupied with a feeling of resentment I had toward him, so I could hardly concentrate on my work at home, let alone in Germany.

In order to make a smooth transition, I decided to spend five days in Europe before this assignment to clear my head. On the fourth day, I visited Rome and the Sistine Chapel. As I gazed at the crucifix of Christ in the chapel, I began to wonder what it was like for people who lived at that time and knew Him. I was embarrassed as I kept peeking and dodging His face, which appeared to be looking right at me. I was ashamed, because I was still in a state of resentment and for four days I hadn't been able to shake it. I didn't like being seen with this overwhelming resentment.

I thought about a number one request I might have for Christ. So, I considered asking Christ to please remove the resentment I was feeling toward my husband to enable me to do a good job in Germany. I quickly scanned everything that was wrong with George. I had been adhering to the No Put-downs rule when talking with him, but now I was filled with resentment. I silently asked Christ to please remove this resentment.

Suddenly I looked at Him more thoroughly and realized that the crucifix represented His suffering. How selfish of me to make a request of a Christ figure in this suffering state. Then I pictured myself asking, "Christ, if you were here today like this, what would be your number one request of me?" The answer I imagined was, "Understand this moment of mine. If for one second you can feel what it was like to be nailed to the cross right in front of people you had healed and helped and loved, then I will feel that my life mattered and your resentment will be released just in that act of total empathy."

As I pictured the faces Christ must have had to look upon as he ached, my resentment was lightened immediately. The urge to put George down was diffused by the comparison. With my resentment reduced, I was able to visualize the work to be done in Germany and mentally prepare myself.

Now the next day I was able to be completely present and understand what the German utility company wanted and needed. I could fully hear their concerns. Frank was trying to tell me why some of our two-way interactive exercises were not appropriate for the German culture. When they had expressed a need to remove one exercise that was too "California" for the German company, I had originally disagreed but came to agree with him. We were aligned and we were ready to present alignment to others. I could focus now, and the relief felt wonderful.

Spiritual Practices as a Way to Manage Oneself Away from Put-downs

Several years ago, I was hired to create a mission and a strategic plan for a chemical company in Kuwait. I read the Koran before going so I could relate to their culture. I was aware of their reverence for Allah, but was impressed by the integration of this spiritual discipline into the business environment. Their practice of hailing called "crying" to Allah at a certain time each day released the resentment that was building up in the sessions of that day. Tensions would rise, values clash, resentment grow, then suddenly at a certain time each day, everyone stopped and hailed Allah. Once the prayers were over, the negative seemed to dissipate, and it was easier to contribute and get back to the business at hand. Meetings flowed and we were much more productive after the tension and resentment had been released.

Then there was the client who was a fabulous artist and woodworker who kept a Buddha on his desk. He used it to release suffering and resentment. He said he used the Eight Paths of Buddhism to release tension several times each morning.

In another example of linking spirituality with success, an Olympic toboggan racer from India was asked on television to what he attributed his incredible success. His comment was that his Hindu spiritual discipline got him through the semifinals because, as the announcer said, "It gave him an inner calm others lacked. The tension had wiped most competitors out." He rarely tobogganed in India because there is little snow, but knowing how to stay calm had enabled him to place on the Olympic team.

There is no way to give equal time to all spiritual practices here, but suffice it to say that having your own mental or spiritual discipline, whether it's listening to that voice within (I call it your second opinion), meditation, physical exercise, or religion, makes a major difference in being able to get past resentments and convert put-downs to requests so your career can blossom. The importance of this simple task is that the consistency of doing it privately in the workplace will provide the inner peace to allow you to direct and lead your career.

As we master the urge to put another down, we will discover our own inner sources to grow our job, empower those around us and transform our workplace. The urge to put others down is particularly strong when there are persons in your workgroup with personality disorders.

Rule 2 Exposes Personality Disorders

Most mission statements and company business plans assume that reasonable, logical minds are in the workplace. This assumption is true for about 87 percent of the people in the workplace. The other 13 percent could have hidden agendas, health problems, or what is called a "personality disorder." According to a December 1999 report by the surgeon general of the United States, 22 percent of the population has a diagnosable mental disorder. These numbers mesh with the 12 to 15 percent of apparent mental disorders that I have observed in the workplace since 1980. Since I am not a psychologist, the most reliable evidence I have of mental or personality disorders in the workplace is the person who cannot keep the Three Rules. Thus the Three Rules have become not just the gauge but also a tool to help middle managers deal with disorders in the workplace. If the middle manager does not recognize mental illness or personality disorder in either his boss or employees, it can be a threat to his or her career.

A key story in a Sunday edition of the *New York Times* was titled "Defining the Line between Behavior That's Vexing and Certifiable." This article named additional certifiable criteria for Antisocial Personality Disorder, Histrionic Personality Disorder, Defiant Disorder, Caffeine Intoxication, Nicotine Dependence Disorder, Obsessive Compulsive Personality Disorder, and Non-Compliance with Treatment.[4]

Unless your goal is to be a psychiatrist or psychologist, getting involved in diagnosing these behaviors will do little to enhance your career. However, Rule 2 is particularly good for exposing personality disorders. Five of the nine general characteristics of a borderline personality are manifested by putting others down. Thus, even if they agree to No Put-downs, people with such a disorder will not be able to maintain that agreement.

A personality disorder is "an enduring pattern of behavior that deviates markedly from the expectations of the individual's culture"—i.e., their inner world is different than the outer world. The borderline personality disorder is indicated by any five of the following nine symptoms:

1. Frantic efforts to avoid abandonment—has difficulty with separate and distinct viewpoints

2. Alternating extremes of idealization and devaluation of self and others (splitting: one day you are wonderful in their eyes, the next day you are terrible)

3. Identity disturbance—unstable self-image varies from arrogant to suicidal

4. Impulsivity in at least two areas: spending, sex, substance abuse, reckless driving, or eating disorders

5. Recurrent self-mutilating behavior

6. Instability due to reactive mood swings

7. Chronic feelings of emptiness

8. Inappropriate intense anger. Hostile attacks or silent rage at random times.

9. Stress-related paranoid symptoms

Successful top-level managers and employees can disguise such a disorder in today's workplace. Many employees with personality disorders do not show acute or bizarre behaviors. In fact, they may be wizards in their work and excellent providers, but they are psychologically unable to be in a relationship of mutual support.[5] The most common practice that I believe affects the day-to-day increasing number of persons with borderline personality disorder in the workplace is the tolerance of gossip and put-downs. This activity creates an environment that seems to allow borderlines to remain behind the put-down.

Borderlines, both as bosses and as employees, can appear to be contributing. Middle managers can gain an extra insight from requiring Rule 2 because it so clearly exposes borderlines. The overwhelming urge to attack and blame others makes the No Put-downs rule next to impossible for borderlines to keep without consistent outside help. Borderlines can gain incredibly high levels of emotional support and then turn on those around them at random, unexpected times.

I experienced a "boardroom borderline" more fully when a man I will call Chuck lived with a woman who was diagnosed as a borderline. Chuck began dating "Linda," a key executive of a software company. Because he had seen her only in her executive role, she seemed like a nice woman for him to date. Shortly after they began dating, however, she was in a rush to make a commitment and live together. Of course it was flattering to Chuck; he thought it meant she loved him and he decided to go for it.

The next month, and a few thereafter, the story changed. As he tells it, "As soon as we moved in together, the love became love and hate intermittently" (symptom 2). In retrospect, he said she was constantly exhausted by having to be in a contributing mode at work and had none left for home.

After a few months, each evening Chuck would become the object of her attack and blame. It wasn't about love at all. What she wanted was someone at home to hate so she could be positive at work.

"The real Linda," he said, "was so endearing and lovable." According to Chuck, they initially had what seemed to be a deep, passionate, and spiritual connection. But the balance of positive and negative interactions tilted more and more toward the latter. He described her "altered states," which occurred on a regular basis (symptom 6)—first she was excessively critical of the government, then of men, and then of him. She was better than everyone else one day, hopeless the next (symptom 3).

He explained how Linda started to make up offenses. Once, while on a vacation with her, he went for a walk. When he returned, she was irate and feeling an inappropriate level of abandonment. She accused him of going off the beach and into the nearby brush to meet someone. Even though he showed her his footprints in the sand, she was still angry. The facts seemed irrelevant and the feeling of abandonment prevailed (symptom 1). Another time, he says, he interrupted her favorite baseball's team game on television to tell her her brother was on the phone. She later accused him of calling her brother just so he could interrupt the baseball game (symptom 9—paranoia). When he showed her the phone bill one month later, she had already engaged in a twenty-four-hour quiet rage (symptom 8). The stories got worse and worse. They became more and more difficult to hear.

Chuck knew that Linda had been abused by her father, and he had an illusion that if he were a little more understanding and loved her and gave her space, her attitude would improve. An insidious effect of the borderline disorder is that it seduces others into thinking they can help. Linda was extremely successful at work and used her performance on the job to invalidate any of Chuck's requests for her to change. "I'm successful at work, so our problems must be your fault." When others saw Linda at community events, they always commented she was so charming and it was obvious to Chuck that they questioned the validity of his stories.

Rule 2 of the Three Rules saved him from that dysfunctional relationship. Once the inappropriate behaviors began, he went to a counselor for help with learning to set limits. He applied the limits to their relationship by telling her of his personal boundary of "No Personal Attacks." When the personal attacks became obsessive and were bordering on physical threats, he had the clear signal he needed to move out. He was able to say, "I love the real you and we had great hope, but I cannot live with the hostile behavior." It allowed him to part in a way that kept his dignity intact.

Linda's board of directors continued to think Linda was a star, but no manager ever had a chance to grow and develop in her department. She constantly put down one manager to the others. When a consultant (one of my partners) told her of this behavior, Linda refused to stop. She said it gave her pleasure. The problem was that it was almost impossible for her to tolerate any real input from another person. She could follow instructions from a board of directors, but she could not consider the pros and cons of ideas from other people below the board level. (Symptom One)

Nevertheless, the company still grew. Linda did everything the board wanted and more. But managers were all treated like gofers, and Linda made all the decisions. The careers of the middle managers stagnated in that setting. The growing company lured managers into thinking their careers would grow, too. Little did they know that there was no real access to their president and that they would be the subjects of regular gossip between their boss and coworkers.

According to Dr. Michael Barrington, president of Phoenix-Bohan, an HMO for behavioral disorders, "working with borderline personalities in the workplace makes you feel crazy. If an employee shows five of the nine symptoms, send them to employee assistance programs, just as you would an alcoholic."[6] The twenty-first century began with two new ways to handle borderlines in the workplace: (1) Employee assistance programs, and (2) the Employee's Disabilities Act now includes physical, mental, and emotional disabilities. According to *Harris v. Oregon Health Services* (September 1999), a borderline personality disorder is considered a mental illness under the Americans with Disabilities Act.[7] This means that managers/supervisors are expected to make accommodations for the borderline just as they are required to do for those who have physical disabilities.

The accommodations required of them are that they make adjustments *unless* the employee is unable to perform the tasks and uphold the Three Rules. If you hold everyone to the Three Rules, you have established that standard and need not be forced to hire or keep disruptive borderline employees. If it's your boss who is the borderline, it's best to start looking for a new job if you don't want your career to be permanently damaged. Remember, only a professional psychological evaluation can determine if a person has a borderline personality disorder, but if someone is unable to adhere to Rule 2, that person will create problems—borderline personality or not.

Rule 2 Helps You Manage a Narcissistic Boss

The feature article in the January/February 2000 issues of the *Harvard Business Review* was titled "Narcissistic Leaders: The Incredible Pros, the

Inevitable Cons," by Michael Maccoby. The Internet Revolution has given rise to this new type of executive—gifted, visionary, productive, and willing to take risks. Narcissists in history also inspired people and shaped the future during the Industrial Revolution. Maccoby says: "Andrew Carnegie, John D. Rockefeller, Thomas Edison, and Henry Ford are narcissistic leaders who exploited new technology and restructured American industry."[8]

"Narcissism" is the term that Sigmund Freud used for this condition, which is manifested by a huge ego, self-involvement, and self-aggrandizement. It was named after the mythical, Narcissus, who died because of his pathological preoccupation with himself. Later Freud realized we are all somewhat narcissistic, so, only professionals can determine if the degree of narcissism present is normal or pathological. According to Maccoby, today's narcissists—people like Jack Welch, George Sovos, Bill Gates, and Steven Jobs—have emerged to restructure worldwide industry via the Internet Revolution. "Productive narcissists have the audacity to push through the massive transformations that society periodically undertakes."[9]

The downside is that narcissists can be emotionally isolated and highly distrustful and thus are vulnerable to times of hostile rage. One Oracle manager described his narcissistic chief executive, Larry Ellisan, this way: "The difference between God and Larry is that God does not believe he is Larry."[10]

Because there are a larger number of narcissistic leaders at the helm of today's corporations, employees and managers must learn how to recognize and work around narcissistic bosses. It's a matter of learning to adapt or leave. The strength of a narcissistic leader is that he or she can lead with great vision and inspire scores of followers. The weaknesses include oversensitivity to criticism, lack of empathy, distaste for mentoring, and an intense desire to compete.

What can middle managers do to recognize these leaders? Try the Three Rules test. If leaders do not contribute to the company mission (if they are building their own empire), if they engage in uncontrollable put-downs during their times of rage, or if they continuously break agreements, they could be narcissistic leaders.

In case you must stay in your job for a while longer, Michael Maccoby's article gives three strategies on how to briefly deal with a boss who is narcissistic, but they are good only for the short term: (a) always empathize with the boss, but never expect any empathy back; (b) give the boss ideas and let him/her take the credit; (c) manage your time: "narcissistic leaders give more orders than one could possibly execute. Carve out free time for yourself when there's a lull in the boss's schedule." In your free time, look for a new job.

Narcissistic leaders are usually very poor mentors. Your career is probably on hold, if not in jeopardy, if your boss takes all the credit, keeps you constantly overwhelmed, and won't mention you or have empathy for you.

Empower Yourself and Others to Diffuse Put-downs

In April and then November 2000 the combined value of all NASDAQ (high-tech) stocks plunged $1 billion. This kind of market uncertainty creates very volatile workplaces, in which narcissistic behavior runs rampant and put-downs are everywhere. Even though it is illegal under Title VI of EEOC to create a hostile work environment, some high-tech Internet start-up companies with narcissistic leaders do not pay attention to that directive. Meanwhile, here is how you can set boundaries and lead yourself regardless of what may be going on around you. You can lead the way by empowering yourself and others to diffuse the put-downs or hostile work environment. If a complaint is real, it can be rephrased into a positive request. If it cannot be converted into a positive request, it is clearly a put-down.

To handle this, you can hold on to Rule 2 and say, "Even though it may seem obvious to you, would you please convert what you just said into a request?" One male president of a radio station said to a female mid-manager whom we'll call Sally: "Don't always be so emotional." This was an all-out put-down (a criticism without hope).

But Sally knew how to handle it. She replied, "Would you please convert that to a positive request?"

"Sure," he said sarcastically. "Please be non-emotional."

"Are you sure that's what you want? It is my emotion and passion for my clients' success that makes me by far your number one producer. Without that passion, I will have no clients," she responded. Sally had a strong grounding because she used the Three Rules in other settings and could keep this exchange light and friendly. She kept asking him to convert his complaint into a positive request.

What he finally came up with the next day was, "Bring your concerns to me in a logical, sequential way so I can understand them and respond to them." She was very glad to hear what he wanted and did as he requested, and their relationship improved immediately.

Not every put-down hides a borderline. But be warned: managers and employees who are intensely focused on the weaknesses of others and who cannot ever seem to convert the put-down to a request do show signs of borderline personality or other problems. These disorders or emotional irregularities fester in a workplace and rob people of the possibility of a positive career—themselves included. It is much easier to require the No Put-downs rule of employees than of coworkers, since you have built-in authority over people who report to you. Borderlines may use their splitting characteristic (extreme idealization and devaluation) between you and their coworkers. They might be very serving and contributing to you at first but may be very subtly cutting to coworkers (like Chuck with his board versus his managers). When a coworker criticizes another employee to you, ask them to convert it to a positive suggestion, and call in the other employee. Most people who use put-downs often cannot tolerate up-front, positive honesty and will choose on their own to find another job.

Weed Out Destructive Employees with Rule 2

A company president whom I'll call Neil asked us to help save a good producer whom no one liked. He wanted to do an alignment between himself and a difficult employee, Donna, who may or may not be a borderline. She so focused on her hate for certain of her coworkers that she kept putting them down. She could not conceal her contempt, and the other managers complained to Neil. I asked Neil why he hadn't terminated her. He explained that Donna did a valuable job for him.

Then I met Donna. She continued with her put-downs. I reminded her of the No Put-downs rule, but she thought it didn't apply to her. "That's for them, not me [sysmptom 2]. My job is to be the heavy around here." When I kept pushing her to say what she wanted from a coworker, rather than what she didn't like, she looked angry and accused me of being a "touchy-feely personnel type." I playfully said, "No Put-downs also applies to you and me," to which she responded, "I'm not going to play these games. I have more important things to do." I said, "Shall we postpone our meeting and work up an alignment between you and your manager another time?" Neil, her boss, had a directive from his board to do this alignment in one week, so time was important to her. Since she had just two days left, she agreed to try to convert her criticisms to requests.

Working effectively with possible borderline managers requires very strict boundaries. This is why strong adherence to the No Put-downs rule was so effective in this case. I reminded Donna of our three written agreements. I said I could finish this project only if she would contribute to the alignment process, convert all put-downs to positive requests, and keep agreements. She finally got back on track in a very patronizing tone and only because the board chair was overseeing the project. After using the Funnel to diffuse her many complaints about Neil, she finally converted to one request:

1. Back up my decisions

   A. Send complainers to me
   B. See and understand my reasons
   C. Discuss with me

Result would be: Complaints about my decisions would stop.

Neil's number one request of Donna was

1. Treat employees with respect no matter what.

   A. Be consistent
   B. Create a positive experience with interactions
   C. If they don't deserve respect, quietly document it and still treat
      them with respect.

Result would be: Complaints would be reduced to two to three a month.

When they met to align their two number one requests, Donna went first. Neil accepted her request to back up her decisions. When it was Neil's turn to tell her his number one request, she became irate and said, "Oh, you want me to be Mary Poppins!"

"No! Don't escalate this."

I intervened with, "Neil was just asking you to treat each person with respect no matter what—not fake glee—just respect."

She was upset by the request and left for a while. Then she came back and argued for a long time that some people don't deserve respect. Neil explained it was too damaging to their business not to respect everyone equally, and he was asking this as his number one request. She reluctantly agreed. Their alignment was signed and a thirty-day follow-up was scheduled. At the end of thirty days, I asked each how the other did.

Neil stretched to adhere to her number one request. She gave him an 80 percent. Donna managed to treat her coworkers with some respect, no matter what. He gave her a 65 percent. All was fine until the next big upset. She went right to visible contempt toward her coworkers and even some clients in public. Neil made a judgment; she got a 0 percent.

Donna was perfect for the job when they first hired her because the company was in financial trouble and she said no to all the poor risks and demanded payment from nonpayers. But, once the company was back on track, her abrasive style was harmful. Since a deep contempt for everyone was her normal state in this workplace, she was uncomfortable with having to treat everyone with respect. When she saw "0" on her evaluation from Neil, she quit. By holding the line, Neil was able to keep Rule 2 in action in his company.

Remember, focus on Rule 2, and 87 percent of your employees will flourish in a workplace of positive requests and continuous improvements. Focus on your own career goals and match your requests of employees to the objectives you want to achieve. You will feel liberated, as will those around you.

7

The Power of No Put-downs

No one can make you feel inferior without your permission.

—ELEANOR ROOSEVELT

Constructive Discontent

The business goal for the 'No Put-downs rule is to create constructive discontent. Constructive discontent means being curious, empathetic and constantly learning in the face of resistance and opposition. It does not imply no disagreement or no complaints. It means seek out the hope in every complaint and find the pearl in the opposition—our opponents often have valuable information for us but it takes emotional intelligence to find it.[1] We could say constructive discontent is criticism with hope.

The Pacific Management Group conducted a survey of ten thousand mid-managers over a ten-year period and asked what, on bad days, is the average time spent focusing on or obsessing over another person's weaknesses? The average answer was 69 percent. Once mid-managers learn how to observe themselves as closely as they observe others, and then use the Three Rules to take responsibility for their own behavior, they will be well on their way to changing that behavior, and they then will be able to find constructive ways to work with both superiors and subordinates to transform their work environment. The key lies in transforming negative comments into positive actions.

Steps for Converting Put-downs into Positive Requests

The objectives for reaching the goal of no put-downs are as follows:

A. Identify the irritation/complaint/offense.

B. Assign a percentage of how much time on a bad day is spent responding to the irritation.

C. If the percent is 20 percent or more, convert the irritation/complaint/offense to a request before it is expressed.

D. Privately release the personal resentment that causes the put-down to get stuck as such.

E. If it contributes, communicate the converted complaint into a positive request to the person who can do something about it.

F. Ask also what you can do to improve.

G. Use the wisdom of the converted put-down to improve the workplace so that people are energized, motivated, and continuously improving.

Put-downs also may eliminate the sacred sense of community and invalidate other people and their contributions to the organization. Many individuals who do not define themselves by their mistakes and missteps are often willing to define others that way. The real losers are the people who engage in put-downs. By focusing on the dark side of others, they do not have a chance to observe and grow from their own failings.

If a company tolerates gossip, blaming, and other kinds of put-downs for a long period of time, the situation will probably not change in a short period of time. Negativity may have become the habitual form of communication. After a workshop on the Three Rules, however, employees tend to help each other become more aware of put-downs. This is a goal for the No Put-downs rule: establish as part of the corporate culture people who keep each other in check in a positive, team-oriented way.

When a business adopts the Three Rules as part of its personnel policies, it is important to have the organization's mission, values, and goals outlined and understood by everyone in the firm. When such objectives are clearly defined, cooperation increases and there is a significant shift away from negativity. People feel involved and empowered when they understand that every contribution counts. More often than not, they devote their energy to promoting the good of the company and moving in a positive direction.

PUT HOPE BACK IN CRITICISM

An aerospace company adopted the Three Rules and used the Funnel and Alignment process to improve business. Steve, the president of the company, was concerned because the company kept missing deadlines for government contracts; and as a result, it was losing business. He said the organization could easily get 25 percent more in government contracts if he could trust his managers. He went through the funnel steps and said that his number one request of all of his managers was that they "operate with **integrity**."

He knew this request for integrity was going to offend them, so he wasn't planning to tell them. He was right. They probably would feel put down if they thought he believed they had no integrity. I asked Steve to outline three verbs to describe what he meant by integrity. He reacted with sarcasm and defensiveness.

"Look it up in the dictionary," he blustered.

It did not matter how the dictionary defined it. What mattered was his understanding of integrity, since he was using it as a gauge for judging his managers.

When Steve did try to define integrity, he could only say what it wasn't. "When a manager brings me a recommendation and then keeps changing it, I can't trust it. When we agree to a deadline and they don't keep it, I can't trust them. They aren't thorough enough."

Steve complained a little longer, then I asked if there was anything he liked about his managers. He conceded that they were all honest and trust-worthy people. His eyes glistened as he said this and then he stopped. He could see that the issue was more a matter of his not being able to trust his people than it was their lack of integrity. Steve realized that he could tell his managers what he wanted from them to increase his trust level without put-ting them down for lack of integrity. In doing so, he came up with a much better and more tangible number one request: "Consistently give me com-plete staff work." His four descriptors were:

A. Outline pros and cons thoroughly.

B. Triple-check all your figures.

C. Make a specific recommendation with a backup.

D. Tell me if your project is going to be late as soon as you know, so I can do something about it.

The result: "I would be able to trust your recommendations and act on them in a timely manner. This would increase our government contracts by 25 percent because I could move more quickly."

For Steve, getting out of the put-down habit meant thinking through what he wanted in positive terms and restating his objectives in a way that did not invalidate his people. Like many presidents, he was probably not going to tell his number one request because he didn't want to offend his employees. Yet, middle managers need to know their bosses' number one request. As a conscientious person, Steve continued to be aware of his need to communicate in positive terms, and he replaced his habitual negative thinking with positive communication. Many, if not most, people will shift to the positive once they realize how destructive their unexpressed criticism is and how productive constructive discontent can be. In this case, the company's government contracts increased by 23 percent.

CREATE SAFETY BY SETTING A ZERO TOLERANCE FOR PUT-DOWNS

When I started my career at Xerox Learning Systems, I was the manager for its national training operations. My first assignment was in the Research Triangle of Raleigh-Durham, North Carolina, an environmental research facility with more than fifty physicists hard at work. For the most part, their intellects were off the charts and their research was unparalleled anywhere in the world. This company treated employees well and tried to give them whatever they requested in order to get high-level work done.

My boss at Xerox Learning Systems was Dick, a superstar in the field of training and development, plus a super salesman. He was such a good salesman that he sold a huge training and development contract to a group of physicists who hated training, development, and sales. Somehow he convinced their general manager that our team would solve all their problems. I had been with the company only two weeks when I had to take five people and lead a tough training expedition in North Carolina. Fortunately, Dick (knowing that the group was irate) gave me some pointers on how to handle attacks from the group. We role-played the scenario several times, and his advice was this: "Do not take it on; keep the energy on the attacker; never defend."

When I first walked through the facility, I learned that something was terribly amiss—mistakes were being made, output had slowed to a crawl, and everyone seemed miserable. Quality research was being done, but productivity and joy had reached new lows. The general manager, whom Dick had sold on our training package, disclosed the terrible truth: People in the company were so hostile that he wouldn't have been surprised if there had been a murder in the labs. Resentment was rampant; rage was barely controlled. These scientists were brilliant at studying the ozone layer and figuring out how to save our air, but they didn't have the time or the tools to communicate with employees. They became complainers instead—the report wasn't typed up right, the material wasn't delivered on time. Furthermore, they had no interest in relating to other people and didn't care about communicating. In fact, they resented being required to attend this weekend seminar.

Fifty-five employees attended the first seminar. Most were scientists, but many technical assistants were also included. They reluctantly agreed to the Three Rules. Two hours into the first day's presentation, a scientist named Earl raised his hand and challenged us. "What kind of cars do you drive?" he asked our team. A few members of our team named their automobiles. With increasing hostility, Earl asked, "What do you get paid?"

"Nothing so far," I replied.

"I think you guys are space cadets and weasels," he snapped back.

By now Earl had broken two of the Three Rules. His questions were obviously those of someone who had decided not to contribute, and he was putting us down to boot. Today I would handle a challenge like that by saying, "Hey, Earl, no put-downs," but Earl was too hostile to back off with just a suggestion. I knew I had to be more direct. All I could remember in the fog of fear was to "focus on them" as Dick had told me.

"Earl," I said, "what is going on with you right now that is leading you to say these things?"

"You California consultants are just out for the money, and all this stuff is bull!" he blustered. His anger was almost choking him.

"Earl," I inquired cautiously, feeling as if I were dodging bullets, "what happened in the past with California or a consultant?"

Earl calmed down a little and explained that a psychologist his company had hired several years before had psychoanalyzed everyone and caused havoc and disharmony.

I was grateful that that Rule 2 had given me a path to get to the source of his hostility. Because we had agreed to the Rules, I had the strength to keep him focused on the real issue and keep all of us from getting overwhelmed by his put-downs. After spending fifteen minutes on the story and the problems of their former psychologist, I explained that we were management consultants, not psychologists, and our goal was to help them reach their goals. We were there to demonstrate tools that they could use to get their employees to support their MBO—Management by Objectives. Once we had identified and dispelled Earl's fear and clarified our MBO-related goals, everything changed.

All Three Rules proved to be a safe tool for the physicists. They were able to grasp the rules right away and apply them, realizing that the rules gave them a consistent way to interface with people who were there to help them clarify their objectives. They didn't have to pal around with people or even like them—they just had to learn to treat them with "civility."[2] The Three Rules cut through years of hostility and got to the heart of the matter. According to Ken Blanchard, "Communication happens naturally when you make things safe."[3]

Gaining Valuable Customer Input

Complaints are not always put-downs. They may be honest attempts to rectify a bad situation. Behind many complaints are some pieces of wisdom. Some companies have a complaint box next to the suggestion box to allow employees to express their ideas about what's going wrong. Astute managers find the hope hidden in the complaints.

One marketing expert, for example, stood in grocery store aisles and asked shoppers for complaints about chicken soup. The most common complaint was that the cans were too large for single people to consume in one sitting. That complaint led to development of single-portion cans, a profitable addition to the soup company's product line. Years of asking shoppers for suggestions had not produced a single usable idea, but asking them to complain gave the company a wonderful new concept. The company continued asking for complaints, realizing that they were a new way to get to the pearls.

To contribute most to a business, however, complaints about people should be handled with agreed-upon communication tools. "Martha isn't doing her job right," needs to be transformed into a positive request like, "I need you to do inventory every month." This helps to create a more profitable and mentally healthy work environment. When a caring concern can be perceived as a put-down, the power of the recipient to create a put-down from a caring concern can be shocking and scary.

Even if you follow the No Put-downs rule every day and are careful to treat others with respect and dignity, you can still occasionally be perceived as criticizing another without hope. Sometimes an oversensitive person in a painful state can distort a kind act on your part into a major put-down.

DENNIS AND THE PERCEIVED PUT-DOWN

I attended a small conference where we agreed to keep confidential everything shared in the session. During our lunch break, a group of us went for a walk. A psychologist—I'll call him Dennis—said his foot hurt a lot and asked if we would all walk slower. Dennis never mentioned his foot during the meeting, but he did share a lot about his work and home life. The day was helpful, and it seemed as if we were all friends when it was over. This was mid-April 1989. In May 1989 I attended an event at my son's school, and as it turned out, Dennis's son and mine attended the same school. I was surprised and delighted to see him there and to make the connection. After we had discussed our sons briefly, I asked how his foot was. He changed the subject and turned away.

The next week I got a letter from him telling me how offensive my comment was; it had disgraced him in front of his in-laws, who were within earshot. The foot problem was considered psychological, and it made him look bad as a psychologist. He went on to say that he would tell others in the community that they could not trust me because I reveal personal confidences in public.

I wrote him back right away to apologize and ask for forgiveness. I felt so bad that I had embarrassed him. I politely and warmly informed him that I had had no idea his foot problem was confidential, since the information had emerged outside the session. I had had no idea the problem was psychological, and I told him how sorry I was, asking if there was any way I could make amends. He did not respond, and he would not speak when I saw him later in public.

Nine years later, one of my coworkers said she had just seen Dennis and told him we were working together. He said, "Don't trust her; she'll reveal confidential information and embarrass you in public." Luckily, my coworker asked me about this, so I was able to explain and show her the letter.

Dennis helped me realize that what may not seem like a put-down to the speaker can feel like one to a recipient of the comment or information. Since so many put-downs happen accidentally, there is no reason (zero reason) to allow a few intentional ones. Dennis got a divorce a year or so after our encounter, so he may have been in a weakened emotional state at the school event. While put-downs can happen even in total innocence, even with caring, concerned intent, we can't afford to do even one little deliberate put-down here or there.

Lead the Way toward Certification and Accreditation

One of the fastest-growing trends in the early twenty-first century was the global impact of International Standards Organization (ISO) 9000 Certification. The ISO is a nongovernmental agency that sets quality standards for companies all over the world. The purpose of the ISO is to help major national and international companies ensure that they are buying supplies from companies that will stay in business for a long time and manufacture high-quality products.

In an elaborate reporting structure, companies are asked to note and record many details about daily procedures. Most of these procedures are routine, normal, and passed on by word of mouth from veteran employees to newcomers. Having to document them was one thing, but having to show "continuous improvement" is where the ISO 9000 challenge begins.

A portion of my work with clients in the past five years has been in supporting their efforts to obtain ISO 9000 Certification (or ISO 9002 if it's engineering-oriented). The most significant obstacle to certification is not a lack of understanding or a lack of concern, it's the inability to focus on processes instead of personalities. In other words, when a working group is assigned to "improve," they usually start by pointing out who does what wrong. The goal for No Put-downs when an organization is trying to improve is to focus on process, not personalities.

AN ELECTRONICS ASSEMBLY COMPANY

A ninety-employee electronics assembly company made parts for Hewlett-Packard (now Agilent Technologies) for twenty-seven years. The company excelled at being customer-focused—so much so that it could anticipate H-P's every upcoming need. The plant was led by the H-P order. As soon as the order was placed, it was posted, and the deadlines were the final authority to all the employees.

Someone once mentioned ISO 9000 to one of the owners of the assembly company, but it didn't seem important. Later, it was announced that H-P was under strict new orders to use only suppliers who were ISO-certified. An H-P inspector would visit in a month. The date came, and so did the two inspectors. The assembly company failed miserably.

Then came the put-downs. The owner/family blamed each other, the managers blamed each other, and the employees blamed each other. Even though this was a Three Rules company, the audit failure proceeded to break down the Three Rules. One of my associates was asked to sign on as acting president to get them unstuck and give the family some time out to resolve other family problems. His instructions were these: "(1) Everyone contributes to the next ISO audit; (2) No put-downs of people. You can put down processes, but each time you do, please identify your solution; and (3) Keep your agreements to improve." He then asked people to E-mail him each process that wasn't effective and suggest an improvement.

They made good use of converting the put-downs to improvements. Once they were away from people and focused on the processes, the job was much easier. A new mission was set: assure a profit margin in every product's life cycle. Then all documenting made sense. "Jo never writes anything down," became "Jo needs to separately document which parts are for H-P and which are for Company Z so we know what each one costs."

Once the corporate culture shifted from defense to let's all improve, life was breathed back into the workplace. People were energized; they had goals to improve upon, and they were united in preparing for their next audit. By 2001, the company passed ISO Certification with flying colors.

A COLLEGE PRESIDENT

A college president in her five-year plan decided that her school would be an AACSB-certified university since many of its degrees were business-related. AACSB is in addition to regular certification and designates a high-level degree college as well. A workshop was set up to plan for the AACSB Certification. Given that the number one goal for the year was "quality education," the president asked me to facilitate the second day of a two-day off-site workshop for all the department heads. She and I prepared an agenda for each of the two days.

By the end of the first day, she called in exhausted and disappointed. She said the group was indignant that she had had the nerve to suggest improving the quality of education—"Weren't we doing that already?" they defensively responded. The entire day was consumed by complaints and defensive explanations of all of the things they were already doing. They started blaming and putting down others, and nothing she did could bring them back on track.

What happened? First, even though she told me she would, she did not use the Three Rules. No one had any direction or commitment to contribute to the day, to keep agreements, or to convert put-downs to something constructive. I had not met any of these eighteen department heads, but I would. The next morning I did know I could count on the Three Rules to bring the department heads together.

At 8:00 A.M. on the second day we began. I said "There are eighteen of you and one of me. Your first day did not cover any of the items on your president's agenda, so we have to go twice as far today. In order for us to do this, I need your agreement on three things: (1) Every one of you will contribute to the items on the agenda; find ways to resolve, improve, and move forward; (2) No put-downs. It's fine to disagree all you want and it's fine to criticize procedures but not people. Convert put-downs to requests and focus on process, not people; and (3) Keep agreements—follow through with whatever you agree to today." Everyone agreed, but I had the feeling that they didn't really mean it.

We covered vision and values, and what it would be like after AACSB Certification. We set goals and objectives and converted their complaints to requests. Although the vision and values, mission and goals went amazingly well, the complaints began again. I had to intervene with one woman about two dozen times. She was so used to criticizing everyone that she knew no other way, and no one else wanted to stop her. No one wanted to be in her line of fire, so her behavior also was poisoning the entire group. I felt that same reluctance, but my reminding her about the No Put-downs rule for the twenty-fifth time must have been the turning point. She left early, and everyone else continued to contribute. By having the No Put-downs rule, we were able to quiet the biggest problem and uncover many excellent ideas for improvements from others. By focusing on procedures and not personalities we were able to move forward.

We went an extra three hours, and by the end of the day everyone had Funnels and Alignments, goals and agreements on what to do differently. Three people were prepared to ask Glenda, the loud one, to listen, respect others' viewpoints, and be supportive. Glenda resigned thirty days later, saying the job was too stressful.

That one little rule, No Put-downs, seemed to be the pivotal point that turned this university group around. The Everyone Contributes rule immediately kicked in, and everyone but Glenda planned to keep the new agreements. Department chairs passed their new goals on to the faculty, and the faculty were enthusiastic once again about its program. They were going for AACSB approval, and that would uplift the career and future opportunities for everyone involved.

CONVERT PUT-DOWNS INTO PROFIT

Mel, a middle manager at a telecommunications company, kept putting down Tim, one of his employees, for not being more analytical. On Tim's performance review Mel checked "below average" on analytical skills. The truth was, Mel was extremely analytical, so he judged others by his standards and not by their own strengths. Tim was flexible, spontaneous, and creative, but Mel did not notice because he was looking for analytical skills similar to his own.

Because this company had adopted the Three Rules, a coworker pulled Mel aside and asked him to quit putting Tim down. But this didn't work for long; Mel would roll his eyes and say sarcastic things like "Whatever" and "Hel-lo"! Then Mel's manager, whom we'll call Sam, insisted that Mel learn to convert his put-downs to positive requests of Tim.

At first Mel argued with this manager, saying that he was "just being honest." Honesty to Mel meant telling people the "truth" about their weaknesses. "You're asking me to sugarcoat the truth, which is like asking me to lie," Mel said with tight lips. Since Mel was new to the company, his manager, Sam, sat him down for a long meeting, saying, "Mel, I can't tell you how many people have told me that they were just being honest when they put someone down. Do you think 'honest' always means something negative? If I said, 'Mel, I just have to be honest with you,' would you be awaiting something positive?"

"Maybe," said Mel with a tight jaw.

"Mel, do you remember our personnel manual with the section about Office Communication Policies?" said Sam, trying a new approach.

"Well, I didn't memorize the whole thing," quipped Mel.

"That's fine, but here on page fifty-eight we have a policy that states our philosophy is to build on strength. To keep this meaningful, we have three agreements that you agreed to when you signed this manual. You agreed to 'Everyone contributes,' 'No Put-Downs,' and 'Keep Agreements.' You have been doing great on contribution—you have helped the supervisors with product certification, and I am sure we will be certified soon. And you have kept your agreements with customers. Regarding Rule 2, though, we need your constructive commentary about how to improve the process. Because we are soon to be product-certified, we are promising our customers continuous improvement. Can you identify one specific way that Tim can improve how he works with you?"

"Yes! He could get conscious and quit making recommendations he knows nothing about. Oh, and he could wipe that grin off his face; quit being late and quit making inappropriate jokes."

"Mel! What do you want Tim to do? State it in the positive—remember, this is our company policy as well as our commitment to improvement. I need your forward direction for Tim."

Sam valued both Tim and Mel and was determined to find a way to get over this impasse. Because it was company policy, Mel agreed to use the Funnel process with the help of another manager who knew it well.

With guidance from his peer, Mel finally completed the Funnel. It looked like this:

Number one request: "Be more analytical on the monthly report."

A. Write a paragraph telling how you got the numbers.

B. List observations you have about the month.

C. Make a recommendation.

Result: "I could make better financial decisions, and we could make $10,000 more per month or $120,000 more per year."

Next, Tim prepared his number one request of Mel and they set a day to meet. Tim was ready for a tone of contempt from Mel. But, when Tim heard Mel's number one request, he looked very relieved. And with the new forward-moving request, Tim was able to visualize what Mel meant. Each step was doable. Tim could respond to clear requests much more effectively than to a put-down, such as "not being analytical enough." Each month Tim wrote the descriptive paragraph, made notes of observations, and gave a recommendation. He was very uplifted to know that Mel wanted his observations and suggestions. Tim's descriptions, observations, and recommendations included the creativity and flexibility that Mel needed to make timely, impactful, financial decisions. Both Mel and Tim were uplifted by this synergy, and Sam was relieved. Since financial decisions were made faster and better, earnings were up by $5,100 by the third month and $6,200 by the fourth. They were on their way to their new profit goal and two jobs were moved toward careers.

GIVE AND RECEIVE CORRECTION WITH DIGNITY: GAP ANALYSIS

Identifying the gap between what is and what we want is called "gap analysis." One goal of the No Put-downs rule is to identify improvements in a non-offensive way by use of the gap. Even when the No Put-downs rule is followed and all criticism is converted to positive requests, some people still feel put down by the requests.

Ron, the board chairman of a large real estate/mortgage company in the Midwest asked me to work with the board and its president, Bob. The board said they were unable to convey desired improvements without offending him.

I met with the seven board members and funneled all their various requests, merging them into an all-encompassing number one request: "Develop your management team." They listed three action descriptions and an outcome. Next, Bob separately identified his number one request of the board (a three-year contract). The board chair and Bob met. Bob began with his request, and they agreed; then the board chair told Bob the board's number one request of him ("Develop your management team").

This infuriated Bob. "Don't they care about financial goals? This is the fastest-growing real estate institution in this part of the state, and all they care about is transforming me into a personnel manager. I'd better get out of here fast. I'm in the wrong place."

Bob argued that money, not people, was the key. They argued for two hours. Bob was saying, "I thought increasing profits was my job, not being a personnel person."

The board chairman replied, "It is! You've done a great job. Keep it up.

How can we improve in one more area now by having more management team development?"

"I already am!" said Bob.

Bob finally started to come around when we used the Funnel as a GAP diagram. There was a very manageable discrepancy (gap) between what he was doing to develop his staff and what the board wanted done. The board was the guiding factor in this case. They could see he was a superstar and he was doing all the work, but the management team was weak and presented a potential problem.

We must have shown Bob the picture of the Funnel twenty-five times over a two-week period. We'd be on other topics, and suddenly his anger would rear its ugly head. "I'm already doing a lot for my employees."

"Yes, Bob, you are. The board only wants a few more actions to build stronger managers. Let's go back to these three small steps on the Funnel." Then he would relax again, seeing that the three steps were changes he could make and they were not a put-down. "There just happens to be a gap between their picture of developing a management team and where we are right now. You are doing steps already—they happen to want more. Nobody is wrong," he was told.

Even though developing teams was not Bob's forte, he knew enough to set up regular team meetings, invite the managers to contribute, and give more positive feedback when appropriate. When we did the six-month follow-up, I asked Ron, the board chair, "How is it going?"

He said, "We're growing like gangbusters." Bob had finally internalized the input without interpreting it as a put-down.

When you prepare a completed Funnel for employees, you have given them a gap analysis, which is a suggested three-step improvement that does not feel like a put-down. It empowers employees to make their own career decisions in amazing ways. Bob stretched and carried out the board's request in spite of his initial contempt. Having the courage to listen to and carry out your boss's requests will create amazing entrepreneurial career opportunities. Their suggestions specifically identified the gap between what Bob was doing and what they wanted him to do. The detailed gap analysis is clearly much more empowering than "Bob, you don't motivate your staff and they are stagnating." Bob's career blossomed when he finally incorporated the suggestions from the board's Funnel/GAP analysis.

Many times we are encouraged to improve basic skills and adopt new ones, but, unfortunately, one important step to improvement is overlooked— HOW is that improvement to be accomplished? The Funnel/GAP analysis is the tool that worked for Bob and the board of his company.

Funnel

Your Name: Today's Date:

1. Develop Your Management Team

SPECIFICALLY:

• What will this person do to meet your request?

• Use a verb to begin each of the three short descriptive sentences.

2a. Set up regular team meetings (first Tuesday every month).

2b. Inspire managers to contribute more ideas and suggestions at the monthly meeting.

2c. Let managers know specifically what they do well on a weekly basis.

SPECIFICALLY:

• How will you know the request has been fulfilled?

• What will be different?

• How will the change be measured?

3. We would hire more salespeople. We would increase sales by 10 percent in ninety days.

Transforming Put-downs into Responsible Communication

First know your strengths, then build on them.

—PETER F. DRUCKER

I have observed that when a middle manager decides to adopt the Three Rules, it is important that he or she have the tools to make the No Put-downs rule a realistic goal. This is important for four reasons. First, it is the only "NO" of the Three Rules, which requires that it offer something to replace that "no"; second, in our culture the media foster put-downs; third, most work groups have never been given effective tools or guidelines in this area; and fourth, the new economy makes responsible communication more important than ever before.

Peter Drucker's *Management Challenges for the 21st Century* concludes with a chapter called "Managing Oneself." "Managing yourself requires taking responsibility for relationships," Drucker says. "First accept others as individuals and know their strengths and values. Second, take responsibility for communication: make sure you let people know what you can be counted on for, what you value, and how you work—and find out the same from them."[1]

The ITS tool allows employees to move from that basic urge to put people down toward taking responsibility for communication. The No Put-downs rule directs employees to do something productive with the pent-up urge to criticize.

ITS Tool—"It's" a Lifesaver When
You Want to Put Down Another Person

The ITS tool can be used when someone (including yourself) gets stuck wanting to criticize another person. ITS can also be used with any work-group as a way to diffuse festering resentments or hostilities. This tool is to be completed individually and privately first, then publicly if appropriate. At your next meeting, pass out the ITS form and follow the instructions precisely.

This exercise diffuses the hostility and/or resentment that coworkers normally develop. They learn to recognize their own strengths and to value the strengths of others. A sense of acceptance and sighs of relief usually fill the room as each person privately, but in the presence of others, releases the urge to put down another and replaces it with his or her own feeling of well-being.

The ITS Exercise

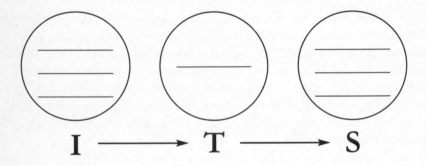

Step 1: Think of someone who irritates you intensely, preferably on the job. If you can't think of someone at your current job, think of someone from a previous job. Write down his or her initials only and keep him or her as your focus throughout the exercise.

_____

(initials)

Step 2: I is for Irritation
With this person in mind, write down the three things he or she does that irritate you the most. For example, the person may be dishonest, inconsiderate, and take all the credit. Be sure to be concise.

1. _____

2. _____

3. _____

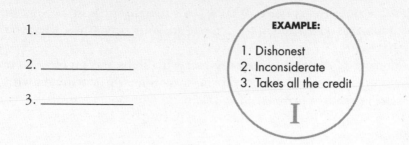

EXAMPLE:

1. Dishonest
2. Inconsiderate
3. Takes all the credit

I

Step 3: T is for Time

Estimate the percentage of an eight-hour day that you spend working directly with this person and dealing with the irritation that he or she causes you—the time you spend avoiding this person, cleaning up after him or her, solving problems he or she created, doing his or her job, thinking about him or her, discussing him or her with those around you, etc. Write that figure on the line below.

_____
(percentage of time)

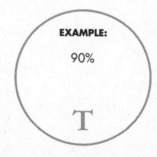

EXAMPLE:

90%

T

Step 4: S is for Strengths

Next to each number, write the positive opposite of what you wrote in the I circle. For example, "dishonest" becomes "honest." Also feel free to write your own word for personal opposite, not just the dictionary opposite. Do not use any "no" or "doesn't" in the S Circle. For example, instead of saying "doesn't take all the credit," say "shares credit."

1. _____

2. _____

3. _____

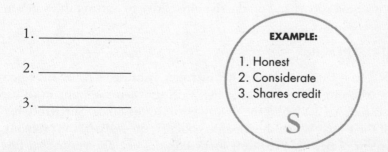

EXAMPLE:

1. Honest
2. Considerate
3. Shares credit

S

Review the three items twice. Would you agree that at least two out of the three items that you wrote in the S circle are **your** strengths—what you bring to the team?

This moment of discovery is usually met with sighs and giggles. Most people are moved to a new level of consciousness when their irritation with another is converted to a personal affirmation.

- Honest

- Considerate

- Shares the credit

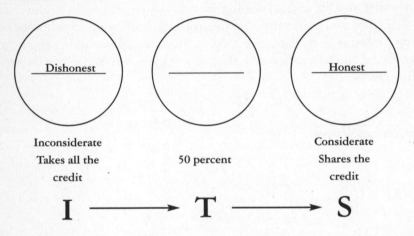

<table>
<tr><td>Dishonest</td><td>————</td><td>Honest</td></tr>
</table>

Inconsiderate		Considerate
Takes all the	50 percent	Shares the
credit		credit

$$I \longrightarrow T \longrightarrow S$$

The ITS exercise is amazingly consistent in identifying the strengths you bring to the workplace and to relationships. At least two of the three will usually be positive qualities that you have to offer others. These are not your only good qualities by any means. If you do the circle with another person, you will come up with three more. This exercise always deepens our understanding of ourselves and our potential. When we understand our own strengths, we feel stronger about making contributions to others and to the organization as a whole. This is a professional and productive alternative to putting them down.

LUCY AND ED—ITS IN ACTION

Lucy was always furious with Ed, her manager, because he never answered her questions thoroughly, always kept her waiting when she went in to see him, and was rude to her when she finally got into his office. She wrote her irritations in the I box. When she thought about it, she realized she probably spent 25 percent of her time stewing about Ed's defects. She wrote that figure in box **T**. Then she wrote the opposite qualities in the S box. When she saw her list of qualities that she wished Ed had—to be thorough, on time, and polite—she realized that she herself had these good qualities. She felt better about herself, stopped fretting so much about Ed's defects, and lost the urge to gossip with her coworkers about how irritated she felt. She never even approached Ed about her irritation.

When you see how much energy you lose by being irritated and realize how much you have to offer, your own mental state improves. You find yourself making good decisions in many areas of your life. You can build much confidence and self-esteem by recognizing your good qualities. When energy shifts toward positive contributions, put-downs are also diminished.

WHEN ITS OPENS NEW CAREER DIRECTIONS

Chet and Louise, a husband and wife team, had progressively developed their Washington nursery business for more than twenty years and planned to retire and turn it over to their son, who had recently finished college. Their son had worked full-time for six months and almost never asked either of his parents for advice or direction. His mother was furious about her son's "aloofness" and took it as lack of respect. The father isolated himself and began developing a separate business to avoid the tension. Finally, the stress was so unbearable that Chet asked me for help.

Chet told me that Louise would not turn anything over to their son, and a cloud of anger was pervading and even deteriorating the business. Employees were leaving, sales were down, and his wife was so stressed that it was affecting their marriage.

During my first meeting with Chet and his wife, I asked Louise what she was doing to make the business successful and, conversely, what she was doing that sabotaged the company. Louise could only name things that she did to make the business successful. In her mind, her son, Jack, did all the sabotaging. Her three most intense irritations of Jack in the I circle were "doesn't understand finance," "doesn't know vendors," and "doesn't greet customers." When asked what percentage of her time she spent in reaction to her irritation with these three items, she said 50 percent. Chet raised his eyebrows at that, since in his estimation she spent 100 percent of her time reacting to her irritations with their son.

Next, we explored the opposite of Louise's complaints. We came up with the positive opposites to her complaints. The three items in the S circle were "understands the finances of the business," "relates well to vendors," and "greets the customers by name." I invited Louise to entertain the idea that this S circle list represented *her* strengths, that these were the strengths *she* brought to the business. The angry owner's eyes began to soften as she contemplated this possibility, and for a moment she let go of her obsession with her son's shortcomings.

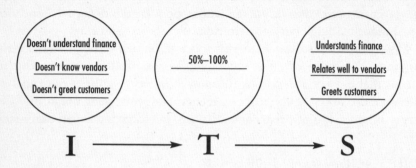

Louise now appeared open to exploring new avenues of thinking, and I was able to ask if she was willing to empower her son by turning over some finance and vendor information to him. She tightened up again. "He'll never get it," she said. "He's just too stubborn."

Knowing a gentle intervention was in order, I asked if I might say something that could be uncomfortable.

"Go ahead," she said.

I cautiously pointed out that *she* seemed stubborn, and yet somehow she had learned the business.

The owner brightened, "Yes, I did learn it all by myself. No one taught *me* the business."

"Is it possible that maybe your son wants to learn on his own too?" I suggested. Her quick retort was that it was a waste for him not to get the benefit of her twenty years of experience. After some discussion, we uncovered that Louise's frustration came from the feeling that her son did not respect her or her years of experience. She was able to see that her hurt and frustration fueled the demands she made on Jack and that that was sabotaging the business. As it became clear what she was doing and the effect it was having on their business and her closest relationships, she sat back in her chair, closed her eyes, and observed how powerless and hopeless she felt at that moment.

I asked Louise if she seeks answers or advice outside herself when she gets stuck in a conflict. "No," she responded firmly. "I don't go to church and I don't pray. We don't have time; we work on Sundays."

"That's fine," I said. "But, there must be something or someone who gave you the courage and strength to learn this business and become the expert you are." The room was quiet for a moment. Her eyes filled with tears as she recalled her source of support: It was her father.

"Dad believed in me and told me so. He told me I could be a successful businesswoman one day and gave me reasons why." As she described her father and his vision of her, Louise recognized how he had empowered her by believing in her, not by instructing her or demanding that she do it his way. Her blue eyes glistened as she spoke lovingly of her deceased father. We began to envision how her dad would have turned the business over to Jack and what steps he would have recommended. Drawing on her relationship with her father, Louise was able to see new possibilities.

As Louise accessed this part of herself—the connection with her dad—the answers began to flow. During the next several weeks, she wrote a three-year plan for transferring the business to Jack, outlining the steps that would allow her to let go of one part of the business at a time. They included Jack's attending weekly meetings with the accountant to learn finance, his getting to know vendors, and a willingness on her part to allow him to use his own style—giving customers a quiet space to look around before they are greeted. She did this with respect for herself, her husband, and her son. She and Chet set a retirement date that would begin with a ninety-day trip around the world.

In his book *A World Waiting to Be Born,* M. Scott Peck says, "There is a small loss of freedom associated with constant self-examination and consciousness. But those who have become accustomed to it have found, as balance that consciousness and civility make for a way of life that is profoundly liberating."[2] Putting others down often robs us of our own opportunity for self-awareness and the freedom that comes with it.

Conscious Communication Tool—
What to Do When You Get Derailed

In the normal course of events, people disagree with one another about many things. When you are working with the Three Rules system, these disagreements especially need to be handled consciously. Potentially explosive, emotional situations can be handled with equanimity without violating the No Put-downs rule.

We can disagree all we want with someone's ideas, thoughts, or opinions, but if we invalidate the person, it changes the atmosphere, making it unsafe for that person to express his or her truth. David Bradford of the Stanford University Graduate School of Business addressed this issue when he wrote, "One of the major problems I see with managers is in their effort to achieve excellence. They don't have basic skills to confront others nondestructively."

Working with the Funnel and the Alignment process and ITS moves us in the right direction, but we can still get derailed when minor problems surface and we do not have the tools to help us cope nondestructively with those problems. We may resort to complaining, gossiping, or blaming one another for real or perceived errors instead of keeping our communications positive. As with Louise, sabotage takes over and our productivity goes out the window.

One of the most emotionally intelligent methods I know for handling conflict is the Conscious Communication process. It allows us to become conscious of our feelings in a constructive way and express them to one another effectively, without injuring the other person's feelings or self-esteem. It finds the "hope" in criticism. It resolves the conflict.

In business, expressing emotions was traditionally considered "unprofessional." Yet feelings are very present in the workplace even if they are disguised. Emotions need to be addressed in a professional way, however. Many executives are notorious for not understanding emotions. According to Robert K. Cooper and Ayman Sawaf, "Emotions are powerful organizers of thought and action and are indispensable for reasoning and rationality."[3] One health-care mid-manager said people in her department had literally been trampled by a merger and were still feeling the effects. This senior manager told the large group, "Get over it." The mid-manager asked later, "How?" Enter the Conscious Communication tool. The tool can help release in an intelligent manner emotions you may be accumulating.

Hostility and abusive behavior are on the rise in the workplace. While old-economy managers say they are afraid to tell the truth to power, the new economy has brought us a greater number of younger managers and narcissists who throw "tantrums." Employers and employees may vent negative emotions in many ways, from swearing and glaring at officemates to the extreme behavior of violence. When negative emotions get out of hand, use the Conscious Communication tool. It is one of the few consistently effective means we know to help people get over hostilities and hurts and move on to more positive ground.

This tool consists of a list of almost one hundred feelings and a communication form asking seven simple questions about one's own feelings and their possible consequences. The chart helps us identify feelings we may be dealing with and need to recognize.

Using the form provides us with a nonthreatening way to let go of feelings that are making us unhappy and nonproductive. It is unlikely that we will choose to confront each other destructively if we have a way to handle our disagreements civilly and with focus on our mutual objectives.

Feelings Chart

Love	Hostility	Betrayed	Isolated
Hate	Confusion	Peaceful	Alone
Anger	Aggravated	Enthusiastic	Independent
Frustration	Protective	Empty	Trapped
Guilt	Possessive	Mad	Powerful
Anxiety	Happy	Sympathy	Needed
Worry	Sad	Embarrassed	Confident
Hurt	Excited	Shy	Wanted
Tired	Surprised	Terror	Secure
Confused	Shocked	Abused	Insecure
Curious	Afraid	Flexible	Cautious
Hopeless	Important	Misunderstood	Vulnerable
Hopeful	Rejected	Proud	Tender
Appreciative	Depressed	Pleased	Rage
Helpless	Nervous	Caring	Accepted
Overwhelmed	Grief	Carefree	Nurturing
Pressured	Inadequate	Fear	Weak
Sure	Disappointed	Mean	Deceived
Unsure	Lonely	Aggressive	Self-Defeating
Satisfied	Bored	Irritated	Disgusted
Relief	Blamed	Justified	Content
Joy	Self-Doubt	Defensive	
Scared	Deserted	Dependent	

Conscious Communication

1. I make myself feel _____
    (use Feelings Chart)

    when _____
    (briefly describe situation)

    _____

2. I am concerned that what might happen is _____
    (what you want changed)

    _____

    _____

3. I would like you to _____

    _____

    _____

4. My goal is _____

_____

_____

5. It seems to me your goal is _____

_____

_____

6. Would you be willing to explore some alternatives to help us both achieve our goals? If "yes" finish with #7. If "no" finish process with thanking him/her for listening to you.

7. Some possibilities I have come up with that may be more effective or harmonious are:

   1. _____

   _____

   2. _____

   _____

   3. _____

   _____

Are any of these acceptable to you? Do you see other possibilities? Listen to response, possibly discuss and thank her/him for listening to you.

MANAGING THE HOSTILE WORKER

Myra was the number one broker in a successful real estate firm. She was powerful and effective with her clients, and they thought she was wonderful. But her staff felt constant hostility when clients were not there or when Eric, the chief broker, left the office. They feared her hostility even more because they suspected she had a gun.

The corporate office had recently adopted the Three Rules and made them part of the employee handbook, along with the forms and tools for Conscious Communication. Everyone was expected to know and use these methods for resolving difficulties.

Three women on the staff went to complain about Myra's hostility. Apparently, Myra had rolled her eyes, slapped down papers, and pointedly slammed doors when she was upset. She rarely stated what she wanted but engaged in constant put-downs. For example, she constantly made rude, negative remarks about Lucy. She called her scatterbrained and incompetent. When one of the other staff people would make a mistake, Myra would contemptuously say, "You pulled a Lucy."

Once Myra threatened to slap Nancy, the receptionist. Lucy heard her and reported the incident to Eric. He investigated the situation by speaking to Myra, but she was at her charming best with him. Nothing was resolved. The office was similar to a dysfunctional family: telling one parent of the other parent's abuses rarely works because they really don't want to know about the problems.

Lucy and Nancy felt let down when Eric could not improve things, so they went to Pam, the human recourses manager at the home office. Pam reminded the women of the Conscious Communication form and helped them fill it out. They used the Feelings Chart to give words to their experiences with Myra and wrote them on the Conscious Communications form in the appropriate places.

The first question on the communication form says, "*I make myself feel . . . ,*" which reduces the possibility of defensive reaction. If we were to say "*you make me feel . . . ,*" it actually would be inaccurate in most cases, but more important, it would create defensiveness in the listener. By owning our own feelings, we are empowered to do something about them. Even in this situation, when Myra allegedly is intentionally trying to hurt Lucy and Nancy, they will benefit from taking charge of their own feelings.

Conscious Communication

LUCY'S COMMUNICATION TO MYRA (NEVER DELIVERED)

1. I make myself feel <u>threatened, intimidated, out of control</u>
   (use Feelings Chart)
   when <u>you glare at me and make condescending remarks, humiliate Lucy,</u>
   <u>tell me you hate people.</u>   (briefly describe situation)

2. I am concerned that what might happen is <u>you're going to shoot somebody,</u>
   <u>maybe me, or sabotage my job.</u>   (what you want changed)

3. I would like you to <u>love and respect people or leave.</u>

4. My goal is to get beyond this and have a happy work environment.

_____

_____

5. It seems to me your goal is to win and to take prisoners [dark side] or to give
your best to the customer [bright side].

_____

6. Would you be willing to explore some alternatives to help us both achieve our goals? If "yes" finish with #7. If "no" finish process with thanking him/her for listening to you.

7. Some possibilities I have come up with that may be more effective or harmonious are:
   1. Make honest amends to those you have harmed.

   _____

   2. Genuinely admit that you are powerless over you anger.

   _____

   3. Go to weekly counseling with an honest, open mind.

   _____

Are any of these acceptable to you? Do you see other possibilities? Listen to response, possibly discuss and thank her/him for listening to you.

This is a subtle but important distinction. The minute we realize that our feelings are under our own control, we gain a new perspective, moving from the stance of victim to the stance of a leader acting on our own behalf. From this perspective, we are less likely to succumb to fear, we avoid sabotage, and we become better able to contribute to our organizations responsibly.

Lucy showed her newly filled out form to Eric, but she had reasons she did not want to present it to Myra personally. Myra had always escalated any minor confrontation with Lucy into full-scale hostility. In fact, Myra's hostility created fear at many levels, and it was beginning to affect the whole organization. The financial goals of the office were no longer being met.

Eric hoped he could ignore the problem and it would go away. But the opposite was happening. The old Werner Ehrhart saying "What we resist persists" was true in this case. Eric resisted acting on the complaints of the staff, and as a result hostility persisted.

Pam, the human resources manager, called a meeting with Eric, her branch manager, and the CEO of the company and showed them the Conscious Communication sheets. Eric said that he would like Lucy and the receptionist to go directly to Myra, but Pam told him it wouldn't work. "No, Eric," she explained. "It is not fair to ask them to go to the hostile person with these issues when they fear physical harm. It's your job." Forced to take a stand, Eric did it well. With the No Put-downs rule and the Conscious Communication tool to enforce company policy, he was able to confront the volatile situation effectively. He filled in his own Conscious Communication form and asked Myra to write out a form as well.

Conscious Communication

ERIC'S COMMUNICATION TO MYRA

1. I make myself feel frustrated, fearful, disappointed
   (use Feelings Chart)
   when I see you have picked on other people in the office or created a hostile
   (briefly describe situation)
   environment.

2. I am concerned that what might happen is most people will quit and that there
   (what you want changed)
   could be lawsuits because of your creation of a hostile environment.

3. I would like you to take responsibility for your anger in the office.

4. My goal is to have a very friendly and fun place to work where people enjoy coming
   into the office each day.

5. It seems to me your goal is to provide the highest possible client service to our clients
   at the expense of the staff.

6. Would you be willing to explore some alternatives to help us both achieve our goals? If "yes" finish with #7. If "no" finish process with thanking him/her for listening to you.

7. Some possibilities I have come up with that may be more effective or harmonious are:

1. <u>When you feel angry, come directly to me.</u>

2. <u>Cooperate with me when I try to mediate a situation, however small it may seem.</u>

3. <u>Treat people with respect no matter how angry you are.</u>

4. <u>Make amends with people when you blow it.</u>

Are any of these acceptable to you? Do you see other possibilities? Listen to response, possibly discuss and thank her/him for listening to you.

Conscious Communication

MYRA'S COMMUNICATION TO ERIC

1. I make myself feel <u>angry, frustrated, and hurt</u>
   (use Feelings Chart)
   when <u>you listen to Lucy and the others when they complain about me.</u>
   (briefly describe situation)

2. I am concerned that what might happen is <u>you will believe them and they don't know</u>
   (what you want changed)
   <u>the pain I have in my wrist.</u>

3. I would like you to <u>be understanding of my pain and health problems.</u>

4. My goal is <u>to serve the clients in the best way possible.</u>

5. It seems to me your goal is <u>to get into everyone's personal feelings.</u>

6. Would you be willing to explore some alternatives to help us both achieve our goals? If "yes" finish with #7. If "no" finish process with thanking him/her for listening to you.

7. Some possibilities I have come up with that may be more effective or harmonious are:

1. Train or terminate Lucy.
   _____

2. Refrain from listening to their complaints.
   _____

3. Let me do my job.
   _____

Are any of these acceptable to you? Do you see other possibilities? Listen to response, possibly discuss and thank her/him for listening to you.

When Myra saw Eric's form and read how other people felt about her, she fumed and swore it was a pack of lies. She had never humiliated anyone in the office; she never picked on people. Myra told Eric she felt hurt, angry, and frustrated that he would even listen to others when they complained about her. Didn't he know she had a terrible pain in her wrist? She wanted him to be understanding of her health problems. She was only trying to serve her clients' needs. Why did he have to get into everyone's feelings all the time? Besides, Lucy needed to be terminated or trained. "Please stop listening to everyone's complaints and let me do my job," she said angrily to Eric.

Eric did not put her down in any way. He reminded Myra that he was only relaying the concerns of the staff, and that the corporate office required that they use this method for dealing with problems of this sort. He agreed to determine whether Lucy needed further training. Myra could not defend against that. She agreed to do the three things Eric asked:

1. She would go directly to him when she felt angry and cooperate with him to the utmost to solve the problem.

2. She would treat people with respect.

3. She would make amends to anyone she blew up at.

For the first month, all was quiet. Eric thought the problem was solved. But by the second month, Lucy, the receptionist, and another staff member began to feel the hostility again. Myra seethed, tight-lipped and furious, behind a closed door, and they were afraid she would blow up any minute.

Myra never went to Eric when she was angry, did not treat the staff with respect, and never apologized or made amends. She did not keep her agreement with Eric to handle her anger according to his requests. The Three Rules and the Conscious Communication process were part of the office policies. Because Myra did not follow them, Eric would have had grounds to terminate her, but sixty days after he reminded her about her three agreements, she went on a six-week sick leave and then resigned.

Ideally Myra and Eric would have done an Alignment Agreement to check in with one another and determine if they were "on course" with the agreements that came out of their Conscious Communication.

Alignment Agreement Follow-up for Myra and Eric

Alignment Date:

Follow-up Date:

Employee: **Myra**   Reviewer: **Eric**

| | | | | This Follow-up | |
Last Follow-up	EE%	ER%		EE%	ER%

Employee Request: Understand my pain.   ☐   ☐
New or Revised

What it looks like: A. Train Lucy.   ☐   ☐

                        B. Refrain from listening to complaints.   ☐   ☐

                        C. Let me do my job.   ☐   ☐

Measurement: Complaints about me would reduce from one a day to one a week.

Signed: _____

Gap Correction:

					EE%	ER
Last Follow-up EE% ER%					☐	☐
Reviewer Request: *New or Revised*	Take responsibility for your anger in this office.				☐	☐
What it looks like:	A. When angry come to me first.				☐	☐
	B. Cooperate in mediation.				☐	☐
	C. Make amends.				☐	☐
Measurement:	Absenteeism would go from weekly to monthly.					

Signed: _____

Gap Correction:

Even without an Alignment Agreement, by Eric's holding to his requests of Myra, he gave the rest of the people in the office a powerful message: "We believe everyone must contribute in our office as well as with clients. We do not tolerate put-downs or hostility, and we insist that people keep their agreements." Within six months business picked up dramatically, and the company expanded into a second office.

Feelings and emotions come up all the time in business situations. Having the tools to work with them not only allows us the opportunity to get through them without wounding anyone but it also expands the opportunity for growth and productivity. It is an exercise in healing and, as such, is very valuable in the workplace. Wounded feelings often translate into sabotage. Learning to manage hostile and resentful feelings in ourselves and others is a powerful skill for middle managers to master.

MANAGING YOUR OWN IRRITATIONS

Lana, a literary editor, had a difficult situation with a prospective client who kept calling her. He left message after message without leaving a number where she could reach him. He was becoming a nuisance. Irritated, Lana complained to her associate about this man's constant demands. She was extremely busy and received dozens of phone calls every day and reviewed hundreds of manuscripts. Her time was valuable, and he was taking up too much of it with his incessant telephone messages.

Her associate asked me, "Do you have any quick tools we could use so she doesn't blow it with this writer? He has a lot of potential, but she can't deal with him just now."

"Do you think she could find five minutes to work with me?"

"Yes."

I asked Lana the questions on the Conscious Communication sheet, and the only thing she needed in front of her was the Feelings Chart. She selected three feelings from the chart and answered the first question on the form by saying she felt irritated, hostile, and mean when he called her nonstop. In section 2, she said she was concerned that she would end up not taking him on as a client and feel mean and hostile about it. In section 3, she stated that she would like him to leave a message telling her when and where he would be available to receive a call back from her.

When Lana thought about statement 4 of the Conscious Communication form, her attitude softened. She understood that her real intention was to help him. She could see how his demanding manner caused her to lose her professional, caring nature. By filling out the Conscious Communication form, she sorted out her feelings and got back to her best self. She was prepared to tell him what she wanted rather than wasting time complaining about him and putting him down to her associates.

As it turned out, the writer and the editor went in different directions, and she did not have a chance to tell him what she discovered from the exercise. But going through the process helped her to return to her own inner place of calm and kindness. The experience helped her to deal with other demanding writers in the future. It got her back in the position to control her career by leading rather than reacting.

Being open, honest, and nonjudgmental is the opposite of putting someone down. It is a gift to both the communicator and the recipient. Though there was no immediate monetary reward for Lana, the Conscious Communication process relieved her stress and increased her ability to let other prospective clients know how she prefers to handle telephone contacts with them.

Company Policies and Procedures for Mandating "No Put-downs"

Many good middle managers have lost their chance for promotion or their whole career because of a sexual harassment charge and/or their inability to lead the outspoken employees toward more professional behavior. The new and growing trend for lawsuits in the workplace is charges against managers for "hostile work environments or intentional infliction of emotional distress." If you have a proactive way to prepare for this, you can stop most hostile behaviors from the beginning: If you do not, the damage can be devastating.

A STATE FOREST SERVICE

One state that values its forests did a long and in-depth search for the perfect director. When Carl came aboard, he restated the mission he was charged with in his contract, which was to manage the forest service like a professional business and make it self-funding and profitable. The mission was communicated regularly. Over a two-year period, he met with every manager, and together they set goals to support the profit-oriented mission. He listened and learned from each and readily included their ideas. There was tremendous buy-in from his top managers.

Next were the mid-managers. The managers told the mid-managers what their new goals were, and the mid-managers were on the front line, coaxing and convincing the employees to become more accountable. By the time the mid-managers received the goals and objectives from the managers, they were stressed because they didn't have much input and many of the objectives seemed unreachable. But it seemed they had to agree to them, and so they did.

At the beginning of year three, each mid-manager was to meet with his or her employees to get the following agreements: that they would work 8:00 A.M. to 5:00 P.M. five days a week; call in sick if they weren't coming so their job could be covered; write a weekly report on activities with suggestions for improvements; stay below budget and prepare to reduce the budget for the next year by 10 percent.

At least 80 percent of the employees began to balk at what they considered demanding requests. The first thing they did was to generate personal attacks on the two key mid-managers. The two mid-managers who had the most employees were so intensely gossiped about and complained about to their manager that one week, when Carl was out of town, the assistant manager took the mid-managers out of their supervisory responsibilities and reassigned them.

When Carl returned he was very disappointed at what his assistant manager had done with the two mid-managers. Together Carl and his manager hired and trained two new mid-managers and brought in our firm to introduce the Funnel and Alignment processes. We, of course, requested that they adopt the Three Rules before we began. They said they couldn't because government personnel polices are fixed and can't be easily changed.

So we trained and prepared alignments for every employee of the two new mid-managers from the largest and most difficult departments. Each employee got to make a request and both mid-managers also made a number one request related to the new profit-oriented goals. Alignment Agreements were collected.

Now, everything was in place—employees had agreed to work the full eight hours each day, write reports weekly, support improvements, be role models for others, focus on work not personalities, answer the phone on the second ring, treat the forest personnel like customers, and so on.

We called in sixty days later to follow up and see how work was progressing and to support the mid-managers in this challenging leadership assignment. We reached only voice mails and received no return calls. Those we finally did reach said, "We can't discuss this." For days I couldn't reach Carl, but I finally got a message from him to meet at a specified time. He was quiet and subdued—not anything like the enthusiastic and hopeful director I had admired for two years as he led toward his mission and goals.

"Carl, my gosh, what is going on?"

"The employees have filed a class-action suit against me and the department for intentional infliction of emotional distress."

"For what?" I gasped.

"For requiring them to be here a full forty hours, for asking them to write reports, stay under budgets, cut budgets, etc. All the mid-managers and manager requests have caused them stresses."

"Carl, you have done everything right. I always knew I'd write a case study about you one day as a role model executive, and you are and have been. How do you function here day to day in this?" I asked.

"Right now, I just put one foot in front of the other and wait to see where this lawsuit goes."

"Do you think it would have made a difference if there was a policy in place that everyone had to contribute, all put-downs had to be converted to requests, and everyone was required to keep agreements—the Three Rules you wanted to use but the state government policy didn't include?"

"Absolutely—that's why the alignments all worked in the meetings, because they had to agree to the Three Ground Rules to attend the seminars. But once the meetings were over, they all went back to minimizing contribution, putting managers down, and not keeping agreements."

"Can I help in any way?"

"I'm not sure; probably not. I can't think clearly right now."

We ended our discussion and a month later when I called, I found he had been transferred to another position in Washington, D.C. That summer I took my family on our third trip to our favorite camping spot in that state. The ranger there, a person we'd come to know, said this was her last week.

The campground was closing because of lack of funding. If I ever had a chance to add to the U.S. or state government personnel policies and procedures, I would implement the "No Put-downs" policy outlined below.

Office Communication Policy and Procedures— "No Put-Downs"

Do not put down any person related to this workplace. Whether in jest or in anger, we ask that you *never* put down another person in this organization, not a coworker, manager, employee, partner, client, vendor, customer, stockholder, supplier, etc.

A put-down is criticism without hope. Teasing and bantering are fun and acceptable, but if the person feels personally less, it is a put-down. Be aware of whom you tease. In the law of physical injury, you "take the victim as he is." This means if he has a previous leg injury and you hit his injured leg, you are liable for the whole thing. Watch for sensitive people.

It is fine to disagree with something someone says or does; it's fine to suggest improvements; it's okay to criticize a process. It's *not* okay to degrade a person. When you are irritated with others in the company (and this certainly will happen), please take the following steps:

- Do not gossip.
- If you feel that someone puts you down, speak up right away with "that hurt" or "that feels like a put-down," or remind them "no put-downs."
- If someone offends you, do not hesitate to resolve it right away:
    A. Use the Feelings Chart to identify your feelings.
    B. Use the Conscious Communication tool to prepare for meeting with the person with whom you have an issue.
      - Go to the person and communicate what you have prepared.
      - Give the person the Eight-Step Checklist for Effective Listening.
      - If you do not feel heard after completing your communication, take someone with you on your second attempt.
      - End the meeting with a signed Alignment Agreement.
    C. If you are the cause of another person's irritation, use the Eight-Step Checklist for Effective Listening to respond.
      - Carefully go over each step, especially Step 3. Acknowledge the person either by feeling his or her feelings or recalling an example of when you felt that way.

- Tell that person what you might have done to contribute to this issue. Acknowledge that your behavior had an impact on the person.
- In Step 7, fill out an Alignment Agreement with a recommended follow-up date.

Rule 3: Keep Agreements

Keep your promises. You are accountable for all you promise.

—THE KORAN

ACCORDING to Don Miguel Ruiz in his book *The Four Agreements,* the most important agreement in life is the First Agreement. "Be impeccable with your word. Your word is the power that you have to create."[1]

This agreement is so important that with just this one agreement you will "transcend to heaven on earth." Keeping agreements generates trust and is the key to leadership. All of us want our leaders to have integrity and keep all of their agreements. Since you are now your own CEO, the responsibility for integrity begins and ends with you. When you know you keep your word, you will feel self-empowered. You probably are already keeping agreements or you wouldn't be a mid-manager. But try being "impeccable" with your word.

What Does Keeping Agreements Mean?

Keeping agreements with another in the business sense usually means the following:

1. Make an agreement only if you have the authority, time, resources, and so on to carry it out. Never make an agreement you don't intend to keep.

2. Once you agree, verbally or in writing, keep your word and just do it.

3. If for any reason you can't do it and circumstances change, contact the person immediately and reset or cancel the agreement.

4. If you forgot the agreement, make amends to the person. Try approaching the situation like the airlines do: they offer coupons for free drinks or free movies if a flight is later than agreed. Carry around coupons for a latte or muffins and give them out when "little" agreements are missed. It can add fun to your department.

Keeping Agreements Builds Trust

In today's global work environment, the criterion for integrity gets clouded. For example, in Japanese tradition, there is no word "escrow" because it is assumed that on a handshake both parties will keep their agreement—personal honor depends on it. In Russia, there is no word for "equity" because individuals never had ownership under Communist rule. The word "entrepreneur" in the Russian translation means "crook."

In Kuwait many expatriate Americans were hired as managers of rebuilding projects. But in Kuwait it is normal to not pay a person for up to six months. Americans became irate and quit, calling the business owners crooks. The owners always intended to pay the Americans, but it was to be in lump sums, not on a weekly basis, as the Americans assumed.

In many countries, "tips" are what we call bribes. Projects are budgeted with a 10 to 20 percent surcharge for bribes/tips. Is it dishonest to pay an official for extra consideration? In our country, yes—in some others, no.

I once interviewed a U.S. bankruptcy judge named Sidney Brooks, in Denver, Colorado. He said there are very few common international rules between countries and as a result, the international courts are packed and stuck. I asked him if there was one rule that could help resolve all the differences.

He thought for a minute and said, "Keeping your word." No country can dispute that, and all contracts require that both parties agree to something. Then I asked him about Rule 1, Everyone Contributes. "What if both sides were asked to help contribute to the resolution so you and other judges aren't always doing all the mediating?"

"That would be wonderful," he said. "I can't even imagine."

"What's it like now?" I asked.

"They take opposite sides, attack each other, and try to win their case."

"What about a No Put-downs rule?"

"We could never expect that," he said. "But it would be nice."

"So the one rule you would like to see to help avoid and/or resolve international conflicts is "Keep One's Word"?

"Yes."

"How about Keep Agreements?"

"Same thing."

Robert Mondavi tells the story of his Italian-born and -raised father who was a role model for Robert. Cesare Mondavi was a representative of family and of trust. "The more I thought about it, the more I realized that my father was not selling grapes. He was selling himself. They were buying my father's word. Cesare Mondavi was called 'good as gold,' and so was his word."[2]

There are many reasons why people from different countries may not trust one another. There may be a historical conflict between nationalities; there may be moral or religious differences between religious groups or ethnic groups. The importance of keeping agreements is that the habit and reputation of keeping one's word can transcend such religious and cultural differences. You may not know what part of the world will enter into your career, but if you keep agreements consistently, you will become trustworthy, which translates in the business world as being extremely marketable.

Local Trust—Trustworthiness Wins Out Time and Again

In my work with thousands of executives, managers, and employees all over the world, I have walked through the hiring decision-making process many times. I have worked with them to list pros and cons of each candidate, to do thorough reference checks, conduct complex written tests, and put them through interactive assessments. Some of these assessments have been designed so that candidates for the mid-managerial positions are asked to handle various emergencies, make judgment calls, deal with irate customers, make technical decisions, write reports, and answer E-mails. Some of these assessments have lasted for eight hours and some include up to twelve candidates at a time. We have also combined technology and intuitive feelings when we tried psychological computerized tests to analyze the candidates' integrity, judgment, and intellect. My grandfather, John Morgan, designed "The Morgan Mental Test" when he was a psychology professor at Northwestern University in the 1940s—so I know that people have been trying to use the testing method to hire managers for more than sixty years.

While witnessing the decision process of whom to promote, over the past twenty years, I've found there is one overwhelming characteristic that is increasingly and consistently the deciding factor. It cannot be easily discovered on a test or during an all-day assessment. That characteristic is trustworthiness, which is not to be confused with blind loyalty. Meaning that, for whatever reason, the hiring person believes and feels that you will keep all of your agreements with him or her and with others. My boss at Xerox used to tell me, "People buy based on how they feel." Trust is an emotion. And it has been my experience that executives select managers based on whether they feel trust.

No matter what the situation, be a person who honors agreements. If you accomplish that, you will find incredible opportunities available to you. Start with agreements to yourself, start with your family—clean up those little ignored agreements. The behavior will filter into the workplace and put you into a leadership position even if your title hasn't changed . . . yet.

Personal Trust—Managing Our Shadow Side

One vice president at PaineWebber, Steve Graves, creates trust from his mission statement. "I give people a sense of security in relation to their money." With this mission, they feel secure, and this allows them to trust him. It was because of this integrity that the local branch manager of PaineWebber spent a full year trying to get Graves to relocate to PaineWebber from Merrill Lynch. As I was working on this chapter, I asked Steve, "Why do you think it's important to keep agreements?"

"Keeping agreements not only gives clients a great sense of security about their money, but it gives me a sense of well-being about what I'm doing," he replied. "I get filled with anxiety if I don't keep an agreement with a client or family member or friend. It's for my own benefit."

Once Steve became known as a guy to trust, the local paper began quoting him about business in Sonoma County, Northern California. Steve would tell only what he knew for sure, and he would share his information in simple layman's terms. In 1999 Cisco Systems bought out a local telecommunications company called Cerent for $7.3 billion. There were about 250 employees with stock options averaging $7.1 million per person. In 2000 Texas Instruments bought Alantro Marconi bought Mariposa etc. These employees were technically oriented but not stock-savvy, so they began looking for a broker. They wanted to do business with a broker who was capable enough to increase their stock and caring enough to speak in a language they could understand. Several spoke English as a second language. While other investment brokers were clamoring for this sudden miraculous business, many of the clients flocked to Steve because he kept agreements and gave them the real sense of security they needed. They trusted him.

Keeping agreements empowers your career, reduces anxiety, and expands the trust people have in you. It also helps you trust yourself. Cooper and Sawaf call trust a key component of emotional fitness. Keeping agreements with yourself is critical to being the leader of your career. If you say you are going to make ten calls a day, or take a class, or recommend a new project—decide on a completion date and do it. Do it with complete commitment and intention because your career is affected by this. Remember—you are your own CEO.

By facing your urge not to keep agreements with yourself, you will come to know what Cooper and Sawaf, in *Executive EQ,* call "our shadow side." It is only in knowing our shadow side that we can identify and remove the obstacles to our career. These obstacles are often revealed when we are rationalizing breaking an agreement to ourselves. Our ability to feel joy is related to our ability to feel sorrow. So, too, our ability to have integrity is related to our ability to face our temper or arrogance or mistrust, and so on.[3]

For example, Kevin is a mid-manager at a fast-growing irrigation company. He loves growing things, being outdoors, and working with customers. Every now and then his temper flares up, and he gets red-faced and tells off someone he works with. This behavior, while it felt good at the moment, was ultimately keeping him from becoming a manager. Others mentioned it, so he made an agreement with himself to "avoid blowups." But that alone didn't work. Just like the Funnel rules, your agreement with yourself must be stated in the positive and have three descriptors and an outcome. So Kevin came up with: "Hold the tension—(a) count to ten; (b) go for a walk; (c) look for the real reason I'm angry. What would be different: people would trust me to do bigger jobs with bigger clients. I would get promoted; I would make more money."

Kevin reset his agreement with himself. He not only counted to ten and went for a walk, but he also began to understand his anger. When possible, he used the ITS form to convert his anger into his strengths. Then he was able to build on those strengths.

The strengths were: he is comfortable with important people; he includes others' opinions; and he is very goal-oriented. Each time he was ready to blow up, he counted to ten instead (sometimes eight, eventually seven, then six), walked away, and repeated, "I am comfortable with important people, I include others' opinions, and I am goal-oriented." He set a goal to sell to larger companies, and since he had the clout to interact with them, his boss agreed with the goal.

When his boss abruptly quit to take a better position, Kevin was ready to be promoted into that slot because he had kept his agreements with himself. As Mahatma Gandhi said, "The only devils in the world are those running around in our own heart. This is where the battle should be fought." Kevin fought his personal inner battle and won.

Leadership and team-building classes can help employees reveal their shadow sides and confront their personal obstacles. Kevin participated in one of these leadership and team-building classes with thirty-six others. Each one of them identified an obstacle to his or her career growth and then spent the first week observing it and the next five weeks gently trying to change it. The trust that develops in a team is refreshing and empowering when all members are working together to keep agreements that overcome personal obstacles. All members are uplifted by the synergy of a common bond of personal and career growth. Everybody wins, agreements are struggled with and kept, company success is used as the measure, and jobs transform into careers—not secretly but right up front.

Implied Agreements

Many implied agreements come with the job of middle manager. Following is a list of 180 of those agreements. No one could possibly follow all of these expectations 100 percent of the time, which is why it is important to agree verbally, and in writing, to all agreements.

180 Implied Middle Managers Agreements

- Give orders clearly
- Tell employees how they are doing
- Develop teamwork
- Defend individuals against unjustified criticism
- Help new members fit into the group
- Consider the feelings of others
- Encourage employees to do their best
- Correct employees when necessary
- Coordinate the work of the group
- Keep group informed on matters affecting their work
- Talk to employees at their desks, if possible
- Accept criticism
- Show the importance of the work

- Study employees to determine their abilities and shortcomings
- Criticize constructively
- Encourage people to "get things off their chests"
- Treat all courteously
- Recognize off-the-job accomplishments
- Set an example
- Show respect for employees and others
- Keep them doing things right
- Show how work ties in with work done in other departments
- Back-up and go to bat for employees when they are right
- Give attention to the shy and lonely
- Train understudies
- Find out how people feel as well as how they think

- Use every possible suggestion offered by employees
- Put every employee on his or her own as quickly as possible
- Tell others of the importance of the group
- Speak to every employee every day, if possible
- Make use of any special skills and abilities
- Explain WHY things are done
- Recognize good and mention it
- Equalize overtime
- Help group clear up conflicts both on and off the job
- Recommend deserving workers for promotion
- Visit employees when they are sick
- Treat all fairly
- Listen

COMMUNICATING EFFECTIVELY

- Explain clearly
- Give reasons for all policies and procedures
- Show and demonstrate, if possible
- Follow up long or doubtful instructions and information
- Have a purpose for every meeting
- Ask questions beginning with "What," "When," "Why," "Who," and "How"

- Conduct effective group meetings
- Encourage employees to express themselves
- Explain thoroughly decisions made at high management levels
- Report progress made in meeting schedules and maintaining quality
- Explain changes before making them

- Give reasons for notices meant to direct or persuade
- Show employees the tools to express themselves effectively
- Keep superiors posted on trends
- Listen carefully to all complaints, using the 8-Step Checklist for Effectively Listening

CONTROLLING EXPENSES

- Get complete explanations of budgets, if prepared by others
- Look for and suggest ways of improving methods
- Find causes of "over" and "under" items in budget
- Encourage suggestions from employees

- Check use of utilities— water, air, gas, and electricity
- Plan to avoid overtime
- Tell employees how the department is meeting cost standards
- Requisition only the supplies needed for efficient operations

- Explain to employees reasons for keeping costs low
- Keep a personal record of critical expense items
- Protect equipment, machines, materials, and property

DEVELOPING SELF

- Recognize exact responsibilities
- Get a clear understanding of new developments in your career field
- Clean up details promptly

- Get pleasure from the accomplishments of others
- Take calculated risks
- Control temper
- Adopt and practice a system of problem analysis for decision making

- Stay informed of new developments in your career field
- Make prompt but not hasty decisions
- Learn the limits of authority

- Improve ability to pass on information
- Plan a course of study; get advice, if necessary
- Weigh the short- and long-term effects of decisions
- Take part in community activities
- Learn the economics of the business

- Seek job improvements
- Learn to do the best you can with what you have got
- Maintain a sense of humor
- Support employees with written notes
- Set goals for self and work to reach them

- Get pleasure from being and working with others
- Use the experience of others
- Schedule personal time
- Get things done by persuasion, not by authority alone
- Develop and use checklists

KEEPING RECORDS

- Learn the reasons for all records
- Keep accurate records
- Improve handwriting, if necessary

- Maintain a records-retention schedule
- Keep written work up-to-date

- Write down messages that are important
- Suggest ways to cut paperwork, but do do the paperwork required

MAINTAINING DISCIPLINE

- Set standards of good work habits and conduct
- Tell what you want rather than what you don't like
- Keep employees informed of what they are to do
- Reprimand when necessary
- Set a good example

- Give clear instructions; use job-training steps
- Follow set procedures in disciplining, but suggest ways to improve
- Encourage employees to offer suggestions of good work habits
- Control absenteeism and tardiness

- Revise standards whenever necessary
- Find out what employees need from you and make sure you provide it
- Reward good work habits with a "pat on the back"
- Put in a day's work for a day's pay

PERSUADING AND GIVING REASONS

- Give reasons for meeting responsibilities

- Ask employees for their input

- Give reasons for rules, policies, and practices

- Ask employees for their agreement to follow through
- Give reasons for offering suggestions
- Ask others for input as to how to be safer

- Give reasons when making requests of superiors
- Ask others if they have suggestions
- Give reasons when seeking the cooperation of other managers for improvement

- Ask superiors what requests they may have of you
- Give reasons for practicing safety on and off the job
- Ask other managers what they suggest for improvement

PLANNING AND ORGANIZING

- Develop a checklist of equipment, materials, and people
- Decide who is to carry out the decision
- Schedule work according to priority
- Identify, locate, and describe any deviations from standard practice

- Recognize when a problem exists
- Gather information on the problem
- Conclude planning with a written list of things to do
- Determine alternative objectives of a decision, then choose the best alternative

- Determine what the problem "is" and what it "is not"
- Anticipate changes and emergencies
- Persuade, if necessary, to get the action required

MAINTAINING QUALITY

- Know the exact quality
- Listen to suggested improvements with an open mind
- Build concern for quality work

- Follow the standards set, but at the same time look for ways of improving them
- Train employees to meet the standards

- Look for and suggest improvements in method
- Cooperate with other department managers to control quality

PRODUCING QUANTITY SCHEDULED

- Develop a list of critical jobs and check them at definite intervals

- Develop a checklist to aid in maintaining supplies of materials and equipment

- Determine responsibility for carrying out schedules and verify that it is understood

- Anticipate bottlenecks and plan what to do to clear them up
- Set up controls and reporting procedures to check on progress

- Anticipate interruptions in utilities and plan what to do to overcome them

- Plan to reduce overtime
- Cooperate with staff departments and managers

PROMOTING SAFETY

- Set a good example
- Check continuously for unsafe conditions, such as improper illumination or unsafe storage areas
- Do not take things for granted

- Take precautions to prevent accidents
- Make your own department an outstanding example of safety
- Anticipate possible safety hazards and plan how to avoid them

- Discourage any horseplay
- Thank employees for safety suggestions
- Understand your rights and responsibilities as a manager under the Occupational Safety and Health Act

TRAINING EMPLOYEES

- Select the right people for the right jobs
- Let the learner outline his or her own training steps
- Prepare to train thoroughly
- Follow up closely until the learner can do as instructed

- Find out what the learner already knows and can do
- Put the learner on his or her own
- Show the learner what he/she will gain by learning
- Rotate employees, when possible, to broaden skills

- Retrain if the learner needs it
- Taper off management as the learner develops skills
- Ask the learner questions beginning with "What," "When," "Where," "Why," "Who," and "How"
- Keep stress in balance

SERVING CUSTOMERS

- Demonstrate that customer service starts with you and works its way out to others in your organization and ultimately to the customer

- Teach others that value-centered customer service is created by the values of the people who provide it

- Build life long customers
- Serve internal and external customers

MANAGING ONESELF

- Stay physically and emotionally fit
- Tap into intuitive skills
- Look for methods of self improvement
- Create vision and mission
- Use visualization
- Take responsibility for relationships

Dealing with Implied Agreements

When I wrote the first draft of this book, I initially sent it to three agents. All three responded and asked for more information, saying they were interested. One agent said she was going to New York to meet with publishers. She said she was going to mention my book and see if there was an interest. I said, "Great." She sent me a contract to look over while she was gone and directed me to her assistant if I had any questions. For thirty days neither of us called the other. Meanwhile, the other two agents were in communication with me asking questions, going over manuscript details, telling me about their agencies, working out contracts, etc. After three weeks of very thorough analysis of the two agents, I selected one. I wrote all three a letter to tell them of my selection.

By now it had been five weeks since I had heard from the first agent. She received my letter and was very upset, proclaiming, "You don't take your own agreements seriously," and "You must understand that in publishing your word is your bond." Apparently, our first telephone conversation in which she suggested mentioning my book to publishers was, in her mind, a verbal contract. Then, based on her assumption that we had this verbal contract, she talked with several publishers, who then asked her to send the manuscript. When she got my letter saying I had selected another agent, she was put in a poor light with the publishers. Does this mean I don't take agreements seriously? No. It means I didn't know we had an agreement. Once I understood this, I felt very sorry about it.

I called her to apologize for whatever role I had played in the misunderstanding. It taught me a lot about the agent/publisher business. On the agent's part, she should have communicated with me more clearly and much more often. On my part, I should have studied the agency/publisher world more thoroughly.

The agent reverted to violating Rule 2, No Put-downs, by accusing me of being a person who does not care about agreements. This is exactly why there are **Three** Rules and all **three** must be in place. Because agents are well trained in eliminating people's work, they get in the habit of criticizing. I found this to be the case with editors, agents, and publishers—also with engineers, accountants, and computer experts. They are trained to identify what *isn't* right. This is helpful most of the time, but learning to criticize *with* hope instead of *without* hope is the key.

A Rule for the Rules

Following the Three Rules yourself means never pointing the finger at others and ridiculing them for not following the rules. If you do that, you are violating Rule 2. The rules are best used individually first, then outwardly. However, the rules should be introduced as a request or a preference—not as a demand or a sermon. Your career will be uplifted when you keep your agreements, but realize that everyone strays from agreements once in a while. We can always encourage others to keep the Three Rules, but putting them down for not keeping an agreement makes us violators of Rule 2.

"Keeping Agreements" Starts with Family

While I have collected and analyzed tens of thousands of agreements between boss and employee, I don't think any of those agreements were as educational to me as those with my three children. You may want to practice the Three Rules with your partner, your children, or your parents to receive some of the career-transforming lessons shown below.

MARK

When my oldest son, Mark, was thirteen, he was getting D's in several classes. His father and I were horrified. Since I was a management consultant and a college teacher, I thought surely I could help him with his studies. We went over spelling, history, practice quizzes, and did great reports. He still got D's. I found he wasn't turning in his homework. It was "cool" to get D's. It was not "cool" to get A's. I tried to tell him about college, and he said he didn't care about college. I was left speechless.

I "sucked it up," as they say, and accepted that grades were not important to him, only to his parents. I remembered all of the middle managers I worked with who needed to get employees to do things the employees didn't think were important. To do this, the managers and employees would do an Alignment. They asked the employees for their number one requests and, in trade, told the employees their own number one requests. Yet, trying to get one another to agree on the importance of the other's request is sometimes a waste of time. We taught them to just agree to do one another's requests and, hopefully, someday they would see why.

Keeping this in mind, I decided to do an Alignment with Mark. I decided if this Alignment process does not work with my son, then I would never use it again, because it is useless if it doesn't work for the tough times at home as well as at work.

When I accepted that Mark did not care about my number one request, I realized I didn't know his number one request. Since he understood the Alignment process from doing it in our family and seeing it in motion with others, he knew what I was doing.

"So, Mark, what is the number one thing you want from me?" He knew right away.

"Drive me to Jason's house two days a week."

My thoughts were racing, "Jason! He is an awful kid who spits, swears, skips school, and lies; how will this ever help Mark with his grades? He'll go to F's. And . . . drive? I don't drive at 3:00 P.M.—I have a full-time job. No way can I rearrange my schedule to pick him up in the middle of the day. But wait—I made an agreement with myself to use this tool. Using this tool means doing whatever the other person wants as long as it's not illegal, immoral, or fattening, and then see if that person will do my number one request."

"Okay, Mark." I finally was able to speak. "I will. How about once a week for a month until I can readjust my schedule and then we'll go twice." I think he said something like "Rad" or "Awesome."

I took a deep breath as I prepared to tell him my number one request of him. I was afraid he'd say no, but I knew that by his getting his number one request, he might say yes. "I want you to get a 2.5 grade point average. That's A's, B's, and C's, nothing below a C." He responded with that "Dennis-the-Menace" chipper voice, "Okay."

LIFE-ALTERING CAREER-TRANSFORMING ALIGNMENT OF 1984

Mark's request of Mary: Drive me to my friend Jason's house two days a week: 3:00–5:00 P.M.

Mary's request of Mark: Get a 2.5 grade point average at school on a 4.0 scale: B–/C+.

RILEY FAMILY NUMBER ONE REQUESTS THE YEAR BEFORE

Riley Family Number One Requests 1983

Mark—12 yrs

Keith—7 yrs
Mary—
George—
Brooke—not born yet

Mark's requests	of George:	Help me fix things.
	of Keith:	Finish games we start; don't quit.
	of Mary:	Drive me more places.
Keith's requests	of George:	Take me to the toy store to spend my own money and push me on the swing.
	of Mary:	Pack my lunch.
	of Mark:	Treat me with respect; don't tease me.
Mary's requests	of Mark:	Do your chores without me asking.
	of Keith:	Treat me as well as you treat the dog.
	of George:	Get me pregnant with a baby girl. ( )
George's requests	of Mark:	Understand the consequences of your actions.
	of Keith:	Admit if you make a mistake.
	of Mary:	Spend quiet reading time with me.

So, when the time came, I drove as slowly as I could from his school to Jason's house, and I picked him up right at 5:00 P.M. or just before. I could see no link between our two requests, and I struggled the hardest I've ever struggled to keep an agreement. I had to face my own dark side: feeling like a bad mother, letting go of control, letting him grow up, and facing my own aging. Such monsters lived in this agreement and in the slow drive, which was now twice a week. I never even asked him if his homework was done.

By the end of seventh grade, he had a 2.68 GPA. More important, he continued to get A's, and B's, and C's during the rest of high school, all through college, and later for his M.B.A. Because of the success of the agreement with my son, I recommitted myself to this process and the Three Rules, and I have Mark to thank. He could always tell the truth to power. And I listened in the nick of time—my power was dwindling under the old way we had been doing schoolwork.

The lesson for middle managers, no matter how irrelevant and unimportant your employee's number one request may sound, is if it isn't illegal or immoral or too costly, just do it. Review the eight number one requests in Appendix B under "What do you want" and see if any of them are impossible. The most difficulty I've had with mid-manager alignments is getting managers to believe the number one request of the employee. As I did with Mark, try doing their request anyway and see what happens.

Now that Mark is a mid-manager, I asked him what he had learned during his own private confronting of homework and grades. He said, "There's very little difference between A's and D's. If you do 90 percent of the work (or so you think) you end up surprised with D's. If you do just 10 percent more (all of the work) you miraculously get A's." Keeping agreements with yourself is the place to start.

KEITH

Keith, my second son, has been steadfast and consistent since he was young. His agreement was to sweep the kitchen, empty the trash, and feed the dog before school. Not a morning went by that he was not the first one up in the morning to sweep even if there were three crumbs on the floor and to empty the trash with only two items. So we knew we had better keep our agreements with him: Allowance to be paid by 10:00 A.M. on Saturday and trash bags and dog food always in supply. I'd find myself running out to the store at night so as not to be caught without trash bags or dog food the next morning. I never taught him—he taught me to keep my half of our agreements—always!

At the end of his junior year in college, he was unanimously elected treasurer of the Industrial Technology Department at Cal Polytechnic University at San Luis Obispo, California. He'd never been in a financial role before, but he accepted the position, which started in May right after the election. The agreement in the treasurer's position was to keep the department financially sound.

While he was celebrating at the end-of-the-year party, he was handed a bill to sign. He had no idea whether they could cover the cost, but it was Saturday night, everyone was very festive, banks were closed, and he had the authority. So he signed. Then he had a knot in his stomach for the rest of the party. On Monday he discovered they did not have the funds to cover it. "Why was it I wanted this job?" he pondered. His peers ignored the problem because they knew he would handle it, and during the summer he figured out how to raise the funds to cover the check. Does keeping agreements mean not having fun? By fall he had learned to integrate the two—integrity and fun. "Parties are more fun if you can afford them," he said.

The message I learned from Keith regarding mid-managers is to make sure you keep your agreements with the employees for the sake of building a culture of integrity. It will pay you back over and over.

BROOKE

Brooke is eight years younger than Keith. As the little sister of two older brothers, Brooke got away with breaking agreements. Not so much with Keith, but with Mark, her dad, and me. We would overlook little things like agreements to clean her room or pay back money. Keith eventually got very upset and pointed out Brooke's inability—or rather her unwillingness—to keep agreements. By the time she was five or six years old, we all tried to emphasize and reward keeping agreements. It was a long, tough struggle, and I saw how being lax early made it very tough later.

When Brooke was thirteen, she had her first outside-world, real test of leadership and keeping agreements and commitments. She and her friend Becca were elected to the eighth grade student council in a K–8 school. They attended a mandatory Student Council Leadership Camp during the summer, and when they returned to school in the fall, they found that eighth-grade student council members were in charge of ecology.

When I picked the girls up each Tuesday after school, they were late and their clothing was stained. Emptying and sorting all the trash on campus and then lifting it up into big bins wasn't what they had pictured as their prestigious role in Student Council. Hand-sorting every partially filled soda can left them with cut hands and wet clothes. Each week the weather was getting colder, and it began to get darker as they sorted the last sticky bunch of cans. I bit my lip the first several Tuesdays as I drove Becca and Brooke home in their silent disappointment. "If I'd known what ecology meant, I wouldn't have run," said Becca, and Brooke agreed. I feared they would quit and never want another leadership responsibility again, but I said nothing. Each day we walked past the family bulletin board with the Three Rules that we called "House Rules." I wondered if Brooke ever thought of them.

Several weeks later the principal stopped me and said, "We are so pleased with Brooke and Becca's new bathroom hygiene program as part of their ecology." "What?" I muttered. "Oh, yes," she continued. "She and Becca are really taking ecology seriously. No one ever addressed bathrooms before, and now everyone is looking forward to the 'Bathroom Hygiene Contest' between boys and girls next month. It will last for a week, include a 'fun day' and there will be prizes for . . ." The details faded away as I fought back the tears. She not only kept her agreement, she also contributed.

We still struggle with agreements, Brooke and I. But at least she knows what agreements are and how to keep them. We celebrate when she keeps them, and she and the boys and I do push-ups when we forget. Push-ups are a discipline measure in the Marines. Brooke's lesson for middle managers is that you shouldn't just suffer through the keeping of agreements. Instead, bring them to life; add to them and make them fun. Your career will blossom by your own consistent choice to keep the agreement.

MAKE CERTAIN YOU KEEP YOUR AGREEMENTS

Just because I teach agreements at home and at work does not mean I am perfect at keeping mine. A president of a manufacturing company—I'll call him Stewart—called me in to work on growing the business ten times in ten years. He was a one-third partner, and the other two partners insisted on this fast growth.

In the first meeting Stewart told me that his number one request of me was to train his secretary, Ruth, to become a personnel director. I agreed. His second request was for me to help managers develop a ten-year plan and then train all managers and supervisors to learn the skills necessary to implement the plan. I agreed to this also. We signed the contract in our first meeting. It was a huge assignment, and I invited four other partners to join me in completing it. One of the partners, Bob, was assigned to focus on working with Ruth. The other three helped set up the seminars and conduct the supervisory and management training. We customized a six-week training program to fit their growth goals.

Bob set up appointment after appointment with Ruth to teach her personnel management skills, but she never showed up. When he caught her by accident, she said she had a headache or was "brain-fried." After at least twenty attempts, Bob started joining us in the mid-management seminars.

The seminars were going according to plan—six weeks long, twelve participants per seminar, each learning to plan, delegate, and resolve conflict. The mid-managers in their six-week sessions each ended with a speech about the specific details and plan as to how they could lead their department to grow by ten times in ten years. Each of the twelve mid-managers was dressed very professionally, they all showed enthusiasm and commitment that the owners had never witnessed before. By listening to these mid-managers, the ten times growth seemed very attainable. All three partners were visibly and emotionally moved by these speeches. At the end, one owner's voice cracked with emotion as he tried to express his appreciation and awe.

Back at work, things were not going so well. The engineers felt their department could not grow because they were unable to fill any vacant engineering positions. It turned out that Ruth had been offended by the manager of engineering, so to "punish" him she would not hire anyone. My associate, Bob, intervened, ran an ad, interviewed five people, and filled two positions.

The next middle manager group was getting ready to give its speech to management and owners when Stewart called me into his office. "I want you and every one of your staff out," he said. "After the speeches today? Right!" I said. "No, now!" he retorted.

"What happened?" I said, in total disbelief since everything was going so well.

"Ruth is very upset that Bob is taking over her job. You agreed to help her become a personnel manager and that has not happened."

"But she canceled all the meetings and refused to get educated on it. . . ."

"My decision is final."

I could go on about how Ruth was playing games and didn't want to learn, but not only would I be breaking the No Put-down rule, the truth was I had agreed to train her to become a personnel manager, and I hadn't kept my agreement.

A year later, their executive vice president called us to see about joining our firm. He said they grew 23 percent the first six months but then dropped back to where they had been. It seemed that Stewart did not enforce the Three Rules equally among his employees, and the company was unable to achieve the growth that the managers desired.

The Power of Keeping Your Agreements

Regardless of what language, your intent manifests through your word.

—DON MIGUEL RUIZ, *The Four Agreements*[1]

IN order for people to keep agreements, the following three things must be established:

1. Be discerning about what you agree to and with whom you agree.

2. Make commitments to yourself and others that will hold up regardless of their immediate circumstances, however dire—and regardless of whether or not they are responsible for creating those situations.

3. Know the exhilaration and career improvement that can occur for you during the toughest stretches of keeping agreements.

THE WINERY—MAKE MANAGEMENT MORE ATTRACTIVE THAN A UNION

If you drive through the beautiful rolling hills of Napa and Sonoma County, you will pass grapevines ripening on sunny hillsides and beautiful wineries that invite you to stop and try the products. Everything looks perfect. But a few years ago there was trouble at a well-known winery there. Union organizers came in and tried to convince the workers to form a union. The owner of the winery, whom we'll call Todd, was surprised and dismayed when the union seemed to be gaining a foothold. He felt personally wounded when many of the workers, whom he had known for years, attended a union information meeting at one of his facilities. "Why would my people want to do this?" he asked. "I give them so much. Who are the ringleaders? What if there is a strike?"

Todd didn't stay stuck in disappointment and resentment, however. One of his agreements with his company was to treat all employees with dignity. This meant he would weigh the pros and cons of any issues they brought to him. To honor his agreement, Todd listened to inside sources who described the complaints of the workers. They were able to identify the major issue: Workers felt that their supervisors did not treat them with respect. They belittled them, would only delegate small tasks and then would renege, gave the workers responsibility but not authority, treated them like children, and did not consider their ideas.

The union representative was discussing hours, vacation, collective bargaining, wage increase, and benefits—basically, he was attempting to address emotional issues by focusing on material things. The owner, however, decided to wage a pro-company campaign. Among his recommendations, he suggested that department managers and supervisors attend extensive training on how to treat employees. He also outlined a vigorous schedule for himself to speak to all employees in person and ask for their support.

Before the union vote, Todd held two open meetings—one in English, one in Spanish—and gave his word that things would change. He looked employees in the eye and said, "I believe I now have a better understanding of the problem. You want more say-so, you want to be treated with dignity by your supervisors, you want more input, and you want to be valued and listened to." Then he agreed to make those changes, and he asked them to cast their vote in favor of the company.

Because Todd had always kept his agreements with them in the past, the employees believed him, and the overwhelming majority gave him their votes 48–9. The newspaper headline read, WINERY EMPLOYEES REJECT UNION STATUS, 48–9. The reason quoted was, "The winery has a good relationship with its employees." In turn, Todd put a program in place to ensure that everyone would be treated respectfully. In handling his labor problem, Todd had unwittingly followed the Three Rules. First, instead of putting the workers down for considering union membership, he diffused his resentment and then set out to resolve their grievances. He made an agreement with them and took steps to keep that agreement. His practice of keeping little everyday agreements in the past paid off when it was time for the "big" agreement.

The strike stopped, but issues later began to fester because the supervisors did not have the skills to fulfill Todd's agreement to treat employees with dignity. Our firm was called in to teach an eight-week supervisory skills course. The owner had made attendance at the sessions mandatory, and some supervisors were resentful because in their minds they were already doing a good job. They had been bottling and shipping wine for years. The wine was good and production was usually on schedule. They believed they already knew how to treat employees to get the job done.

As usual, we began the course by explaining the Three Rules for the session, and by the time we began to apply those rules in class, their objections faded away. They understood that Todd was not just imposing the Three Rules on them arbitrarily, but that he, too, was following them. He was particularly fixed on keeping his agreement to address the employees' complaints.

We worked for several weeks, helping each supervisor Funnel and Align the employees' goals with his or her own. Employees found that working in this way on the production of goals with their supervisors empowered them more than the union meetings had. For the union advocates in this case, sabotage had been much more exciting than being productive. In fact, I learned that none of the three union advocates had ever been very productive workers.

For the most part, the agreements in this case were highly successful. Todd kept his agreements, so employees were motivated to keep theirs. Having a president like Todd makes middle managers' careers much easier to lead. He leads the company; you lead your career. Word spread that Todd's winery was a Three Rule company, and creative, entrepreneurial, opportunistic people applied to work there. Their growth has been successful beyond their highest set goal.

BEWARE OF AGREEMENTS WITH PEOPLE WHO CAN'T KEEP THEIRS

Loretta was a very successful decorator and the owner of a furniture store in the Silicon Valley. They called her the furniture magnate. Her secret ingredient was that she always kept agreements. I'm not sure if it was her upbringing or her own strong values, but she took all agreements very seriously. Her problem was in assuming others would keep theirs.

She hired us to assist the store in creating a strategic plan. We met weekly to establish a mission and values for her company, and all full-time employees were involved in its creation. The company's mission became, "Enliven the spirit of every home." One of the ten values they came up with was, "Keep all agreements with customers, coworkers, and suppliers." She did Alignments with all her employees and got an average of 91 percent on the follow-ups.

Her business grew to include a second branch in San Francisco, and she started dating another company owner in Silicon Valley. Time passed and I didn't see Loretta for two years.

The next time I heard from her, she was married, pregnant, and very troubled about some problems she was having. She told me about her husband—we'll call him Clark—and how they had made some agreements before getting married. He agreed to help around the house daily (empty dishwasher and trash) and make the monthly house payments. She agreed to give him lots of personal space and make the 20 percent down payment on the house. She made the down payment, and they moved in. Weeks and months passed, but he never did any chores. Clark said it was beneath him.

They went to counseling, and when the counselor heard the story he asked Clark, "Why didn't you keep your promise to empty the dishwasher and take out the trash?" Clark said, "I just promised it so we could get married—people do this in business all the time. I didn't really mean it!"

Then, after the first year, he announced he wasn't going to pay the monthly payment anymore. "But this was our agreement," Loretta said. "I paid the down payment and you pay the monthly payments."

"I changed my mind," was his response.

"He has a double standard—I must keep all my agreements, but he doesn't have to," she told me. "He devalues my down payments and brags about his monthly payments. Each week he devalues a new part of me—my hair, my nationality, my line of work, my relatives, my friends, and the books I read. At the same time he overvalues each of those in himself.

"He keeps every agreement with his board of directors and then comes home and blatantly violates our agreements. He's real paranoid that I'll stop working and he'll have to support the baby and me. I had to sell the San Francisco store to spend more time with the chores at home and prepare for the baby. He was so loving at first, but now he goes back and forth from mean to nice, then on to very mean and compensatory nice."

"Why did you marry him?" I asked.

"I wanted a baby and a family."

She went on to describe how awful and abusive his behavior had become. She said he would turn angry and hostile over irrelevant things.

"What's he like with managers and his employees?" I asked.

"He seems to pick one at a time and criticize them until they can't stand it anymore and they quit."

"Is there a huge gap between his salary and anyone else's?"

"Yes."

"How's the company doing?"

"Same. It keeps slowly growing. He's really brilliant at his job. He can guess things before they happen. He's a futurist, but he can't build managers."

I then asked her what she was going to do.

"You know me, old 'keep your agreements,'" she said. "I want to get help to make it work, but I also want others to learn from this. I don't want to keep it a secret anymore. I do want to learn to deal with it."

After five weeks of consultation with a psychologist, his diagnosis was that Clark had a narcissistic borderline personality disorder. According to Paul Henning, Ph.D., MFCC in Southern California who specializes in narcissistic personality disorders, "Narcissists have an exaggerated sense of importance. Concerned with their own self-promotion, they show disdain for others while upgrading themselves."[2] Loretta was pregnant and felt stuck.

Clark is still effective in his job reporting to the board of directors and the stockholders. But, middle managers, beware: be very careful that your career is not dependent on a mutual relationship of support with this type of boss.

Be sure whomever you make agreements with has the capacity to carry out the agreements you make. Maintaining the "Keep Agreements" rule over time will identify those who are not capable of keeping agreements and allow them to get help. You will then be able to lead the 85 to 87 percent who are able to keep agreements. Keeping agreements with one another creates a healthy, functional workplace—one that fosters meaningful careers.

MAKE COMMITMENTS THAT WILL HOLD UP

Michael Sullivan, the president of Flex Products, Inc., took the company public. Below is a list of the Standards of Behavior that he lived by and inspired others to live by as well. Take note of number 10; this is the epitome of the goal for keeping agreements.

FLEX PRODUCTS STANDARDS OF BEHAVIOR

1. The same **standards** exist for all members.

2. We believe in our **community values** and we live by them.

3. Our work is to create an **environment** that will lead to sustained success for the **company**. We will not deflect ourselves with irrelevant detail and micro management.

4. Membership in this group is based on achievement, contribution, and sustained performance.

5. We make **decisions** consultatively; management decisions represent a single voice, backed by the commitment of all members.

6. We are guided by a **vison** that is clearly enunciated in a current, comprehensive **strategic plan**. The **vision** and the **plan** are shared with all employees.

7. We **communicate** openly and **support** and **trust** one another. We are committed to win together, not at the expense of any team member. We pick each other up if one falls.

8. We acknowledge the limitations of what we know.

9. The **company** and our own **team** must be **learning organizations**; we review, analyze, and learn from all of our experiences.

10. We take **responsibility** for what we say and do and honor our **commitments** to one another. We respect the effort and energy that others dedicate to meeting our commitments.

11. We allow for disagreements and don't personalize differences.

12. We are explicit about what we want to accomplish when we are working together: our **objectives** are clear.

13. We test our decisions against one **benchmark**: "Will this make **our company** a better **company** for all stockholders?"

Flex Products grew and went public, and Michael sold his interest and began putting on seminars in partnership with me. I noticed that he either kept or reset even the smallest agreement without any effort.

One bank client we worked with to outline mission and values had the sixth week devoted to each mid-manager giving a speech about how he or she could lead their department to increase the profit margin. Michael said, "I'll videotape them." I said, "Great."

The videotape project was a monster; getting the right camera, getting the right setup, electrical outlet, and parts. It was far beyond what either of us expected. Filming all twenty-four speeches on a hot day without air-conditioning—not to mention making and distributing copies—was very difficult. I had no idea what was going on behind the scenes because Michael never complained to me until we had the finished product. The speeches were so moving that the president, our client, said viewing them gave him a lump in his throat. He also said that after viewing the speeches, he could see that he was able to let go and let the managers take over. His new agreement was to delegate. Every time the bank manager forgot to keep his agreement to delegate, we would remind him how Michael kept his agreement to video-tape the speeches, and he would reaffirm his agreement.

Several of Michael's employees were in a college class I taught called *Quality Management and Productivity* the next year. They were filled with stories of what it took to keep agreements. Those kept agreements made regular people magnificent. Kept agreements transform managers into leaders. Michael Sullivan's kept agreements earned millions of dollars for him and all those associates with his company.

Managing at the mid-manager level is much like parenting. You outline tasks to be done, set deadlines and goals, but at the same time you must be civil, possibly supportive and respectful, maybe even empowering. Review your Mission Statement exercise from chapter 5 and see what you wrote in the section about how you want to be remembered as a manager. My guess is there is some combination of "good leader" and "be supportive." Each of these qualities is enhanced by keeping agreements. One of the most impactful lessons that employees and children get in life comes from the power of keeping agreements.

VICK AND BEN—FACING A BROKEN AGREEMENT

It's not only the day-in, day-out keeping of agreements that is so lesson-oriented. When you hold on to an agreement gently and respectfully in plain sight of the other parties involved, they begin to recognize their broken agreements. Broken agreements provide very valuable insight and information to ourselves and others.

Vick gives us the story on this point. He was a manager of a food distribution company who could not move his career forward and couldn't figure out why. He set goals, organized, delegated, and taught all his employees what to do, but every morning the mistakes left over from the evening shift created much turmoil. Starting every morning in turmoil was sucking the energy from Vick and his team.

Each morning he went early to meet with the night shift supervisor and covered every item. The night supervisor and employees seemed surprised by their increasing number of mistakes. The truth of the situation was that everybody loved the night supervisor, Ben, but no one wanted to tell Vick that Ben slept every night during his shift because he had a good family and a bad gambling habit. The drivers didn't mind because they didn't really want a "boss" around, so they got to be more lax too. They were all buddies and liked it that way. Finally, a concerned driver told Vick that Ben was sleeping on the job.

While Vick liked Ben and knew the others did too, he felt that as a mid-manager, a part of his job was "tough love"—but not "mean love." The company's mission stated they were "lean and clean." Tiptoeing around an on-the-job sleeper who was sabotaging Vick's career was not clean; it was wasting money and was indirectly supporting Ben's gambling habit.

Vick did not want to hire a detective or come at night himself to catch Ben. This was too negative, too expensive, and too much like police tactics. Since the company was a Three Rule company and used the Alignment process regularly, Vick did a normal alignment with Ben.

Vick's number one request of Ben was this: "Lead the drivers to be a problem-solving team." The action items were "Make sure they resolve all the problems from the evening as soon as they occur," "Ask for input from other drivers in the warehouse," and "Emphasize and reward clean work areas and quickly resolved problems." What would be different? "Four out of five mornings when the day shift starts, we would have zero problems left over from the night shift."

Ben couldn't think of a number one request from Vick (which is an indicator of a possible problem). When people cannot think of a single thing they would like to improve, it is suggested they use the word "continue" and use it as a chance to tell their boss what it is they appreciate so much. Ben's number one request was, "Continue to give me autonomy in managing the warehouse." Ben could come up with only one verb statement: "Let me resolve the problems." Ben's list was short and incomplete.

After thirty days, an auditor sent out the Follow-Up Form (see below) to both Vick and Ben. Vick marked 25 percent for Ben. For the first week, Ben led the drivers to be a problem-solving team, but for the remaining weeks, everything was back to usual. Ben gave himself a 90 percent based on the first week. He ignored the last three weeks.

Alignment Agreement

Please Print

Organization: Today's Date:

Employees Name: Employee's Job Title:

Reviewer's Name: Follow-up Date:

INSTRUCTIONS: Before writing, Reviewer first hears the Employee's complete request, then it is discussed and agreed upon by both. Reviewer then clearly and concisely prints the Employee's request in full, and signs in agreement. Employee then hears the Reviewer's complete request, they come to agreement, Emloyee prints the request, and signs the form.

EMPLOYEE'S REQUEST (PRINTED BY THE EMPLOYEE)

1. The #1 item _____ wants from _____ is:
   Employee's Name   Reviewer's Name

   _____

   _____

2. Specifically what will the Reviewer do to meet your request?
   A. _____
   B. _____
   C. _____

3. How will you know the request has been fulfilled; how will you measure the change? _____

   _____

I agree to begin on _____ Signed _____
                    Date   Reviewer's Signature

REVIEWER'S REQUEST (PRINTED BY THE EMPLOYEE)

1. The #1 item _____ wants from _____ is:
   Reviewer's Name   Employee's Name

   _____

   _____

2. Specifically what will the Employee do to meet your request?
   A. _____
   B. _____
   C. _____

3. How will you know the request has been fulfilled; how will you measure the change? _____

   _____

I agree to begin on _____ Signed _____
                    Date   Employee's Signature

Ben was about to lose his job if something didn't change. It was up to him. Vick never mentioned the sleeping. He only mentioned the three weeks Ben didn't perform. Vick, on the other hand, got 100 percent on his number one request from Ben. Vick kept his agreement with Ben, and Vick held Ben accountable for his request. Vick then did a very important thing: he did not mention gambling or sleeping because it would cause defensiveness, and he did not try to "help." By holding just to the agreement, Vick created a life-transforming event for Ben. Vick asked Ben, *"What do you suggest?"*—a key question to ask in the case of an unkept agreement.

In that safe, but not overnurturing, environment in which Ben had room to see the consequences of his behavior, Ben told Vick about his other job and about his gambling debts. They agreed to a one-week leave of absence while Ben made a choice about his job. Ben returned from the week off not only ready to improve his career but he had also reunited with his estranged wife and child. He now gives talks to service clubs about his gambling recovery process. He credits Vick for the most caring and high-integrity intervention imaginable—"He just sat there with me as we looked at my 100 percent score for him right next to his 25 percent score for me. Vick asked what I suggested."

Keeping agreements calls for others and ourselves to be the best we can be. You can transform your career and those of others around you by keeping your agreements and asking others to keep their agreements.

KEEP AGREEMENTS IN FAMILIES

When my sons return for visits, our favorite memories and stories seem to be about overcoming obstacles to the Three Rules. One story had to do with my son Mark keeping an agreement about earning money before going to an amusement park. Mark had a habit of spending money as soon as he earned it.

Mark had asked if, in two weeks, he could go to an amusement park. We said yes but he would have to use his own money, not borrow any. But on the night before the event Mark had no money. He had already spent what he had earned. He asked for a loan, but that would violate the agreement. My heart was aching for him. I wanted him to go, and it would have been so easy to give him the money, but we'd done that too often, and it was time to be firm about our new agreement to earn money before you spend it. Most important, we'd made a specific agreement regarding his earning the money for the amusement park.

Mark asked how he could earn $25 by morning. We've often paid the kids 10 cents a minutes or $6 per hour for back massages. He massaged our backs until we couldn't take it any more. Then he polished the two cars—in the garage at midnight, weeded the hothouse, and polished the silver. By three or four in the morning, he had earned the money.

I ached to watch him do this and leave for the amusement park so tired, but years later, we have a warm laugh together about it. From that point on, Mark *always* had a savings account. Perhaps now that he's a mid-manager at a large bank, he understands in the deepest sense the value of saving. When you hold your employees, your children, and yourself to keeping tough agreements, transformation can occur.

Making Agreements with Grown Children

Appendices IA, IB, and IC (pp. 307–309) show some additional examples of middle managers wrestling with making agreements they can keep with adult children. Notice the pattern of parents wanting adult children to do more chores and adult children wanting more rapport with parents.

Keeping Agreements against All Odds

Bankers Trust of New York was preparing for a new organizational structure that would give many of its investment bankers a great deal of independence. The investment bankers were soon going to change their role and become almost like independent contractors. The bank president wanted to have a system in place that aligned him with them toward the same goals before the new structure was announced.

In 1983, *Office Automation and Administration*[3] magazine published my article about a new kind of performance-appraisal process that was decentralized. After reading my article about the performance-appraisal alignment process and knowing her president's wish, Vice President Susan Lawly called and asked me to send the materials so she could use the system as their new performance appraisal system. I did so, and Susan conducted seminars so all the investment bankers could go through the course and be prepared for a meeting with the president by having their number one request in hand.

Susan said they had been working so much on their own, she wasn't convinced that the president and investment bankers would actually keep their agreements, even if they told their number one request to each other and agreed to fulfill them. She asked me to come to New York to sit in on each Alignment meeting between the twelve investment bankers and the president. I was to help clarify the agreement, be a witness to their making agreements, and support their keeping the agreements.

We set up a January date far in advance because it was rare to have them all in the same building on one day. Meanwhile, my number one request of my husband, George (that he get me pregnant with a baby girl) materialized. Being two and a half months pregnant wouldn't prevent me from going to New York, so I kept the date I agreed to.

The new campaign launch was set to begin on a Monday after the Alignments were completed. The president and vice president wanted to be very sure about the mutual goals and agreements before letting the managers increase the independence of their roles. I took a red-eye flight from San Francisco to New York on Tuesday evening, arriving Wednesday morning. Since the meetings were set for all day Thursday, I had time to spare. I went to the Motherhood Maternity Shop and bought a full supply of winter and summer maternity clothes. I returned to my room at 4:00 P.M. to review the paperwork in preparation for the Bankers Trust meeting.

By 5:30 P.M. I was interrupted by heavy labor pains. As the hours passed and the pains got worse, I called my old junior high friend, Tina, who is now a well-known and respected director of a Planned Parenthood facility. After talking me through all of the symptoms, in a firm, calm voice she told me exactly what to do—let nature take its course and don't call a doctor. That's what I chose to do. Without going into all the gory details, I spent the night having a miscarriage, in terror, and with zero sleep.

By 6:00 A.M., I had to start dressing for my 7:00 A.M. breakfast meeting with New York Bankers' Trust vice president Susan Lawly. I had no time to prepare or review all the information. I met Susan for breakfast at my hotel. For an hour and a half she told me about what was going on at Bankers Trust. Surprisingly, I felt more present than I'd ever been in a client meeting. I kept correctly anticipating what she'd say next.

Toward the end of the meeting, when she'd covered each person with whom I was to meet, she mentioned that she had a son. Just before we were to leave at 8:40 A.M., I said "Susan, last night I had a miscarriage, so it's tough to walk. Can we have all twelve people come to one spot where I'll be instead of me going to the different offices?" With empathy and focus she said, "Sure. I'm sorry." We began the day and didn't discuss it again. The meetings continued to be incredibly clear. I could anticipate problems; I seemed to know just what to ask. I have never felt as clear—almost clairvoy-ant—and confident in my work as I did that day.

At 4:30 P.M., I left to get to my hotel and return all the maternity clothes before catching my flight. I silently cried on and off all the way home. But, having kept my agreement against all odds made the grief much easier. It was healing for me to have to keep my agreement. Knowing the level at which you can perform moves a career to new levels. Wallowing in the grief would have wasted the great gift of clarity I was given that day.

That same year I received a holiday card from Susan. She said she told her employees that I'd had a miscarriage the night before our meetings but kept the agreement with them nonetheless. That became their example for keep-ing agreements. I was surprised, because in the struggle to keep this agree-ment, I've always thought it helped me more than it did them.

11

Creating Agreements That Work

It takes courage to stand up and speak. It takes more courage to sit down and listen.

—WINSTON CHURCHILL

Celebrate What Agreements Are Kept — Reset Those That Are Not

Because commitments are directly related to corporate profit and specifically designed to empower employees, a carefully monitored step-by-step system combining regimentation, professionalism, and sensitivity is critical.

The Follow-up Tool

The Alignment Agreement Follow-up is used to assist mid-managers in keeping agreements as well as requiring it of their employees and managers. The purpose of the follow-up tool is to ensure that agreements are kept and corporate profit goals are met or exceeded. It is a tracking process to monitor the commitments that were established to reach these profit goals.

HOW TO USE THE ALIGNMENT AGREEMENT FOLLOW-UP — JOHN AND PAUL REVISITED

When John and Paul were able to overcome put-downs and clearly state what they wanted from one another, they were well on their way to achieving their company's goals. However, following up is essential to maintaining kept agreements.

John's making a request of Paul to take a stand and be a leader ("Build a model, make a video, show everyone how to build it, set a schedule, hold them to it") was a wonderful surprise for Paul. It gave him the permission he needed to take charge and lead. Paul was totally empowered to step up and do just that.

Sixty days after their Alignment Agreement, I flew to Seattle for an informal pre-follow-up. I dropped in unexpectedly on Paul. His secretary said, "He's in a disciplinary meeting with an employee; he'll be out soon."

Alignment Agreement

Please Print

Organization: **Manufacturing Fortune 500**   Today's Date: **9/16**

Employee's Name: **Paul**   Follow-Up Date: **11/1**

Reviewer's Name: **John**   Consultant:

INSTRUCTIONS: Before writing, Reviewer first hears the Employee's complete request, then it is discussed and agreed upon by both. Reviewer then clearly and concisely prints the Employee's request in full, and signs in agreement. Employee then hears the Reviewer's complete request, they come to agreement, Emloyee prints the request, and signs the form.

EMPLOYEE'S REQUEST (PRINTED BY REVIEWER)

1. The #1 item _____**Paul**_____ wants from _____**John**_____ is:
   <small>Employee's Name</small>   <small>Reviewer's Name</small>

   let me have input on goals.

2. Specifically what will the Reviewer do to meet your request?
   A. Meet with me before setting deadlines.
   B. Ask me when I think we can meet it.
   C. Include me in goal setting meetings with executive staff.

3. How will you know the request has been fulfilled; how will you measure the change? We'd make 90 percent of deadlines.

I agree to begin on ___**9/16**___ Signed _____
                      <small>Date</small>   <small>Reviewer's Signature</small>

REVIEWER'S REQUEST (PRINTED BY THE EMPLOYEE)

1. The #1 item _____**John**_____ wants from _____**Paul**_____ is:
   <small>Reviewer's Name</small>   <small>Employee's Name</small>

   for Paul to take a stand and lead.

2. Specifically what will the Reviewer do to meet your request?
A. _Build a model._
B. _Make a video and show everyone._
C. _Set a schedule and hold them to it._

3. How will you know the request has been fulfilled; how will you measure the change? _We'd make 90 percent of deadlines. We'd save 10 percent in material._

I agree to begin on ____9/16____   Signed _____
                          Date   *Employee's Signature*

When Paul was given the authority to take the lead, he excelled. I saw the model, watched the video, and heard the hum of busy, communicating employees. Their on-time orders were looking good, and he had led the group to 70 percent production deadlines. "How's John doing?" Paul laughed a confident and caring laugh. "Well, he tries." At ninety days I returned for the final follow-up. The scores were not matched. John's overall score for Paul was 60 percent; for himself 90 percent. Paul's score for both was 90 percent.

Alignment Agreement Follow-up for John and Paul

Alignment Date: **4/10/01**

Follow-up Date: **7/10/01**

Employee: **Paul**   Reviewer: **John**

Last Follow-up EE% ER%	This Follow-up EE%	ER%
Employee Request: *New or Revised* — Let me have input on goals.	90	90
What it looks like: A. Meet with me before setting deadlines.	☐	☐
B. Ask me when I think we can meet it.	☐	☐
C. Include me in goal setting meetings with executive deadlines.	☐	☐

Measurement: We'd make 90 percent of deadlines.

Signed: _____

Gap Correction:

Last Follow-up	EE%	ER%		EE%	ER%

Reviewer Request: Take a stand and lead. | 60 | 90 |
New or Revised

What it looks like: A. Build a model.

                          B. Make a video and show everyone.

                          C. Set a schedule and hold them to it

Measurement: We'd make 90 percent of deadlines.

Signed: _____

Gap Correction:

I asked John why he gave Paul only a 60 percent when orders were 70 percent on time and he was leading the way. "He's too soft with them; he never yells." Using John's request of Paul, however, is an easy way to reconcile the request with performance. Here is how John's requests and Paul's performance matched up.

- Build a model—yes, there it is

- Make a video—there it is

- Show everyone how—here's the training schedule

- Set a schedule—here's the schedule

- Hold them accountable—here are all the disciplinary documents

When I pointed out to John that he had never asked Paul to yell and it might not be accurate to score Paul on that basis, he said, "Let me take a look." The fact was, the follow-up revealed that Paul had kept all his agreements and deserved to be scored accordingly. Tight follow-up is an essential tool for making sure that mid-managers are acknowledged when they have kept their agreements. The follow-up keeps managers from moving the score line further so that no one ever feels the accomplishment of something.

Let's take a look at the other half of the John/Paul alignment. John had stretched very hard to keep his agreement with Paul. It took everything he had to ask for Paul's input about deadlines, instead of telling him when they were. It bothered John intensely to invite Paul to planning meetings. (This was his dark side.) John was obsessed with control, so relinquishing it was very difficult. He kept saying he couldn't do it, and I kept reminding him it was the only way he could expect Paul to step up and lead the group to 70 percent production deadlines. John's future career depended on his ability to fight his "shadow."

Czeslaw Milosz, a Nobel laureate, said, "What has no shadow has no strength to live."[1] Ignoring dark moments gives them added power and creates obstacles to our success. Facing our shadow side gives us strength to move forward, be successful, and be free of our self-imprisonment. John was able to maintain control and let Paul have some input on the goals.

John got only 90 percent on Paul's score sheet, but 99 percent in my book. The success of their alignment was very profound. In ninety days, the company went from 0 to 70 percent of deadlines met. For an earth-moving, equipment-manufacturing company, this was a miracle. John and Paul were written up in the *New York Times*—front page of the Business section.

The importance of setting agreements is enhanced by the importance of keeping agreements. This is the only tool I have ever known that documents agreements in a way that empowers people to do great things in the name of keeping their agreements. During the past thirty years, corporations and individuals have become, to some extent, opposing forces. Synthesis, the alignment and merging of two opposite forces, can renew the partnership and go a step further toward creating a healthy one. An independent third party should conduct the follow-up, so that true synthesis can occur. Like a CPA audit, a follow-up must be firm in recording agreements but not involved emotionally.

How can this be accomplished? The follow-up process begins when the completed, signed, and dated Alignment Follow-up sheets are given to an Alignment auditor. Upon receipt of the completed, signed, and dated Alignment sheets, the auditor will schedule a follow-up for ninety days after the first date recorded on the Alignment Agreement form. After ninety-days, the Alignment sheet is given to the reviewer and the employee separately to fill in the eight boxes on the column that describes them (EE—Employee or ER—Reviewer). If they are not filled in and returned within forty-eight hours, the auditor should meet separately with each individual to assist in this process and document the time.

When both employee and reviewer forms are complete (by E-mail, fax, or voice mail), the auditor returns them simultaneously to the other party and to the reviewer's boss. The reviewer or his/her boss then takes appropriate steps to bridge any gap between the two scores.

AGREEMENTS THAT ARE NOT KEPT NEED TO BE RESET

Dawn was the highest-paid paraprofessional troubleshooter in an engineering firm. She harbored hidden feelings of inadequacy because, although she was extremely competent, she possessed neither an engineer's license nor a college degree. To overcome these feelings, she longed for recognition and acknowledgment from her boss, Glen.

Glen complained that he lost billable hours listening to Dawn explain, complain, and give lengthy dialogues of her problem clients and difficult investigations in the field. In the Funnel process (see chapter 5) he changed this complaint to a request. Instead of asking the same questions repeatedly, would Dawn "keep a record of his answers, then work more independently to solve some of the problems on her own?" When asked, "What would be different?" he replied, "I'd be able to bill thirty hours per week instead of twenty-five."

When it was Dawn's turn, she was not totally honest in her request, because her real issue was with wanting recognition to overcome her hidden feelings of inadequacy—which is embarrassing to ask for. So instead she asked for "varied clients." Glen, believing that this was the way Dawn wanted to be treated, granted her request for a more varied client base.

During a ninety-day follow-up meeting, Dawn was asked if she had followed through on Glen's request that she begin to solve her own problems in the field. She belittled the agreement, changed the subject, and said she was too busy for this game. The auditor stuck with the question and E-mailed a request for a follow-up score as to how they both did on their agreement. Dawn was given twenty-four hours to score Glen and herself. Through the follow-up process, Dawn was finally able to admit that she had not, in fact, kept her agreements with Glen (0 percent). Instead, she had continued to run into Glen's office and complain and explain, as before.

Admitting that we have not kept our word can open a stuck mind to new levels of understanding. In this case, new understanding led to a renewed request from Dawn that was more honest. She discovered her own need to be recognized for her expertise as a troubleshooter, particularly as the only non-degreed, non-licensed engineer. She asked to have her role as a troubleshooter announced at a staff meeting, to be introduced to the clients as such, and to be allowed to train a new paraprofessional, thus giving her the recognition and esteem she sought.

Dawn's real desires were out in the open, and Glen no longer had to listen to long narratives, which were Dawn's subversive way of demanding recognition. Both parties were now winners, and the company benefited with five more billable hours per week from Glen and seven more billable hours per week from Dawn.

What Alignment Auditors Reveal in Follow-ups

When the auditor meets individually to complete follow-up sheets, it isn't always a one-minute stop. When follow-ups are not completed, there is usually some reason for the delay. Most often it is resistance on the part of the employee/reviewer to look at a dark side of themselves.

When many follow-up sheets are collected, they can become the manager's monthly report. They also offer a percentage indication as to who is keeping profitability and respecting goals, who isn't, and to what degree.

SOME THINGS TO LOOK FOR IN ALIGNMENT AGREEMENT FOLLOW-UP FORMS

1. Are 95 percent of employee requests asking for recognition, respect, or freedom?

2. Are reviewer requests related to the corporate goals?

3. Are both reviewer and employee keeping their agreements? What percentage of the time?

4. Are all employees being reviewed?

TIPS FOR ALIGNMENT AGREEMENT FOLLOW-UP

1. Weekly staff meetings should include goals of every employee and reviewer.

2. Alignment Follow-ups should be done every ninety days.

3. Strategic planning sessions should be held annually, at the same time each year.

4. One-on-one conferences should be held within forty-eight hours whenever a gap of twenty or more points is recorded between employee's and reviewer's scores.

5. Scores within twenty points of each other should be celebrated.

6. New number one goals should be recorded for a new alignment (most often the same alignment continues).

THE NEED FOR ALIGNMENT AND FOLLOW-UP

1. To be sure that you will meet your goals and live by your mission

2. To keep your workplace growing, both financially and mentally

3. To keep integrity alive and well in the corporation

4. To consistently reach through negative patterns by reducing the demanding person to just one request and to be clear with it (e.g., John)

5. To consistently break through codependent patterns by forcing the codependents to come forward with at least one genuine request for themselves (e.g., Paul)

6. To transform your job into a career

FOLLOW-UPS CAN LEAD TO SUCCESS

You recall the winery president, Todd, who promised his employees he would make sure the dignity issue was addressed when he asked them to vote non-union. The account below shows how the follow-up tool was the only tool refined enough to really make the dignity promise hold.

Todd was following his promise to make sure his supervisors treated employees with respect. He used the follow-up form to make sure that the Alignments were kept between all supervisors and employees. In spite of this process, the quality department was being rocked with emotional outbursts. The issue was dignity. Carla, the quality control department manager and assistant winemaker, used the Funnel to make her number one request known to Joyce, the quality control supervisor: "Empower your employees and treat them with dignity." In turn, Joyce asked Carla to keep her informed every day of what was going on. Carla and Joyce made an agreement to honor each other's requests as per Todd's company-wide promise. Although ninety days is the normal time frame to Follow-up Alignments, in cases of urgency, a thirty-day time frame is often set. This was the case with Carla and Joyce because Todd had an agreement to keep that all employees would be treated with dignity and Joyce was not doing it.

Alignment Agreement Follow-up for Joyce and Carla

Alignment Date: **4/10/01**

Follow-up Date: **7/10/01**

Employee: **Joyce**   Reviewer: **Carla**

		This Follow-up	
Last Follow-up EE% ER%		EE%	ER%

Employee Request: *New or Revised*	Keep me informed each day.	90	85
What it looks like:	A. Meet with me at 8:00 A.M. daily to let me know what's up.	95	88
	B. E-mail me on any new events during the day.	85	82

Measurement: We'd be more efficient in the lab.

Signed: _____

Gap Correction:

		EE%	ER%
Last Follow-up EE% ER%			

Reviewer Request: *New or Revised*	Lead the way for your employees by empowering them and treating them with dignity.	90	5⅓
What it looks like:	A. Admit you haven't been honoring dignity in the past.	95	16
	B. Commit to weigh the pros and cons of their suggestions.	90	0
	C. Speak in a respectful tone.	85	0

Measurement: Management would take note and acknowledge us for resolving the volatile lab situation.

Signed: _____

Gap Correction:

Unfortunately, within a few weeks the employees in the department were complaining about things getting worse—they were not treated with respect or dignity. Todd asked Carla to get to the heart of this problem. Carla met with Joyce and reminded her of the A-B-C part of her agreement that they had set—specifically, "Admit you were disrespectful in the past and want to move on and improve." Joyce called a meeting of the quality control lab employees the next day. Now it was up to Joyce to fix the problem. She stood up and said to her quality control employees, "There have been outbursts and blowups and you, you, you, and I have been at fault." She did admit her own mistake, but she literally pointed her finger at each person as she said *"you,"* blaming them in a most humiliating manner. Then Joyce asked for suggestions, but there were none. She closed the meeting by putting up a poster, "Six Points of Good Human Relations," and saying that everyone was to follow it. Later, one person brought up the possibility of a suggestion box, but Joyce overrode the idea quickly, stating that they were too small of a department. The blowups in the quality control lab stopped, but anger seethed beneath the surface.

At the urgent thirty-day check-in point, the auditor followed up on the agreement process that Joyce and Carla had initiated. They each graded the other on keeping their agreements, assigning percentages to how well the requests were followed. Both Carla and Joyce gave Carla a high grade on keeping her agreement to inform Joyce about current developments. But when it came to Carla's request that Joyce lead the way to empowerment, there was a wide discrepancy. Joyce thought she had done a good job and gave herself a 90 percent on empowering employees. Carla gave her only 16 percent.

Todd asked me to audit the follow-up for Joyce and Carla. When Joyce saw the low score her boss had given her, her face turned pale and her eyes filled with tears. She began to chatter nervously about all she had done: she said, "I admitted I was at fault, I held meetings, put up guidelines, and have not blown up at anyone lately." Then she launched into a harangue about how stupid the employees were. She was obviously experiencing anxiety.

I touched Joyce's shoulder gently to bring her back to the present and asked her to be silent for a moment so we could regroup. "Your personality is not on trial here, Joyce," I told her. "It's just that Carla made a request that you empower and treat employees with dignity. There's a gap between how you both perceive the results. Are you willing to look at the gap between your scores and Carla's to find out what Carla was looking for? It's not a matter of who is right. It's a question of exploring what each of you sees here."

This calmed Joyce down so Carla could now explain that Joyce did admit to her employees that she was at fault, which earned her sixteen points. However, she sabotaged her effort to empower them by casting blame when she said, "You and you and you are at fault too." Also, she did not weigh the pros and cons of putting in the suggestion box. "Joyce, while you may have thought you spoke in a respectful tone, that was not the perception of your staff." To clarify what each side wanted and what had been achieved, they went over each item on the follow-up form.

	Score by Carla ReviewER (%)	Score by Joyce EmployEE (%)
Empower and treat employees with dignity:	5⅓	90
A. Admit you haven't been honoring dignity in the past	16	95
B. Weigh the pros and cons of their suggestions	0	90
C. Speak in a respectful tone	0	85

Joyce had a strong will to understand the process and improve. So in spite of the embarrassment and discouragement this incident brought her, she had the courage to say, "Show me what you mean. I think I must have a blind spot."

Carla gave careful examples, and slowly Joyce became aware of how she was sabotaging her department by obsessing about errors and harshly blaming others for mistakes. Eventually she saw that she had an overcontrolling side to her. She admitted that she thought her way was better than the steps Carla had outlined in the Alignment.

We were working very hard during the meeting on defining dignity and giving examples. In learning to respect her workers, Joyce discovered that she needed to give *serious* consideration to others' ideas and suggestions. Consideration means weighing the pros and cons of what someone said. No matter how stupid or irrelevant she thought the worker's suggestion or complaint was, she as the supervisor was to think over the pros and the cons very carefully.

In the supervisors' class that week, they practiced with each other taking on roles as if they were rehearsing for a play. Inez, taking the role of vineyard worker, told Joyce, who played the role of Inez's supervisor, that she thought it would be a good idea to pick grapes at night so it wouldn't be so hot. Instead of giving her some snide answer or blurting out what a terrible idea she thought it was, Joyce role-played dealing with the idea respectfully by taking time to evaluate it fairly. "Well, we'd certainly be cooler," she agreed, and she even asked her to tell more about the idea. After about five seconds, she said, "The pros are it would be cooler and create two shifts; the con is that we may have to install about a million dollars' worth of outdoor lights. And if we did that, the price of wine would be so high, we might lose our customers." By taking a moment to give Inez's suggestion some thought and offering her a fair and balanced answer, Joyce was learning to add to the worker's sense of self-respect instead of stripping it away with a rude comment. Her answer also contained information that added to Inez's knowledge of how the business works.

The lights wouldn't be coming on in the vineyard scenario, but the lights had come on for Joyce. As she learned from her experience, she realized how to improve her skills. She learned that dignity means in "consideration of," which means taking time to weigh the pros and cons of what people suggest. She stretched herself to take that small but powerful step in dealing with her own department.

Giving consideration to employees' thoughts and ideas helped Joyce transform the quality control department. She went back to her group and replicated the processes she had learned in class with Inez. She admitted that her overcontrolling way was hurting everyone. She told them of her commitment to change and asked them to support her new ways. There was a silent awe that day as the energy moved in the room. The staff in the quality control department was ready to stop creating unnecessary chaos and to improve their own behavior. They moved right ahead by making agreements among themselves to honor each other's number one requests. This freed the employees to quit playing sabotage games and be ready to contribute their best efforts to achieving the department's goals. They began to refocus on wine quality with renewed enthusiasm. Todd made sure that the last midmanager holding out on dignity was corrected. His agreement was kept. The union never showed up again in his winery.

I saw Joyce in a mall a few years later. She spoke incessantly and enthusiastically about that Alignment: "I will never forget that 5 1/3 percent that was next to my 90 percent. I just couldn't see what I was doing. It still isn't 100 percent natural, but every day I now ask myself, 'Did I really listen? What can I improve?' I have to make a little effort each day, but we have the most wonderful department now. Just seeing my blind spot was life-changing. I have the Three Rules on my wall because every tough situation relates to one of them."

THE UNSEEN INGREDIENTS IN QUALITY WINE

As a result of the employee/management alignment, the quality of the wine improved, which was very meaningful to the winery as a whole. Joyce had always been a wonderful quality-control person, highly talented and conscientious at setting, knowing, and monitoring standards. But she had been sabotaging the department by alienating her employees. When dignity was added as the extra, unseen ingredient in the wine, quality goals were achieved regularly. Better wine meant increasing their winning of Harvest Fair awards—widely publicized events that added to sales and the winery's reputation.

Little by little, one person and one situation at a time, other departments in the winery put the Alignment and Follow-up to work. Of course, problems continued to arise, but Rule 3 proved to be an effective tool for keeping the winery's agreement with its employees. One of the most beautiful aspects of the rules is that anyone can use them. When they are in place as ground rules for behavior in the company, new employees understand them from their very first day on the job.

Lead Yourself and Others to Win-Win—A Tool to Agreements

Agreements that are set as a resolution to a conflict seem to carry extra weight. In the winery example above, President Todd's agreement to make sure dignity was shown to every employee was born out of a close call with a union and a strike. If Todd had casually told an employee over a beer, "We'll take care of that dignity thing," it would have been a whole different strength of agreement.

When you live the value of keeping your word, you learn not to make agreements casually or lightly. One of the best workplace tools I know that will keep you from over-committing to employees, coworkers, customers, or vendors, is the Eight-Step Checklist for Effective Listening. Many mid-managers put these Eight Steps on a business card–size paper and keep it in their wallet for immediate access.

The Eight Steps of Listening—A Tool for All the Rules

Everyone has experienced the frustration of trying to get a point across while the other person is preoccupied. Perhaps that other person is really listening intently, but if he or she is looking away, toying with things on a desk, or acting bored, we do not feel as if we have been heard. Sometimes our own level of concentration is so intense that we really do not hear 100 percent of what another person is saying or understand what they mean.

Of all the tools that support achieving all Three Rules, none is quite so full of impact and consistently used as the Eight Steps of Listening. The important thing about effective listening is that it can be used when enacting any one of the Three Rules. Listening is the key in contribution, converting Put-downs, and creating and solidifying agreements.

Eight-Step Checklist for Effective Listening

#1 PAY ATTENTION; INTEND TO UNDERSTAND
* Focus attention on the person; do not interrupt.
* Maintain eye contact, sit forward, and lean toward the speaker.
* Take in the whole picture.
* Tell and demonstrate to the person that he or she has your full attention.

#2 SUMMARIZE WHAT YOU HAVE HEARD (USE FEELINGS CHART)
* Repeat back in your own words what you heard. "Let me see if I understand. You are feeling . . . because . . . is that correct?"
* Use words that create pictures and feelings.

#3 ACKNOWLEDGE FEELINGS
* Ask how the person feels about the situation.
* Show awareness of the speaker's concern: "I understand how you feel." or "I can see your frustration."
* Tell about a time you had similar feelings or describe a similar situation.
* Suspend your own biases about the situation.

#4 ASK CLARIFYING QUESTIONS
* *Who* . . . is involved?
* *What* . . . have you said?
* *Where* . . . did you get that idea?
* *Why* . . . is this happening now?
* *How* . . . did you arrive at that conclusion/idea/agreement?

#5 ASK FOR THE OTHER PERSON'S SUGGESTIONS FOR RESOLUTION
* How would you recommend that this be handled?
* What would you like to see done?
* Ask for all relevant information.

#6 PRESENT YOUR POSITION
* If the suggestion above is suitable, tell the person: "That sounds like a good idea." Make sure the message is consistent; body language matches the verbal component.
* If the suggestion in #5 is not suitable, present your position: "I hear your suggestion and I have another point of view. What we might do is . . ."
* Collaborate: "Your suggestion works nicely in these areas. I'll support you. Can you support me in these areas?"

#7 DECIDE ON SPECIFIC COURSE OF ACTION AND FOLLOW-UP (USE *ALIGNMENT AGREEMENT*)
- "Now, let's see, I will . . . and you will . . . okay?"
- Ask: "Do you need additional support? How and in what form?"

#8 THANK THE PERSON
- Evaluate the conversation: Were you both heard and understood? Is the solution win-win?
- "I really appreciate your coming to me with your concerns."

If someone comes to you, whether it is with a threat of major strike or a small complaint about another person, you can use this Eight-Step tool to: (1) minimize the commitments you make; (2) maximize the possibility that the person with the complaint will resolve his own issue; and (3) make sure that if you do make an agreement, it is one that will affect your leadership role and your career positively as well as the other person's.

Let's review a law office situation that could have ended with a burdensome agreement in Chelsea's lap. Without the Eight Steps, Chelsea may have made one of those gnawing time-consuming agreements to help Marilee. With Eight-Steps, Marilee resolved her own conflict and Chelsea maintained her leadership position, protected her time well, and empowered a frustrated employee.

WHEN A COWORKER DOESN'T LISTEN

Marilee was fed up with a noisy officemate. The woman would not stop talking loudly even though Marilee repeatedly asked her to hold it down. Marilee had no real authority to do anything about it directly, so she went to Chelsea, her boss, to ask her to help. But Chelsea ignored her too.

Marilee filled out a Conscious Communication form and went back to Chelsea. Here's what her form stated:

1. I feel helpless, disappointed, and betrayed when you [Chelsea] ignore my requests for help in getting a quiet workspace.

2. I am concerned that my work will suffer and that I will feel unappreciated, overwhelmed, and alone in trying to get conditions to change.

3. I want you [Chelsea] to help by taking a stand with the other attorney.

4. My goal is to keep the workspace quiet and businesslike.

5. It seems to me that your goal is to stay out of the conflict and leave me alone to solve it, which I cannot do effectively.

6. Some possibilities I have come up with that may be more effective or harmonious:

   a. You [Chelsea] would speak to the other attorney about his noisy secretary.

   b. Put up partitions in the office.

   c. Give Marilee a private office.

Chelsea was familiar with the Eight-Steps of Listening. When Marilee came in with her problem and her Conscious Communication form, Chelsea applied the Eight-Steps of Listening. See where the shift occurs from disappointment to empowerment.

Step 1: Pay Attention
- Focus attention on the person; do not interrupt

- Maintain eye contact, sit forward, lean toward the speaker

- Take in the whole picture

- Tell and demonstrate to the person that they have your full attention

Chelsea gave Marilee her full attention. She focused on Marilee and did not interrupt. She leaned forward in her chair while Marilee spoke and maintained eye contact, taking in the situation in a friendly, interested manner. She could see that Marilee was really upset.

Step 2: Summarize
- Repeat back in your own words what you heard. "Let me see if I understand. You are feeling . . . because . . . is that right?"

- Use words that create pictures and feelings (use the Feelings Chart).

Chelsea let Marilee know she was listening by following Step 2, repeating Marilee's concerns in her own words. "Let me see if I understand," she began. "You feel frustrated because you can't concentrate? The noise in the office aggravates you?"
Marilee replied in the affirmative.

Step 3: Acknowledge Their Feelings

- Ask how the person feels about the situation.

- Show empathy for the speaker: "I understand how you feel."

- Tell about the time you had a similar feeling or describe a similar situation.

- Suspend your own biases about the situation.

Chelsea went on to Step 3. "I understand that you felt helpless and betrayed when I ignored you the first time you tried to bring this matter to my attention, right? I remember going to Tom once with my request for a new computer, and he ignored me. I felt so angry. I understand."

Step 4: Ask Questions

- "Who is involved?"

- "What have you said?"

- "Where did that thinking come from?"

- "Why is this happening now?"

- "How did you arrive at a conclusion/idea/agreement?"

Chelsea moved to the fourth listening step and asked the appropriate questions: "How long have you felt this way?"

Marilee knew she was being heard now, and responded calmly, "It started three months ago. In spite of being asked to quiet down, Joyce continued to speak in a very loud tone."

"Why do you think this is happening now?"

Step 5: Ask for the Person's Suggestions

- "How would you recommend that this be handled?"

- "What would you like to see done?"

- "Ask for relevant information."

Chelsea moved to Step 5 of listening: "What are some suggestions of what you would like us to do about the situation?"

Marilee suggested, "We could put up partitions in the office or give me a private office. Maybe we could talk to Joyce's boss."

Step 6: Present your Position

- If any of the suggestions in Step 5 are suitable, tell the person: "That sounds like a good idea." Make sure the message is consistent, that the body language matches the verbal component.

- If the suggestions in Step 5 are not suitable, present your position: "I hear your suggestions, and I like 1 and 3 the best."

- Collaborate: "I'll support you in the partition idea and in talking with Joyce's boss." "Marilee, I'll speak with Joyce's boss and the office manager too and ask about partitions."

Step 7: Decide on Specific Follow-up

- "Now let's see, you will talk with Fred and Sue about partitions. I will back you up by giving you the go-ahead."

- Ask: "Do you need additional support? How and in what form?"

Chelsea applied the seventh step: "You can speak to the office manager today if you like. Okay? And if that doesn't work, you can speak with Joyce's boss when he returns from his trip and let him know we talked. You might ask Joyce politely one more time to modulate her voice."

Marilee readily agreed. Now that Chelsea was backing her in the matter, something would be worked out by Marilee.

Step 8: Thank the Person

- Evaluate the conversation: were you both heard and understood? Is the solution win-win?

- "I really appreciate your coming to me with your concerns."

Chelsea found the eighth step to be the easiest of all: "Thank you for bringing this to my attention, Marilee. I feel we can find a win-win solution, don't you?"

Chelsea went to the office manager with the problem and asked her to move Joyce's desk or do something to let Joyce know she was too loud. When the office manager spoke with Joyce, she learned that Joyce was slightly hard of hearing. The solution was simple. They purchased an inexpensive telephone for Joyce's desk that amplified the sound so she could hear better. And her loud voice decreased by many decibels. They also put up a divider between Joyce's and Marilee's desks, and the noise problem was resolved to everyone's satisfaction. Marilee could work in peace, Joyce could hear, Chelsea kept her valuable secretary. The firm spent much less on new equipment than it would have spent on hiring a new secretary.

A PERSONAL APPLICATION

Ironically, I was dealing with a family matter the same week I was working on this chapter. Many people today are trying to balance their personal and professional lives, so I'll include this example to demonstrate using Eight-Step Checklist for Listening at home as well as at work.

George is my ex-husband. He and I might still be married if we'd had the Eight-Step Checklist Listening during our marriage, but we began to use them later, after our divorce. We live very close to each other; and, at the time, our daughter, Brooke, was visiting him every other weekend. Sometimes we have disagreements and communication gaffes with the schedule.

One day I was thirty minutes late taking Brooke to his house. When I got back to my house, there was an irate message from him on my answering machine. "You are selfish and irresponsible and don't give a damn about anyone else. I am really upset with you. You ruined my whole @#$*& evening. I hope you are satisfied!" And he slammed down the phone. I was surprised because Brooke had informed me that she and her father had no plans that night and she thought being thirty minutes late was not a problem.

The next day I made an appointment to meet George at his office. Though he was still angry, he agreed to try the Conscious Communication process and Eight-Step Checklist for Listening. Our daughter's schedule would be an ongoing part of our lives; he would try anything to improve the way we handled it.

George wrote on the form, "I feel angry, frustrated, abused, and trapped when my plans are ignored."

Of course, I wanted to tell him right away my feelings but by following the Eight-Steps I held the tension and listened to his feelings. My job was to summarize them. "You said you are angry because Brooke was late, and I'm not honoring your plans." (Steps 1 and 2.) George nodded.

Then I said, "I totally understand because I have a business partner who always ignores our time commitments and it makes me furious." (Step 3.)

Next I asked a question from Step 4: "Why is this coming up now?" (Quietly fuming, I thought, "Why has he rarely mentioned it in the past? I bet his new girlfriend is behind all this.")

George explained that it had been festering for a while, but now he was learning to express his feelings. I could feel myself softening, but I stuck to the steps.

Following Step 5, I asked him to suggest how I could improve the situation.

"Don't make Brooke responsible for communicating. You call me yourself and inform me of any changes," he replied.

I nodded with agreement and relief. It was hard listening, summarizing, and acknowledging with my own emotions on hold. But I knew it would be worth it. When we got to Step 6, it was my turn to present my viewpoint. I could not seem to keep the tears out of my voice, but it was *my* turn. "George, I always saw us as working together in a high-level partnership," I said, my voice cracking. "I'd hoped we would cover for each other and always have Brooke's best interests as our number one priority. We would tell each other in a positive way what wasn't working."

George hadn't been perfect about keeping our agreements either, and I went on to tell him my point of view. "Last week you dropped Brooke at the swimming pool with three of her friends and drove away before they had a chance to find out that the pool was closed. I covered for you, George. I didn't blame you or put you down in front of her. I picked them up and got them ice cream, even though it made me late for my evening class. I didn't put you down about it, I just informed you. It seemed like something we should do—a silent part of our coparenting."

George was listening intently to me, and when I mentioned this incident, his manner softened and the anger went out of his eyes. This gave me courage to go on. "I'm sorry for the inconvenience last night, and I agree to communicate directly. Of course that will work better for both of us." I told George that Brooke had not remembered that she and her father had plans that evening. In fact, she told me there would be no problem getting to his house late. Of course, I should have called him to confirm.

George and I agreed to talk directly from that moment on. This was our follow-up (Step 7). It took the burden of communication off Brooke, who was too young to take on that responsibility, and cleared a way for us to work together more successfully as her parents. Plus, we, her parents, broke our marriage agreement, which is why we are divorced. It is our responsibility to work at visitation—not Brooke's.

Adhering to Step 8 of listening, I sincerely thanked George for going through this process with me. We both knew we had accomplished something important in that brief meeting. It was not altogether comfortable for either one of us, but our relationship smoothed out afterward, and all three of us benefited.

Listening actively and meaningfully is much easier with a map—the Eight-Step map. We get into trouble when we forget to use it. It's a sort of "catch-22," when we are really upset and need the Eight Steps the most, we almost always forget them. I keep them with me all the time and review them when going into a sticky situation. More mid-managers have used this tool with success than any other tool. It gives you the guidance to lead almost any tense situation to an aligned and win-win conclusion. Whoever knows these steps ends up leading the meeting. But more important, it creates an opportunity for the person you are listening to to solve his or her own problem. Notice that at Step 5 George resolved the problem. Middle managers really empower their employees when using all Eight Steps of this tool.

Conflict Resolution

For five years I have been gathering conflict resolution procedures from different organizations. As a professor of conflict resolution to mid-manager master's degree students at the University of Phoenix, Sonoma State University, and the University of Portland, I have assigned hundreds of these working adult students to bring in and demonstrate the step-by-step procedures used by their organizations to resolve conflict.

Their samples involved public agencies, HMO's, public utilities, the USPO, Charles Schwab, PriceWaterhouse, telcommunications companies, Bank of America, Xerox, accounting firms, law offices, General Electric, Pacific Gas and Electric, Cellular One, and many other types of companies, large and small. After searching for similarities and differences class after class, one similarity was very revealing. In every case, the person with the complaint was supposed to seek resolution by going directly to his or her boss. Yet in a majority of the cases, the problem was with the boss. So the person either stuffed the problem or gossiped instead of going over the boss's head and risking revenge.

I began a survey asking each student to bring in any policies or practices for the first step in the grievance procedure—was there any guideline as to how to approach the boss with a complaint? In almost all cases, there was no first-step procedure. If there was one, it was outlined as: "Write a one- to three-page description of your complaint" which is a one-way communication format.

We can conclude that most grievances that went all the way to the top did so because they didn't get handled at the first stage. The reason they weren't handled at the first stage was usually because they did not have the tools to take an issue to a boss and expect to have it resolved.

I started bringing my mid-manager students the Conscious Communication tool (including the Feelings Chart and the Eight-Step Checklist for Listening). I asked them to try these techniques at their workplace. All at the same time, twenty groups of working adults tried this out at their work-places.

Since most conflicts are built on grievances and most grievances are directed against another person or that person's decision, the Conscious Communication form was exactly what employees needed for that first step of issuing a grievance. But much more important and dramatic in their findings was the impact of the Eight-Steps Checklist for Listening when used by the person against whom the grievance was filed. While it is very helpful to use the Conscious Communication tool on an aggrieved employee, even if they don't use it, a genuine use of the Eight-Steps Checklist for Listening did "miracles" to resolve these conflicts.

The Eight-Steps Checklist for Listening is a stand-alone tool. When someone comes to you upset and points the finger, the Eight Steps will diffuse and redirect and resolve. Remember the television station and Tim, whom the salespeople were angry with in chapter 5? He used the Eight Steps and diffused the anger. By Step 5, Sara came up with the solutions and took action to fix them. Tim found he didn't have to pretend he felt compassion. He just had to do the Eight Steps.

Middle managers, like Tim, discovered that they are empowered to resolve their own conflicts. Manager after manager from the M.B.A. conflict resolution reported that he or she felt so much more in control of their jobs by having a tool to register a complaint or receive and resolve one from another.

Other mid-managers remarked about the leadership role they felt when they could offer the Conscious Communication tool and the Eight-Step Checklist for Listening to others who were in conflict. By having these tools to resolve their own conflicts, mid-managers felt their leadership position expand as CEO of their own career. Resolving conflict in a healthy, professional, consistent way creates empowered leadership for mid-managers.

12

Successfully Introducing the Three Rules to Your Workgroup

Being real and true to yourself builds personal power, personal power expands one's field of power.

—ROBERT K. COOPER and AYMAN SAWAF, *Executive EQ*

T HE when, where, why, who, and how you introduce the Three Rules at work has a lot to do with their success. While this chapter will cover many possible methods that have been successful in implementing the Three Rules in the past, nothing is as critical as custom-designing the introduction of the Three Rules in a way that uses your strengths and moves toward your personal mission as well as toward the company goals.

Before introducing the Three Rules to your workgroup, clarify your personal mission and the company's mission. What is your boss's number one request? What are your employees' number one requests? What are three of your strengths? How can you build on those strengths? What should you contribute?

According to *Executive EQ: Emotional Intelligence in Leadership and Organizations,* "Being real and true to yourself builds personal power,"[1] personal power expands one's field of power.

As a baby boomer, I remember the selfish era when we said, "I just have to be me,"—usually referring to being late, rude, or sloppy. Conversely, the quote from *Executive EQ* refers to being our best selves—our self-awareness, inner guidance, respect for others, personal mission, personal responsibility, or spiritual connection. The best self is, of course, what we want to use to introduce the Rules.

If your personal mission is to integrate who you really are into your work and to speak the truth, then introduce the Three Rules directly and clearly from the heart. If your company mission is to "make a billion more in aught four," and people are wasting time, acting undisciplined, and needing direction, try direct order. Or, if you like to have fun at work, try the playful method. To introduce the rules at work, use the format that is most aligned with who you are and what your personal mission states.

Many, many human resource managers, executives, and middle managers who have decided to use the Three Rules and then hesitated to introduce them to the group say this: "The employees are not ready for this." What they really mean is, "I am not prepared for this." But you are prepared because you have your mission, strengths, know your boss's and employees' number one requests, and have what it takes now to lead.

While Peter Drucker tells us to "build on strengths," Mother Teresa tells us to keep building on them even in the face of discouragement. Once you have examined the many different formats to introduce the Three Rules, remember—the introduction should still fit you. As a mid-manager, don't forget to consider the urgency of the situation and the needs of your employees. Below are various methods to introduce the rules to a workgroup: Direct Order, Direct Request, Policy Method, Win-Win, Group Input, and Consensus Building.

A. Direct Order

A direct order is usually short and to the point. It tells what you want done but does not tell how. It is usually top down, does not require input to the order but does require getting everyone's attention. Direct orders can be military style, playful, or matter-of-fact.

1. MILITARY STYLE

In the early 1940s, both my mother and my father worked at Goodrich Tire and Rubber Company in Akron, Ohio. She was an executive secretary to the president; he was a mechanical engineer. The story of how they met has become part of family holiday skits and laughs—but all these years the message about a military-style direct order has been consistent in their story.

Mr. George Vaught was hired to take the place of a controller who had supposedly been too lax, indecisive and indirect. George knew his first directives would have to be understood, received, and carried out by all if he was to command a strong leadership position over his employees and improve the value of the stock. With the onset of World War II, Vaught had to take charge quickly.

Margaret Clark, my mother, was his executive secretary. After three months of just observing, her new boss asked her to take dictation and then type and distribute his first directive: "Effective Monday—all desks are to be faced north." Burton Morgan, my father, had a chance to ask Mr. Vaught why. Mr. Vaught said, "It's important to establish the power of command. And my goal is to double the stock value in one year." My father then bought as many shares of stock as he could afford at $7 per share.

The military order was issued on Friday. No one moved the desks. Over the weekend, George had a moving service come and move everybody's desk to face north. By Monday morning, he had their attention. Both my parents recall he was not popular, but he was in command.

Both my parents and their longtime friends from Goodrich still recall that day and the positive impact of a direct order, along with the great sense of security and well-being it gave. The employees wanted to contribute to the war effort, and George wanted to make a profit doing so. Not that facing the desks north would stop the war, but having a strong leader was just what they needed. By the end of one year, the stock value had gone up to $100 per share.

If there has been a financial crisis, a shooting incident or threat, a death, or any kind of turmoil, a direct order may come as a welcome directive after the crisis is over and people are wanting to get back on track. Again, the method of introduction is determined by your needs as well as the needs of your employees.

2. PLAYFUL STYLE

Sometimes charismatic, fun leaders can get away with direct orders because they blend them with a fun and playful management style. The best example I know of this is Paul Orfalea, also known as "Kinko," founder and builder of Kinko's 24-hour Copy Centers.

Twenty-five years ago I met Kinko when he was just a kid with five printing stores. He and I were part of a group of post-college kids who had a summer off and lots of time on our hands. For three months we all spent each day together; I didn't even know Kinko worked. We rented sailboats, played volleyball, rode tandem bikes, hiked, swam, body-surfed, visited every relative of his in the San Fernando Valley. All this time he made five daily phone calls and joked with someone on the other end of the line. The rest of us didn't pay much attention to Kinko's five daily calls.

By Labor Day I had an opportunity to attend Kinko's company picnic. I couldn't believe my eyes—attending the event were twenty employees plus families, totaling more than fifty people. They all loved Kinko. He had the perfect nickname for each of his five managers. He called one manager who wore saddle shoes Two-tone, and the name held even when he wore sandals. There was Timber, Dan-the-Man, Fur Hair, and so on. Kinko was Paul's nickname, since he had very curly hair.

Kinko was always teasing in a non-offensive way, never putting anyone down. He was funny and fun, and the kids of the employees all played games along with the adults. I found myself chugging in the beer-drinking contest and running in potato sack races with an intensity I had never thought possible. At the end of the picnic, he closed with a few jokes and lots of hugs and then challenged them all to get the numbers up.

After the group returned to work and school, the rest of us lost touch, but since Kinko and I have similar birthdays, we have maintained our friendship throughout the years by calling each other every year on December 1 to say "Happy Birthday" and to touch base for the important job of exchanging funny stories.

For twenty-five years, I have had the chance to watch his direct-order/loving and fun mixture grow his business. Kinko has always had the rule of five calls: once it was five copy centers, then it was five copy center directors; next it was five regional directors over five local directors over ten stores. He had five perfect nicknames for five directors when he'd tell them to get the numbers up . . . after telling a joke or two.

Today Kinko has a family that skis, travels, and plays together, and he just has to make five calls to the five global directors of the ten international regional directors who are over the fifty country cluster directors, over the 250 countries, over the 750 national regions, over the 1,500, etc., etc., down to the Kinko's in your town. He calls the five global directors to tell a few jokes, use their affectionate nickname, and tell them to get their numbers up.

Kinko made "getting numbers up" fun and light as he built a billion-dollar global business.[2] So—as middle managers, you may enjoy the direct-order/playful method as well when introducing the Three Rules. To help implement them successfully, keep the Three Rules in front of people, on the wall, and give reminders that appear in light moments.

3. MATTER-OF-FACT STYLE IN ONE-TIME SEMINARS

Sometimes when you have a one-time seminar to conduct, you can just say, during this seminar, I want you to contribute, not put anyone down, and keep any agreements you make. Put the Three Rules on the wall and move on to direct order.

B. Direct Request

A direct request is not as blunt as an order, but it still makes a strong point. It is much more detailed than the direct order. The direct order is "face north" or "get your numbers up," and it leaves the "how" to the individual.

In the direct request mode, you let the group know this is important and spend much time describing why and how these Three Rules would be carried out. Below is an example of what a direct request meeting may be like to a workgroup.

If you are using The Three Ground Rules for a one-time meeting, speech or seminar, and you prefer direct request to direct order, your introduction of them would go more like this:

Three Rules Speech

Welcome to our class/seminar/meeting on _____. Our goal is for each of you to leave here with _____ e.g., full understanding of how to invest your assets in the next six months, or new tools you can use to avoid lawsuits in your company, etc.

My job is to clearly and succinctly facilitate the comprehension of this material. What I need from you to assist me in doing this is to keep these Three Rules for the duration of the meeting:

1. **Everyone Contribute**—Before you share, ask yourself if it will contribute to the group. Conversely, if you have something you know would help, insist on saying it.
2. **No Put-downs**—Disagree all you want, but do not personally put down another person in this room.
3. **Keep Agreements**—Whatever you agree to do after today—**do**.

Now ask: How many of you are willing to keep these Rules? Get a show of hands. Respectfully and comfortably remove anyone who does not choose to follow these Three Rules. This is touchy only if you or they take it personally. If you respect their wish not to follow the Rules, schedule another time to meet with them, one on one.

Introduction to a Workgroup

A company-wide effort to adopt the rules might be initiated by the president, who presents them first to the managers, then at a general meeting or by a manager or mid-manager directly to their workgroup. The speech is the same. All of the guidelines need to be set out that first day with the announcement, here are the new Three Rules for the organization:

1. Everyone Contributes
2. No Put-downs
3. Keep Agreements

Everyone Contributes

First, I'd like to ask each of you to contribute every day to this workgroup. If each of you search for daily improvement, then we meet our goals and enjoy our work along the way. Find out how your job affects the financial success of this company; find out your supervisor's most important goal, and make it a priority every day to contribute to its achievement. When continuous improvement is respected by all employees, it is the best source of success available. The best asset we have is you and the contribution you make. The value you get from this workgroup/company is what you put into it. So the first agreement is to contribute to the workgroup/company.

No Put-downs

The second agreement is never to put down anyone else, no matter how different they may be from you, how wrong you think they are or how much they offend you. None of us will invalidate anyone else personally. You can disagree all you want with someone's idea or procedure, but putting someone else down makes it unsafe for others to tell the truth and robs *us* of good suggestions. If you are angry with a coworker, client, or vendor, work to broaden your own understanding. Anger can lead to constructive discontent—it can also motivate one to take action to improve. Hostility in the workplace is illegal and it can be defined much differently than anger. Hostility is anger aimed at another person in a vengeful way. Never do anything hostile or vengeful in the workplace. Instead, use the tools in our personnel handbook—Conscious Communication, the Eight-Step Checklist for Listening, and lead the way toward positive constructive action.

Keep Agreements

Make your word matter.

   a. Make an agreement or a promise only if you intend to keep it. If you say, "I'll call you back tomorrow," then do so.

b. Make only those agreements that contribute to the company and simultaneously honor people's dignity. To threaten revenge does not fit the Keep Agreements category; promising oneself to withhold any expertise or extra effort from the company does not fit. What does fit is an agreement to yourself or others to be on time, to cover certain items and so forth.

c. Make sure that "keeping" agreements is balanced between you and others; they keep their agreement with you and you keep yours with them.

d. When you see that you have broken an agreement (missed a deadline or forgotten to call back), acknowledge the agreement, and either reset a new one or make it up to them in another way.

e. Keep to contracts. Or, if you can't, make timely changes that benefit both parties.

NOW: Ask "How many of you are willing to follow these Three Rules from this time forward?"

- **Wait** until all hands go up.
- Look around to double-check.

If there is someone who does not raise his or her hand, ask that person to reschedule a time to meet with you or another designated person. Don't fire or judge him or her. Temporarily and immediately remove this person from the situation. No matter how uncomfortable this is, you set the tone for integrity to the Three Rules by your compassionate and firm stand at this critical moment. After attendees agree, by a show of hands, the speaker may continue with all other agenda items. Notice the immediate change in the group.

C. Policy Method—Including the Three Rules in Policy Manuals

Looking at values, statements, missions, and goals, we often find the Three Rules in various forms. Review yours and make sure it covers contribution, respect, and integrity—most do. You can then use this format as a basis for the Three Rules in your company and your department. This gives you more clout as the leader of the rules—because they were derived from the company mission. See chapter 5 for three samples of company mission and values and determine which items address one of the Three Rules.

Below is the method used by some companies to clarify the Three Rules as part of their ISO 9000 continuous improvement procedures. This is usually done along with one of the other verbal introductions. The Jetronics Company has generously allowed us to use its manual:

Jetronics Company Employee Manual (continued)

2017 Continuous Improvement Policy

Jetronics' policy of continuous improvement is part of every employee's job. Every employee contributes to the success of Jetronics. Suggestions for improvement are always welcome.

Jetronics' policy of continuous improvement means we all work together as a team and support each person's contribution to our success.

We continuously strive to improve the quality and efficiency of our business. We each continually look for ways to improve our processes and products.

Some examples of what every employee can do that creates improvement are **contribute, convert**, and **keep agreements.**

Contribute

1. Contribute by offering your suggestions for improvement in a positive manner.
2. Contribute in meetings by looking for solutions, acknowledging other viewpoints and having an open mind.
3. Contribute by setting personal goals to support Jetronics' mission, values, and quality statement.
4. Contribute by supporting other employees and their goals as appropriate.
5. Contribute by providing honest, positive acknowledgment of the successes of others.
6. Contribute by taking personal responsibility to ask for and get the support you need to be successful.

Convert

1. Convert complaints, including inspection rejects, into suggestions for improvement.

2. Convert negative personal attacks into positive requests for improvement. Whether in jest or in anger, never put down another person associated with Jetronics, not a coworker, manager, or customer. It is fine to disagree with something someone says or does, but it is not fine to degrade that person.

   When you are irritated with others in Jetronics (and this certainly will happen), try to resolve your conflict directly. The Jetronics' Policy of Continuous Improvement involves everyone taking responsibility for his or her part of successful teamwork.

Keep Agreements

1. Agree only to what you can. If you are not able to keep your agreement, inform and reset the agreement.

D. Using the Win-Win Style of Introducing the Three Rules

Win-win is another approach you may want to use to introduce the Three Rules to your workgroup. The win-win format is a frame of mind that constantly seeks mutual benefit in all human interactions. It means agreements or solutions that are mutually beneficial and satisfying. Win-win is based on the paradigm that there is plenty for everyone. Issues do not have to be resolved your way or my way; there is a better way—a higher way. (Not "my way or the high way," the higher way.)

Thus, groups will sometimes want to challenge the Three Rules, and they will change them. This is rare, but it's always good to be prepared. With the idea that there is plenty for everyone, you can add rules and expand the current three. In order also to keep integrity in what you want, you can ask to keep the Three Rules intact—if the group uses words like "accountability" instead of "keep agreements," that's fine.

Win-win doesn't mean you give up; it means you speak your truth—others speak theirs—and the result will often be better than either side by itself.

E. Introducing the Three Rules with Group Input

To foster group input, a winery was trying to encourage a team approach throughout the company. The managers decided to hold a series of meetings in which they were trying to "roll out" the Three Rules. They decided to get input from the group as to how a meeting about rules should be conducted. Each manager was to discuss with his or her workgroup the suggested Three Rules and ask for the group's input or additions. To begin the meetings, the managers asked the employees to come up with ground rules for the roll-out meeting on ground rules. For their meetings, three groups were to create rules. Two other groups came up with their own rules for meetings, as follows:

MEETING RULES (GROUP 1)

1. No one gets into trouble for speaking his mind.

2. No put-downs. Everybody's opinion counts.

3. Be a good listener; be positive.

4. We will not discuss specific personal issues.

5. Everyone agrees to be accountable to the company values.

6. Everyone should try to formulate concerns into specific requests. All requests will be responded to.

7. Raise your hand to be recognized.

While this list lacked "Everybody Contributes," it seemed the seven rules would be enough to do the job.

RULES FOR MEETINGS ON RULES (GROUP 2)

1. No retribution—speak out without fear.

2. No put-downs—everyone's opinion counts.

3. Everyone contributes.

4. Express concerns as specific (actionable) requests.

5. Don't try to solve individual personnel problems. Those are for private, one-on-one resolution.

6. All requests will be responded to—now or at a future meeting.

While this set of rules did have "Everyone Contributes," it did not have "Keep Agreements"—so they let me add it and we had seven. A third group decided to have just one rule: They wanted to use the Native American "talking stick"—the person who holds the prescribed object speaks. Having the freedom to have their own department ground rules gave the group the freedom needed to cooperate with the overall Three Rules for the company. As the months and years passed and new employees came, most departments ended up simplifying and using the Three Rules. But the win-win approach was a way to keep everyone involved along the way.

A seasonally oriented irrigation supply company was experiencing dramatically busy seasons followed by very slow, dead time that lasted for months. The manager felt the staff needed codes of conduct that would work for them in both extremes. First, they agreed to the Three Rules as their manager suggested. When they were in the slow season and had time to think about it, they added the following:

CODE OF CONDUCT

I. We will assume people's actions will arise out of good intentions.

II. We will resolve issues at the lowest level possible (by going directly to the source first).

III. We will treat each other with courtesy and respect, with a willingness to apologize and to forgive.

IV. We will own the problem and provide assistance to resolve it.

V. We will consider anyone we come in contact with as our customer.

There are probably many other "rules" that can be effectively used, but the only trouble is that spontaneous new rules don't have all the systems in place to make them happen. Twenty years of developing systems to support the Three Rules has made them more effective than a possibly "better" four or five rules that have little supporting structure.

If your team comes up with five new rules that have no structure to carry them out, you may want to suggest to one of the people who want them that he or she develop a structure for keeping them. Also remember; in the win-win approach you need to have what you want, so you could have **both** the Three Rules and a Code of Conduct. That's what the irrigation supply company did, and it was a win-win all around: Three Rules and a Code of Conduct. The Three Rules were required; the Code of Conduct was recommended.

F. Consensus Building with the Three Rules

Consensus is defined as the opinion arrived at by most of those concerned. Many managers prefer to manage by consensus because they can assure support for their direction. Mr. Vaught at Goodrich pushed for consensus by having his employees' desks moved over the weekend after they failed to follow his command. Kinko had consensus already because he was fun and lovable and he made people laugh. His employees followed him because they wanted more of that good feeling he created. Most managers, in the day-in/day-out decisions and directions, often need to work toward building consensus.

1. POLITICAL CONSENSUS BUILDING

Some people think of politics when they hear the word "consensus." For example, in *All Too Human*, by George Stephanopoulos, one gets the idea that President Bill Clinton rarely led from his own conviction—he led from what the polls said the latest public opinion (consensus) was on that subject.[3] Elected officials most often are expected to represent the viewpoint of others and are not asked to lead but rather to represent. What they usually represent is their desire to be reelected. There is often a lack of measure of whether elected officials were successful or not.

When I was a planning commissioner, I was mildly reprimanded by the city council for making decisions against the recommendation of the staff. I based my decisions on new information from the protesting group who presented its position in person at the meeting. The council thought that planning commissioners should already have their minds made up just by reading the notes from the staff and not be influenced by their own convictions or by information from concerned citizens.

The political systems that stress popular opinion and controlled consensus have their place in society, but they are not included in this book. This book is called *Leadership Begins with You*. It does not center around the idea that leadership begins with public opinion polls.

2. BUSINESS EXECUTIVE—TIGHTLY CONTROLLED CONSENSUS BUILDING

Many executives have learned that consensus is important and have also learned the steps to look like they are building consensus. Unfortunately, they have a very difficult time letting go of full control. The good news is that more often than not the executive consensus builder has a vision and a mission and is closely watched on this path by both a board and a staff of managers. Controlled consensus building was best outlined in the following front-page article from *Investors Business Daily*, by Morey Stettner: "Five Key Ways Executives Advise on Building Consensus among Managers."

"Lay the groundwork; meet with supervisors or leaders first, then present the Ground Rules and ask for their thoughts. Next, meet with the whole group and include the ideas from the earlier meeting." (Paul Snyder, Chairman of Snyder, a hospitality company in Buffalo, NY)

"Defer to the experts," says Jerry Shoft, general manager of an industrial tool manufacturing company in Connecticut. "Let the expert then resolve all the disagreements. Consensus isn't everyone agreeing which way to go as much as getting everyone to acknowledge and accept the expert's view."

"Define your role," says Lesley Mallow Wendell, manager of Options Inc., a Philadelphia career and human resources consulting firm. "Make it clear to the group you want their input, but don't tell them any final decision will be made with the total consensus. Try: 'I'd like your input before this decision gets made'."

"Stick to a schedule." According to manager Wendell, "Announce a date by which all opinions must be in—then keep it."

"Limit the participants," is the advice of a manager at Bob Evans Farms, an Ohio restaurant chain. "When making big decisions, stick to just three people, then agree all three must agree for us to go ahead."[4]

According to *Forbes*, December 1999, the new 45-year-old CEO of Hewlett-Packard, Carly Fiorina, says she listens to the input and then reminds the person she appreciates the input, but she will make the final decision.[5] (By Sept. 2000 Carly was named chairman of HP with a $3 million signing bonus.)

If this style is comfortable for you, then by all means use it. If leadership is to begin with you, it must begin with your style. Control is not always negative, as some would have you think. If you can lead best with some degree of control, then use it.

3. MANIPULATED CONSENSUS—TRY THIS IF YOU WANT A JOB, NOT A CAREER

In *Work Would Be Great If It Weren't for the People*, Ronna Lichtenberg gives many subversive tips for getting what you want in the workplace. Some examples are leapfrogging over the boss's head, or sucking up to a coworker you are in battle with (who is also needy for compliments)—telling how good he was at something, then getting what you want from him. She also makes the suggestion to "pretend to be supporting" a protégé when that person is excelling, then you stay in control. One more—"pay attention in times of flux so you can vie for a higher position."[6]

This book covers the idea of "making office politics work for you." The problem with this technique is that it fits the seventh sabotage category called "builds empires." Some people have brought in the Three Rules via leapfrogging, sucking up, pretend support, or political regrouping in crisis. However, while such an approach means you can lead in the short run, it requires high personal attachment and intense concentration on activities that do not contribute to your career.

This may be fun but as we know, "empire building" sabotages your own career as well as the company.

4. DIALOGUE AND SYNERGY—WONDERFUL WHEN IT HAPPENS

In *The Seven Habits of Highly Effective People* Stephen Covey lists "Synergize"* as Habit #6.[7] His conviction is that if Habits 4 and 5 (think win-win and seek first to understand and then be understood) are in place, then synergy will occur. Synergy is when the result created by the group is greater than the sum of the parts. The natural reproductive laws of nature are the epitome of synergy, where $1 + 1 = 3$. Synergy in consensus building often means transformation. Instead of discussing something as a transaction, synergy can change the assumptions. Synergy cannot be dictated however, because it naturally evolves from a safe space where healthy dialogue is occurring.

Dialogue is a process that goes beyond any one individual's understanding. Dialogue is not like discussion. Discussion is like Ping Pong™; a back and forth effort to win. In order to ensure dialogue, a group of people must treat each other as colleagues in a mutual quest for deeper insight and clarity.[8] You may ask that each person contribute to the mutual quest and treat each other as colleagues, which can then provide the framework to build consensus. Synergy and dialogue saved a winery during a surprise grape shortage because the general manager had already created a synergistic, problem-solving think tank as his management team months before.

Mike Hardy, a former mid-manager at Gallo, a chief operating officer at Rodney Strong, Windsor Vineyards, and Klein Family Vintners, and then general manager at Round Hill Cellars, made a bold move at one of these

---

*Trademark of Franklin Covey Co. Used with permission. All rights reserved.

wineries. He was tired of resolving conflicts between managers, so he set a mission to transform them into a problem-solving think tank. I was brought in to facilitate this process a week at a time.

The group liked the idea of being invited to be a part of his think tank, so they all agreed right away to the Three Rules. Then they added some new rules, like—always consider the whole winery, not just your department, and everyone offer some input toward decisions. We were going through 8:00 A.M. management meetings every Wednesday with this new format. Each Wednesday, Mike would bring one topic for the team to discuss in the think tank format.

One Tuesday in 1993, rumors circulated that there was going to be a major Chardonnay grape shortage. By Wednesday at 6:00 A.M., headlines in the local paper read: CHARDONNAY GRAPE SHORTAGE PREDICTED. By Wednesday at 8:00 A.M., at their regular weekly meeting with the think-tank style already in place, the group miraculously rose to the occasion. The problem was presented by Mike in his usual simple phrase format: "Today's subject is the Chardonnay grape shortage." Next, each person gave his or her observations and data about this shortage, which was written on a large flip chart. Next, Mike collected possible solutions: decrease the orders; change the goals; sell more Merlot; order grapes from Chile and Peru; increase the price; decrease the price, and so on.

With all managers sitting in the same space with the same information, a plan was created in a very short time that included almost all of the recommendations. Thus, one department was not burdened with the full responsibility of responding to the crisis. The team spirit was a miracle to watch. All turfs disappeared; all rules were kept. More important, all ideas were considered, and the result was far better than any individual could have created. In the end, this winery emerged with flying colors and high profit during the grape shortage when other winery stocks plummeted.

Let's compare this to Robert Mondavi Winery in 1993, during the same shortage: Mondavi is a visionary winery executive with a contagious charismatic style. The Napa County people love him because he is one of theirs. He was "thrown out" of his family winery and became a hero on his own. His romantic and passionate contribution to grape growing in Northern California is commendable, but he is not a consensus builder.

The *New York Times* describes *Harvests of Joy* like this: "Mondavi recounts the story of how, almost single-handedly, he changed the way Americans think about wine."[9] For Mondavi, that visionary, single-handed success worked, and he has a huge and delighted following. Mondavi's style can help us distinguish charismatic direction from the group consensus synergy. During the 1993 Chardonnay shortage, however, Mondavi stock plummeted.[10]

One person alone, no matter how charismatic and miraculous, cannot synergize. If you are a charismatic visionary and have a popular following, you may not need group consensus. Mike wanted and thrived on group consensus—and so did his managers. The Three Rules are the context for group consensus, dialogue, and synergy to occur. Rather than use the group consensus to agree to the Three Rules, it may be more helpful to do what Mike Hady did: use the Three Rules to create a think tank that will be used for group consensus on other topics. Once people have experienced the dialogue and synergy that are possible in full group consensus, they usually embrace the Three Rules without a second thought. In most cases, employees are thankful for the Three Rules and will eagerly embrace them.

5. WHEN NOT TO USE CONSENSUS BUILDING

While there are times when charismatic visionary leadership doesn't work (like when Chardonnay grapes are gone), there are also times when group consensus doesn't work. The main time not to use it is when you do not have the authority or the inclination to go in a new direction. If you are not willing to be redirected, don't use it. Try Direct Request, Direct Order, or Win-Win—but not Consensus Building.

In my first job as a middle manager, I worked for the Institute for Professional Development in Irvine, California. This company contracted with the University of Redlands to create and manage their off-campus college degree programs for working adults. I had just received my Ph.D. in management when I was given the job to manage the Business Degree programs, hire faculty, design curriculum, and assure a certain percentage of profitability.

My first assignment on the first day was to terminate two instructors by Wednesday. I made the mistake of using the consensus method of termination. I gathered as much information as possible to make sure I understood why their performance was jeopardizing accreditation, getting low scores from students, and not up to the Institute for Professional Development's standards.

On Wednesday at 5:00 P.M., we three met (both instructors and myself). I worked toward consensus so they would both agree with their termination. As we were halfway through, I felt this nausea in my stomach. They were never going to agree with me. Why should they? They both agreed to improve and make the necessary changes. I said I thought it was too late, but I appreciated their willingness to change.

The next morning, Thursday, they both came to work as usual. My "group consensus" method of firing had not worked. I had led them to believe they had a choice when they didn't. The result was, I had to terminate them both again the next day. Trying to be "nice" can be harmful to those you are supposedly nice to. This experience was one of the foundations for the tools for the Three Rules. It's through mistakes in that first mid-manager job that so many concepts became clearer. All the Ph.D. management courses did not teach those front-line lessons.

G. Short-Term Detachment to Regain Group Support

By willing to detach from the Three Rules if necessary. You can always keep to them privately no matter what. But every once in a while a group really wants to have no rules or they have a whole different set of rules, like the Code of Conduct above. If you have been too controlling, you may have lost your chance to get agreement on the Three Rules or on anything, for that matter. If this is the case, let them create the rules. Just having rules that the group agrees on is better than no rules or forced, unkept rules. Presenting what looks like only *your* rules may jeopardize the chance of your employees' ever following them. You may need to let go of the Three Rules for now and see what your people develop. In any case, you will win because you will learn more about your employees' needs and perspectives. In his *Harvests of Joy,* Robert Mondavi says listen to and appreciate critics—they have a lot to teach you. Employees will win because they will feel empowered by having genuine input. As time passes, the rules will take shape to fit your wishes. When the employees create the rules, you may ask them to rotate responsibility for enforcing the rules.

On family vacations, we used to take our three children and often other families with children. Since our vacation spot is on an island, everyone's contribution was critical. I felt like a drill sergeant enforcing, insisting that one child made ice each morning, one put away dishes, one made sun tea, one set the table, one washed dishes, one hung towels in a certain place, one chopped vegetables, etc. It was all on a chart, but enforcement was a misery for me. So we rotated the "heavy" job each day. The heavy had to remind everyone about their chores.

Little Keith was the best "heavy" because he just went down the list in a detached way—just reminding—just for that day. And he was only eight or nine years old.

Employees can be very creative if you let them. Some use the Three Rules as the agenda outline for meetings—an effective way to organize and carry out a meeting.

PERSONAL DETACHMENT

Remember—*you* are not the Three Rules. You are a manager who is trying to *implement* the Three Rules. When you incorporate these rules in your department, you will be vulnerable to someone saying, "You didn't contribute; that was a put-down; you broke an agreement." But don't let it get you down. Remind them that you are also wrestling with the Three Rules for yourself. You do not proclaim to be "the Three Rules." Because you take them on simultaneously when you are enacting them, you are working on them in tandem with your employees. They are to be used first and foremost privately and internally.

In my first job, I taught eighth grade at McKenny Junior High in Tempe, Arizona. One of the rules was "no gum in class." Personally, I didn't care if they had gum in class, but it was part of the school's rules, and my job was to carry out the school's rules. I always corrected students with gum, but in a detached way, "Uh-oh, gum—one check mark."

One Saturday I was in the produce section of the local grocery store. A student from another class rushed up to me, "Mrs. Riley, there is someone in the meat section chewing gum." They thought my whole life was making sure no one on the planet ever chewed gum. I don't mind if people don't follow the Three Rules either. If someone in the meat section puts someone down there is no Three Rules police to stop it. Ideally, the Rule 3 will serve as a little reminder to ourselves to check how we do in situations.

If you can personally detach from the Three Rules, it will be easier to use all the above formats. By designating others to enforce them, or being lighthearted about it, or casually making it one of several direct orders, or including the rules in your mission or values, or having it in a personnel manual, you allow some personal detachment and give space to the group to follow your lead.

H. Laying the Foundation for Putting the Three Rules in Place

Some mid-managers have told me they tried privately using the Three Rules for a few months before introducing them to the group. They claimed it gave them an in-depth understanding of the personal courage it takes to keep an agreement with yourself to keep the Three Rules. They said it also adds a compassionate dimension to their introductions of the Rules by telling of their own wrestling with them. This invites and leads other people to try them too.

Keeping the rules requires self-discipline, not finger-pointing. When you can be receptive and appreciative, gentle and lighthearted when reminding others, then keeping the rules will become natural and easy. Remember, more people died in battle over differing views over religious rules than any other reason. Don't let anyone get too righteous or too rigid. If they all agree that they want five rules, then have five rules. Agreeing on rules is more important than using only the Three Rules themselves.

Many different formats will work to introduce the Three Rules to your workgroup. The goal here is to introduce the Three Rules in a format that fits your strengths, convictions, values, mission, and goals. Whether you try the Goodrich Tire, Kinko, Robert Mondavi, or Mike Hardy method, remember the Nike slogan too—"Just do it!"

13

Generating Buy-in to the Rules

Change is inevitable; growth is optional.

—MICHAEL O'BRIEN, Author, Philosopher

Everyone Contributes: Management by Objectives (MBO)

When I was in graduate school getting my Ph.D. in management under the advisorship of Peter Drucker, I was transformed by his Management by Objectives (MBO) approach. MBO is a management method that requires the manager to set specific, measurable goals with each employee and then periodically discuss his/her progress toward these goals.[1] Drucker was and still is the "Father of Management," a best-selling author and one of the most sought-after consultants in the country. I attended his classes at night while working in a civil service job, and I got speeding tickets driving home after classes, because I was so inspired by the difference MBO would make in my workplace.

"Management by Objectives" began with Luther Gulick in the mid-1930s and was used solely in government agencies. By 1940, the concept of MBO was applied to the private sector. A profound distinction occurred as MBO was applied to business—it became immediately evident that results-oriented, real MBO required "self-control."[2] For the first time, the objectives were not just goals but something that had to be reached. Because government work did not require making a profit, it was easier to drift away from stated objectives toward activities that might not contribute. MBO subtly addressed the corporate law of entropy discussed previously. If everything in the universe (including a company) is always losing available energy, there should be an infrastructure in place that increases energy; otherwise the company will disintegrate by the law of nature.

MBUO—Management by Unstated or Unclear Objectives

An example of management by unstated or unclear objectives happened to me as a junior administrative assistant in the personnel department of the City of Los Angeles, just before learning about MBO. My first assignment was to work on a brochure that would entice clerk-typists to accept positions in the Los Angeles Police Department (LAPD). My objective seemed clear—fill LAPD clerk-typist positions. Right away, I interviewed and photographed three senior clerk-typists at LAPD and got quotes about why they liked their job. I independently searched and found a graphic designer in L.A. city hall to have brochures made to go to employees on the clerk-typist list. When they received their LAPD clerk-typist offer, they also could see the career potential there. The sixth week after the brochures went out, all LAPD clerk-typist positions were filled.

I was very excited about my six-month performance review. I anticipated a good score, if not a celebration. The three overall performance review rating categories available in the City of Los Angeles at that time were: (1) Competent, (2) Improvement Needed, and (3) Incompetent. To my stunned disappointment, my overall review rating was "Incompetent." I was devastated and could hardly speak. When I said, "But what about the brochure and filling the positions?" The boss said I did it too hurriedly. The person before me had been working on it for two years, therefore doing the brochure by myself and scurrying around to get it produced made others nervous. I was numb. This devastating performance review took place on a Friday, and I spent the whole weekend feeling depressed and helpless.

I was amazed later by how many other people had experienced similar situations—being judged on unspoken objectives when they believed the spoken objectives were the ones that counted—then finding out after diligent effort that you were working on the wrong goals. Was my goal to contribute to the complacency of civil service workers or to fill LAPD jobs with qualified people? My mentor, Los Angeles councilman Howard Finn, said, "Find out what you have to do to bring up your review score, not what you did wrong."

On Monday I went to my supervisor and asked, "What do I need to do to get a higher score?" I summarized his complaints about me: "You said I walk too fast, talk too much, joke around too much, and just seem to be scurrying around all the time." "That's correct," he said. "You make others nervous—you finished the brochure too fast—it made so-and-so look bad."

"So to explain this in terms of what I *should* do, do you want me to walk slower, talk less, joke around less, and keep movements to a minimum . . . and work slower?" As his head nodded very slowly up and down, my dignity was restored. "I'm not incompetent," I realized. We just had different objectives. I wanted to fill those positions. He wanted me to act like a civil service worker. The objective was to fit in, not to fill positions.

"In MBO," says Drucker, "achieving a desired result is from the willingness or buy-in of both the manager and employee to contribute to the same objectives. It is the ability to have self-control, to know that we are making the right contribution and to be able to lead ourselves to make the right contribution. Acting like a civil service worker may be right for this government agency, but it is not right for the business world.

"In MBO, the manager should ask, 'What should this organization hold me accountable to contribute in the next year? Two years? What specific assignments in this position make the greatest contribution?' Unless these questions are brought to the surface, there is no buy-in. MBO must determine the right concentration of effort. Self-control shows the buy-in on both the part of the manager and the employee. MBO is not planning. It is a *tool* for planning. It is a decision-making process, setting priorities and goals, and getting people to discipline themselves to initiate and direct their work toward the goals and purpose."[3] This term, "self-control," from the 1980s, is called "buy-in" in 2000.

After I had experienced the civil service, misaligned performance review, MBO seemed so simple: Start with the mission, set financial goals for the whole organization, then break them into objectives for each department. Once each department knows its objectives, managers, supervisors, and individual contributors know their part, and they will do their part and be judged against stated, clear objectives. Perfect!

I left my civil service job and went to work in the private sector. The first two companies I worked for were either vague on objectives or vague on carrying out the objectives. I thought this was unique to these companies. Now I was confused—why aren't these businesses more clear on their objectives? MBO is so good—why aren't companies implementing it?

Luckily for me, I was trained by Drucker to choose the right goal. He always said, "Pay attention to which goal you are achieving." The lack of "paying attention to which goal you are achieving" was something that I was unprepared for. It was most blatant when I was asked to teach "Goal Setting for Managers" at what was then a large leasing company that had a new MBO program. I was now a business consultant, and the company contracted with me to get buy-in or commitment from employees and managers for the new MBO plan.

It turned out that this West Coast leasing company had just finished a two-year, very expensive MBO program when an East Coast consulting company came in and got input from all managers to outline a full professional, easy-to-read, well-documented, accurate MBO program. I was the local consultant hired to maintain it. The MBO program began with a strategic overall objective that necessitated a shift from ROI (Return on Income) to ROA (Return on Assets).

The first six-week seminar included twelve managers. In the first day of the first seminar, I asked the managers to fill out the questions in Appendix E-1: "What is the mission of our leasing company? What is your department's number one objective? What is your number one goal?" This exercise seemed appropriate, since the MBO program was in place, plus the company had been written up in *Business Week* magazine that same month. The magazine reported that the firm had recently shifted its strategic objective from return on income to return on assets. It was a major shift that affected every level of the organization. When I asked the managers what was expected of them in order to facilitate this change, none had a clear understanding or could even identify the objectives.

Why had they not bought in to the change? If they had bought in, wouldn't they be asking what new goals they needed to accomplish to contribute to the new strategic objective? The president himself had bought in to it without another thought when the board of directors decided to make the change. He took it for granted that because everyone had input to the MBO plan, they would automatically have buy-in. Why didn't they?

Not one manager in that room was aware of his or her piece of the shift from ROI to ROA. No one had read the article or knew the number one request of their boss. Two of the twelve knew their boss's number one request of them in general terms. They never *agreed* to the goals. They were handed the MBO goals after their slight input. This is not an attack on this president or the leasing company. This situation simply represents the era of the 1980s and 1990s. This scenario was repeated over and over, within many organizations. Why didn't they care about MBO? The leasing company was bought out by Ford Motor Company two years later, and I set out to discover why people didn't buy in even when they had input. What I learned first was the difference between input and buy-in. What I learned second was how to motivate, empower, and ensure that others buy in to the right goal.

Input Versus Buy-in

Input is like participation. It is possible to have positive or negative input. You can leave fingerprints in paint, shoot someone, file a lawsuit, harass a coworker, and you'll have input. Some naïve middle managers will ask for slight input, like what color to paint the work areas, and expect everyone to buy in to painting it because they "helped" select the color.

Input does not guarantee commitment toward the company goals. It is neutral, yet it's almost impossible to have buy-in without input. Input is a critical ingredient, but it does not guarantee buy-in. Buy-in, on the other hand, assures contribution to the right objectives and the self-control to achieve them. ("Self-control" was a 1940s term used by Drucker in his first MBO book. In his 1999 book he calls it "managing oneself" and calls for immediate action in this area.[4])

In almost every case of a company with an MBO program, people did have input—lots of input. This was the big thing in the 1980s—get employee input and involvement. But since not all input assures buy-in, MBO was not a two-way agreement between managers and employees. It was a one-way document handed from boss to employee. This was a difficult discovery for me because I did not want to criticize my mentor's MBO idea. But this diligent search for what was missing in MBO had to be completed.

Rule 1: Everyone Contributes (to the right goal) almost single-handedly alters the way companies can do MBO in the twenty-first century. Once employees had to picture themselves contributing to objectives and committing to them, it was apparent that they needed to experience benefits as well. Employees needed to help lead the way to their objectives. They also wanted to be able to voice their needs in order to accomplish these objectives. Anyone leading people to anything will need certain agreements, assistance, support, and supplies. You can never lead your career if you set out to accomplish other people's goals and ask them for nothing in return. You may need more direction, less direction—more responsibilities, more authority, more informality, more input, more communication, fewer instructions, less interference or more training.

If you do not ask for anything, you run the risk of experiencing an incompetent performance rating, as I did at the Los Angeles personnel department. I could have asked for graphics assistance, help with interviews, and samples of other brochures. I could have been informed that a much slower pace was expected. I might even have been informed about the battle between personnel and LAPD and told that the personnel department was intentionally going slow on filling these positions because of some interoffice conflicts.

If you are contributing to your boss's objective, tell him or her what you need in order to achieve buy-in. If you are assigning objectives to others, find out what they need from you to buy in to your objective. Many executives argue this point with me and ask, "What do you mean, ask employees what they want? They get to keep their jobs—that's what they get." My favorite playful response is, "Well, you won't be able to keep yours if you think that's all people want in trade for these aggressive goals." Then they either kick me out or we achieve a nice rapport.

MBO with clear objectives and some input still isn't the perfect situation. It tells people how to contribute, but does not encourage their buy-in. How can a civil service agency assure buy-in to increased goals and objectives?

MBTWO (Management by Two-Way Objectives) — Public Works Department

Not all government agencies have misplaced contribution goals. One county public works agency director incorporated the Three Rules into his agency, and it transformed the whole department. By clarifying the right contribution and stretching to keep agreements even when they seemed insignificant, this agency became a model for Rule 1 (Everyone Contributes) and Rule 3 (Keep Agreements).

This public works agency was headed by a well-respected and well-liked director who was voted "Public Works Man of the Year." Even though he was ready to retire, Don Head was willing to apply the Three Rules in order to increase the buy-in from his department heads. They were all doing reasonably well in their departments, but he wanted to see visible improvement in all departments and eliminate entropy.

The tool he used to get buy-in for his new, improved public works department was the Funnel and Alignment Process demonstrated in chapter 5. Below are excerpts from an article I coauthored with Don Head,[5] who took a stand to improve the quality of every bridge, road, sewer facility, and transportation in his county and wanted buy-in for his stand. Our goal together was to get the right input necessary from all six departments in order to get their buy-in, and to take the right actions to reach Don's new quality program. I was so impressed to see a public agency really get buy-in from both top and middle management that I felt an article was needed to vindicate public service.

Our work began with the Three Rules to which all agreed. Buy-in can't even be a subject to consider until the Three Rules are set. To get buy-in through mutual agreements, Don first gave each of his managers time to privately identify the number one request of him personally. After agreeing to their requests, Don told them his number one quality request. His requests of his top six managers were these:

Manager 1: Increase reliability on budgets. Check every request to see if there is a less expensive or better way.

Manager 2: Motivate and lead your staff. Give them more authority.

Manager 3: Prepare to become an assistant department head. Particu-
            larly learn how to give speeches.
Manager 4: Keep regular hours. Set an example.
Manager 5: Personally walk on and under to inspect every bridge in
            this county.
Manager 6: Get more involved with the board of supervisors.

In return, each of the six managers made his or her request known
to Don:

Manager 1: Meet once a month for thirty minutes on a specific day
            and time.
Manager 2: Meet twice a month for thirty minutes.
Manager 3: Coach me on political aspects of the job.
Manager 4: Set priorities.
Manager 5: Keep me informed on agreements you make with my
            foremen.
Manager 6: Delegate more projects involving the board.

Don understood that by keeping the agreements he would create the buy-
in required for the increased quality of the public works program. Six Alignment Agreement forms were filled out, each with Don and one manager
writing the other's request. Twelve agreements were set in motion—six for
Don and one for each manager.

Don was known as a big thinker in the public works field. He is very similar to many people in high positions who are big thinkers. It was the "little"
things that completely surprised him in this process. Let's take Manager 5.
Don asked Manager 5 to personally walk through and observe, touch, feel,
smell every bridge in the county. Manager 5's request was that Don keep him
informed about any agreements Don made with his foremen. Thirty days
into the alignment process, I asked Don, "Did you make any agreements
with bridge and road foremen?"

"I don't know," he said with some irritation. This subject was not on his
mind.

"What's your guess?" I asked. Don glared at me in silence. It was as if he
didn't know why I was intruding into his space. Luckily his phone rang, so I
could start breathing again. Standing in the face of a powerful person's anger
can hinder one's breathing! I had a chance to collect my thoughts and continue. "Don, your agreement with Manager 5 was to inform him whenever
you make agreements with his foremen. I realize you are not used to doing
this, but I want you to consider two things:

1. This is the number one request that Manager 5 has of you, and he worked hard to clarify to you what is so important to him, and

2. Your number one request of Manager 5 is to personally walk on, touch, and observe every bridge in the county by year end, and all he needs you to do is to have you tell him your agreements with foremen."

"That just isn't important. What I say to foremen is not related to checking bridges," he said.

"Then why did you sign this Alignment Agreement that said you would inform him?"

Don was a man of his word. And when I showed him the Alignment form he had signed just thirty days earlier, he paid attention.

"What does he mean by 'agreements with foremen'?" Don asked.

Fortunately, we had described what that meant. When Don thought about it, he realized he had made agreements with Manager 5's foreman twice. He jotted down the incidents and said he would call Manager 5 and tell him of his agreements with foremen, and he did.

Thirty days later I visited Don again to see if he had met with Manager 1. Manager 1 was diligently reviewing the reliability of the budget numbers, but two months had passed and there had been no meeting with Don. "Don, do you recall agreeing to meet every thirty days with Manager 1?"

"Yes. I have an open-door policy, and he can come in here anytime he wants. If he wanted to meet, we would have met." Just before Don turned back to his paperwork, he said with a smirk, "Okay. What did I forget?"

"Your agreement. Remember when you spent all that time clarifying to Manager 1 the details of how he could increase the reliability on the budget? Here it is—you wanted to have backup explaining each item so that when you were in front of the board of supervisors, you could respond to any questions. When you were in the last board meeting and they asked about budget items, did you have answers?" I asked, looking at his Alignment agreement at what he asked of Manager 1.

"Actually twice now, it went really well—best ever, and I thanked Manager 1 afterward."

"Good, he's doing your number one request. Now, his number one request of you that he spent a long time thinking through and risked asking for was for you to meet with him once a month, on the second Tuesday at 9:00 A.M. Here is his request—thirty minutes—in your office. Have your secretary confirm first so I know we have a set-aside time."

"Look, I can't baby these people."

"Then why did you agree to do it?"

"Because it was such a small thing in exchange for all the budget help," he said.

"If it is so small, why don't you do it?" I asked.

"Because I just can't believe this is that important to him."

"Do you think he lied?"

"No, I just don't think he really knew his number one request."

"Don, that's why you paid me. We had a seminar. People spent two hours trying to clarify what they wanted from you. Then they went to the trouble to tell you, and they stretched to meet your huge, big-thinking goal."

My meeting with Don was on the first Monday of the month, just in case he had forgotten the Tuesday meeting. He called his secretary to tell her to call Manager 1 and set up the 9:00 A.M. appointment for the next day. Since Don had missed the first meeting, Manager 1 was a little let down, but he still had a long agenda of items and he needed uninterrupted time with Don. I wasn't in the meeting, but I can't help but think synergy occurred. After that meeting, Don selected this manager to be the new assistant public works director.

Each manager's request got more buy-in from Don, and as they saw Don buying in to their requests, they bought in to his public works department improvements in impressive ways. When Don made it through the six-month trial period, he said, "For forty years, I have been managing people thinking I had an open-door policy. But I never really set aside specific time or a way for real input from people; I never really thought they might want these types of items. I wish I had known this before."

In the past, Don had been resisting his staff's input and they were resisting some of his goals. Their buy-in was greatly increased when he bought in to their requests. Each week his secretary scheduled an uninterrupted meeting with those who wanted it. Five of the six managers were in very high alignment with Don; their scores on the follow-up were all above 85 percent.

Manager 4 asked Don to set priorities. This manager had some heart problems, and he believed that feeling everything was urgent had caused him to have a heart attack. He thought that if Don could prioritize, it would help him be more relaxed about which project to do next. Don agreed. Don's number one request of Manager 4 was that he set a good example for his employees by coming in on time and keeping to a one-hour lunch. Manager 4 would not agree to that. He said that since his heart attack, he must exercise at lunch and get nine hours of sleep, and he just couldn't change his schedule.

Synergy occurred because they were having a genuine dialogue. Instead of grumbling about the manager not agreeing, Don said, "Great! I hate setting priorities. So how about if you keep the hours you have now, and I'll keep letting managers set their own priorities as long as they know the number one goal." They both laughed and had a hearty agreement. "I don't have to do this, and you don't have to do that." This is what we call Advanced Alignment. Remember, 12 to 15 percent will not be able to align and/or keep all of the Three Rules. There's room for them, too.

Both Don and Manager 4 were relieved. They bought in to something bigger and better than their requests. They bought in to their partnership and mutual respect. Input into their part of the objectives created buy-in. Five of the six managers bought in and achieved the goals. They were motivated by Don's buying in to their requests. Each day I drive over the Don Head Bridge on my way to work. I often recall the core statement that *Water Engineering Management* quoted from Don after this process: "Issues viewed as trivial by one participant are often significant to the other."[6] Amen.

MBTWO (Management by Two-Way Objectives) — A Private-Sector Company

Frank, a Fremont, California, electronics distributor, saw the twenty-first century technology ready to explode and thought he'd better be prepared. He had owned a very successful business for twenty-five years that consistently produced and was still growing. But he was ready to move on to other things in life and wanted the business to support his very comfortable retirement. The question was, How could he get other people to care as much about the business as he did? How could he get them to reposition the company to grow in the technology market? He was the owner, but a very generous management profit bonus and employee profit bonus made it seem co-owned—to him but not to the employees.

He decided to work toward ISO 9000 Certification to position the company to last for twenty-plus more years. Frank attended several Total Quality Management (TQM) conferences. One was the American Society for Quality Control (ASQC) conference in San Jose, where I was the keynote speaker, recommending Funnel and Alignment to guarantee buy-in to quality improvement goals. Frank decided to immediately implement an ISO quality program in his company. The first thing he did was to offer a free quality workshop to the management team. No one attended. After all, they already felt like they were doing quality work, and the mere suggestion of it was a slight to many people.

Frank called me and asked for a copy of the slide I'd shown about why quality programs fail:

- Threaten the status quo

- Create reaction/resistance

- Force pseudo-integration and acceptance

- Lead to subconscious sabotage by both managers and employees

- Give few accurate clues to why it failed

He knew that the buy-in was the missing ingredient; although it was hard for him to understand that his employees, for whom he had done so much, were not loyal to this *program*. We had to keep reminding him that it wasn't personal. It was simply a law of physics: for every action there is an equal and opposite reaction. An action to push a new program invites an action against the new program. Frank recalled times in his life when ideas were imposed on him and when he had often felt like rebelling. When he finally could accept the image of scientific theory and not take it personally, we could embark on a buy-in program.

All the employees were invited to attend a general meeting at which the quality program was briefly overviewed and the idea of finding out their personal requests right from the start was shown. The Three Rules were established first. A pattern in the employees' requests of their managers was very interesting. Four out of five employees who reported to one manager, all said they wanted him to use their ideas or act on their input. Patterns for number one requests are helpful improvement tools for building quality managers. This manager realized he should acknowledge their input or they would never buy-in to ISO 9000 or quality improvement.

A key ingredient to getting to buy-in was the Three Rules. All employees agreed readily to the rules because they really did want to contribute and improve the quality of the company. Like many new programs, this one started with great fervor, and an overwhelming majority of the employees felt very enthusiastic. They used the Funnel and Alignment process, and each identified and agreed to improvement in their work processes (as per ISO 9000 guidelines). They had an 89.1 percent, which was the average score in follow-ups for keeping their agreements with one another. Frank decreased his time there to one day a week, so he could embark on a graduate school program that was taking much of his time outside the organization. He did not do Alignments with his three managers.

His three managers had input in the ISO, but they did not have buy-in. Much of the initiative was lost and ISO 9000 Certification went to the back burner. Employees slipped back into their old habits, and Frank had to drop the graduate program and come back to work.

By round 2, there were some conflicts and complaints to be dealt with in the group. Luckily they had the Three Rules in place and as a result they had a tool to resolve conflict. Because these tools and the rules were already in place, two meetings of two hours each was all it took to resolve the conflicts and refocus the group with a new resolve to keep the "continuous improvement" process so they could get ISO-certified. They had just lost a major order because of not being ISO-certified. Two of the three managers were in major conflict. By agreeing earlier to the Three Rules, they agreed to use the Conscious Communication tool to work through discord and back toward contribution. Otherwise, the company would never achieve ISO Certification and would lose valuable business opportunities.

One mid-manager, Ed, was very outspoken, expressed anger and frustration regularly, and, unfortunately, offended several employees. However, he was great on the phone with customers. Jack, Ed's manager, was very professional in his expression and did not like to see so much energy wasted in anger. Ed was the number one contributor to the sales success in the company, however, so previously Jack had never complained about Ed. Now it was improvement time. Jack used the No Put-down alternative, the Conscious Communication tool. Ed listened with the Eight-Step Checklist for Listening. Something shifted. Jack felt that he was being heard, and Ed was happy to have someone stand toe to toe with him.

Then they reversed roles. Using the Conscious Communication tool, Ed told Jack that he felt frustrated and angry when Jack acted over concerned with being politically correct. After finishing the form, Jack used the Eight Steps and admitted that he was very controlled and actually should express himself more. Ed admitted he was overly abrupt and should be more considerate. Then Jack said, "I'm kind of glad you are outspoken because it's a good model for me." Ed agreed that he was glad Jack was politically correct, because it meant he didn't have to be.

The resistance between the two melted. Jack gave Ed the support needed for Ed to finish the policy and procedure manual for ISO 9000. Jack felt a great release from all the pent-up control, and the rest of the management team breathed a sigh of relief. When people find an alternative to put-downs, a feeling of creativity and support permeates the group. Jack and Ed then decided to buy the business from Frank. With their partnership aligned, their joint buy-in to ISO, and a long and healthy future for the business, Frank was finally free to retire.

Frank now lives in Maui and sends clever E-mails to Jack, Ed, several others, and myself on the cc list. Jack and Ed have built the company beyond what any of us thought possible, but not until there was buy-in. Buy-in to grow the business and buy-in to own the business—buy-in is about the truth. When the truth is present, people buy in with incredible fervor. In the twenty-first century, people demand truth and need faster and safer ways to achieve it.

When I asked Edward Deming, quality guru, "How do you get buy-in for Total Quality Management?" he answered, "Set up a win-win for them. Win-win means both contribute—and both get what they want. Middle managers have the opportunity to create buy-in from both above and below. The same tool can be used to achieve full buy-in from both your boss and your employees."

The message here is that you will have all the buy-in you ever thought possible if you remember one main rule—to know the number one thing each person wants that you need buy-in from, and do that number one thing.

To get buy-in to the Three Rules, outline the contribution you need from others. Find out from them how you can contribute to them. *Never guess* (or second guess)—*ask* and then *do*. Once you have made your requests of others and understand specifically what they have identified they need from you, you are ready to make the two-way MBO agreement called the MBTWO. Keep your agreement with them and require that they keep their agreement with you. Focus on what the other person has requested, and revel in he or she doing what you requested. You'll know you earned this leadership experience, and a career environment will replace your job environment.

Rule Two: Big-Time Buy-in

While MBO is much about buying in to Contribution (Rule 1) and Keeping Agreements (Rule 3), it does not cover the second rule, No Put-downs. Many executives today have excellent missions, values, goals, and objectives all spelled out and continuously updated. Company missions appear everywhere. Similarly, there is a much greater attempt today to keep agreements with employees. Keeping agreements has been most apparent with the large number of high-tech companies going public and transforming employees into millionaires. This process demonstrated to employees that the "you will be entitled to part of the profit" promise was kept. But the No Put-downs rule has appeared as the Achilles' heel in the high-tech growth arena and demanded to be followed.

One chief executive officer whom we'll call Pete shows us the millions of dollars that can be gained by adding the No Put-downs rule to actions, even when the individual may not want to give up put-downs. Pete had the courage to be coached and is reaping the reward.

Pete grew up in a lumber town and lived a rough and tough childhood. Taking potshots and throwing verbal "bullets" was part of his culture. It was fun and everyone did it. He was an exceptionally smart young man and became one of the youngest managers ever in technology. He was extremely intelligent, so college came easy. Being the visionary he was, Pete could see the explosion that was coming in technology back in 1980, when he took over as the general manager of a division of his company. At the time, the company had $60 million in net profit. If he could position his company to include all technology markets, he envisioned the growth and set a goal to grow to $600 million in twenty years. Also, he was a very high-integrity person and would turn down million-dollar deals if they were not ethical. His word was good and everyone knew it.

He had one fatal flaw—he couldn't resist putting people down. Because he was so intelligent, others sometimes seemed like dummies to him. Because he was so ethical, others seemed like crooks. Calling people dummies or crooks was not conducive to building a management team that could help grow his division from $6 million to $600 million in twenty years.

Rich, a professor/consultant, was Pete's coach. While Pete "bought in" to the No Put-downs rule for his employees, his own behavior was not so easy to change. Each week Rich would meet with Pete on several issues, but always working to convert put-downs into requests.

The Professional Growth Plan was what began the buy-in process for Pete. He was using it to replace the company's performance review system. Whenever Pete was tempted to express contempt or skepticism, he was coached by Rich to convert it into a request. As Pete saw feedback from managers to whom he had made requests, he reflected, "It is these little things that add up to major changes in employee behavior."

Rich knew Pete "bought in" to the No Put-downs rule when he made the Funnel and Alignment part of the company's annual merit review system. This way, Pete was forcing himself to buy in to No Put-downs. There is no place in the Alignment process for a put-down. Correction, improvement, criticism with hope—yes! Put-downs—no. But Pete still has Rich come by monthly to make sure he doesn't slip. Real change requires regular discipline.

By 2000, Pete's company has won the award for fastest-growing company in its field three years in a row. And its profits are not just $600 million— they were $700 million for 2000. Rich says Pete's buying in to Rule 2 was the point of transformation. And he knew it wasn't a one-time thing. It was a sabotaging habit that he was committed to overcome. He had the courage to seek help and keep being coached on it for ten years. Knowing our blind spots and having the courage to repair them can be the key to leadership and a meaningful, successful career.

Commitment to all Three Rules will usually reveal one rule that is a struggle to keep. If we buy in to only two of the rules, we will not advance in the most impactful, career-growing direction possible. By buying in to all three rules, no matter what, we allow our strengths to show up and we can build on them, and what we didn't see then, we then can see. These factors combine to give us an incredible liberation to contribute successfully.

14

Jump-starting the Rules with a Three Rules Performance Appraisal System: The "Professional Growth Plan"

> Unless you try to do something beyond what you have already mastered, you will never grow.
>
> —RALPH WALDO EMERSON

To take hold and really be infused into the workplace, the Three Rules should become part of the infrastructure of the company. For years companies have been searching for a performance appraisal system that would ensure productive buy-in from employees and offer an objective way to pay for productive performance. This chapter will outline a performance appraisal system that jump-starts the Three Rules right into the core systems of your workgroup and your company.

Feeling very dissatisfied with the literature on performance reviews, my associates and I have professionally researched the subject of performance appraisal since 1983[1] and have written books, articles, and materials that reflect our findings. The first franchisee of our consulting company to distribute a Three Rules performance appraisal was Dr. Rich Noland in Salem, Oregon. Dr. Noland coauthored an article with First Technology Credit Union CEO Tom Sargent about this "amazing new process."[2] Other articles were published on the subject, and responses to these have been the core of our consulting practice for twenty years.

In October 1999 we published our sixteenth article on results from our most current performance appraisal research. This article was coauthored by two human resources professionals, Dr. Jack Kondrasuk and Wang Hua, with the help of students. It appears, in the *American Journal of Compensation and Benefits* and is titled, "If We Want to Pay for Performance, How Do We Judge Performance?"[3]

In the 1999 research, 70 percent of human resources directors called by students said their reviews were successful at measuring performance. Conversely, only 20 percent of middle managers who are on the front line and in the trenches day in and day out said that these various reviews work for them. Why the discrepancy?

HR people usually develop or purchase a review system. Even if they don't develop or purchase it, they are responsible for its successful application. They judge success by completed and returned forms, reasonable comments, and the overall absence of complaints. But there is a conflict of interest here. It is in their best interest to announce it is a successful review system because they are ultimately responsible for its success. Since we interviewed only the HR directors, we accumulated only their viewpoints. Other surveys in the past, asking mid-managers if performance reviews help, show only 20 percent satisfaction. This inadvertently helped me tremendously in observing just how far HR has distanced itself from the middle manager.

To lead your own career, I personally recommend that you do not leave it to the HR manager to determine your performance review process. In the twenty-first century the HR person has many other priorities—lawsuits, sexual harassment issues, expanded benefits, more and more compliance, safety requirements, OSHA, E-mail monitoring, etc. HR is no longer the best place to look for a performance appraisal system that could capture the best of your employees' energy and focus it toward your mission and goals—you are.

In *Executive EQ: Emotional Intelligence in Leadership and Organizations,* the author concludes: "The basic ingredients are inside your heart and your head. You are the leader. You are the process."[4] "You must *be* the change you wish to see in the workplace," says Mahatma Gandhi.[5]

Middle managers are the front line—"in the trenches," living with the day-to-day entropy and sabotage and the resistance to wonderful visions, missions, and objectives. I want to present to you the most tested, refined, and successful tool of all that I have tried. It's a tool that includes all the Three Rules, fights all eight sabotages, reverses entropy, and empowers you and your employees to the mission and to lucrative financial rewards and meaningful careers. This is a twenty-first-century performance appraisal system called the Professional Growth Plan. It incorporates the Three Rules into the infrastructure of your workgroup via a performance appraisal process. If used between you and your boss, as well as between you and your employees, this process can transform your managerial tasks into a lucrative and meaningful career.

The Professional Growth Plan

The Professional Growth Plan (PGP), once called the Systemix Performance Appraisal, was originally designed and distributed to corporations by Xerox's Learning Systems (XLS) Division. In 1979, I was one of the Ph.D. researchers with a budget of several million dollars allocated to identify what motivated employees and what skills were inherent in almost all jobs. With a research base of $25,000 and respondents from all over the country and all levels of jobs, a skills list similar to the one that follows was developed. In 1981, XLS went out of the training and education business, and we acquired the rights to the research. While it has been updated to include more technology and more self-management, the basic skills and instructions are founded on statistical validation of what motivates people to be productive.

This tool is helpful to middle managers because it allows you to escape the constant meetings where managers ask you to be on a committee to redesign the performance appraisal form and trust this form to identify contribution, convert all put-downs to requests, and ensure that agreements are kept. If you are interested in using this for a large group or for salary calculations, E-mail us for more detailed instructions at mriley@sonic.net.

Meanwhile, for you and a few employees, follow the instructions in this chapter. You will notice that the Funnel and Alignment are part of the PGP. You already know how to use this tool from earlier chapters.

The Professional Growth Plan incorporates the Three Rules—everyone contributes, no put-downs, and keep agreements. The PGP has been used in hundreds of companies for more than twenty years, so the problems have been resolved and you can trust the form. And most important, it has a follow-up feature to measure the financial impact of each person and the mentally healthy culture that is being created. These assessments can be on a monthly or quarterly basis.

The Professional Growth Plan treats every employee as a *professional* in his or her work; *growth* is about the future, about doing more, better, and faster; *plan* is its part in the company's strategic business plan. Whatever review system you use should include these basic objectives: (1) to improve contribution, (2) to implement your goals and objectives, (3) to increase employee retention and (4) to decrease sabotage. The PGP incorporates these concepts in the following four simple steps:

Pre-Review

Please Print

Organization: Today's Date:

Employee's Name: Employee's Job Title:

Reviewer's Name: Follow-Up Date: 8/1/01

I. WHAT SKILLS ARE MOST IMPORTANT TO THIS JOB?

_____ a. Quantity of work

_____ b. Consistently using time efficiently/effectively

_____ c. Applying technical knowledge appropriately

_____ d. Generating new ideas or suggestions

_____ e. Making timely decisions

_____ f. Foreseeing and solving problems

_____ g. Providing quality customer service

_____ h. Planning, organizing, and delegating work

_____ i. Properly operating and caring for equipment

_____ j. Providing sound training and direction

_____ k. Making sound judgments

_____ l. Effectively communicating with others in written or verbal form

_____ m. Consistently creating effective teamwork

_____ n. Motivating and assisting other staff members

_____ o. Applying operating policies and procedures prescribed for the job

_____ p. Meeting goals, objectives, and commitments

_____ q. Following through on tasks, activities, and responsibilities

_____ r. Observing safety requirements

_____ s. Maintaining good attendance and punctuality

_____ t. Managing oneself

_____ u. _____

II. WHICH SKILLS DOES THE EMPLOYEE PERFORM WELL?

_____ a. Quantity of work

_____ b. Consistently using time efficiently/effectively

_____ c. Applying technical knowledge appropriately

_____ d. Generating new ideas or suggestions

_____ e. Making timely decisions

_____ f. Foreseeing and solving problems

_____ g. Providing quality customer service

_____ h. Planning, organizing, and delegating work

_____ i. Properly operating and caring for equipment

_____ j. Providing sound training and direction

_____ k. Making sound judgments

_____ l. Effectively communicating with others in written or verbal form

_____ m. Consistently creating effective teamwork

_____ n. Motivating and assisting other staff members

_____ o. Applying operating policies and procedures prescribed for the job

_____ p. Meeting goals, objectives, and commitments

_____ q. Following through on tasks, activities, and responsibilities

_____ r. Observing safety requirements

_____ s. Maintaining good attendance and punctuality

_____ t. Managing oneself

_____ u. _____

Pre-Review
Rudy's Form

Please Print

Organization: N/A

Today's Date: 5/1/01

Employee's Name: Rudy

Employee's Job Title: VP Manufacturing

Reviewer's Name: Jim

Follow-Up Date: 8/1/01

I. WHAT SKILLS ARE MOST IMPORTANT TO THIS JOB?

__3__ a. Quantity of work
__2__ b. Consistently using time efficiently/effectively
__2__ c. Applying technical knowledge appropriately
__*3__ d. Generating new ideas or suggestions
__2__ e. Making timely decisions
__2__ f. Foreseeing and solving problems
__1__ g. Providing quality customer service
__2__ h. Planning, organizing, and delegating work
__3__ i. Properly operating and caring for equipment
__2__ j. Providing sound training and direction
__3__ k. Making sound judgments

__2__ l. Effectively communicating with others in written or verbal form
__2__ m. Consistently creating effective teamwork
__2__ n. Motivating and assisting other staff members
__*1__ o. Applying operating policies and procedures prescribed for the job
__2__ p. Meeting goals, objectives, and commitments
__2__ q. Following through on tasks, activities, and responsibilities
__3__ r. Observing safety requirements
__2__ s. Maintaining good attendance and punctuality
__2__ t. Managing oneself
____ u. _____

II. WHICH SKILLS DOES THE EMPLOYEE PERFORM WELL?

__✓__ a. Quantity of work
__✓__ b. Consistently using time efficiently/effectively
____ c. Applying technical knowledge appropriately
__✓__ d. Generating new ideas or suggestions
__✓__ e. Making timely decisions
__✓__ f. Foreseeing and solving problems
____ g. Providing quality customer service
____ h. Planning, organizing, and delegating work
____ i. Properly operating and caring for equipment
____ j. Providing sound training and direction
____ k. Making sound judgments

____ l. Effectively communicating with others in written or verbal form
____ m. Consistently creating effective teamwork
____ n. Motivating and assisting other staff members
____ o. Applying operating policies and procedures prescribed for the job
____ p. Meeting goals, objectives, and commitments
____ q. Following through on tasks, activities, and responsibilities
____ r. Observing safety requirements
____ s. Maintaining good attendance and punctuality
____ t. Managing oneself
____ u. _____

* Compare to Jim's form

Pre-Review
Jim's Form

Please Print

Organization: N/A

Employee's Name: Rudy

Reviewer's Name: Jim

Today's Date: 5/1/01

Employee's Job Title: VP Manufacturing

Follow-Up Date: 8/1/01

I. WHAT SKILLS ARE MOST IMPORTANT TO THIS JOB?

__2__ a. Quantity of work

__2__ b. Consistently using time efficiently/effectively

__2__ c. Applying technical knowledge appropriately

__*1__ d. Generating new ideas or suggestions

__2__ e. Making timely decisions

__2__ f. Foreseeing and solving problems

__3__ g. Providing quality customer service

__3__ h. Planning, organizing, and delegating work

__2__ i. Properly operating and caring for equipment

__2__ j. Providing sound training and direction

__2__ k. Making sound judgments

__2__ l. Effectively communicating with others in written or verbal form

__2__ m. Consistently creating effective teamwork

__2__ n. Motivating and assisting other staff members

__*3__ o. Applying operating policies and procedures prescribed for the job

__3__ p. Meeting goals, objectives, and commitments

__2__ q. Following through on tasks, activities, and responsibilities

__2__ r. Observing safety requirements

__2__ s. Maintaining good attendance and punctuality

__3__ t. Managing oneself

____ u. _____

II. WHICH SKILLS DOES THE EMPLOYEE PERFORM WELL?

____ a. Quantity of work

____ b. Consistently using time efficiently/effectively

____ c. Applying technical knowledge appropriately

__✓__ d. Generating new ideas or suggestions

____ e. Making timely decisions

__✓__ f. Foreseeing and solving problems

____ g. Providing quality customer service

____ h. Planning, organizing, and delegating work

____ i. Properly operating and caring for equipment

____ j. Providing sound training and direction

____ k. Making sound judgments

__✓__ l. Effectively communicating with others in written or verbal form

____ m. Consistently creating effective teamwork

____ n. Motivating and assisting other staff members

____ o. Applying operating policies and procedures prescribed for the job

__✓__ p. Meeting goals, objectives, and commitments

____ q. Following through on tasks, activities, and responsibilities

____ r. Observing safety requirements

____ s. Maintaining good attendance and punctuality

____ t. Managing oneself

____ u. _____

* Compare to Rudy's form

Step 1. Pre-Review Part I—What Skills Are Most Important to This Job?

On this form listing a range of job-related skills, both the reviewer and the employee assign a 1, 2, or 3 to each skill, based on how important that skill is to the employee's job. There is a limit of five 3's. No limit on 1's and 2's.

Skills most important to the employee's job will be discussed in the review. In this chapter is a "Pre-Review" form listing various job skills. It is completed by both employee and reviewer separately before the review meeting. At the review meeting, both will discuss the relative importance of each skill to the job. The employee is not discussed at this point, just the job.

It is crucial that each person sees how the other views the job. Very often, low morale develops when an employee spends all his or her energy on developing skill X, and then at promotion time an employee performing skill Y gets the promotion. With the Professional Growth Plan, both the supervisor and the employee rate priorities and define important job activities. It's a win-win situation.

Step 2. Pre-Review Part II—Which Skills Does the Employee Perform Well?

Discuss the job tasks that the employee performs best. In this step, the pre-review form offers the same list of job-related skills as in Step 1. Again, before the meeting both parties have separately checked five areas in which each feels the employee is strong. From "a" to "t" will be five check marks (✓). In the Professional Growth Plan forms and meeting there is no discussion of the employee's weaknesses. You may think it's Pollyanna-ish to tell people their strengths but not their weakness, and that it's unrealistic. Remember—our aim is to transform jobs into careers and to increase productivity, not to judge and criticize. We usually criticize based on what behaviors in others expose our own negative patterns. Thus criticism is of little or no value.

In our Xerox Learning Systems survey of 25,000 employees, they were asked what motivated them to do a good job. The overwhelming majority said, "Recognition." If recognition is built firmly into the review, success will occur. Recognition is the main function of Step 2. Further, the employee's weaknesses are handled in Step 3—goal setting. In Step 3 corrective action is taken by converting all complaints into requests.

Step 3. Identify Your Number One Request

This is the heart of your creative entrepreneurial opportunity. Before the Professional Growth Plan meeting, the supervisor and the employee separately perform essentially similar tasks. They each fill out the Pre-Review form and a Funnel sheet. The Funnel and Alignment process has been shown throughout this book, but in the PGP process, the Funnel is placed on the back of the Pre-Review form.

Next, each prepares to tell the other what he or she could do to contribute to his or her career. If asked point-blank "What do you want?" an employee might say something vague like he or she wants "more communication." But in preparing ahead for the PGP meeting and using the Funnel questioning process, the employee's request becomes much more specific. For example:

The number one thing I need from my supervisor to make me more productive is: Meet with me every Wednesday, 11:00–11:15, to give me feedback on certain tasks I perform, particularly scheduling, cost estimates, and inventory.

How achieved? Using verbs to introduce each of the three:(a) **Tell** me how I am doing on scheduling, (b) **Show** me how close I am on cost estimates, and (c) **Inform** me if I am saving any money with our new inventory control process.

What would be different? I would be well under budget, and missed deadlines would decrease by approximately 25 percent. For the Eight Most Common Requests employees make of their supervisors, see Appendix B.

In a separate office, a reviewer also prepared Steps 1, 2, and 3 in advance. One reviewer request was:

The number one thing I want from you that will help us reach our profit goal is: Write up a daily schedule and plan every afternoon for the next day.

How achieved? Using a verb (a) **Include** the priorities for the day, (b) **Decide** who works which machine, and (c) **Estimate** time on each machine and allow some down time.

What would be different? We'd get production started at 7:00 A.M. each day instead of 8:00 A.M., and 90 percent of deadlines would be met. For some examples of what managers have wanted from employees, see Appendix A. By now both parties have filled out Step 1, Step 2, and Step 3 (Funnel) in preparation for their Performance Review meeting.

Step 4. Alignment Meeting

In the Alignment meeting, the Pre-Review forms of the two parties are compared. Discrepancies are acknowledged but not changed. To establish dignity (weigh the pros and cons), the reviewer is to consider and acknowledge the employee's view of the priorities of their job, even if different. The employee does not change his or her form to match that of the Reviewer.

Next, the employee tells the reviewer what's on his Funnel and if accepted, the reviewer writes it down in detail and signs it. Then the reverse—the reviewer tells employee his or her number one request. The employee writes it down and signs. The Alignment form goes into the pending file of the PGP auditor for follow-up within ninety days.

Pre-Alignment Funnel

Your Name: Today's Date:

What is the Number One Thing the Other Person Can Do to Contribute to Your Career?

GOAL:
Stated in a positive way, the number one item I want from _____ is:

1.

SPECIFICALLY:
- What will this person do to meet your request?

- Use a verb to begin each of the three short descriptive sentences.

2a.

2b.

2c.

SPECIFICALLY:
- How will you know the request has been fulfilled?

- What will be different?

- How will the change be measured?

3.

Alignment Agreement

Please Print

Organization: _____   Today's Date: _____

Employee's Name: _____   Employee's Job Title: _____

Reviewer's Name: _____   Follow-Up Date: _____

INSTRUCTIONS: Before writing, Reviewer first hears the Employee's complete request, then it is discussed and agreed upon by both. Reviewer then clearly and concisely prints the Employee's request in full, and signs in agreement. Employee then hears the Reviewer's complete request, they come to agreement, Employee prints the request, and signs the form.

EMPLOYEE'S REQUEST (PRINTED BY REVIEWER)

1. The #1 item _____ wants from _____ is:
          Employee's Name   *Reviewer's Name*
   _____
   _____

2. Specifically what will the Reviewer do to meet your request?
   A. _____
   B. _____
   C. _____

3. How will you know the request has been fulfilled; how will you measure the change? _____
   _____

I agree to begin on _____ Signed _____
            Date   *Reviewer's Signature*

REVIEWER'S REQUEST (PRINTED BY THE EMPLOYEE)

1. The #1 item _____ wants from _____ is:
          Reviewer's Name   *Employee's Name*
   _____
   _____

2. Specifically what will the Employee do to meet your request?
   A. _____
   B. _____
   C. _____

3. How will you know the request has been fulfilled; how will you measure the change? _____
   _____

I agree to begin on _____ Signed _____
            Date   *Employee's Signature*

Alignment between the employee's responsibility to contribute to the strategic plan and the employee's specific career request is very different from the mutual goal-setting concept of the 1980s. Mutual goal setting was used to get employees to buy in to corporate goals, i.e., to have employees help establish their own work goals. While for some employees the corporate goal may indeed be top priority, 95 percent of employee requests come from their own personal career needs (recognition, challenge, security, etc.). These needs are the employee's truths about what must happen in order for him or her to be genuinely interested and focused on company goals. The lie is to pretend that every employee cares only about profit and productivity. The truth is that if employees get their career growth needs met, they are much more conscious of and committed to their company's financial goals and objectives.

Our research has shown that most employees prefer to have executives and owners establish corporate goals. They are the ones who have an overview of the market, the economy, and the competition. The employee usually welcomes a strategic plan, especially one that comes from a value-based mission statement.

In mutual goal setting of the 1980s and 1990s, the strategic plan was often changed by the time everyone contributed. There remained hardly any resemblance to the original goal, which may have been, for example, 10 percent net profit after taxes. The owner and the executives have a legitimate right and obligation to set the goal. The productive and effective place for employees and supervisors to have input is to tell what they need in order to accomplish their part of the already set strategic plan.

The Professional Growth Plan in Step 4 first compares the employee and reviewer priorities written in Step 1 and the strengths they each checked in Step 2. After comparing 1 and 2, they go to their Funnels. The Funnels are intended to align manager and employee vis-à-vis their goals. Step 4 is the result of the two merged Funnels and the Alignment Agreement form. Either Appendix L or X may be used for this. If it's new, try Appendix L for careful steps. When you become familiar with the process, go right to Appendix X, Alignment Follow-up, so you are ready to follow up within ninety days. Both Appendices L and X represent a combination of what both parties want in order to achieve the profit goals.

The employee always goes first; therefore, item 1 on the Alignment Agreement represents an employee request. If the supervisor agrees, they write the employee's request on the Alignment Agreement. Employee items are likely to be quite different from employer requests and can usually be categorized as respect, recognition, or freedom, although those three words are rarely used. In our research and consulting since 1979, we have gone over thousands of employee requests. Ninety-five percent of the time, employees ask for recognition, respect, or freedom, in their own terms, in exchange for carrying out the corporate goal. By being asked to make an individual request on his or her own and by having it heard, written, and responded to by his or her supervisor, the employee is touched in the way Naisbit calls for in his 1999 book, *High Tech High Touch*.

Item 2 on the Alignment Agreement is the Reviewer's number one request. Supervisors almost always request more, better, or faster. Reviewer requests are very different from employee requests. Thus, the Alignment sheet is aligning what the employee wants with what the supervisor wants from him or her. It is an illusion to pretend that employee and reviewer would have a truly mutual goal. In the early Management by Objectives programs the supervisor's request is agreed to by the employee, thus the term "mutual." This does not touch the employee and does not guarantee buy-in.

So, alignment in the Professional Growth Plan combines and lines up the separate and unique requests of employee (Goal 1), then the reviewer (Goal 2). The reviewer's requests relate to their responsibility to meet the corporate goal. Employees' requests inform management of their individual career or motivational needs. This eliminates the need for management to have to figure out how to motivate employees. The employees will tell you themselves, but only if they have the opportunity to be guided through the Funnel process to very clearly and thoroughly let the supervisor know exactly how to fulfill their requests so that they truly feel touched and acknowledged.

Once the meeting has occurred between employee and reviewer and the Alignment Agreement Follow-up form is complete, the agreement (one page) is given to the auditor or whoever is documenting the follow-up dates. Both parties are E-mailed or faxed or handed an Alignment Follow-up form (Appendix Y) and asked to fill in their scores. The employee fills in scores in eight boxes in the left column, the Reviewer in the right (Appendix Z). The auditor merges scores and returns them to both. If there is a gap of twenty points or more, the low scorer writes in the reason for the gap (see Appendix Z).

The next step varies, based on the manager. Some managers document and chart scores to record trends; others let the Employee and the Reviewer deal with the result. But in most cases the Reviewer and the Employee either make a new number one request or agree to continue with the original.

The Professional Growth Plan begins with a healthy corporate mission and financial goals. The executive staff identifies and aligns their requests with company goals. Then it is used by every manager, supervisor, and employee in the organization.

The PGP is an anti-entropy, productive, two-way communication process, which is used to take the company's mission, goals, and objectives and tie them to each individual in the company. Simultaneous to spreading the profit goals, it diffuses employees' sabotaging behaviors and offers employees a chance to be their own creative entrepreneurial opportunist.

The Professional Growth Plan provides the following:

1. Identifies at least one career-enhancing request of each employee

2. Clarifies and simplifies the most important contribution the employee can make

3. Opens the minds of employee and reviewer, even if only for a brief time

4. Shifts criticism into productive requests

5. Creates a meeting of the minds between boss and employee

6. Ensures contribution by tying employees' activities to the profit-oriented objectives of their managers

7. Creates productive dialogue and often synergy

8. Eliminates many opportunities for sabotage

9. Quantifies self-analysis by the follow-up to the aligned goals every ninety days

10. Rewards those who kept their agreements, corrects those who didn't

11. Creates data for a monthly corporate culture report by listing all the employees' number one requests and all the follow-up scores

12. Encourages both parties to speak their truth

13. Liberates both boss and employee to be creative entrepreneurial opportunists

14. Replaces an outdated performance review system

15. Converts to more numerical ranking, if needed, to determine salary percent

16. Institutionalizes self-analysis and continued improvement

Enacting the PGP

One human resources mid-manager—we'll call her Nita—at a high-tech manufacturing company, conscious of the importance of performance reviews but generally reluctant to be confrontive, adopted the Professional Growth

Plan for her workgroup. She hired my former associate, Bill Gittins, to assist her. Bill is now Director of Human Resources for London's Marconi plc, a global communications giant. Yet he still recalls like it was yesterday the details of facilitating the PGP at Jim's company six years earlier. Details are in his 1995 *Plant Services* article.

Bill suggested that Nita involve top management in the new review process. Nita then asked two of the executives if they would agree to an experimental practice review between the two—Jim (the president and owner) and Rudy (the vice president of manufacturing). With a slightly patronizing tone they agreed. Jim said, "We've worked together for twelve years and know each other's job and personality as well as our own. But we'll go through the steps to help you out."

Separately using the Pre-Review form before their meeting, Jim marked item *o* on "applying procedures" as a 3 (most important) for Rudy's VP manufacturing job. Rudy marked item *o* as a 1 (least important) to his job. Meanwhile, Rudy marked item *d* "generating new ideas or suggestions" with a 3 (most important) for VP manufacturing and Jim gave item *d* a 1 (least important) for the VP manufacturing position.

Next, in Step 2, each separately checked the five things they thought Rudy did best. Then, they each prepared in the Funnel their number one request of the other. Jim's request was "apply job-costing procedures." Rudy's number one request of Jim was "go through the chain of command—let me make ideas and suggestions for my employees." Now they were ready to meet.

During their review meeting, Nita and Bill asked them to place the two review forms side by side. They were startled to discover the gaps in what they each thought was most important skills for the VP manufacturing position. Rudy was surprised in Step 1 to see the gap where his boss ranked "applying procedures" (item *o*) high and Rudy marked it low. But in the meeting Jim was able to tell Rudy how consistent and accurate job-costing procedures directly affected labor and inventory as well as ISO 9002 Certification. Rudy just hadn't seen the particular job-costing form as important even though Jim had mentioned it before. The gap got Rudy's attention.

Jim was taken back to see the gap in item *d*, "generating new ideas and suggestions." Jim liked MBWA (management by walking around), and enjoyed troubleshooting and giving suggestions himself, so he didn't need Rudy to do it. But in the performance review meeting, Rudy was able to tell Jim that giving suggestions directly to his employees in the plant interfered with Rudy's authority and made his job difficult. For twelve years, Jim thought this was helping Rudy.

In the Funnel part of the Professional Growth Plan, Rudy's number one request was for Jim to "follow the chain of command" (delegate), and Jim's request of Rudy was to apply the job-costing procedures every day. Both agreed, filled out an Alignment form and a Follow-up form. Rudy's new stock options were to be determined by how many days he turned in a complete and accurate job-costing sheet to Jim. Jim's board would increase his stock options based on Rudy's scores of how Jim did on Rudy's number one request to "delegate day-to-day problem-solving decisions and ideas to Rudy."

The PGP process was then used as the performance review system for assembly-line employees and their managers. Stock options were awarded in place of salary increases for employees who scored 80 percent or higher on the follow-up. At the time, stock options didn't mean much, but having the PGP in place kept bosses and employees communicating about the right subjects in the right way.

The careers of this employee group, as well as those of Nita, Jim, and Rudy, were built slowly and professionally over the next few years. By 2000, theirs was another high-tech company that made millionaires out of hundreds of employees from the stock options they had been given back in 1995. Fortunately, there was a way to monetarily reward those who contributed in the most efficient manner, those who converted put-downs to requests, and those who kept agreements. These careers were not just meaningful, they were lucrative.

This Professional Growth Plan has successfully replaced the old performance appraisal in hundreds of companies throughout the United States. What is new is the discovery of how closely linked the PGP is to the Three Rules; thus it becomes the most effective way to integrate a Three Rules culture into normal business routines.

Worst Case

Let's say that the Three Rules got a bad reputation in your workgroup. This happened with many Total Quality Management programs in the early nineties. Someone before you tried to force TQM on everyone, got righteous and dictatorial, and eliminated any chance for success. Let's say this happened with the rules. No problem. You never have to even mention the Three Rules as such. Just use the Professional Growth Plan (PGP) in place for or in addition to your performance review system. The PGP guides boss and employee to clarify contribution, has no place for put-downs, builds on strengths, and documents whether agreements are kept. The use of this tool ties in with all the rules, flushes out sabotage, and rewards employees who contribute. When you use the PGP with your boss, you can request the number one thing from your boss that will best enhance your career. This is a creative entrepreneurial opportunity to map out a career for yourself. The PGP performance review will balance the energy and the entropy of the workplace for you.

Tailoring the Rules for You

Recently I was giving a speech about contribution, converting putdowns, keeping agreements, and the Professional Growth Plan. One attendee who had been nodding off on occasion raised his hand immediately at the end. Since I was very aware that he had been nodding off, I noticed when he volunteered, so I called on him. He was delightfully candid in spite of having a few coworkers and one manager in the room.

"I get exhausted thinking I have to have all this energy and work so hard, never get pissed off, keep all my agreements, and fill in all these forms. It's too much. What about simple things like just repairing shoes?"

I offered some oversimplified answer like, "Then in the simple life, if it's shoe repair—even if you go at a snail's pace—just make sure you do the most important thing first. Like, fix the shoe on time before dusting the shop."

Because the PGP and the Three Rules are so carefully documented, with step-by-step instructions, even the most antisocial accountants or engineers have made great strides with people and even achieved synergy. You can also achieve financial rewards by following the instructions on how to communicate with coworkers, just like Jim and Rudy.

Thus, the wide diversity in contribution is not just about gender and race; it is about style, energy, and personality. Both the procrastination of the turtle and the chaos created by the hummingbird can be sabotaging if they are not aligned with one another and with the objectives and mission of the workgroup.

Discovering and building on your strengths to reach your goals, is the challenge of the twenty-first-century manager, according to Peter Drucker. Resentment, contempt, and exhaustion usually are created when we are neither building on our strengths nor moving toward our personal mission. Think back to José, the shipper at the winery. His personal mission was a sense of daily accomplishment at work. Here he contributed much more when his focus was in line with the winery's focus—100 percent accuracy on labels. It didn't require any more energy—just a slightly different focus. His new focus reversed his entropy and transformed his job into a career.

Tailor the rules and tools to your own pace. "Emotional intelligence is the ability to sense, understand and effectively apply the power and acumen of emotions as a key source of human energy."[6] Successful application simultaneously reduces entropy and sabotage and creates synergy, inner peace, and profitability.

15

Second Opinion:
A Tool for Inner Wisdom

There is something within you that knows much more than you know.

—CAROL GOMAN, *Creativity in Business*

What lies before us and what lies behind us are small matters compared to what lies within us. And when we bring what is within out into the world, miracles happen.

—HENRY DAVID THOREAU

THE twentieth century left many people in mental and emotional turmoil in the workplace. According to the American Institute of Stress, the cost of stress-related problems as of 2000 is more than $200 billion.[1] Headlines are filled with articles about increasing incivility, rudeness, and hostility in the workplace. Mid-managers are called upon to respond more quickly and effectively to increasing outside criticism and decreasing outside guidance. New tools are being used by successful managers to lead their workgroups and their own careers out of the chaos. We can be our own most trusted inner adviser if we use a technique I call Second Opinion to lead our careers.

While "empowerment" is a worn-out word, self-empowerment is fresh and fits the new century. The Second Opinion (Inner Solution) tool yields immediate success and genuine self-empowerment. After the Three Rules are in place, employees and managers alike have the sense of security that allows them to explore the Second Opinion exercise. With fears allayed, openness to new ideas can be pushed to the forefront.

"Second opinion" in the medical field refers to getting another viewpoint from a second doctor as to whether the diagnosis from the first doctor is the best one for you. The same is also true within us. A viewpoint from our "upset side" or blind spot isn't going to contribute much and may cause harm. Since we can't always identify our mentally unstable or unconscious state, using Second Opinion can move us toward a healthier perspective.

There appears to be an inner wisdom in managers that comes from somewhere, otherwise they would not be managers. By tapping that wisdom and calling upon themselves, managers have been able to experience incredible personal mastery and financial success. This self-empowering, consistently successful tool for managers has been used hundreds of times.

The Second Opinion concept can sometimes take on a spiritual quality, even though spirituality is not always a comfortable topic in business circles. Sir John Templeton, the financial guru and founder of the famous Templeton Fund, wrote several books, one called *The Humble Approach*. In it he says, "I attribute a large part of my own formula for success to the power of prayer in my daily life. In fact, I began all my shareholders' meetings asking God to use us as a clear channel for his wisdom and love."[2] He continues to receive international and financial rewards. His humble approach is worth consideration.

Years ago, when faced with a financial business dilemma beyond my current state of mind to solve, I took the opportunity to call Mr. Templeton at his office in Nassau. To my surprise, Sir John answered the phone himself. I shared the situation with him and his response was, "Get a full professional financial audit. Then when you go to bed that night, ask God over and over what to do. In the morning you will have your answer." I did, and I was given an answer that contributed far more than my nervous thinking.

Recently I had a chance to ask Sir John how people can tell if the answer from their inner Second Opinion is really their higher self or just ego. He said that asking again and again will give you better odds at receiving a response and the answer of the higher self "will give you a peaceful feeling because you will know it is right."[3]

I have also asked four other spiritual leaders the same question. "How do you know if the answer from the Second Opinion is really our higher self and not our ego or lower self?"

- "If the answer gives you a peaceful feeling, it was God's viewpoint. If it creates anxiety or tension, it was your ego answering."[4]
  —Father Joseph Otté, Catholic priest

- "I can tell from the consequences. If they are unhappy, I know God is saying to change direction. If the consequences are joyous, God is saying, 'Frank, you're right on track.'"[5]
  —Reverend Frank Kimper, Methodist minister and Course in Miracles instructor

- "You never really know for sure, and that's what gives us humility."[6]
  —Marianne Williamson, author of *The Healing of the Soul of America, 1997*

- "When you have God's [Second Opinion] answer, you stop whatever you are thinking of doing. It has awe."
  —Neale Donald Walsch, author of *Friendship with God*, in Denver, Colorado, 1998[7]

In a 1908 book by John D. Rockefeller, the reader can tell he used a similar process to the Second Opinion, but he called it his "inner-advisor."

> To our great surprise, business came in upon us so fast we hardly knew how to take care of it . . . Then and indeed for many years after, it seemed as though there was no end to the money needed to carry on and develop the business. As successes came, I seldom put my head upon the pillow at night without speaking a few words to myself from this wise inner advisor . . .
>
> "Now a little success . . . Look out, or you will lose your head—go steady."
>
> These intimate conversations with myself I'm sure had a great influence on my life.[8]

The Second Opinion tool works in conjunction with all of the Three Rules. We multiply our contribution many times over when we allow the Second Opinion to contribute to us and then to the rest of the organization. The Second Opinion also keeps us focused on our best self so we are not as likely to revert to put-downs of others or ourselves. Finally, when we keep our agreements to listen to our inner guide, as did Rockefeller, we are deeply empowered to lead our career and those of others toward success. Both of these powerful financial magnates, Rockefeller and Templeton, nearly a century apart, agreed on the humble approach—humble because one listened, powerful because one acted on the higher guidance.

Graced by hundreds of clients who have used this tool, I have discovered that this inner side of ourselves yields valuable insights into our habits and behaviors and can be a wise resource for solving our daily dilemmas. This exercise is intended to broaden one's source of information and enhance decision-making ability and capacity. I have known people to make very wise financial decisions through Second Opinion consultations that otherwise may have been missed. And don't forget, the Second Opinion can move us to a more mentally healthy viewpoint even when we are overtaken by our negative emotions.

Many people have strong spiritual dialogue through religious practices or other similar disciplines. If this is true for you, you may not need the Second Opinion exercise.

How to Get Your Second Opinion

In order to conduct a Second Opinion exercise, it is important to follow each step. First, picture that you are about to meet a very wise person who has watched you and loved you every second of your life. Visualize that this wise person is your biggest advocate and fan and wants you to succeed and be happy. Write out five questions you would ask this wise person. Make sure the questions are open-ended (not simply yes or no) and are career-related. For example:

1. Why am I so upset?

2. What do I need to be aware of?

3. What question should I ask?

4. What is my blind spot?

5. How should I contribute?

Do not judge whether the "wise person" is familiar with the subjects of the questions. Just write five pure questions you would like to have answered.

Leave space under each question for a written answer.

1. _____
   _____
   _____
   _____
   _____

2. _____
   _____
   _____
   _____
   _____

3. _____
   _____
   _____
   _____

4. _____
   _____
   _____
   _____
   _____

5. _____
   _____
   _____
   _____
   _____

- Ask yourself who the first person was in your life that you felt cared for you and wanted you to have your life's desires. This person could be a parent, a grandparent, an aunt/uncle, teacher, priest, minister, coach, brother, or sister. Preferably someone who is no longer around.

- Select the one who had the most positive, supportive influence—the one with whom you no longer have personal contact, either because of distance or perhaps even death. Close your eyes as you consider your choice.

- Next to the name you have chosen, write the familiar name you called that person (your grandmother's name is Helen and you called her "Mimi"). This will become your Second Opinion person for now.

Note: If the moving back and forth between open and closed eyes is a problem, ask another person to read you the questions and write down your answers.

- Get into the role of your Second Opinion person. In a moment you will close your eyes again and act as though you are in his or her shoes, wearing his or her clothes, in his or her skin. Act as if you are in a play and your role is to be that person. Breathe as he or she would breathe; take on that person's posture, mannerisms, and facial expressions. Stay present with your eyes closed. In your new role, describe yourself in at least ten ways. For example.
  - I am 5'10".
  - I weigh 135 pounds.
  - I have brown hair.
  - I spend a lot of time in the garden.
  - I laugh a lot.

- I like to wear blue clothes.
- I have freckles all over.
- I have on a blue hat.
- I love my students.
- I am mechanically inclined.

Address the question to the Second Opinion person by using their "familiar" name ("Mimi"). **"Mimi, what do you think/feel about Susan?"** In your role as Second Opinion, write the answer on your sheet of paper. For example:

"Susan's a free spirit; she has a sharp mind; I love her; she was always my favorite.

She is   A. Creative

          B. Responsive

          C. Logical

          D. Compassionate"

"Mimi, would you be willing to answer some questions that Susan has today?"

If yes, proceed. If no, ask when would be a better time. It is important that the initial steps be done exactly according to the directions. The first steps create the quality that this tool will provide in the future. Here's how it works.

- Look at the five previously written questions.

- Close your eyes for one minute; pay attention only to your breathing.

- Breathe in through your nose and out through your mouth.

Open your eyes just long enough to read the first question, then close your eyes as you repeat the question silently. Answer the question in your Second Opinion role. Do not labor over the answer, but accept the first thing that comes without discarding any information. Open your eyes and write down the answer that came to you.

Continue to feel the role of your Second Opinion person. Breathe into the feelings and thoughts that this person had for you. Now look at the second question, and close your eyes and wait for a natural response from your Second Opinion. Write down the answer. Then continue the same process for the remaining questions.

Review the answers and observe your emotional responses. Do you feel anxious or peaceful? If you feel anxious, this may not be the best tool for you. If you feel peaceful, get a photograph of your Second Opinion person and keep it near you. Be comforted knowing you can call upon your Second Opinion in tight spots along your career leadership journey.

Below are two case studies that illustrate the unique and detailed use of the Second Opinion in the workplace.

TERRY—DIRECTOR OF HOUSING (REVISITED)
A DEEP, CARING MAN WHO DESPERATELY WANTED TO INTEGRATE HIS LIFE AND HIS LIVELIHOOD

> **Happiness is that state of consciousness which proceeds from the achievement of one's values.**
>
> —DALAI LAMA

Terry was a manager in a public university who claimed he had no joy in his work. He still felt that his work and who he was as a person were separate. When we started our session, we restated the seven steps he had created out of the personal mission statement exercise two weeks before.

Mission: To integrate my true self with my work and have joy in my work.

Objective: A. Expose my thoughts to others.

B. Initiate contact with staff; don't always react.

C. Do things I enjoy: take walks, read, etc.

D. Observe the difference between enabling and empowering.

E. Create a budget in a positive manner.

F. Observe behaviors of others who are sabotaging.

G. Develop a daily spiritual dialogue.

For the next few weeks he deliberately attempted the integration of his work and his true self on the job. The first thing was to find a higher level of truth in his interaction with people. (This related to items A, B, D, and F of his mission.)

In his job as student housing director, he was required to make decisions that were frequently emotionally charged. Deep in his heart, he often knew the best solution, but he sometimes withheld his opinion. He told himself he didn't want to upset people. He would often wait and not reveal the answer for a long time, rationalizing that it would be better for them to wait. As we worked together, Terry discovered the true reason for his hesitation to provide the answers. It was not so much to alleviate others' upset, but more so that his own discomfort would diminish. He reasoned that it was all in the name of being a nice guy, but in reality he was trying to protect himself from the personal discomfort. But "comfort is killing me," he murmured.

For the next few weeks he worked from his seven objectives list. He had specific goals to achieve. He needed to reorganize his department, which he had hesitated doing because "so-and-so" might get upset. The next week he saw this protective behavior as codependency and enabling. This insight gave him the courage to stop tiptoeing around his people and, instead, help them to reorganize.

At the beginning of each week's meeting, Terry wanted us to close our eyes and ask a higher power to guide and direct us. At the same time, it was difficult for him to relate to God as the higher power because as a young boy he was taught that God sometimes punished people who were bad. It was very difficult for him to be open and ask for help from a God who might punish or hurt him. Intimidated by God, Terry decided that the way he could bring spirituality to his job was to find some outside source that did have a positive influence on him.

I would like to stress again that I have rarely found anybody in any management position who didn't have someone who empowered and encouraged them. So, I asked Terry, "Who in your life empowered you to be a manager? To be what you are? To go to college? To be a dad? To do all the things that you are doing?" Well, Terry thought about it and replied, "Oh, yes, my basketball coach. Yes, my coach, Len."

Terry had a lot of distress that day and was searching diligently for answers. He wanted answers to his questions—a "right now" resolution to his dilemma. The Second Opinion exercise seemed right, so he was willing to give it a try. If he could ask an all-knowing guru, what would he want answered? He came up with the following five questions:

1. How do you know if something is an opportunity or a trap?

2. Do I need to get into an honest exchange with George? (a coworker)

3. How should I respond to Sue? (a difficult employee)

4. How can I maintain enthusiastic, genuine energy?

5. Why do I repeatedly censor myself and hold myself back?

To assist in the role for the Second Opinion exercise, Terry moved into another chair that was to represent Len. Then Terry closed his eyes and pretended he was Len. I asked him what it was like to be Len. He said, "Oh, well, if I were Len . . . I am about six foot. I have three children. I am a real family man. I have a little bit of a stomach. I'm a real friendly guy, and I teach history."

"Good," I said. "I have some questions to ask you. Will you answer these questions?"

"Sure," he commented, now adopting the character of Len, eager instead of hesitant and fearful. Then Terry and I began to role-play.

One at a time, I repeated the five questions to Terry and recorded his answers. This is how he answered:

1. "Len, how do you know if something is an opportunity or a trap?" I asked, in the role of Terry.

   "If it's 'win-win' it's an opportunity. If it's 'lose-lose' it's a trap. If you win, it's okay too. You are not a loser and don't deserve to lose." Terry answered, as through the eyes of Len.

2. "Len, do I need to get into an honest exchange with George?" I asked.

   "As soon as you first see evidence that George wants you to both win. Otherwise, don't play. Terry, you have an overdeveloped sense of responsibility. If George won't respond, it's just too bad. Let it go!"

3. "Len, how should I respond to Sue?" I asked again as Terry stayed in the role of Len.

   "Same as with George. Start small and see if it is reciprocated. Then go further. Do the 'win-win' test. Don't make big commitments without successive responses. Like coaching, use a game plan. When a player doesn't play, try a new player."

4. "Len, how can I maintain enthusiastic, genuine energy?"

   "Be realistic on the goals. See the progress the players make, even if you aren't winning. Come up with an operational definition of success at each level. When it is met, acknowledge it. This is how to tell who's on the team: those who practice every day whether they want to or not. Those who ask how they can make a difference, do. Those who don't, often act out of entitlement."

5. "Len, why do I censor myself over and over and hold myself back?"

"Like Moses, you are afraid of your power. You keep testing your truth by the reactions of others, and that invalidates you. Keep your eyes on me, Len."

I asked if there was anything else Len wanted to communicate to Terry. He had a few other comments and brought closure. Then we counted slowly from three to one and Terry, no longer in the role of Len, moved back to the other chair. He had adopted Len as his spiritual partner. Spiritual dialogue (Goal 7 in his personal mission) was now on track.

Terry looked ten years younger. He said he was so moved to feel connected with Len and to know he could tap into that dialogue at any time. His eyes glistened. He now seemed at peace before returning to what had been a previously stressful working environment.

His concern the next week was about his department's budget. His people were fighting with each other; they all wanted a bigger piece of the pie. They were jealous of each other and accused him of favoring one over another. The date to turn in the budget was fast approaching. What Terry wanted to do was set the budget himself and move on. He wasn't looking for input from the fighting employees. At some level the employees didn't want to provide input either. Most weren't versed on budget issues and were used to Terry accepting full responsibility for the budget anyway. What they wanted was to make sure nobody else was getting a better deal.

Their "empire-building" territorial conflicts didn't contribute and were filled with put-downs. Their attitudes "sucked from the space"! Thus, the first order of business for Terry was to have a staff meeting and institute the Three Rules. The employees grumbled at first, but soon agreed when they realized that Terry was serious. It was rare that he made requests of them, so they stopped their bickering and decided to welcome his leadership.

The next week we went back to the dialogue between Len and Terry. What Terry had discovered from playing the role of Len was to handle the budget the way that Len coached basketball—by expanding his thinking. Instead of a one-year budget, Len helped expand Terry's thinking, and Terry soon decided to communicate his five-year budget plan to the staff.

Terry said he felt empowered when he met with his staff to discuss the budget. "Let's think about where we want to be in five years." Terry told the staff. With guidance from Len, plus a team following the Three Rules, Terry was actually able to get them excited about the budget, just like Len had encouraged the basketball team before the big game. Suddenly the one-year budget was no big deal. People weren't fighting over it anymore; it was just one-fifth of the whole picture. More importantly, overall synergy had occurred and promised to grow and continue throughout other team endeavors.

Terry not only found a peaceful way of establishing the budget for one year, but he also created enthusiasm for his five-year budget plan and a renewed synergy in the office. Every step of the way, when Terry had meetings or filled out forms, if he was stuck he would seek Len's advice, asking, "What would Coach Len do?" Terry was starting to integrate a deeper part of his life into his work.

As Terry continued, so did his new discoveries. At that point I asked, "How did you feel about that budget process?"

Something moved. There was a little quiver in his shoulder as he said, "Well, it was nice."

"What's that twitch in your shoulders?" I asked. "You just reacted in your shoulders."

"I'm not sure," he replied with a question in his voice.

I decided to give him a Feelings Chart that listed a wide range of feelings. I said, "What's the most likely feeling that you just had in your shoulders?"

He went over the chart and gasped a bit. Then he said, "Joy. I guess that was joy."

"What is it that you did with the joy?" I asked.

"Well, I don't know; I didn't know it was joy."

I discovered with Terry, as with many other people, that it is often difficult for them to recognize joy.

Terry was surprised, saying, "I thought joy was more intense, louder, more active." But he began to discover new qualities of joy, the deep sort of inner joy that comes when you are in close communications with your Second Opinion. His joy came as a surprise, but it was peaceful and gentle—it stopped in his shoulders. In fact, after having identified his true feelings of joy, Terry wanted to quit blocking so much of the full emotional experience.

We were about three months into our weekly sessions before he started to consistently discover that fuller experience of his own personal joy. Our original goal of working together was to get results on his mission: integrate his real self with his work while experiencing more joy on the job. He was integrating his real self. Now it was important to discover what joy truly felt like. It was joy that he felt when he was in partnership with Coach Len getting his employees to go for a five-year goal instead of a one-year objective. "They got enthusiastic, and we were all enjoying greater success."

As the sessions went on, he had other goals to achieve. One was a conference he planned to attend, and his goal was to speak his truth. Every year he went to this conference, he would sit quietly and observe the glib people talking "to" or "at" instead of truly sharing "with" those attending, but this year Terry had a different goal. He wanted to contribute to the conference and share his truth. Sure enough, an opportunity came up, and he eagerly responded. At first a few people glared. But afterward, several people came up to him, touched his arm, and said, "I loved what you said. I really heard you and I agree."

As Terry dialogued with Len on a regular basis, the spirit of Len was integrating into Terry's daily life. For example, Terry was a perfectionist who believed his self-worth came from his "perfect" accomplishment of each task. Although it was out of character for Terry to be late, one day he showed up fifteen minutes after our scheduled meeting. It was his choice. He made a judgment call to stay in another meeting that he felt was important. As he was driving to our meeting, knowing that he was late, he began to mentally beat himself up for his deliberate decision to be late, heaping on the self-doubt and guilt. But, in that opening (sometimes it's in our errors that we grow), he connected with his true spiritual side. In the car he said out loud, "I am a partner with God, and he's the managing partner, and I feel his presence. It started as Len, but it's really God. I feel a partnership." He listened to his Second Opinion, and came to the liberating realization that it was okay to be late.

When he got to the meeting fifteen minutes late, I hardly even noticed the time. We had been working since fall, but today was a beautiful spring day, and Terry was wearing a shortsleeved shirt to accommodate the heat. We were sitting at the meeting, and he was sharing with me his feelings during the drive to my office. As he was telling the story, I noticed that his arms had goose bumps, on them and I asked, "What is that, Terry? What are you feeling in your arms?"

Looking down he said, "Oh, joy—that is joy!" It didn't get blocked at his shoulders anymore. He had truly accomplished his goal: to have joy in his work. In the car by himself, when he knew he was working with his spiritual partner, he had the confidence to choose comfort over doubt and guilt. His partnership had allowed him to make a wise decision and feel good about it. We talked about it several times in the session and every time he spoke of it, the hair stood up on his arms and the goose bumps appeared. For the second time, he had a physical way to recognize the joy. Even if emotionally he didn't feel it or mentally know it, his arms gave him the signal that he was experiencing joy.

What I learned from Terry was this: when we make ourselves a place where joy can show up—it shows up! And if we make ourselves a place where joy can show up, we are inspired to contribute from that deep place within. Leading from the joy within integrated Terry's life and his livelihood. A year after Terry had established a pattern of daily contact with his Second Opinion, a colleague sent me an article from a newspaper in the Pacific Northwest town where Terry was the director of housing. The headlines and lead story were about how the incredible increase in student housing standards had transformed this university to the level of an Ivy League college. As Terry transformed, so did an entire university.

GREG—A GENERAL MANAGER
A VIETNAM VETERAN WHO PROMISED HIS DECEASED AIR FORCE BUDDIES HE WOULD BE HAPPY IN LIFE IF HE MADE IT—BUT NOW HE COULDN'T KEEP HIS AGREEMENT

Greg was the manager of a security protection company. Every day of his life was about lists, tensions, goals, and meeting other people's needs. Greg felt that he'd never had a chance to think about who he was and what he wanted. He was fifty years old and had survived piloting a helicopter in Vietnam, so he had a real appreciation for being alive. He had seen a lot of his buddies die in Vietnam, and he felt a passionate need to enjoy life. As he was the only survivor of his pilot group, he felt he owed it to his buddies to at least enjoy life. It was a promise they had all made together—whoever lived would enjoy life for the rest who had helped to make that possible.

Since Greg was the only one spared, he felt a heightened reason to contribute and be happy, yet a nagging part of him—his dark side—was obsessed with procrastinating. Greg managed a branch office with the goal of receiving promotions in order to progress up through the normal ranks. Even though his life was about structure and completing the list, he was not meeting weekly goals and he experienced little joy.

When Greg signed up for consulting services, he asked, "Please help me create joy in my life and, at the same time, reach over 90 percent of my goals." After working with Greg for several weeks, we established short-term goals and objectives and together celebrated his success. We also assisted him in working through issues with his employees, yet something was missing— we failed to achieve the depth that was necessary for Greg to integrate his work with his life. Greg agreed to try the Second Opinion exercise in order to achieve more depth. First he listed five questions he would like answered. Next, we worked toward identifying a possible Second Opinion person for Greg.

"Who empowered you, Greg, to be where you are today? Something happened to make you think you could be a branch manager, a dad, a pilot, a husband, and all these things that you are." At first Greg said that a certain teacher had helped him, then he said his mom, but neither of them seemed to fit. Preferring one's Second Opinion to be on the other side, and knowing

Greg could always pick up the phone and ask for his mother's advice directly, we continued the search. Suddenly, Greg remembered his grandpa, whom he called Pawpaw.

I asked Greg if he had ever meditated. He said no, but he was willing to try the Second Opinion exercise. Greg closed his eyes for a second. Feeling uneasy, he quickly opened them to look around, but then closed them once more. I could tell he was struggling. However, we had had consistent, successful, professional experience over time with setting and meeting goals, so Greg decided not to give up now. Though he was clearly nervous, he finally managed to close his eyes and take the risk.

The first of his five questions was, "What does my son want from me?" Second question, "Will I ever move back to Austin?" Third, "Will I be able to keep my job at this protection service company?" Fourth, "When should I move the office to Dallas?" The fifth question remained unasked.

I wrote down the questions, we closed our eyes, and I asked Greg to introduce me to Pawpaw as though he were here. "Pawpaw has six children and he is very devoted to them. All of his children have turned out very well—a brigadier general, a postmaster general, my mother, and all the other successful siblings. Pawpaw is mainly a farmer who raises chickens and a fairly good mechanic on the side. He is always tinkering or working to get food for the family. He is a very loving man, very present for his wife and family."

Then Greg shifted and he was now in the role of Pawpaw. He began, "Well, I'm about five foot eight, and I am overweight, weighing about 230 pounds. I am a farmer and I dress in farmer clothes. I have very white hair. I love my grandchildren a lot, and I really like Greg. Greg is a very special grandchild because he is a good boy. He always does the right thing. He is very active and busy building things. I care a lot about him."

I asked Pawpaw if he could offer some advice for Greg.

"Yes," Greg said in the role of Pawpaw.

My first question presented to Pawpaw was, "What does my son, Jason, want from me?" I read the question in my new role as Greg so he could be in the role of Pawpaw.

The answer he got was to "Show tough love. Tell him in a gentle, loving way that he looks like a man, he is a man, and now it's time to grow up and be a man." The anger disappeared from Greg's voice and Pawpaw's wise words took over. I wrote the answers so Greg could stay in the Second Opinion role as Pawpaw.

As we became more familiar with Pawpaw, I continued to ask Greg's remaining questions. "Will Greg move to Austin?"

"No, your daughter will, but the rest of you won't." Greg was almost shocked as he answered this question in the role of Pawpaw. Many of his goals had to do with moving back to Austin. He seemed relieved, somewhat peaceful at the answer.

The third question got a quick and definite answer. "Yes, you will be able to keep your job."

The fourth question was, "When should we move the office to Dallas?"

"May first, a firm May first of this year." Greg didn't want to move April 1. The corporate office had suggested June 1. But he had never taken his own stand, he just kept listening to other people's opinions. When he got into the role of Pawpaw, Greg became firm and took a stand: He knew that May 1 was the right time to move.

Pawpaw didn't need to know the facts about the business or the move. Greg already knew the facts. Pawpaw's perspective gave Greg the inner strength he needed to take a stand and make a decision. Because Greg had never done any meditation before, he was a little bit hesitant compared to others who were more deeply moved when remembering their Second Opinion person. We counted from three back to one, and he slowly opened his eyes to consciously come back into the room. I asked him how he felt.

"Peaceful and relaxed," he replied.

I observed that Greg had made a habit of nervously running through goals, looking around, somehow always preoccupied—rarely fully present. In the past, he had not been able to stay with one subject more than a few minutes. Now, for the first time, Greg was totally relaxed and peaceful. I looked back at his original goal: to create joy in his life and reach 90 percent of his goals. Greg remembered what joy felt like, and he basked in his newfound experience of it, seeming not to notice the small tear in his eye.

When Greg spoke with his boss, the boss agreed immediately with the May 1 moving date, and while he never exactly said, "I'm glad you made a decision and took a stand" his actions certainly indicated his approval. He told everyone at corporate the new date and immediately lined up the necessary resources to make it happen.

"I made the decision, but Pawpaw's assistance helped so much," Greg thought to himself. While Greg believed procrastination to be his challenge and constantly fought it, his real career block was being afraid to make a decision. Pawpaw helped give him the extra courage he needed. The Second Opinion perspective also gave Greg joy, direction, and strength. I have yet to find someone who does not have these resources available within. The twenty-first century requires tools for peace and inner strength to be able to respond quickly and effectively. Middle managers can be their own most trusted adviser if they use and practice their skills.

Five years later, I called Greg to see if he continued to use Pawpaw as a

Second Opinion. Before I even got the question started, Greg said, "Mary, I have Pawpaw's picture right here on my desk. I use him every day for the courage to make decisions. It has changed my whole concept of my work. It's fun now. I don't procrastinate, but I must ask Pawpaw for something almost every day. No one knows why I have this picture of my grandpa resting before me, keeping me company. I've been meaning to call you for years to tell you how this is working."

Group Setting and Second Opinion

The really valuable thing is intuition.

—ALBERT EINSTEIN

The Second Opinion exercise was requested by a Palo Alto venture capital company. There were twelve members whose main task on a regular basis was to decide which businesses they would invest in, which entrepreneurs they would back and partner. They had many analytical tools to determine return on investment, show five-year projections, best- and worse-case scenarios, alternatives, contingencies. They had been mostly successful, but they wanted to develop their intuitive abilities.

We spent just three hours having all twelve go through the Second Opinion exercise in a group. Each one privately identified his Second Opinion person and five questions. Then we did a short meditation and visualization, and they role-played their Second Opinion person while another asked the five questions. At least three of them were teary during the process and said they had a profound connection. One said he just could not identify a person who influenced him; one said he could not visualize or role-play. But the other ten received valuable, specific insights to use in their decision making.

When we went around the room at the end of the session, each of the ten who used it told the group their newly received advice. The group was astounded at the clear and seemingly accurate advice the others were recounting.

A BEST-SELLER REFLECTS SECOND OPINION

For well over a year, *Tuesdays with Morrie*[9] has been on the top ten best-sellers nonfiction list. Mitch, the author and main character in the book, had an English professor, Morrie, who was very instrumental in his life, but Mitch had not seen Morrie since college graduation. When they reconnected,

Morrie, the professor/coach, was seventy-eight and dying of Lou Gehrig's disease. Morrie had an influence on Mitch as he had encouraged and prepared Mitch for his career as a sportswriter. Although they were 700 miles apart, Mitch and Morrie spent every Tuesday together. Because Morrie was dying, there was a sense of urgency that helped Mitch pay attention to his wisdom. Mitch was stressed and feeling that his life had lost meaning, and he was about to lose the woman he loved because she saw his shallowness. Fortunately she was able to see changes in Mitch through his talking with Morrie and rekindled their love.

In their last meeting, Mitch sobbed, "When you are gone, whom will I ask for advice?"

Morrie said, "Picture me asking you the questions because now you have the answers." Morrie would become Mitch's Second Opinion person.

OTHER REFLECTIONS ON A SPIRITUAL OPINION

In Ken Blanchard's book *Leadership by the Book*,[10] he also takes Second Opinion to the workplace. However, his Second Opinion is Jesus and the tools are (a) the Twelve-Step Program used for Alcoholics Anonymous and (b) the Bible. For those who do have a good spiritual dialogue with Christ and for whom Christianity or the Twelve-Steps is their path, this book is great.

A large number of managers and employees I have encountered have had what I call "spiritual incest," or negative Christian experiences. They have lived through a childhood that either made them fear or not connect with or respect Christ and/or God. While I love the way Christianity works for Ken Blanchard and the others in Blanchard's book, many are still seeking to find spiritual connections that can be used in the workplace and are conducive to all traditional religions as well as New Age religions. What is our common ground?

Many managers get spiritual connections from nature. The goal here is to integrate who you are in your spirit and soul with the work that you do. As theologian, author, professor, and priest Matthew Fox says, "Integrate your life and your livelihood."[11] The Second Opinion can be used in addition to traditional religious or spiritual connections or instead of them. What's important is to stay connected with our inner wisdom and our spirit. The higher the technology, the higher the need for inner connection, i.e., high tech / high touch!

Conclusion from a Second Opinion

We are what we repeatedly do.

—ARISTOTLE

For several years I have been working on this book, with the challenge for middle managers always on my mind. I have watched tools come and go over the past twenty years and have selected the best tools I know and put them into this book to create your mid-managers' toolbox. I first began research in the field of management in 1975. Now globalization and technology have so profoundly changed the available information and variations of management tools that the old is barely recognizable. My job has become selecting among a vast array of tools—not simply learning them.

As it came time to write a conclusion for you, to summarize, to recommend further study, I was stumped. I could only picture more technology, more globalization, more, better, faster everything. I felt stuck. Then my mind scanned the tools I have presented in this book. Would one of these work? So I decided to use the Second Opinion exercise. The person I decided to use as my Second Opinion was my grandfather, John Brooke Morgan, whom I never knew.

In order to get acquainted with Grandfather John, since he died in 1945, before I was born, I decided to dig out a popular book he wrote in 1939 called *How to Keep a Sound Mind*.[12] As I was reading it, I recalled all that I had been told about Grandfather John. He died at age fifty-seven of pneumonia; he was a well-known and very popular psychology professor at Northwestern University back when psychology was a new and often misunderstood science. I recall my grandmother once telling me that he was originally trained as a Methodist minister and when he switched to psychology, his mother ostracized him from the family, never speaking to him again.

From the descriptions of Grandfather Morgan, I knew he was wise, humorous, and compassionate. My father, Burt, has always had Granddad's photograph in his office, where he has been an entrepreneur and executive for forty-plus years. (My own father had possibly used this Second Opinion exercise, without calling it such, to help him make many successful decisions.)

As I read Granddad's book, I was profoundly taken by the issues covered, similar to the issues that are very present in today's workplace. The three issues we see today that he discussed in his book regarding "wholesome living and vocation" in a mentally healthy environment are these:

1. *Habits*: "Mental health is dependent in large part upon the formation of certain mental habits and the elimination of certain others."

2. *Choice*: We have choice, and "it's just about as easy to form the beneficial habits as it is to fall victim to the detrimental habits, if the person involved can be given a clear conception of their relative significance."

3. *Education*: "The practice of those habits which bring mental health is just as enjoyable, or more so, than the practice of pernicious mental habits which lead to mental disease. It is ignorance that does the damage."[13]

I did the five questions exercise to verify once more the value of the Second Opinion exercise and present the best possible conclusion to this book. My fourth of the five questions was this: "Grandfather John, if you were here today, what would you want the readers of this book to know?" Here is what came through as I pictured his response: The quoted parts are from his book.

Your generation has done an astounding job with education. The information you have in the twenty-first century about vocation, psychology, worldwide religion, science, medicine, and technology is beyond the highest form of education we could have ever imagined in the 1940s. Here's the change. Where I wrote "#3, Education" above that "ignorance does the damage," delete that. *Ignorance is not the cause of damage today—choice is.*

Simultaneous to all this vast education and information you have created, you have created an equal amount of diversions—fast food availability, antidepressants, video games, television, hours lost on the Internet searching for meaningful connections. We had diversions too, of course, but your diversions have stayed equal with your information. Thus, the percentage of making the right choice has not improved since 1940. People are choosing diversions even when they know better.

In 1940, let's say we had 40 tools and 40 diversions. Now you have 4,000 tools and 4,000 diversions. We have not escaped the one bottom-line issue: choice. In fact, choice has been simultaneously magnified by the increase of education and diversions. Having more tools would have helped much more if they weren't accompanied with more diversions. We always get back to "you choose." This book is about "leadership begins with you" and it does. It begins with the choices you make each day. I would have called this book *Leadership Begins with Your Choices.*

I repeat a quote: "Wisdom is knowing what to do, virtue is doing it." In the 1930s and 1940s we worked so hard on education that when we knew something, we automatically did it—chose it. But now with an overabundance of knowledge, education and wisdom, your generation is left to wrestle with virtue: why should one do the right thing? In Hinduism it's karma that keeps us choosing wisely, but that's a religion and I gave up religion. This is your challenge: to choose the right rule, the right tool, the right value, the right path for you.

Perhaps this is why sixty-plus years later, the individual more than ever before is his or her own leader. As Stephen Covey says, "Act or be acted upon." If you do not choose to lead, you will be led. Covey's Habit #1 is Be Proactive. "People who end up with good jobs are the proactive problem-solvers who act with principles."[14] We are no longer at the mercy of someone else having to inform or educate us. We have all the access to all the information we will ever need.

If you choose to be the leader of your career, now is the perfect time to make that choice. If you don't choose, you lose. If you are not ready to choose your career yet, at least choose which voice to listen to—the "Second Opinion," not the "shadow self." Consciously choose which voice to listen to. Then choose one action each day toward your personal mission and goal and it's yours. You'll become that natural leader whom others will naturally follow. Choose often, and choose consciously.

16

Why Mid-Managers and Employees
Need the Rules Now and in the Future

Better for most of us, despite the risks, to leap into the future. And
to do it sooner rather than later.

—JOHN KOTTER, Harvard Business School

Globalization and the Need for Simple World Rules

Mid-managers will be profoundly affected by the changes that will be created by the Internet Revolution for the next ten years. They need a simple and effective guidepost more than ever before. Simplicity is the new competitive advantage—only simpler companies and simpler workgroups "will be able to cut through enough clutter, churn and complexity to compete effectively."[1] The future will include more globalization, more technology, a new generation of workers and a clashing of religions and cultural values.

A World Crash

On October 31, 1999, Egypt Air Flight 990 with 217 passengers routed from New York City to Cairo plunged unexpectedly and suddenly into the Atlantic Ocean. Shortly after the announcement of the crash, a reporter informed the world that the Egyptian government had asked the United States to do the investigation. In two weeks, pieces of wreckage were gathered from the area, the "black boxes" were rescued, and the researchers interpreted a recording of a pilot saying an Islamic prayer and concluded that it may have been the pilot's prayer before suicide. Speculation was rampant. This crash and its aftermath are an example of global miscommunication and how little countries, cultures, and religions understand one another. What people failed to realize is that in the Islam religion it is a sin to commit suicide.

The United States' suggestion of suicide led to a retaliating accusation by the pilot's cousin that the United States was making this into a "cheap soap opera." The relatives of the pilot felt that the United States rushed to judgment, misunderstood the Islamic prayer, and was insensitive to the fact that suicide is a sin in the Islam culture. The Egyptian government angrily accused the United States of trying to cover up its own terrorist activities and its own defect in the American-made jet.

If the Three Rules had been applied to the Egypt/U.S. discord over the crash of Egypt Air, here's what could have occurred. Under Everybody Contributes, the goal would have had to be mutually defined. Was the goal for the United States to quickly give a rough determination of why the plane crashed? Was the goal to have a U.S. and Egyptian team research the crash and come up with two or three possible scenarios and then rank them? Once the goal was established, the contribution from each side could have been determined.

One could argue that both sides thought they had contributed. Egypt deferred to the United States to conduct the research, since the crash was in the U.S. vicinity and that procedure would expedite getting information to the grieving families. The United States complied in a timely and efficient manner—which was thought to be a contribution. If the goal was to make a timely determination, then the United States and Egypt both contributed to achieving the goal. With 20/20 hindsight, Egypt should never have deferred to the United States to do the research and then criticized it, and the United States should never have made such sensitive judgments without collaborating with Egypt and having a better understanding of the impact such statements would have. In this situation the United States and Egypt were both "sucking from the space." The United States was [putting-down] offending the Islam religion, and Egypt was [putting-down] U.S. technology.

Victim Position 1—Most major conflicts today are a fight for the victim position. The United States felt unappreciated because Egypt asked them to investigate. They felt as though the job had been done at high cost, and now Egypt didn't like the answer and attacked, making accusations regarding U.S. airline technology and soap-opera mentality.

Victim Position 2—Egypt deferred to the United States to do the research in order to have it be timely and more efficient, since it was a U.S. plane near U.S. territory. Then Egypt felt the United States abused Egypt by making quick, unfounded judgments that attacked their country's religion and culture and betrayed its trust in the research. Whether the conflict is between employee and manager or country A and country B, the future clearly needs simple global guidelines. Mid-managers will have more foreign-born employees in higher positions of technical expertise and more customers from unfamiliar cultures.

Whether it's cultural, governmental, corporate, or personal positioning—our continents are no longer allowed the luxury of seeing each one's inhabitants as solely separate and uniquely functional. We are all connected, and governments, corporations, and employees who recognize this fact will be much more successful in the global marketplace. Let's examine some of those companies, their products, and people to see how they are prepared to serve worldwide consumers.

A WORLD CAR

Toyota's 2000 Echo is considered a world car, meaning that it changes little from country to country. Toyota was looking for a model that could be the same all over the world. Its instrument console is in a pod, positioned on top of the dashboard, that allows the steering to be on either side.

Until 2000, cars were built with steering on one side or the other, depending on the country—left for Canada, right for England, and so on. There were six basic world features: four-door, air-conditioned, under $12,000, stereo/CD, comfy bucket seats in front, and 34/41 mpg. Ford also has a legitimate "world car," meaning it changes little from country to country. A huge number of the world cars are in a world city—Singapore.

A WORLD CITY—THE SINGAPORE MODEL

Singapore gives us another dimension of why companies need the Three Rules for the future. Singapore is extremely clean and prosperous and visibly integrates the major religions and nationalities of the world. The streets are clean because no one is allowed to spit or chew gum or drive a car that is more than ten years old. It is prosperous because business guidelines are clearly spelled out and bribes are not allowed. On any street, equal space and acknowledgment are given to Hindu temples, Muslim mosques, Christian churches, Jewish temples, and Buddhist ashrams.

The rules of Singapore are not biased toward any particular religion or nationality, so no one is personally put down in the rule process. When people encounter traffic jams with one another, I noticed they restate the rule to one another rather than flip them off or call them a name. For example, "This is the turning lane only," "no parking on this side." When most people focus on the systems that are operating within the rules, personal put-downs are rare. The unique blend of productiveness and respectful tolerance sets Singapore apart from all other cities. While the long list of rules and the consequences may not fit other countries today, Singapore does show us why countries will need rules in the future.

Singapore provides us with a model that gives evidence to why mid-managers will need the Three Rules in the future more than ever—rules can balance productivity and individual dignity in a company the way they can in a world city. Most companies, like countries, go too far one way or the other: too pushy on goals or too lax with behavioral problems. The Three Rules can help the mid-managers who are at the forefront by keeping these pushy/lax opposite tendencies balanced. Companies who get too profit-oriented can be destructive to managers and employees' mental health. They will tempt unions and create major grievance-procedure systems. Companies who are too lax on rules invite employees with personality disorders to run the ship and become codependent. Profits that are not put in the forefront will also suffer. Good managers either leave or find a way to keep the "Singapore balance."

A WORLD SERVICE ORGANIZATION

Rotary International is a worldwide service club in 162 countries with two million members. One common bond to all Rotarians, regardless of nationality or religion, is the "4-Way Test." This is the value agreed upon to become a member. The 4-Way Test says "in all things I do, I will make sure it: (1) is the truth; (2) is fair; (3) builds goodwill and better friendships; (4) benefits all who are concerned."

Shortly after the Gulf War, I was asked to conduct a management program in Kuwait. While in Kuwait, I attended a Rotary Club meeting that was in English, had a few women in attendance and was much like a U.S. Rotary meeting. Since the U.S. was on Kuwait's side in the Gulf War, all was smooth as expected, even though I didn't have my Rotary card or pin with me.

A week later, I scheduled a meeting in Cairo, Egypt, on my way home. Cairo had a series of random shootings of U.S. tourists shortly before my arrival. I went to the hotel in town that sponsored the weekly Rotary meeting, still without my pin or my Rotary membership card. Because I was a Rotarian, they assumed I was telling the truth (Test 1), so they let me sign in to attend and purchase a lunch ticket.

It was a hot day, and I wore a red shortsleeved blouse and a beige suit. I felt out of place because I was the only woman, and they didn't allow women to be full members. I didn't speak a word of their language, but luckily they spoke mine. I was tense, knowing they were not a country known for being overfriendly to the United States. This Rotary service club, the 4-Way Test, and our presence together transcended the conflicts between governments. Others in attendance included two men from Israel, one from Jordan, and several from Saudi Arabia. The Rotary Club four rules are already integrating very different nations. I thought four is fine, but what about three?

To be fair and to build better relations (Tests 2 and 3), they introduced me in English and asked me to say a few words to the group (most of them understood English, but the meeting had not been in English). I said, "I'm so grateful to be included, and even though I speak and look different, since we all share the 4-Way Test, I see how we are really all the same." They nodded and I felt at home. I relaxed and enjoyed the lunch. When the meeting was over, an older gentleman who spoke very good English told me that this club didn't just have to overcome my gender, nationality, language difference, and forgotten pin and card, the members also had to tolerate my profession.

"What's wrong with my profession?" I asked carefully.

"I realize you were introduced as a professor and consultant, but women who wear red and who show their elbows are considered prostitutes!"

Oops! Even though I had read the entire Koran[2] before making this trip, I still didn't know about elbows and red. Having common rules was the key to this incident of global tolerance.

A WORLD PARTY

Six billion people all over the world were drawn together through global media technology on New Year's Eve and New Year's Day 2000. Woven together by satellite television, the world's nearly 200 countries in twenty-four time zones became a jamboree of diverse cultures. Handel's Hallelujah Chorus was performed, Buddhist monks prayed for peace in Japan, a German choir sang in Israel, and Pope John Paul II gave thanks for humanity's triumphs and asked for forgiveness for its sins. In India, the Dalai Lama joined thousands of Hindu holy men on the banks of the Ganges. Meanwhile, Premier Yeltzin of Russia resigned and a week-long hijacked plane drama in Afghanistan came to a peaceful end. We were all able to be aware of these events because of the globalization of information and technology.

The Three Rules are big enough to include globalization but small enough to focus on the work at hand. The mid-manager of the new century is no longer simply a part of one workgroup in one company. He or she is part of a global system that has been deeply changed by technology. The world crisis, the world car, the world city, the world service club, and the world party are only a few reasons we need to adopt non-offensive language, common rules, and a simple map so we can face global entropy, regardless of the circumstances. The opportunities from a global economy and workplace can be much more easily tapped into if we can find common ground. Common rules—whatever they are—are a necessity for profitable and healthy world connection.

Technology and the Mid-Manager

While the future is unpredictable, it promises longer lives and increasing unification of nations. But genetic engineering, intoxication with technology, and globalization of business will produce ethical dilemmas and conflicts that were unimagined a century ago. According to John Naisbitt in *High Tech High Touch: Technology and Our Search for Meaning*, "Technology feeds our pleasure centers physically and mentally, but its intoxication is squeezing out our human spirit, intensifying our search for meaning."[3]

The technological genetic manipulation of plants and animals alerts us that humans could be next. While Naisbitt says that Hindus, Buddhists, Muslims, and Jewish leaders he interviewed do not see it as a threat to God's absolute power, some Christian leaders think the charges of playing God against bioengineering and genetic engineering have some truth. Man's search for spirituality is at an all-time high. A special issue of *Business Week* on November 1, 1999, was titled "Religion in the Workplace."[4] Case after case showed how spirituality was being drawn into the workplace. Naisbitt would argue that the isolation and intrusion of technology into our inner world has magnified the search for meaning.

According to Naisbitt, technology has allowed children and adults to shoot and kill on a regular basis with no apparent consequences. But Naisbitt says there are consequences. First, he believes, four out of five children who play video games are addicted to them. This, he says, carries with it all the characteristics of any other addiction. Overfeeding of our pleasure centers daily creates an unconscious choice to be part of entropy in the workplace.

Second, playing war games causes compassion fatigue. The normal compassion one feels watching a friend get hurt is so overstimulated in war games that a person becomes numb to the real pain of real people. According to some news reports, the Littleton, Colorado, gunmen who killed classmates and teachers before taking their own lives in April 1999 played war games for many long hours before their school shooting rampage. But even more poignant, many people who first saw the gunmen had no naturally fearful reaction—one thought it was a senior gag, another didn't even flinch when hearing, "They have guns."

The workplace is likely developing higher and higher numbers of people who are intoxicated by technology. One manager refers to his role in today's uncertainty as being the "designated driver." "I have to keep my own disorders in check so I can drive the workgroup through theirs." The one thing you can do is keep your focus in light of so many diversions. Leadership in the future will not require amazing skills and charisma. Instead, the mid-manager who stays focused on the goals through all the diversions will come out on top in tomorrow's workplace.

If your employees are addicted to alcohol, sex, gambling, or technology, are mentally ill or performing religious rituals at work, you cannot be the social worker, minister, or technology police. Your job is to uphold the Three Rules, and those who cannot follow them will be weeded out. This contributes tremendously to both the acting-out employee and the rest of the workgroup. Employees and coworkers are empowered and motivated by a leader who respectfully reminds them of the rules and return to the rules when he or she gets off course. An employee who resists rules and goals may say you are mean. But holding people to their goals and agreements takes compassion—compassion for your own future and compassion for the future of your colleagues.

> My advice is to fall in love with your future. That's what I've always done and it works.
>
> —GEORGE BURNS

Workplace Behavior

All civilizations are based on having rules that make humans act civil to one another. According to M. Scott Peck in *A World Waiting to Be Born*, civility is "organizational behavior that is ethical and consciously motivated."[5] This means that to be civil we must check our values and be alert.

A healthy organization, says Peck, whether it's a marriage, a family, or a business corporation, is not one that has no absence of problems. As mentioned earlier, it is one that is actively and effectively addressing or healing its problems. A corporation that is blind to its own problems cannot be healthy. Mental health is the ongoing process of actively and effectively addressing problems in order to achieve our own personal best. Two cornerstones of civil organizational behavior and mental health are:

1. The capacity for both individual and corporation to distinguish between legitimate (healthy) suffering and that which is unnecessarily escalated.

2. The willingness to bear (meet head on and work through) that suffering which is a proper portion in our individual and organizational lives.

"It is extremely important for us to understand that conflict in human affairs is healthy and normal. Conflict is an inescapable part of life and not inherently uncivil. It is the essence of civility to deal with conflict in our organizational lives through respectful discussion and clarification. Conflict is uncivil only when it is hidden, unnecessarily adversarial or blown out of proportion."[6]

There seem to be increasing incivilities in the workplace, and human resources experts blame managers and managers blame technology. Managers can do something about the incivilities; technology itself won't solve the problem. The upcoming challenges to middle managers are dealing with behaviors that range from daily incivilities to workplace violence to mental illness and the spiritual void that employees are searching to fill.

Workplace Violence—The Ultimate Incivility

Workplace shootings have forced managers to adopt or establish rules that will prevent workplace violence. A day trader killed nine and wounded thirteen at two brokerage firms, then killed himself. In Pelham, Alabama, a worker was charged with killing two coworkers at their office and then killing a third person where the perpetrator used to work. In Honolulu, a copier repairman killed seven coworkers at a Xerox office. A Seattle man walked into a boat repair company and shot four employees, then fled after killing two.

Workplace violence of all kinds has dramatically increased in recent years—but mass shootings have definitely demanded our attention. Experts say there are common threads to these terrifying episodes, and perhaps even lessons that can prevent reoccurrence. Jack Levin, director of the Burbank Center on Violence at Boston's Northwestern University, says, "These are usually cold-blooded executioners. The killer typically blames others for injustices done to him. Most workplace violence is against managers and supervisors. . . . The number of bosses killed by disgruntled workers or ex-workers has doubled during the 1990s." Levin continues, "When people who are already on the margin begin to feel that no one cares about their problems, some will [become violent]."

Robert Baron, a professor of management and psychology at Rensselaer Polytechnic University, offered this recommendation for how to reduce workplace violence: "Employers need to be more compassionate in their handling of workers, particularly those who are troubled or facing termination." Unfortunately, we cannot tell managers or employees how to feel. We can only suggest that they act a certain way. In dealing with some employees, managers may feel intimidated, angry, fearful for their lives—and justifiably so. But to lead the way to a new system of order, the manager and employers can be asked to *act* in a respectful manner.

Regardless of how a manager feels, he can still try to make his contribution clear, treat everyone with dignity no matter what, and keep agreements. Keith Headman models this for us at Charles Schwab, dealing with a gunman.

THE MID-MANAGER AND THE GUNMAN AT CHARLES SCHWAB AND COMPANY

Rules 2 and 3 are what gave courage and successful techniques to Keith Headman in handling a disgruntled employee with a gun. In one of my M.B.A. Conflict Resolution night classes, a student, Keith, who is the vice president of security at Charles Schwab's San Francisco Corporate Center, wrote about the drama of spending two hours on the phone with a gunman in the Charles Schwab Portland, Oregon, office. Notice how Keith felt fearful, but acted compassionately.

The man who answered my phone call to Portland, Oregon, was the gunman. I'd just heard about a gunman who shot two people as he entered the Charles Schwab building and I was calling to ask about the details. He demanded to know who I was and then he decided to prove to me that he was serious. He fired off several shots to prove his point. Thus began the most scary and most satisfying negotiation of my life.

It appeared that this man was seeking revenge and was mad at several different types of businesses. He was mad at the women he felt got him fired, insurance companies, and banks. Strangely enough, our firm [Charles Schwab] had no connection with any of his targets. The real issue at hand was that he was holding four people at gunpoint and my immediate job was to begin negotiating for their safe release.

He made specific demands regarding the police outside and how he was afraid of them storming the office. As we talked I knew the main thing I had to do was to keep him calm and talking to me. If he was doing this he was not shooting anyone. There was a serious power imbalance in this negotiation. Not only was he holding people at gunpoint, to make it more difficult, these were people I knew personally. He also had multiple weapons and had shown he was not afraid to use them. He had already demonstrated this by shooting two people as he entered the building. He had another very serious advantage; I was 800 miles away. As we talked I realized he had almost all the advantages at the moment. However, I had one thing going for me, I was removed from the immediate situation and was able to remain calm and think clearly.

It was necessary to quickly and confidently gain a rapport with this man. I needed to show him I could be trusted and that I was a man of my word. These two items are critical to any successful negotiation [Rule 3]. If at any time he felt I was not dealing with him in a fair manner or that I was trying to trick him, I knew he would not hesitate to shoot someone to prove his power.

It was imperative that I treat his thoughts and comments with respect [Rule 2]. Even if I didn't feel it, I could still treat it as such. I took his demands seriously. If at any time he felt that I was criticizing him or any of his ideals at the time I knew I would lose him. I had to listen, take notes, read between the lines on what he was telling me and hope that I did not say the wrong thing. All this had to be done while thinking on my feet.

As this continued to unfold I was bouncing back and forth between negotiations with the gunman and providing critical information to the police department negotiator. After two hours I finally had him agreeing to release one hostage and give up one weapon. Throughout this entire ordeal I found myself reminding myself to ask questions and then just shut up and let him talk. I gathered far more information this way.

It was through this type of technique and my willingness to listen to what he was saying, not so much how he was saying it, that we were finally able to reach a very successful resolution. After two hours he released one hostage and one weapon. At this point the police team took over and began negotiating with him. After four hours he released all the hostages and was taken into custody. A very tired and gratified team realized one important thing. We all had one thing to be very thankful for: no one had been hurt since these negotiations had begun. There would never be a need to play Monday morning quarterback and second-guess our decisions.

The outcome? A dangerous and tragic situation ended on a very happy note and everyone was able to go home to his or her loved one that night.[7]

Keith did not know about the Three Rules at the time he wrote this report. Yet, coincidentally, the key to dealing with this gunman and saving lives was making the gunman feel he could trust Keith and that Keith would uphold his word to him.

You gain strength, courage and confidence by every experience in which you really stop and look fear in the face.

—ELEANOR ROOSEVELT

In several M.B.A. classes my students conducted research on common facts about workplace violence. In their final project, these were the three most common facts about workplace violence.

1. The perpetrator doesn't just snap.

2. There are frequent and escalating warning signs seen by the first line supervisor.

3. Early intervention is usually possible with **proper training and communication**.

These common facts about workplace violence point out some challenges for middle managers. The middle manager is on the front line and is the one most likely to see the signs of potential violence. If the mid-manager has the proper training to intervene early, he or she has an incredible opportunity to develop the emotional skills that many executives lack and simultaneously lead the workgroup in a more positive direction.

EARLY WARNING SIGNS OF WORKPLACE VIOLENCE

1. Direct or veiled verbal threats and put-downs

2. Intimidation of others

3. Paranoid behavior

4. Splitting—holds people as wonderful one minute and terrible the next

5. Inability to deal with dialogue or constructive criticism

6. Erratic mood swings

7. History of violent behavior

8. Extreme interest in weapons

9. Being a loner

10. Moral righteousness

How can a mid-manager be expected to know if a behavior is just a vexing, uncivil behavior where the individual is unable to work through legitimate suffering or a certifiable disorder? Middle managers need to focus on the goals and the broken agreements, and in that way weed out workers who cannot successfully contribute. They need the companies to adopt the Three Rules now so they can have the infrastructure to work through behavior problems and redirect the situation appropriately. Whether it is the Three Rules or any rules, insist that your management adopt and back up in action agreed-upon rules. You are on the front line. You are the leader and this is what you need to lead.

Basic Everyday Incivilities and the Mid-manager's Role

The workplace violence examples discussed earlier are the dramatic cases that make the news. Many people argue that these are just a few, rare examples. But national visibility of these few examples has had an impact on companies. For example, a food preparation company controller called me last week to ask what to do about an employee who threatened to "come back with a gun" and shoot his supervisor. There was no president in office, the owner was out of town, and she was left to handle the situation. She called the sheriff and filed a report, and the disgruntled employee quit and hasn't returned. The controller and supervisor were still scared weeks later and not sure what to do.

A university night school program had an angry student respond in an abusive tone when the receptionist said the counselor he was scheduled to meet was not there. Her tone was patronizing and interpreted by the student as a put-down. This escalated when the student said, "What kind of customer service is this?" After she then mumbled to a coworker, he yelled at them both. Next she announced she was going to call security. She did, and he was escorted out. I happened to have been a guest speaker who arrived early and heard the whole interaction. I can only say that given the actual words spoken, her response seemed overdramatized. However, the fear that has crept into the workplace was what I believe led to the call for security.

With unclear rules for the workplace, violence is even more imminent as we see small episodes like this escalate quickly to fearful reaction. If in that split second one of the two parties had said, "Let's both work toward resolution here," or one could have privately converted the put-down to a respectful request, each situation could have had a much more positive ending.

Our local paper has a workplace Q&A section. In it an employee said, "I'm afraid of a coworker who seems potentially dangerous." The advice given in the answer section was, "And where is the top management? Go on the Web and get information or call in a consultant." Most mid-managers don't have accessibility to consultants. But these scenarios remind us all that we need some guidelines for workplace violence that can reduce workplace fear, which is the more predominant issue.

While most of the shooting cases have been employees shooting managers or perceived managers, managers and supervisors also threaten employees. Normally, violence is measured on the part of the receiver. Some violence occurs to employees just by how their bosses communicate. According to a Web site from the Center for Non-Violent Communication, Sylvia Haskvitz, M.A., director, (www.cnvc.com), violent communication is defined as "shame, blame and criticism placed on another person because your own needs are not being met."

Below is a chart of behaviors that can become uncivil. This chart also appears in chapter 6 in the put-downs discussion.

What Managers and Supervisors Do that Threatens Employees[8]

LIGHT GRAY
Abrasive

1. Silence
2. Glaring eye contact: "the look"
3. Brevity or abruptness
4. Snubbing or ignoring people
5. Insults and put-downs
6. Blaming, discrediting, or discounting
7. An aggressive, controlling manner
8. Threats about the job
9. Yelling and shouting (including overuse of caps or exclamation marks on E-mail)

DARK GRAY
Abusive

10. Angry outbursts or loss of control
11. Physical threats

A   B   C   D   E

Lower Intensity	Higher Intensity
Subtle	Obvious
General	Personal
Rare	Frequent
Private	Exposed

As a middle manager, you cannot change the behavior of everyone else and certainly not that of your boss's boss, but you can use the Three Rules to make sure workplace abuse in your area is decreased to lighter shades of gray and lower intensity. This is an excellent opportunity for you to lead your workgroup away from the fear caused by abrasive or abusive behavior and toward the contribution they can make. In *Out of Crisis*, Edward Deming's eighth point for quality is "Drive out fear."[9] The Three Rules and the tools are all designed to help you drive out fear and build a workplace system that fosters contribution, respect, and integrity.

According to Neale Walsch's best-seller, *Conversations with God*,[10] he asked God for laws about fear. God's answer was this : "The First Law is: You can be, do and have whatever you can imagine. The second law is that you attract what you fear."

In my 1990 book, *Corporate Healing: Solutions to the Impact of the Addictive Personality in the Workplace*,[11] I had a similar recommendation. The term "codependent" was popular then, used to describe managers and employees who were engaged in a negative symbiotic relationship. The job of the manager ten years ago and today is to focus on goals and objectives. This focus is healing for the employees. If you are fearful, you invite fear. If you focus on contribution, others around you are more likely to focus on that as well.

A client of mine who had his own business for several years had two sons he wanted to bring into the business. One son became vice president of administration, but the other was very heavily involved in drugs. The father, whom I'll call Dick, went through all sorts of programs for relatives of addicts. He came to the conclusion that a job was the best medicine for his son, whom he loved dearly.

Dick assigned his addicted son to be vice president of sales. He did not tell him not to use drugs, he just asked him to be at work at 8:00 A.M. Each week Dick outlined goals, customers, and so on. At first the son agreed to the job just so he could have money to buy drugs. He would stay out late and have headaches in the morning. With people relying on him and goals he needed to achieve, he began to get to bed earlier. This led to less time to use. Soon he wanted to spend money on a nice car and clothes to enhance his sales and earn more money. In time, about eight to nine months, the high of the substance abuse dropped far below the "high" of being successful, reaching goals, feeling dignity and self-respect.

Workplace violence and the incivilities that lead to it could overwhelm a mid-manager. We all need a common, simple place to go in uncertain times.

Public Conflict Resolution

"Conflict is an organizational fact of life. Customers complain, co-workers bicker, unions demand. We can hide it, control it, fight it, squash it or avoid it, but we cannot eliminate it."[12] If we want to lead our careers in an era of violence in the workplace, we had better take public action to acknowledge conflict, make it a source of growth and creativity, and plan our careers to include resolution strategies.

"Public" here doesn't mean loud; it means up-front, honest, communication. Recently, I read an article about the 1999 Cleveland, Ohio, Business Hall of Fame selecting my quiet and low-key high school friend Dave Daberko, now the CEO of National City Corporation. Known as "Money Man," Dave was described as a very creative leader in building one of the largest banks in America. When asked what was the key to the successful acquisitions that built the bank, he said, "Clear communication from the start and dealing openly and honestly with employees." The article says Dave's emotional intelligence is his key attribute—he's conscious about his employees.[13]

"Daberko's mix of hard-nosed leadership and intelligent concern for his employees, shareholders and customers distinguishes him from his contemporaries. He likes to talk about the business with his employees and hear from them—a compassionate leader." I called Dave, after twenty-five years, to congratulate him on his success and to ask him what he thought about workplace violence. This was his off-the-cuff response: "We've driven so much to improve productivity and keep economic expansion, but we've also asked more and more of our employees. We've substituted winning for fun. We need to make the workers' environment better with things like open quarters, flex time—we need to give employees a chance to be themselves, to foster mental well-being. The pressure is so great. Bottom line—we must understand the point of view of the employee." Dave exemplified Stephen Covey's habits 4, 5, and 6 without ever mentioning Covey. In *The Seven Habits of Highly Effective People*, Stephen Covey says, the first three habits are private, but 4–6 are public. Dave's win-win approach (Habit 4) came through in his focus on employee mental well-being in balance with company productivity. He has had that emotional intelligence needed to avoid workplace violence. Although known for making the bank number one, he isn't really a money man, he's a win-win man.

Habit #5: "Seek first to understand and then be understood," was the most obvious in Dave's final summary. "Understand the point of view of the employee." In Ken Keyes's *Handbook to Higher Consciousness*, he refers to the "instant consciousness doubler."[14] This means the minute you can view something from another's perspective, you instantly double your consciousness. When managers understand employee concerns like Dave does, and when employees understand the concerns of managers, there is a delicate balance and a successful career for both.

Finally, Habit #6, is to Synergize. Synergy is the opposite of conflict and violence. It is that close-connected feeling of contribution and success that uplifts all to a higher place than any one individual could go. Daberko's induction into the Business Hall of Fame was not the result of financial decisions alone; it was all about having the synergy that came from well-balanced financial and emotional health.

Determining what to build privately and what to build publicly are important distinctions for managers leading their careers. If you keep your dealings public, they will be trusted and corrected. Once you get private in leading people, you are vulnerable to enabling them and, thus, vulnerable to workplace entropy. Having healthy visible ways to resolve conflict is critical.

There is also a lack of agreed-upon ways to handle emotions in the workplace. As a result, they often are not handled. Emotional anchors are what some employees have said they experienced when their company became a Three Rule company.

Workplace Spirituality and Emotion

In the November 30, 1999, issue of *USA Today*, the cover story was about the increasing number of children in the United States today who are taking antidepressants. The photo was of popular seventeen-year-old Bridget Frese who recalled distinctive terror of depression since age thirteen. Her father, Dr. Fred Frese, a psychologist and vice president of the National Association of Mental Illness, agreed with many psychiatrists today—that the main reason children have unprecedented rates of depression was because they lack "emotional anchors." The second photo in the cover story article showed Bridget Frese serving communion to her class in a special Mass for teens designed to give children emotional anchors.

Distinguishing Spirituality from Religion

When former nun and religious historian Karen Armstrong left religious life, she described herself as "freed of the burden of failure and inadequacy."[15] Armstrong then became one of the foremost British authors and commentators on religious history. Her study of religion revealed something that surprised her—human beings are spiritual animals. Spirituality has been the way humans try to find value and meaning in life. "Religion, on the other hand," says Armstrong, "has been abused and often robs people of spirituality." There is one very significant point she makes about God. It seems that the idea of God is remarkably close to ideas in religions that developed quite independently. Religions have tried to own God, define Him and punish people for not following their definition. Her religion caused her to fear God. In order to feel her own spirituality, she had to leave the church and get to know God on her own.

A recently completed research project by McKinney and Company, Australia, shows that when companies engage in programs that use spiritual techniques for their employees, productivity improves and turnover is greatly reduced. According to A *Spiritual Audit of Corporate America* published by Jossey-Bass in October 1999, employees who work for an organization they consider to be spiritual are less fearful, less likely to compromise their values, and more able to throw themselves into their jobs. Says coauthor Jan Mitroff, "Spirituality could be the ultimate competitive advantage." Sixty percent of those polled for the book said they believe in the beneficial effects of spirituality in the workplace, "so long as there's no bully-pulpit or promotion of traditional religion."

Unfortunately, religions have a history of righteousness, bullying, killings, and such, so the term "religion" has given spirituality and God a bad reputation in some circles. Famous philosopher Martin Buber (1878–1965), realized that the term "God" had been soiled and degraded, but he refused to relinquish it. "Where would I find a word to equal it, to describe the same reality? It bears too great and complex a meaning for too many sacred organizations." The word "religion" can imply rituals and rites that have violated others.[16]

Private Versus Public Displays in the Workplace

What is common to both workplace violence and workplace religion is that they both reflect public displays of private matters that are usually not appropriate in the workplace. Like a library, a workplace is somewhat sacred in that we each leave our homes and our personal lives and come to an agreed-upon place to quietly perform agreed upon tasks. Our religious preferences and emotional states are not part of the agreement. It's not that they are wrong, but their primary place for expression is not necessarily in the workplace.

A capsulated version of this honoring of sacred space occurred on a flight I took from New York City to Cleveland. As the plane was halfway down the runway, there was suddenly a bloodcurdling scream from a disheveled woman passenger holding a baby. The scream was so loud the captain could hear it in the enclosed cockpit. He made an instantaneous decision to abort the takeoff and made a quick but careful right-hand turn off the main runway. He calmly announced that the plane would return to the gate and take-off would be delayed. Meanwhile, the passengers were buzzing about how scary the situation was and how nervous we felt. We developed a bond as we shared our anxieties with one another.

About ten minutes later, two security guards came to escort the lady and the baby off the plane. The lady stood up and said to the security guards, in a tone we could hear, "I'm okay now. I'd like to stay here and try again." We passengers en masse nodded a resounding no, and many said in unison, "No way." The decision was final. She resisted at first, but then the security guards took her out the door.

Our space had been violated. Her emotional outburst, while it may have been justified, was not appropriate. She thus inflicted her behavior on other passengers. She completely "sucked from our space" security, safety, and forward movement. The group's agreement about the space violation was intense and final but still compassionate. We were sorry for her pain, but we knew this was not the place to heal it. The pilot said it all as we left for our second takeoff: "This plane is leaving for Chicago. If you do not wish to go, speak now or forever hold your peace!"

When the "Everyone Contributes" rule is in place, it means *everyone*. If one person sucks from the space, it can take from everyone. Workplace conflict, resolution, and spirituality can contribute to the space. When workplace conflict is violent or individual spirituality becomes religious bullying, then it no longer contributes. Who decides this should not be a charismatic issue. In others words, the personality of the leader should not determine what religion is okay, what outbursts are okay, or what antidepressants are okay. The values, mission, goals, and rules should decide. When you have outlined the goals, rules, and values, it is much easier to get agreement as to what contributes and what doesn't. "In a company that truly manages by its values, there is only one boss, the company value."

At the well-known clothing store, the Gap, the following values are outlined in eight languages:

1. Everyone counts.

2. Every difference makes a difference.

3. Own it.

4. Do it—done.

5. Less is more—simplify.

6. Take the smart risk.

7. Do it better every day.

8. Do the right thing.

Having real values diffuses violence because people have a way to express themselves in a culture that says everyone counts.

Private Spiritual Growth

In Stephen Covey's *The Seven Habits of Highly Effective People*, he says the first three habits should be private. These are: (1) Be proactive; (2) Begin with the end in mind (set up a personal mission); and (3) Do first things first.[17]

New laws demand that hostile action be eliminated. No Put-downs must be used everywhere. Public expression of intense negative emotion or bullying religion does not generally "contribute" to the sanctity of the workplace.

Most of the tools for the rules are geared toward a private, personal use of the rules simultaneously with taking them to the workgroup. If we need to wait until we have mastered the Three Rules to take them to our workplace, we will never get it done. We can jump-start the Three Rules today if we are willing to work on them privately and simultaneously with the asking of others.

The New Generation Millennials

The 250 Cisco high-tech global employees who became millionaires epitomized all Three Rules. The employees consistently and quietly contributed to the technical and financial success of the company. One of the employees who was my student in a morning class often attended class in spite of having worked all night. I noticed he never complained. Of the 250 employees, 50 percent were born outside of the United States. As a rule, perhaps because they are more cautious and uncertain in a different country, non-American employees tend to put down and sabotage much less than Americans. Third, the ultimate in kept agreements was bestowed on the employees by the company when the stock options they were promised came through. They had been told that if they contributed, they would be rewarded when the company was rewarded.

The new generation of workers and managers will have more variety of values as more nationalities enter the workplace. Engineers and technicians are being imported at high rates to help build our high-tech companies. In addition to the increasingly global and technical nature of today's employees, there are also some new theories about the next generation of employees. Born between 1982 and 2002, the next generation has been named *millennials* by generation historians. According to Neil Howe, who cowrote *Generations: The History of America's Future: 1584–2069*, millennials are civic-minded, optimistic, and team-oriented. A feature article headline described them in this way: LATEST GENERATION VALUES RULES, COOPERATION, AND RESPONSIBIL-ITY. They have high moral expectations and are considered to be like their great-grandparents. A 2000 high school graduating senior in her valedictorian speech announced, "We are the first generation that is more conservative than our parents."

Frank Gregorsky, publisher of the newsletter *Love Those Millennials* and coauthor of the Website *www.millennials.com* has been studying them for two years. He says, "By contrast to their parents and grandparents, these millennials know how to be declarative and outspoken without having a bad attitude."

In short, the millennials contribute; they are respectfully outspoken and honor agreements. This generation has low tolerance for poor leadership and bad morals. A CNN survey showed that 50 percent of millennials think Clinton should have been removed from office after the Lewinski scandal. If we want to be able to relate to this upcoming generation as their managers, their coworkers, or part of our family, we need to prepare common ground that fits them and us. Hopefully, they will come up with a new, improved list of ground rules that fit their future. Meanwhile, the Three Rules are a place to start that will take us right into the core of the future generation.

Jason Nastke, who is two years past the millennial border in age, is right on in his values. This community college student witnessed a town meeting in Valatre, New York, where one citizen shoved another into a window during an argument over where to put a new water tank. In protest, nineteen-year-old Nastke ran for mayor, and he won! His millennial-type platform was "politics can be polite." Since his election, things in Valatre are much more civil. He is described as a very civil servant. "He's got the village back on track," cheers one citizen. The Bible says, "Let the children lead the way." Perhaps the millennials are doing just that—leading us back to civility.

Mid-managers need the Three Rules now and in the future because some dramatic changes are already taking place. We are no longer one country with a mere 300 million people. Globalization gives us 200 countries and 6 billion people that can affect us. Technology is invading our lives and leaving us spiritually empty and looking for meaning in the workplace. The effect of the spiritual emptiness is threefold—some are taking antidepressants to cope, some are seeking religion in the workplace, and some who are at their wits' end are acting out violently. Mid-managers will be those leading these issues in the forefront of the workplace.

Why does a middle manager need the Three Rules in order to lead his career and those around him? He needs the Three Rules to stay focused on goals and have the tools to resolve whatever gets in the way of transforming his own jobs into a career.

YOUR MID-MANAGERS LEADERSHIP TOOLBOX
APPENDICES (TOOLS)

Letter	Name
A	Typical Top Manager Requests
B	Most Common Employee Requests
C	Conversion of Most Common Put-Downs
D	How to Delegate
E-1	Clarifying Contribution
E-2	Determining Company Mission
E-3	Personal Contribution Analysis
F	Credit Union Employees
G	Non-material Rewards Requested by Credit Union Executives
H	Funnel
H-1	John—Funnel
H-2	Paul—Funnel
I, IA, IB, IC	Family Requests
J	ITS (blank)
K	ITS (Louise's)
L	ITS (John's)
M–1, 2, 3, 4	Personal Mission Statement Exercise
N	Examples of Company Values
O	Pre-Review (blank)
O-1	Pre-Review (Rudy's)
O-2	Pre-Review (Jim's)
P	8 Steps Checklist for Effective Listening
Q	Feelings Chart
R	Conscious Communication Form (blank)
S	Lucy's Intended Communication to Myra
T	Eric's Communication to Myra
U	Myra's Communication to Eric
V	The Alignment Agreement Follow-Up between Myra and Eric
W	180 Implied Middle Manager Agreements
X	Alignment Agreement (blank)
X-1	Alignemnt Agreement—John and Paul
Y	Alignment Agreement Follow-Up Form (blank)
Y-1	Alignment Follow-Up—John and Paul
Z	Alignment Follow-Up—Joyce and Carla

The Professional Growth Plan™

Typical Top Manager Requests

What Do You Want?	What Will Your Employee Do?	What Would Be Different?	When Should It Happen?
Motivate and develop your staff.	A. Set clear goals. B. Find out what is needed from you to reach goals. C. Follow through—acknowledge and reward.	We would decrease turnover from 40% to 20%.	By February 1
Keep track of materials.	A. Inventory your materials every day. B. Request needed materials at least three days before. C. Lock your materials cabinet when you leave the office.	We would be able to support the needs of the managers to get the product out the door 24 hours before deadline.	By February 15
Socialize only during your lunch hours.	A. Remain at workstation during business hours. B. Talk only business on the phone. C. Be a role model.	We would complete 25% more transactions weekly.	By January 15
Clean up your station before you leave at night.	A. Put floormat in place. B. Wipe down work area. C. Put tools in toolbox.	We would be ready to begin working by 7:00 A.M.	By January 22
Let me know about problems before they become crises.	A. Give me a weekly report on any problems you see in your work area. B. Give me recommendations to solve your problems. C. Follow through on solutions to problems.	There would be no union grievances.	By January 31
Prioritize your tasks.	A. Meet with me once a week, Mondays at 8:00 A.M. B. Give me weekly accomplishments each Friday. C. Ask me if you get confused.	Inventory would have a 24-hour turnaround.	By January 15
Take responsibility for your hostility in the workplace.	A. If you feel hostile, take a walk; go outside. B. Before criticizing, count to ten, rephrase. C. Focus on your part in the problem.	People would come to you for help each day.	By June 1

The Professional Growth Plan™

Most Common Employee Requests of Middle Managers

What Do You Want?	What Will Your Supervisor Do?	What Would Be Different?	When Should It Happen?
More responsibility	A. Put me in charge of the data processing input section. B. Let me call for repairs. C. Let me train the new person.	Errors would drop below two per week.	By August 11
More independence	A. Tell me the goal you want, then trust me to do it my way. B. Trust me to do it my way. C. Let me come to you if I need help.	I'd get the production out on time.	By February 5
More recognition	A. Tell me when I have done a good job handling a customer complaint. B. Let me know when customers express being pleased with my service. C. Include my name on reports I write.	I'd know the standard and thus satisfy customers sooner. You'd get no more than one complaint monthly.	By September 1
Better communications with me	A. Meet with me in your office every Wednesday from 9:00 to 9:15 A.M. B. Discuss my job with me. C. Let me know how I'm doing.	I'd get work done sooner and have time to work on the emergency plan.	By August 5
More training	A. Teach me more about our new rental equipment. B. Send me to the course at the local college. C. Get an extra manual for me.	I'd be more efficient with the equipment and more able to explain its use to others.	By March 21
More input on goals	A. Include me when you write out biannual goals for my department. B. Ask me what timeline I see as realistic. C. Let me review goals before publishing.	I would reach all my goals.	By April 26
Go through the chain of command	A. Talk to me before discussing problems or requests with my group. B. If one of my employees comes to you with a problem, send him or her to me. C. Advise me of agreements you make with someone from my group.	I could measure progress on an ongoing basis with my knowledge of activity by project members. We could get the product out under budget and on time.	By May 15
Keep me informed	A. Keep me better informed about division and company-wide business. B. Let me attend the monthly meetings. C. Give me copies of memos that affect my department.	I'd meet my deadlines.	By June 6

The Professional Growth Plan™

Conversion from Most Common Put-downs of Middle Managers to …

Most Common Employee Requests of Middle Managers
Rule 2: No Put-downs, i.e., Convert All Put-downs into Complaints.

Original Put-Down of the Middle Manager	What Do You Want Your Supervisor to Do For You?	What Will Your Supervisor Do?	What Would Be Different?	When Should It Happen?
He's a control freak.	Delegate more responsibility.	A. Put me in charge of the data area. B. Let me call for repairs. C. Let me train the new person.	Errors would drop below two per week.	By August 11
She makes me nervous every time she comes by.	Allow more independence.	A. Tell me the goal you want. B. Trust me to do it my way. C. Let me come to you if I need help.	I'd get the orders out by 5:30 each day.	By February 5
He's obsessed with the negative.	Give more recognition.	A. Tell me when I have done a good job handling a customer complaint. B. Let me know when a customer says they are pleased with my service. C. Include my name on reports I write.	I'd know the standard and thus satisfy customers sooner. You'll get no more than one complaint monthly.	By September 1
She has zero tact or communication skills.	Maintain better communications with me.	A. Meet with me in your office every Wednesday from 9:00 to 9:15 A.M. B. Discuss the items on my agenda. C. Let me know how I'm doing.	We'd get ISO 9000 certification by December 31.	By August 5
He expects people to just do the job with no training.	Supply me with more training.	A. Teach me more about our new rental equipment. B. Send me to the course at the local college. C. Get an extra manual for me.	I'd be more efficient with the equipment and more able to explain its use to others without calling you.	By March 21
She's so paranoid she doesn't trust anyone's opinion but her own.	Let me have more input on goals.	A. Include me when you write out biannual goals for my department. B. Ask me what timeline I see as realistic. C. Let me review goals before publishing.	I'd reach all my goals we agree to.	By April 26
He's a loose cannon with no respect for boundaries.	Go through the chain of command.	A. Talk to me before you discuss problems or requests with my group. B. If one of my employees comes to you with a problem, send him or her to me. C. Advise me of agreements you make with someone from my group.	I'd measure progress on an ongoing basis with my knowledge of activity by project members. We could get the product out under budget and on time.	By May 15
She is secretive about what is going on.	Keep me informed.	A. Keep me better informed about division and company-wide business. B. Let me attend the monthly meetings.	I'd meet my deadlines.	By June 6

How to Delegate

1. Explain the purpose of the job that needs to be done, and why that job is important.

2. Explain what results are expected.

3. Define authority—parameters of the operation.

4. Get agreement on a deadline.

5. Ask for feedback—establish mutual understanding of what needs to be done.

6. Provide for controls—along the way, ensure the job is being done right.

7. Provide for support—make sure it is the support your employee wants.

8. Acknowledge and give recognition to employees who have completed an assignment.

Clarifying Contribution

A. What is my company's business?

_____

_____

B. What are my company's goals?

_____

_____

C. How does my department contribute to company goals?

_____

_____

D. What is the most heavily weighted goal for my department?

_____

_____

E. What can I do to make sure the department goal in "D" (above) is reached?

_____

_____

F. How would I, my manager or an outsider be able to verify that we have accomplished the goal in "D" (above)? Will it be measurable? What will be the results?

_____

_____

G. What is my manager's #1 request of me regarding my part of the #1 goal?

_____

_____

H. Given A–G, my most important goal is: (make sure it is specific, measurable, attainable, realistic, and tangible)

_____

_____

Determining Company Mission

A. Do we have a company vision? One year, 5 year? Use if your company does not have a published mission.

_____

B. Do we have a company mission?

_____

C. Are we working to develop one?

_____

D. What are our company values?

_____

E. What are our company goals?

_____

F. Do we have a plan of how to get there? May I see it?

_____

G. How does our department contribute to the company goals?

_____

H. What do I think I can do to contribute to the goals in "E" above?

_____

I. How does my manager think I can best contribute to "E" above?

_____

J. How would my manager or an outsider be able to verify that I significantly contributed to "E" above? (Will it be measurable? What will be the results?)

_____

Personal Contribution Analysis

A. Who am I?

_____

B. What are my strengths? Am I concentrating on them?

_____

C. How do I perform? Is something amiss in how I perform?

_____

D. How do I learn? taking notes? reading? Do I act on this knowledge?

_____

E. What do I need to know?

_____

F. Where do I belong? Alone or in a team, as subordinate or as manager?

_____

G. What are my values? What do I do in a Value Conflict?

_____

H. What is my contribution? What should my contribution be? Does this fit my strengths?

_____

I. Where and how can I have results that make a difference?

_____

J. What results have to be achieved to make a difference?

_____

K. What habits of mine sabotage my career?

_____

L. How can I take better relationship responsibility?

_____

   1. How can I allow others to have their strengths?

_____

   2. How can I take better responsibility for communications?

_____

M. Where can I improve my manners?

_____

N. What is my plan for the second half of my life? Have I begun creating it?

_____

Source: Adapted from Drucker's _Management Challenges for the 21st Century_, Final chapter, "Managing Oneself." 1999

NON-MATERIAL REWARDS REQUESTED BY CREDIT UNION EXECUTIVES

1. Let me know the priorities each week.

2. Give me cross-training.

3. Let me have input on goals—ask my opinion.

4. Speak in a respectful tone of voice—especially in front of a customer.

5. Meet with me every Tuesday from 3:00 to 3:15 P.M. to discuss my job.

6. Have someone else do the mail once a week.

7. Give me board minutes 48 hours ahead of time.

IN EXCHANGE FOR NEXT STEP
OFFERING ANOTHER SERVICE TO CUSTOMER

NON-MATERIAL REWARDS REQUESTED BY CREDIT UNION EXECUTIVES

1. Treat me like a professional—trust my actions as long as results are on target.

2. Give me the authority to go with responsibility (e.g., if you require a 6 percent dividend, don't blame me for decrease in income).

3. Follow chain of command. Deal with me—not my employees.

4. Sign the enclosed employment contract act.

5. Change my title from branch manager to general manager.

6. Accurately reflect active field of membership—not just original sponsor group.

7. Handle policy issues and long-range planning. Leave day-to-day problems to me.

IN EXCHANGE FOR AN INCREASE TO $50 MILLION IN ASSETS

The Professional Growth Plan ™

Funnel

Your Name: Today's Date:

What is the Number One Thing This Can Do to Contribute to Your Career?

GOAL:
Stated in a positive way, the number one item I want from _____ is:

1.

SPECIFICALLY: **2a.**
- What will this person do to meet
  your request?   **2b.**

- Use a verb to begin each of the   **2c.**
  three short descriptive sentences.

SPECIFICALLY: **3.**
- How will you know the request
  has been fulfilled?

- What will be different?

- How will the change be measured?

The Professional Growth Plan ™

Funnel

Your Name: **Paul**   Today's Date: **9/16/99**

GOAL:
Stated in a positive way, the number one item I want from ____**John**____ is:

1. Let me have input on goals.

SPECIFICALLY:

• What will this person do to meet your request?

• Use a verb to begin each of the three short descriptive sentences.

2a. Meet with me before setting deadlines.

2b. Ask me when I think we can meet it.

2c. Include me in goal setting meetings with executive staff.

SPECIFICALLY:

• How will you know the request has been fulfilled?

• What will be different?

• How will the change be measured?

3. We'd make 90% of our deadlines.

The Professional Growth Plan ™

Funnel

Your Name: **John**   Today's Date: **9/16/99**

GOAL:
Stated in a positive way, the number one item I want from _____**Paul**_____ is:

1. Take a stand and lead.

SPECIFICALLY:
• What will this person do to meet your request?

• Use a verb to begin each of the three short descriptive sentences.

2a. Build a model.

2b. Make a video and show everyone.

2c. Set a production schedule and hold them to it.

SPECIFICALLY:
• How will you know the request has been fulfilled?

• What will be different?

• How will the change be measured?

3a. We'd make 90% of our deadlines.

3b. We'd save 10% in materials.

Family Requests
Five Family Alignment Agreements Used by Middle Managers at Home

NUMBER ONE REQUESTS

1.
Mother and Junior College Son Who Lives at Home

Son's Request: 1. Talk "with" me not "at" me.
   A. Sit and talk thirty minutes daily.
   B. Acknowledge me.
   C. Do things together.

Result: We would get to know each other better.

Mother's request: 1. Improve citizenship at school and home.
   A. Start listening.
   B. Allow others to have private conversations.
   C. Finish tasks without me reminding you.

Result: Grades would improve, you'd feel better about yourself, you'd increase friends and have more freedom.

2.
Middle Manager and Live-In 21-Year-Old Working Daughter

Daugher's Request: 1. Communicate more; discuss our days.
   A. Ask me about my day.
   B. Talk three or four times a week, five to ten minutes.
   C. Do things together; movies; shopping, etc.

Result: We'd be closer.

Mother's request: 1. Do your share of work around the house.
   A. Wash dishes three times a week.
   B. Pick up your belongings.
   C. Dust and vacuum weekly.

Result: I will be in a better mood because I won't have to do everything alone.

Family Requests (*cont.*)
Five Family Alignment Agreements Used by
Middle Managers at Home

NUMBER ONE REQUESTS

3.
Middle-Manager Mother and Grown Daughter with Young Children

Daughter's request: 1. Help me with mothering.
                    A. Call to see how we are.
                    B. Get together one to two afternoons per month.
                    C. Try something new together.

Result: We'd make plans together for fun adventures.

Mother's request: 1. Act more like a guest in my home.
                    A. Watch your children at all times.
                    B. Clean up before you leave.
                    C. Call before coming over.

Result: My attitude will improve.

4.
Husband and Wife (Both Middle Managers)

Wife's request of middle-manager husband: 1. Leave work at office for weekends; (don't bring work home on weekends).
                    A. Let others do extra work.
                    B. Delegate more.
                    C. Leave it at office on Friday.

Result: We'd do more things on weekends; we'd have more balance.

Husband's request of Middle manager wife: 1. Go on vacation together spontaneously.
                    A. Pack.
                    B. Don't tell anyone.
                    C. Go.

Result: We'd be more balanced.

Family Requests (*cont.*)
Five Family Alignment Agreements Used by
Middle Managers at Home

NUMBER ONE REQUESTS

5.
Middle Manager Father and Teenage Daughter

Daugher's Request: 1. Be more calm about my homework.
    A. Control temper.
    B. Understand.
    C. Help.

Result: Better grades; less stress and arguments.

Father's Request: 1. Discuss issues in a calm, logical manner.
    A. Present your position.
    B. Acknowledge the feelings.
    C. Listen to my point of view.

Result: Less arguments, more stable relationship; we'd get along.

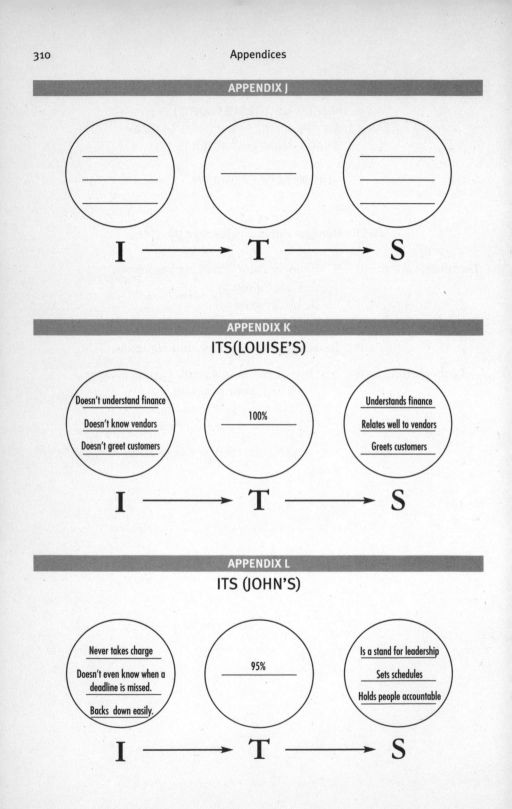

APPENDIX J

I ⟶ T ⟶ S

APPENDIX K

ITS(LOUISE'S)

Doesn't understand finance
Doesn't know vendors
Doesn't greet customers

100%

Understands finance
Relates well to vendors
Greets customers

I ⟶ T ⟶ S

APPENDIX L

ITS (JOHN'S)

Never takes charge
Doesn't even know when a deadline is missed.
Backs down easily.

95%

Is a stand for leadership
Sets schedules
Holds people accountable

I ⟶ T ⟶ S

Mission Statement Worksheet

MISSION STATEMENT EXERCISE

By following the suggested 4 steps in Process One below, you will begin writing a personal mission statement that will inspire you and will provide direction and guidance for your life. Remember that a personal mission statement is as much discovery as it is creation. Don't rush it or set rigid timetables for yourself; rather, go slowly through the process, ask yourself the right questions, and think deeply about your values and aspirations.

PROCESS ONE

The Creation of a Personal Mission Statement

A meaningful personal mission statement contains two basic elements. The first is what you want to be—what character strengths you want to have, what qualities you want to develop. The second is what you want to do—what you want to accomplish, what contributions you want to make. The third is what you want to have—what possessions, money, and so forth that you wish to have.

Note that it is relatively easy to identify the things we want to *have*; for many of us, that list will be the longest. It's important to keep in mind, however, that legitimate power and the highest levels of human happiness and fulfillment originate from the best.

Step 1 Identify an Influential Person

An effective way to focus on what you want to be and do is to identify a highly influential individual in your life and to think about how this individual has contributed to your life. This person may be a parent, work associate, friend, family member, or neighbor. Answer the following questions, keeping in mind your personal goals of what you want to be and do.

Who has been one of the most influential people in my life? _____

_____

Which qualitites do I most admire in that person? _____

_____

_____

What qualities have I gained (or desire to gain) from that person? _____

_____

_____

Step 2 Define What You Want to Be, and Do, and Have

What I'd like to be: _____

_____

_____

_____

_____

What I'd like to do: _____

_____

_____

_____

_____

What I'd like to have: _____

_____

_____

_____

_____

Step 3 Define Your Life Roles

You live your life in terms of roles—not in the sense of role-playing but in the sense of authentic parts you have chosen to fill. You may have roles in work, in the family, in the community, and in other areas of your life. These roles become a natural framework to give order to what you want to do and to be.

You may define your family role as simply "family member." Or, you may choose more specific roles, such as "wife" and "mother" or "husband" and "father." Some areas of your life, such as your profession, may involve several roles. For example, you may have one role in administration, one in marketing, one in personnel, and one in long-range planning.

Examples:

Wife/Mother, Manager—New Products, Manager—Research, Manager—Staff Development, United Way Chairperson, Friend.

Husband/Father, Salesman—Prospects, Salesman—Financing/Administration, March of Dimes Regional Director, Friend.

Define up to seven life roles and then write these roles in the space provided. Next, project yourself forward in time and write a brief statement of how you would most like to be described in that particular role.

By identifying your life roles, you will gain perspective and balance. By writing these descriptive statements, you will begin to visualize your highest self. You will also identify the core principals and values you desire to live by.

Roles

Statement

Step 4 Write a Draft of Your Personal Mission Statement

Now that you have identified your life roles and defined what you want to be and do, you are prepared to begin working on your Personal Mission Statement.

In the space provided below, create a rough draft of your Mission Statement. Draw heavily upon the thinking you've done in the previous three steps. Carry this draft with you and make notes, additions, and deletions before you attempt another draft.

_____

_____

_____

_____

_____

_____

_____

_____

_____

_____

_____

_____

_____

_____

_____

_____

_____

_____

_____

_____

_____

Examples of Company Mission and Values

ADVANCED FIBER COMMUNICATIONS:
- We will treat *all* individuals *fairly*, ethically, and with *respect.*
- We are a company built and sustained by people who are *customer-oriented*, empowered *risk-takers, team players,* and *results driven.*
- We strive to be recognized as a leader in communication technology with products that improve the quality of life in our customer communities.
- We base our *decisions* on the critical *balance* of customer expectations, shareholder return, and the *well-being* of our people.
- We will continuously strive to improve the quality and efficiency of our business.
- *We will make it fun!*

FLEX PRODUCTS:
- The Golden Rule
- Personal Development
- Innovation
- Initiative and Recognition
- Standards of Excellence
- Teamwork
- Fulfillment and Balance

KLEIN FAMILY VINTNERS:
- We are committed to the pursuit of excellence.
- We take pride in our company, its people, and its products.
- We strive to achieve 100% customer satisfaction.
- We offer our employees a stable yet challenging workplace and treat all employees with dignity.
- We are committed to building an open, honest, and trusting work environment.
- We are dedicated to quickly identifying business problems and finding solutions.
- We consider the environmental impact of all our operations.
- We are committed to providing shareholders with a superior return and pride of ownership.
- Our goal is to be the best-managed company in the wine industry now and in the years ahead.

Pre-Review

Please Print

Organization: Today's Date:

Employee's Name: Employee's Job Title:

Reviewer's Name: Follow-Up Date:

I. WHAT SKILLS ARE MOST IMPORTANT TO THIS JOB?

____ a. Quantity of work

____ b. Consistently using time efficiently/effectively

____ c. Applying technical knowledge appropriately

____ d. Generating new ideas or suggestions

____ e. Making timely decisions

____ f. Foreseeing and solving problems

____ g. Providing quality customer service

____ h. Planning, organizing, and delegating work

____ i. Properly operating and caring for equipment

____ j. Providing sound training and direction

____ k. Making sound judgments

____ l. Effectively communicating with others in written or verbal form

____ m. Consistently creating effective teamwork

____ n. Motivating and assisting other staff members

____ o. Applying operating policies and procedures prescribed for the job

____ p. Meeting goals, objectives, and commitments

____ q. Following through on tasks, activities, and responsibilities

____ r. Observing safety requirements

____ s. Maintaining good attendance and punctuality

____ t. Managing oneself

____ u. _____

II. WHICH SKILLS DOES THE EMPLOYEE PERFORM WELL?

____ a. Quantity of work

____ b. Consistently using time efficiently/effectively

____ c. Applying technical knowledge appropriately

____ d. Generating new ideas or suggestions

____ e. Making timely decisions

____ f. Foreseeing and solving problems

____ g. Providing quality customer service

____ h. Planning, organizing, and delegating work

____ i. Properly operating and caring for equipment

____ j. Providing sound training and direction

____ k. Making sound judgments

____ l. Effectively communicating with others in written or verbal form

____ m. Consistently creating effective teamwork

____ n. Motivating and assisting other staff members

____ o. Applying operating policies and procedures prescribed for the job

____ p. Meeting goals, objectives, and commitments

____ q. Following through on tasks, activities, and responsibilities

____ r. Observing safety requirements

____ s. Maintaining good attendance and punctuality

____ t. Managing oneself

____ u. _____

Pre-Review
Rudy's Form

Please Print

Organization: N/A

Employee's Name: Rudy

Reviewer's Name: Jim

Today's Date: 5/1/01

Employee's Job Title: VP Manufacturing

Follow-Up Date: 8/1/01

I. WHAT SKILLS ARE MOST IMPORTANT TO THIS JOB?

__3__ a. Quantity of work

__2__ b. Consistently using time efficiently/effectively

__2__ c. Applying technical knowledge appropriately

__*3__ d. Generating new ideas or suggestions

__2__ e. Making timely decisions

__2__ f. Foreseeing and solving problems

__1__ g. Providing quality customer service

__2__ h. Planning, organizing, and delegating work

__3__ i. Properly operating and caring for equipment

__2__ j. Providing sound training and direction

__3__ k. Making sound judgments

__2__ l. Effectively communicating with others in written or verbal form

__2__ m. Consistently creating effective teamwork

__2__ n. Motivating and assisting other staff members

__*1__ o. Applying operating policies and procedures prescribed for the job

__2__ p. Meeting goals, objectives, and commitments

__2__ q. Following through on tasks, activities, and responsibilities

__3__ r. Observing safety requirements

__2__ s. Maintaining good attendance and punctuality

__2__ t. Managing oneself

_____ u. _____

II. WHICH SKILLS DOES THE EMPLOYEE PERFORM WELL?

__✓__ a. Quantity of work

__✓__ b. Consistently using time efficiently/effectively

_____ c. Applying technical knowledge appropriately

__✓__ d. Generating new ideas or suggestions

__✓__ e. Making timely decisions

__✓__ f. Foreseeing and solving problems

_____ g. Providing quality customer service

_____ h. Planning, organizing, and delegating work

_____ i. Properly operating and caring for equipment

_____ j. Providing sound training and direction

_____ k. Making sound judgments

_____ l. Effectively communicating with others in written or verbal form

_____ m. Consistently creating effective teamwork

_____ n. Motivating and assisting other staff members

_____ o. Applying operating policies and procedures prescribed for the job

_____ p. Meeting goals, objectives, and commitments

_____ q. Following through on tasks, activities, and responsibilities

_____ r. Observing safety requirements

_____ s. Maintaining good attendance and punctuality

_____ t. Managing oneself

_____ u. _____

* Compare to Jim's form

Pre-Review
Jim's Form

Please Print

Organization: N/A   Today's Date: 5/1/01

Employee's Name: Rudy   Employee's Job Title: VP Manufacturing

Reviewer's Name: Jim   Follow-Up Date: 8/1/01

I. WHAT SKILLS ARE MOST IMPORTANT TO THIS JOB?

2   a. Quantity of work   2   l. Effectively communicating with
2   b. Consistently using time   others in written or verbal form
    efficiently/effectively   2   m. Consistently creating effective
2   c. Applying technical knowledge   teamwork
    appropriately   2   n. Motivating and assisting other
*1   d. Generating new ideas or   staff members
    suggestions   *3   o. Applying operating policies
2   e. Making timely decisions   and procedures prescribed for
2   f. Foreseeing and solving problems   the job
3   g. Providing quality customer   3   p. Meeting goals, objectives, and
    service   commitments
3   h. Planning, organizing, and   2   q. Following through on tasks,
    delegating work   activities, and responsibilities
2   i. Properly operating and caring   2   r. Observing safety requirements
    for equipment   2   s. Maintaining good attendance
2   j. Providing sound training and   and punctuality
    direction   3   t. Managing oneself
2   k. Making sound judgments   ___ u. _____

II. WHICH SKILLS DOES THE EMPLOYEE PERFORM WELL?

___ a. Quantity of work   ✓   l. Effectively communicating with
___ b. Consistently using time   others in written or verbal form
    efficiently/effectively   ___ m. Consistently creating effective
___ c. Applying technical knowledge   teamwork
    appropriately   ___ n. Motivating and assisting other
✓   d. Generating new ideas or   staff members
    suggestions   ___ o. Applying operating policies
___ e. Making timely decisions   and procedures prescribed for
✓   f. Foreseeing and solving problems   the job
___ g. Providing quality customer   ✓   p. Meeting goals, objectives, and
    service   commitments
___ h. Planning, organizing, and   ___ q. Following through on tasks,
    delegating work   activities, and responsibilities
___ i. Properly operating and caring ___ r. Observing safety requirements
    for equipment   ___ s. Maintaining good attendance
___ j. Providing sound training and   and punctuality
    direction   ___ t. Managing oneself
___ k. Making sound judgments   ___ u. _____

* Compare to Rudy's form

Clear Office Communication©

Eight-Step Checklist for Effective Listening

#1 PAY ATTENTION; INTEND TO UNDERSTAND
- Focus attention on the person; do not interrupt.
- Maintain eye contact, sit forward, and lean toward the speaker.
- Take in the whole picture.
- Tell and demonstrate to the person that he or she has your full attention.

#2 SUMMARIZE WHAT YOU HAVE HEARD (USE FEELINGS CHART)
- Repeat back in your own words what you heard. "Let me see if I understand. You are feeling . . . because . . . is that correct?"
- Use words that create pictures and feelings.

#3 ACKNOWLEDGE FEELINGS
- Ask how the person feels about the situation.
- Show awareness of the speaker's concern: "I understand how you feel." or "I can see your frustration."
- Tell about a time you had similar feelings or describe a similar situation.
- Suspend your own biases about the situation.

#4 ASK CLARIFYING QUESTIONS
- *Who* . . . is involved?
- *What* . . . have you said?
- *Where* . . . did you get that idea?
- *Why* . . . is this happening now?
- *How* . . . did you arrive at that conclusion/idea/agreement?

#5 ASK FOR THE OTHER PERSON'S SUGGESTIONS FOR RESOLUTION
- How would you recommend that this be handled?
- What would you like to see done?
- Ask for all relevant information.

#6 PRESENT YOUR POSITION
- If the suggestion above is suitable, tell the person: "That sounds like a good idea." Make sure the message is consistent; body language matches the verbal component.
- If the suggestion in #5 is not suitable, present your position: "I hear your suggestion and I have another point of view. What we might do is . . ."
- Collaborate: "Your suggestion works nicely in these areas. I'll support you. Can you support me in these areas?"

#7 DECIDE ON SPECIFIC COURSE OF ACTION AND FOLLOW-UP (USE *ALIGNMENT AGREEMENT*)
- "Now, let's see, I will . . . and you will . . . okay?"
- Ask: "Do you need additional support? How and in what form?"

#8 THANK THE PERSON
- Evaluate the conversation: Were you both heard and understood? Is the solution win-win?
- "I really appreciate your coming to me with your concerns."

Clear Office Communication©

Feelings Chart

Love	Hostility	Betrayed	Isolated
Hate	Confusion	Peaceful	Alone
Anger	Aggravated	Enthusiastic	Independent
Frustration	Protective	Empty	Trapped
Guilt	Possessive	Mad	Powerful
Anxiety	Happy	Sympathy	Needed
Worry	Sad	Embarrassed	Confident
Hurt	Excited	Shy	Wanted
Tired	Surprised	Terror	Secure
Confused	Shocked	Abused	Insecure
Curious	Afraid	Flexible	Cautious
Hopeless	Important	Misunderstood	Vulnerable
Hopeful	Rejected	Proud	Tender
Appreciative	Depressed	Pleased	Rage
Helpless	Nervous	Caring	Accepted
Overwhelmed	Grief	Carefree	Nurturing
Pressured	Inadequate	Fear	Weak
Sure	Disappointed	Mean	Deceived
Unsure	Lonely	Aggressive	Self-Defeating
Satisfied	Bored	Irritated	Disgusted
Relief	Blamed	Justified	Content
Joy	Self-Doubt	Defensive	
Scared	Deserted	Dependent	

Clear Office Communication©

Conscious Communication

1. I make myself feel _____
   (use Feelings Chart)
   when _____
   (briefly describe situation)
   _____

2. I am concerned that what might happen is _____
   (what you want changed)
   _____
   _____

3. I would like you to _____
   _____
   _____

4. My goal is _____
   _____
   _____

5. It seems to me your goal is _____
   _____
   _____

6. Would you be willing to explore some alternatives to help us both achieve our goals? If "yes" finish with #7. If "no" finish process with thanking him/her for listening to you.

7. Some possibilities I have come up with that may be more effective or harmonious are:
   1. _____
   _____
   2. _____
   _____
   3. _____
   _____

Are any of these acceptable to you? Do you see other possibilities? Listen to response, possibly discuss and thank her/him for listening to you.

APPENDIX S

Clear Office Communication©

Conscious Communication

LUCY'S COMMUNICATION TO MYRA (NEVER DELIVERED)

1. I make myself feel <u>threatened, intimidated, out of control</u>

   <small>(use Feelings Chart)</small>

   when   <u>you glare at me and make condescending remarks, humiliate Lucy,</u>

   <small>(briefly describe situation)</small>

   <u>tell me you hate people.</u>

2. I am concerned that what might happen is <u>you're going to shoot somebody,</u>

   <small>(what you want changed)</small>

   <u>maybe me, or sabotage my job.</u>

3. I would like you to <u>love and respect people or leave.</u>

4. My goal is <u>to get beyond this and have a happy work environment.</u>

5. It seems to me your goal is <u>to win and to take prisoners [dark side] or to give</u>

   <u>your best to the customer [bright side].</u>

6. Would you be willing to explore some alternatives to help us both achieve our goals? If "yes" finish with #7. If "no" finish process with thanking him/her for listening to you.

7. Some possibilities I have come up with that may be more effective or harmonious are:
   1. <u>Make honest amends to those you have harmed.</u>

   2. <u>Genuinely admit that you are powerless over you anger.</u>

   3. <u>Go to weekly counseling with an honest, open mind.</u>

Are any of these acceptable to you? Do you see other possibilities? Listen to response, possibly discuss and thank her/him for listening to you.

APPENDIX T

Clear Office Communication©

Conscious Communication

ERIC'S COMMUNICATION TO MYRA

1. I make myself feel frustrated, fearful, disappointed
   (use Feelings Chart)
   when I see you have picked on other people in the office or created a hostile
   environment. *(briefly describe situation)*

2. I am concerned that what might happen is most people will quit and that there
   could be lawsuits because of your creation of a hostile environment. *(what you want changed)*

3. I would like you to take responsibility for your anger in the office.

4. My goal is to have a very friendly and fun place to work where people enjoy coming
   into the office each day.

5. It seems to me your goal is   to provide the highest possible client service to our clients
   at the expense of the staff.

6. Would you be willing to explore some alternatives to help us both achieve our
   goals? If "yes" finish with #7. If "no" finish process with thanking him/her for listening to you.

7. Some possibilities I have come up with that may be more effective or harmonious are:
   1. When you feel angry, come directly to me.

   2. Cooperate with me when I try to mediate a situation, however small it may seem.

   3. Treat people with respect no matter how angry you are.

   4. Make amends with people when you blow it.

Are any of these acceptable to you? Do you see other possibilities? Listen to response,
possibly discuss and thank her/him for listening to you.

Clear Office Communication©

Conscious Communication

MYRA'S COMMUNICATION TO ERIC (delivered)

1. I make myself feel angry, frustrated, and hurt
                          (use Feelings Chart)

   when you listen to Lucy and the others when they complain about me.
                          (briefly describe situation)

2. I am concerned that what might happen is you will believe them and they don't know
                                              (what you want changed)
   the pain I have in my wrist.

3. I would like you to be understanding of my pain and health problems.

4. My goal is to serve the clients in the best way possible.

5. It seems to me your goal is   to get into everyone's personal feelings.

6. Would you be willing to explore some alternatives to help us both achieve our goals? If "yes" finish with #7. If "no" finish process with thanking him/her for listening to you.

7. Some possibilities I have come up with that may be more effective or harmonious are:
   1. Train or terminate Lucy.

   2. Refrain from listening to their complaints.

   3. Let me do my job.

Are any of these acceptable to you? Do you see other possibilities? Listen to response, possibly discuss and thank her/him for listening to you.

The Professional Growth Plan™

Alignment Agreement Follow-up between Myra and Eric

Alignment Date:

Follow-up Date:

Employee: **Myra**   Reviewer: **Eric**

	This Follow-up	
Last Follow-up EE% ER%	EE%	ER%

Employee Request: Understand my pain.   ☐   ☐
New or Revised

What it looks like: A. Train Lucy.   ☐   ☐

B. Refrain from listening to complaints.   ☐   ☐

C. Let me do my job.   ☐   ☐

Measurement: I can serve clients better.

Signed: _____

Gap Correction:

	EE%	ER
Last Follow-up EE% ER%		

Reviewer Request: Take responsibility for your anger in this office.   ☐   ☐
New or Revised

What it looks like: A. When angry, come to me first.   ☐   ☐

B. Cooperate in mediation.   ☐   ☐

C. Make amends.   ☐   ☐

Measurement: We'll have a friendly, fun office.

Signed: _____

Gap Correction:

Implied Middle Managers (Agreement)

- Give orders clearly
- Tell employees how they are doing
- Develop teamwork
- Defend individuals against unjustified criticism
- Help new members fit into the group
- Consider the feelings of others
- Encourage employees to do their best
- Correct employees when necessary
- Coordinate the work of the group
- Keep group informed on matters affecting their work
- Talk to employees at their desks, if possible
- Accept criticism
- Show the importance of the work

- Study employees to determine their abilities and shortcomings
- Criticize constructively
- Encourage people to "get things off their chests"
- Treat all courteously
- Recognize off-the-job accomplishments
- Set an example
- Show respect for employees and others
- Keep them doing things right
- Show how work ties in with work done in other departments
- Back-up and go to bat for employees when they are right
- Give attention to the shy and lonely
- Train understudies
- Find out how people feel as well as how they think

- Use every possible suggestion offered by employees
- Put every employee on his or her own as quickly as possible
- Tell others of the importance of the group
- Speak to every employee every day, if possible
- Make use of any special skills and abilities
- Explain WHY things are done
- Recognize good and mention it
- Equalize overtime
- Help group clear up conflicts both on and off the job
- Recommend deserving workers for promotion
- Visit employees when they are sick
- Treat all fairly
- Listen

COMMUNICATING EFFECTIVELY

- Explain clearly
- Give reasons for all policies and procedures
- Show and demonstrate, if possible
- Follow up long or doubtful instructions and information

- Conduct effective group meetings
- Encourage employees to express themselves
- Explain thoroughly decisions made at high management levels

- Give reasons for notices meant to direct or persuade
- Show employees the tools to express themselves effectively
- Keep superiors posted on trends

- Have a purpose for every meeting
- Ask questions beginning with "What," "When," "Where" "Why," "Who," and "How"

- Report progress made in meeting schedules and maintaining quality
- Explain changes before making them

- Listen carefully to all complaints, using the 8-Step Checklist for Effectively Listening

CONTROLLING EXPENSES

- Get complete explanations of budgets, if prepared by others
- Look for and suggest ways of improving methods
- Find causes of "over" and "under" items in budget
- Encourage suggestions from employees

- Check use of utilities—water, air, gas, and electricity
- Plan to avoid overtime
- Tell employees how the department is meeting cost standards
- Requisition only the supplies needed for efficient operations

- Explain to employees reasons for keeping costs low
- Keep a personal record of critical expense items
- Protect equipment, machines, materials, and property

DEVELOPING SELF

- Recognize exact responsibilities
- Get a clear understanding of new developments in your career field
- Clean up details promptly
- Improve ability to pass on information
- Plan a course of study; get advice, if necessary
- Weigh the short- and long-term effects of decisions
- Take part in community activities
- Learn the economics of the business

- Get pleasure from the accomplishments of others
- Take calculated risks
- Control temper
- Adopt and practice a system of problem analysis for decision making
- Seek job improvements
- Learn to do the best you can with what you have got
- Maintain a sense of humor
- Support employees with written notes
- Set goals for self and work to reach them

- Stay informed of new developments in your career field
- Make prompt but not hasty decisions
- Learn the limits of authority
- Get pleasure from being and working with others
- Use the experience of others
- Schedule personal time
- Get things done by persuasion, not by authority alone
- Develop and use checklists

KEEPING RECORDS

- Learn the reasons for all records
- Keep accurate records
- Improve handwriting, if necessary

- Maintain a records-retention schedule
- Keep written work up-to-date

- Write down messages that are important
- Suggest ways to cut paperwork, but do do the paperwork required

MAINTAINING DISCIPLINE

- Set standards of good work habits and conduct
- Tell what you want rather than what you don't like
- Keep employees informed of what they are to do
- Reprimand when necessary
- Set a good example

- Give clear instructions; use job-training steps
- Follow set procedures in disciplining, but suggest ways to improve
- Encourage employees to offer suggestions of good work habits
- Control absenteeism and tardiness

- Revise standards whenever necessary
- Find out what employees need from you and make sure you provide it
- Reward good work habits with a "pat on the back"
- Put in a day's work for a day's pay

PERSUADING AND GIVING REASONS

- Give reasons for meeting responsibilities
- Ask employees for their agreement to follow through
- Give reasons for offering suggestions
- Ask others for input as to how to be safer

- Ask employees for their input
- Give reasons when making requests of superiors
- Ask others if they have suggestions
- Give reasons when seeking the cooperation of other managers for improvement

- Give reasons for rules, policies, and practices
- Ask superiors what requests they may have of you
- Give reasons for practicing safety on and off the job
- Ask other managers what they suggest for improvement

PLANNING AND ORGANIZING

- Develop a checklist of equipment, materials, and people

- Decide who is to carry out the decision

- Schedule work according to priority

- Identify, locate, and describe any deviations from standard practice

- Recognize when a problem exists

- Gather information on the problem

- Conclude planning with a written list of things to do

- Determine alternative objectives of a decision, then choose the best alternative

- Determine what the problem "is" and what it "is not"

- Anticipate changes and emergencies

- Persuade, if necessary, to get the action required

MAINTAINING QUALITY

- Know the exact quality

- Listen to suggested improvements with an open mind

- Build concern for quality work

- Follow the standards set, but at the same time look for ways of improving them

- Train employees to meet the standards

- Look for and suggest improvements in method

- Cooperate with other department managers to control quality

PRODUCING QUANTITY SCHEDULED

- Develop a list of critical jobs and check them at definite intervals

- Anticipate bottlenecks and plan what to do to clear them up

- Set up controls and reporting procedures to check on progress

- Develop a checklist to aid in maintaining supplies of materials and equipment

- Anticipate interruptions in utilities and plan what to do to overcome them

- Determine responsibility for carrying out schedules and verify that it is understood

- Plan to reduce overtime

- Cooperate with staff departments and managers

PROMOTING SAFETY

- Set a good example
- Check continuously for unsafe conditions, such as improper illumination or unsafe storage areas
- Do not take things for granted

- Take precautions to prevent accidents
- Make your own department an outstanding example of safety
- Anticipate possible safety hazards and plan how to avoid them

- Discourage any horseplay
- Thank employees for safety suggestions
- Understand your rights and responsibilities as a manager under the Occupational Safety and Health Act

TRAINING EMPLOYEES

- Select the right people for the right jobs
- Let the learner outline his or her own training steps
- Prepare to train thoroughly
- Follow up closely until the learner can do as instructed

- Find out what the learner already knows and can do
- Put the learner on his or her own
- Show the learner what he/she will gain by learning
- Rotate employees, when possible, to broaden skills

- Retrain if the learner needs it
- Taper off management as the learner develops skills
- Ask the learner questions beginning with "What," "When," "Where," "Why," "Who," and "How"
- Keep stress in balance

SERVING CUSTOMERS

- Demonstrate customer service starts with you and works its way out to others in your organization and ultimately to the customer

- Teach others that value-centered customer service is created by the values of the people who provide it

- Build life long customers
- Serve internal and external customers

MANAGING ONESELF

- Stay physically and emotionally fit
- Tap into intuitive skills

- Look for methods of self improvement
- Create vision and mission

- Use visualization
- Take responsibility for relationships

The Professional Growth Plan™
Alignment Agreement

Please Print

Organization: _____   Today's Date: _____

Employee's Name: _____   Employee's Job Title: _____

Reviewer's Name: _____   Follow-up Date: _____

INSTRUCTIONS: Before writing, Reviewer first hears the Employee's complete request, then it is discussed and agreed upon by both. Reviewer then clearly and concisely prints the Employee's request in full, and signs in agreement. Employee then hears the Reviewer's complete request, they come to agreement, Emloyee prints the request, and signs the form.

EMPLOYEE'S REQUEST (PRINTED BY REVIEWER)

1. The #1 item _____ wants from _____ is:
                   Employee's Name   *Reviewer's Name*
   _____
   _____

2. Specifically what will the Reviewer do to meet your request?
   A. _____
   B. _____
   C. _____

3. How will you know the request has been fulfilled; how will you measure the change? _____
   _____

I agree to begin on _____ Signed _____
                       Date   *Reviewer's Signature*

REVIEWER'S REQUEST (PRINTED BY THE EMPLOYEE)

1. The #1 item _____ wants from _____ is:
                   Reviewer's Name   *Employee's Name*
   _____
   _____

2. Specifically what will the Employee do to meet your request?
   A. _____
   B. _____
   C. _____

3. How will you know the request has been fulfilled; how will you measure the change? _____
   _____

I agree to begin on _____ Signed _____
                       Date   *Employee's Signature*

The Professional Growth Plan™
Alignment Agreement
PAUL'S FORM

Please Print

Organization: Manufacturing Fortune 500　　　Today's Date: 9/16

Employee's Name: Paul　　　　　　　　　　Employee's Job Title: Manager

Reviewer's Name: John　　　　　　　　　　Follow-up Date: 11/1

INSTRUCTIONS: Before writing, Reviewer first hears the Employee's complete request, then it is discussed and agreed upon by both. Reviewer then clearly and concisely prints the Employee's request in full, and signs in agreement. Employee then hears the Reviewer's complete request, they come to agreement, Emloyee prints the request, and signs the form.

EMPLOYEE'S REQUEST (PRINTED BY REVIEWER)

1. The #1 item _____Paul_____ wants from _____John_____ is:
   _{Employee's Name}　　　　　　　　　_{Reviewer's Name}

   let me have input on goals.

2. Specifically what will the Reviewer do to meet your request?
   A. Meet with me before setting deadlines.
   B. Ask me when I think we can meet it.
   C. Include me in goal setting meetings with executive staff.

3. How will you know the request has been fulfilled; how will you measure the change? We'd make 90% of deadlines.

I agree to begin on ___9/16___ Signed _____
　　　　　　　　　　　Date　　　　　　　　　　　*Reviewer's Signature*

REVIEWER'S REQUEST (PRINTED BY EMPLOYEE)

1. The #1 item _____John_____ wants from _____Paul_____ is:
   _{Reviewer's Name}　　　　　　　　　_{Employee's Name}

   for Paul to take a stand and lead.

2. Specifically what will the Reviewer do to meet your request?
   A. Build a model.
   B. Make a video and show everyone.
   C. Set a schedule and hold them to it.

3. How will you know the request has been fulfilled; how will you measure the change? We'd make 90 percent of deadlines. We'd save 10 percent in material.

I agree to begin on ___9/16___ Signed _____
　　　　　　　　　　　Date　　　　　　　　　　　*Employee's Signature*

The Professional Growth Plan™
Alignment Agreement Follow-up

Alignment Date:

Follow-up Date:

Employee: Reviewer:

This Follow-up

```
┌──────────────────────────────────┐
│  Last                            │        EE%      ER%
│  Follow-up   EE%        ER%      │        ☐        ☐
└──────────────────────────────────┘
```

Employee Request:
New or Revised

What it looks like: A.   ☐   ☐

                       B.   ☐   ☐

                       C.   ☐   ☐

Measurement:

Signed: _____

Gap Correction:

```
┌──────────────────────────────────┐
│  Last                            │        EE%      ER%
│  Follow-up   EE%        ER%      │        ☐        ☐
└──────────────────────────────────┘
```

Reviewer Request:
New or Revised

What it looks like: ☐   ☐

                                              ☐   ☐

                                              ☐   ☐

Measurement:

Signed: _____

Gap Correction:

The Professional Growth Plan™

Alignment Agreement Follow-up (for John and Paul)

Alignment Date: **5/10/00**

Follow-up Date: **8/10/00**

Employee: **Paul**   Reviewer: **John**

This Follow-up

	EE%	ER%

Last
Follow-up   EE%   ER%

Employee Request: Let me have input on goals. | 90 | 90 |
New or Revised

What it looks like: A. Meet with me before setting deadlines. | ☐ | ☐ |

                          B. Ask me when I think we can meet it. | ☐ | ☐ |

                          C. Include me in goal setting meetings with | ☐ | ☐ |
                             executive deadlines.

Measurement: We'd make 90% of deadlines.

Signed: _____

Gap Correction:

Last
Follow-up   EE%   ER%

Reviewer Request: Take a stand and lead.   EE%   ER%
New or Revised

What it looks like: A. Build a model. | 60 | 90 |

                         B. Make a video and show everyone. | ☐ | ☐ |

                         C. Set a schedule and hold them to it. | ☐ | ☐ |

Measurement: We'd make 90% of deadlines.

Signed: _____

Gap Correction:

The Professional Growth Plan™

Alignment Agreement Follow-up for (Joyce and Carla)

Alignment Date: **4/10/01**
Follow-up Date: **7/10/01**
Employee: **Joyce**   Reviewer: **Carla**

		This Follow-up	
Last Follow-up EE%	ER%	EE%	ER%

Employee Request: *New or Revised*	Keep me informed each day.	90	85
What it looks like:	A. Meet with me at 8:00 A.M. daily to let me know what's up.	95	88
	B. E-mail me on any new events during the day.	85	82
	C. Give me copies of relevant information	90	85
Measurement:	We'd be more efficient in the lab. Complaints would go from 5 per week to 1 per month.		

Signed: _____

Gap Correction:

		EE%	ER%
Last Follow-up EE%	ER%		

Reviewer Request: *New or Revised*	Lead the way for your employees by empowering them and treating them with dignity.	90	5⅓
What it looks like:	A. Admit you haven't been honoring dignity in the past.	95	16
	B. Commit to weigh the pros and cons of their suggestions.	90	0
	C. Speak in a respectful tone.	85	0
Measurement:	Management would take note and acknowledge you for resolving the volatile lab situation. Complaints would be reduced from 5 per day to 1 per month.		

Signed: _____

Gap Correction: Joyce needs to admit **she's** not been honoring dignity and weighing the pros and cons in a respectful voice.

Notes

CHAPTER 1

1. Robert K. Cooper and Ayman Sawaf, *Executive EQ: Emotional Intelligence in Leadership and Organizations* (New York: Perigee, Berkeley Publishing Group, 1997), 17.
2. Patricia Wiklund, *Taking Charge When You're Not in Control* (New York: Ballantine Books, 2000), 29.
3. Peter Drucker, *Managing in a Time of Great Change* (New York: Truman Talley Books/Dutton, 1995).
4. John D. Rockefeller, *Big Business: Economic Power in a Free Society* (New York: Doubleday, Page, 1908), 144–145.
5. George Zimmer, president of the Men's Warehouse, University of Phoenix, Commencement Speech, 1998.
6. Peter Drucker, *Management Challenges for the 21st Century* (New York: Harper Business, 1999), cover.

CHAPTER 2

1. Richard Pascale, Mark Milleman and Linda Gioja, *Surfing the Edge of Chaos* (New York: Crown Business, 2000).
2. Peter Senge, *The Fifth Discipline: The Art and Practice of the Learning Organization* (New York: Doubleday/Currency, 1990), 239.
3. Victor Frankel, *Man's Search for Meaning* (Boston: Washington Square Press, 1984), 75.
4. John D. Rockefeller, *Big Business: Economic Power in a Free Society* (New York: Doubleday, Page, 1908), 145.
5. Speech by Kaiser Permanente public affairs director at Santa Rosa Rotary Club meeting, January 2000.

6. Robert K. Cooper and Ayman Sawaf, *Executive EQ: Emotional Intelligence in Leadership and Organizations* (New York: Perigee, Berkeley Publishing Group, 1997), 50.

7. Edward Deming, *Out of Crisis* (Cambridge, Mass.: MIT Center for Advanced Engineering, 1986), 23–24.

8. Richard Carlson, *Don't Sweat the Small Stuff at Work* (New York: Hyperion, 1999), 5–282.

9. Dale Carnegie and Associates, *How to Win Friends and Influence People: The Leader in You:* (New York: Simon and Schuster, 1993), 17.

CHAPTER 3

1. Conversation with Bob Galvin, San Francisco, St. Francis Hotel, October 2, 1998.

2. John Naisbitt, *High Tech High Touch: Technology and Our Search for Meaning* (New York: Broadway Books, 1999), 91.

3. Ibid.

CHAPTER 4

1. Chris Evans, *Breaking Free of the Shame Trap* (New York: Ballantine Books, 1994), 102.

2. Gordon Bethune and Scott Huler, *From Worst to First: Behind the Scenes of Continental's Remarkable Comeback* (Somerset, N.J.: John Wiley and Sons, 1998), 130–133.

CHAPTER 5

1. Peter Drucker, *Management Challenges for the 21st Century* (New York: Harper Business, 1999), 180–183.

2. Robert Mondavi, *Harvests of Joy* (San Diego: Harcourt Brace, 1998), book cover.

3. Stephen R. Covey, *The Seven Habits of Highly Effective People* (New York: Simon and Schuster, 1989), 131. Covey reference to Roger Merrill, *Connections: Quadrant II Time Management*, 131.

4. Mary Manin-Morrissey, *Building Your Field of Dreams* (New York: Bantam Books, 1996), 33.

5. Dierdre Fanning, "A Spiritual Healer for the Workplace," *New York Times*, June 10, 1990, 1.

CHAPTER 6

1. Kathleen Ryan and Daniel Oestreich, *Driving Fear Out of the Workplace* (San Francisco: Jossey-Bass, 1991), 132–133.

2. Deborah Tannen, *The Argument Culture: Stopping America's War of Words* (New York: Ballantine Books, 1998), 71–76, 97.

3. Dalai Lama, *Ethics for the New Millennium* (New York: Penguin Putnam, 1999), 82.

4. "Word for Word: Defining the Line between Behavior That's Vexing and Certifiable," *New York Times*, December 19, 1999, 7.

5. Diagnostic criteria from *DSM-IV*, (Washington, D.C.: American Psychiatric Association. 1994), 280–281.

6. Conversation with Dr. Michael Barrington, University of Phoenix, October 1999.

7. *Harris v. Oregon Health Services*, Portland, September 1999.

8. Michael Maccoby, "Narcissistic Leaders: The Incredible Pros, the Inevitable Cons," *Harvard Business Review* (January/February 2000), 68.

9. Ibid., 69.

10. Ibid., 70.

CHAPTER 7

1. Robert K. Cooper and Ayman Sawaf, *Executive EQ: Emotional Intelligence in Leadership and Organizations* (New York: Perigee, Berkeley Publishing Group, 1997), 101–105.

2. M. Scott Peck, *A World Waiting to Be Born: Civility Rediscovered* (New York: Bantam, 1993), 4–5.

3. Ken Blanchard, *Managing by Values* (San Francisco: Berrett-Koehler, 1997), 86.

CHAPTER 8

1. Peter Drucker, *Management Challenges for the 21st Century* (New York: Harper Business, 1999), 184–185.

2. M. Scott Peck, *A World Waiting to Be Born* (New York: Bantam Books, 1993), 27.

3. Robert K. Cooper and Ayman Sawaf, *Executive EQ: Emotional Intelligence in Leadership and Organizations* (New York: Perigee, Berkeley Publishing Group, 1997), xxxiii.

CHAPTER 9

1. Don Miguel Ruiz, *The Four Agreements* (San Rafael, Calif.: Amber-Allen Publishing, 1997), 79–80.

2. Robert Mondavi, *Harvests of Joy* (San Diego: Harcourt Brace, 1998), 147.

3. Robert K. Cooper and Ayman Sawaf, *Executive EQ: Emotional Intelligence in Leadership and Organizations* (New York: Perigee, Berkeley Publishing Group, 1997), 175.

CHAPTER 10

1. Don Miguel Ruiz, *The Four Agreements* (San Rafael, Calif.: Amber-Allen Publishing, 1997), 79–80.
2. Paul Hennig Ph.D., MFCC, *www.lei.net8080/dml/Odyssey/NPD.htm.*
3. Mary Riley, "Toward Better Performance Reviews," *Office Automation and Administration* (July 1983), 28–30.

CHAPTER 11

1. Cooper and Sawaf, *Executive EQ: Emotional Intelligence in Leadership and Organizations* (New York: Perigee, Berkley Publishing Group, 1997), 174.

CHAPTER 12

1. Robert K. Cooper and Ayman Sawaf, *Executive EQ: Emotional Intelligence in Leadership and Organizations* (New York: Perigee, Berkley Publishing Group, 1997), 65.
2. DeLuca, *Start Small Finish Big* (New York: Warner Business, 2000), 270.
3. George Stephanopoulos, *All Too Human: A Political Lesson* (New York: Little, Brown, 1999).
4. Morey Stettner, *Investors Business Daily*, October 11, 1999, front page.
5. Quentin Hardy, "The Cult of Carly," *Forbes*, December 13, 1999, 141.
6. Ronna Lichtenberg, *Work Would Be Great If It Weren't for the People* (New York: Hyperion, 1998), 37–64.
7. Stephen Covey, *The Seven Habits of Highly Effective People* (New York: Simon and Schuster, 1989), 66.
8. Peter Senge, *The Fifth Discipline: The Art and Practice of the Learning Organization* (New York: Doubleday/Currency, 1990), 10.
9. Robert Mondavi, *Harvests of Joy* (San Diego: Harcourt Brace, 1998), 291. Cover quote by Frank Prial of the *New York Times*.
10. Ibid., 285–291.

CHAPTER 13

1. Gary Dessler, *Human Resource Management* (New Jersey: Prentice Hall, 1997), 357.
2. Peter F. Drucker, *Toward the Next Economics* (New York: Harper and Row, 1981), 78.
3. Peter F. Drucker, *Management Challenges for the 21st Century* (New York: Harper Business, 1999), 163.
4. Ibid.

5. Don Head and Mary Riley, "Be a Boss and Listen," *Water Engineering Management (The Magazine of Applied Water/Wastewater Technology)*, (July 1989): 47.
6. Ibid., 49.

CHAPTER 14

1. Mary Riley, "Toward Better Performance Reviews," *Office Automation and Administration* (October 1983): 28–30.
2. Tom Sargent and Rich Noland, "Performance Appraisals: New Process Makes Reviews Something to Applaud, Rather Than Dread, by Both Supervisor and Employee," *Credit Union Management* (March 1988): 14.
3. Jack Kondrasuk, Mary Riley, and Wang Hua, "If We Want to Pay for Performance, How Do We Judge Performance?" *Journal of Compensation and Benefits* (September/October 1999): 35–40.
4. Robert K. Cooper and Ayman Sawaf, *Executive EQ: Emotional Intelligence in Leadership and Organizations* (New York: Perigee, Berkeley Publishing Group, 1997), 272.
5. Ibid., 273.
6. Bill Gittins and Mary Riley, "The Power of Positive Reviewing," *Plant Services Magazine* (May 1995): 79.

CHAPTER 15

1. Bill Jensen, *Simplicity—The New Competitive Advantage in a World of More, Better, Faster* (Cambridge, Mass.: Perseus Books, 2000), 38.
2. John Templeton, letter to author, April 22, 2000.
3. Telephone conversation with John Templeton, April 8, 1993.
4. Father Joseph Otté, retired priest of St. Eugene's Catholic Church, Santa Rosa, California. In a series of weekly sessions (similar to *Tuesdays with Morrie*), 1984–1986.
5. Reverend Frank Kimper, retired Methodist minister and teacher of "The Course in Miracles," 1995–2001. Phone conversation, June 12, 2000.
6. Marianne Williamson in answer to a question author posed from the audience at a Copperfield's book signing and author presentation, Santa Rosa, California, 1992.
7. Neale Donald Walsch, in a conversation in Denver, Colorado, following his presentation in July 1998.
8. John D. Rockefeller, *Big Business: Economic Power in a Free Society* (New York: Doubleday, Page, 1908), 46.
9. Mitch Albom, *Tuesdays with Morrie: An Old Man, a Young Man, and Life's Greatest Lesson* (New York: Doubleday, 1997).

10. Ken Blanchard, Bill Hybels, and Phil Hodges, *Leadership by the Book: Tools to Transform Your Workplace* (New York: William Morrow, 1999).

11. Matthew Fox, *The Reinvention of Work* (San Francisco: HarperCollins, 1994).

12. John Brooke Morgan, *How to Keep a Sound Mind* (New York: Macmillan, 1939), 249–268.

13. Stephen Covey, *The Seven Habits of Highly Effective People* (New York: Simon and Schuster, 1989), 76.

14. Ibid.

CHAPTER 16

1. Bill Jensen, *Simplicity: The New Competitive Advantage in a World of More, Better, Faster* (Cambridge, Mass.: Perseus Books, 2000), Introduction.

2. *The Koran*. Translated by N. J. Dawood (New York: Penguin, 1990).

3. John Naisbitt, *High Tech High Touch: Technology and Our Search for Meaning* (New York: Broadway Books, 1999), 268–269.

4. Michelle Conlin, "Religion in the Workplace," *Business Week* (November 1999): 150–155.

5. M. Scott Peck, *A World Waiting to Be Born* (New York: Bantam, 1993), 5–6.

6. Ibid., 305.

7. Keith Headman, "Dealing with Conflict Resolution in My Workplace," paper prepared for a University of Phoenix M.B.A. class (Conflict Management Systems), October 1999.

8. Kathleen Ryan and Daniel Oestreich. *Driving Fear Out of the Workplace* (San Francisco: Jossey-Bass, 1991), 132–133.

9. Edward Deming, *Out of Crisis* (Cambridge, Mass.: MIT Center for Advanced Engineering, 1986), 24.

10. Neale Donald Walsch, *Conversations with God* (New York: Putnam and Sons, 1997), 54.

11. Mary Riley, *Corporate Healing: Solutions to the Impact of the Addictive Personality in the Workplace* (Deerfield Beach, Fla.: Health Communications, 1990), 11.

12. Cathy Costantino and Christina Sickles Merchant, *Designing Conflict Management Systems* (San Francisco: Jossey-Bass, 1996), 3.

13. Bob Batchelor, "Money Man," *Inside Business* (October 1999): 60–61.

14. Ken Keyes Jr. and Penny Keyes, *Handbook to Higher Consciousness: The Workbook* (Coos Bay, Oregon: Love Line Books, 1989), 98.

15. Karen Armstrong, *A History of God: The 4000-Year Quest of Judaism, Christianity, and Islam* (New York: Alfred A. Knopf, 1993), viii.

16. Ibid., 387.

17. Stephen Covey, *The Seven Habits of Highly Effective People* (New York: Simon and Schuster, 1989), 61.

Bibliography

Albom, Mitch. *Tuesdays with Morrie: An Old Man, a Young Man, and Life's Greatest Lesson.* New York: Doubleday, 1997.

American Psychiatric Association. *Diagnostic Criteria from DSM-IV.* Washington, D.C., 1994.

Armstrong, Karen. *A History of God: The 4000-Year Quest of Judaism, Christianity, and Islam.* New York: Alfred A. Knopf, 1993.

———. *The Battle for God.* New York: Alfred A. Knopf, 2000.

Autry, James A. *Confessions of an Accidental Businessman.* San Francisco: Berrett-Koehler Publishers, 1996.

Bartholomew. *I Come as a Brother: A Remembrance of Illusions.* Taos, N.M.: High Mesa Press, 1986.

Batchelor, Bob. "Money Man." *Inside Business.* October 1999. pp. 60–61.

Bellman, Geoffrey M. *Getting Things Done When You Are Not in Charge.* New York: Berrett-Koehler Publishers, 1992.

Bethune, Gordon, and Scott Huler. *From Worst to First: Behind the Scenes of Continental's Remarkable Comeback.* Somerset, N.J.: John Wiley and Sons, 1998.

The Bible. King James Version. New York: Macmillan, 1987.

Blanchard, Ken, Bill Hybels, and Phil Hodges. *Leadership by the Book: Tools to Transform Your Workplace.* New York: William Morrow, 1999.

Blanchard, Ken, and Michael O'Connor. *Managing by Values.* San Francisco: Berrett-Koehler Publishers, 1997.

Brokaw, Tom. *The Greatest Generation.* New York: Random House, 1999.

"The Growing Presence of Spirituality in Corporate America: Religion in the Workplace." *Business Week.* November 1, 1999.

Carlson, Richard. *Don't Sweat the Small Stuff at Work.* New York: Hyperion, 1999.

Carnegie, Dale, and Associates. *How to Win Friends and Influence People: The Leader in You.* New York: Simon and Schuster. 1993.

Carter, Rosalynn. *Helping Someone with Mental Illness.* New York: Random House, 1998.

Chopra, Deepak. *How to Know God.* New York: Harmony Books, 2000.

Conlin, Michelle."Religion in the Workplace." *Business Week,* November 1, 1999. pp. 150–158.

Cooper, Robert K., and Ayman Sawaf. *Executive EQ: Emotional Intelligence in Leadership and Organizations.* New York: Perigee, Berkeley Publishing Group, 1997.

Costantino, Cathy A., and Christina Sickles Merchant. *Designing Conflict Management Systems.* San Francisco: Jossey-Bass, 1996.

Covey, Stephen. *The Courage to Change.* New York: Simon and Schuster, 1999.

———. *Principle-Centered Leadership.* New York: Summit Books, 1990.

———. *The Seven Habits of Highly Effective People.* New York: Simon and Schuster, 1989.

Covey, Stephen, Roger Merrill, and Rebecca R. Merrill. *First Things First: To Live, to Love, to Leave a Legacy.* New York: Simon and Schuster, 1994.

Crandall, Rick. *Break-Out Creativity: Bringing Creativity to the Workplace.* Corte Madera, Calif.: Select Press, 1997.

Credit Union Management. "Performance Appraisals: New Process Makes Reviews Something to Applaud, Rather Than Dread, by Both Supervisor and Employee." March 1988.

DeLuca. *Start Small Finish Big.* New York: Warner Business, 2000.

Deming, Edward. *Out of Crisis.* Cambridge, Mass.: MIT Center for Advanced Engineering, 1986.

Dessler, Gary. *Human Resource Management.* New Jersey: Prentice Hall, 1997.

Drucker, Peter F. *The Effective Executive.* New York: Harper and Row, 1966.

———. *Management Challenges for the 21st Century.* New York: Harper Business, 1999.

———. *Managing for Results.* New York: Harper and Row, 1964.

———. *Managing in a Time of Great Change.* New York: Truman Talley Books/Dutton, 1995.

———. *The Practice of Management.* New York: Harper and Row, 1948.

———. *Toward the Next Economics.* New York: Harper and Row, 1981.

Ehrlich, Gretel. *Question of Heaven.* Boston, Mass.: Beacon Press, 1997.

Evans, Chris. *Breaking Free of the Shame Trap.* New York: Ballantine Books, 1994.

Fisher, Roger, and Alan Sharp. *Getting It Done; How to Lead When You're Not in Charge.* New York: Harper Business, 1999.

Foundation for Inner Peace. *A Course in Miracles.* Tamalais, Calif.: author, 1976.

Fox, Matthew. *The Reinvention of Work.* San Francisco: HarperCollins Publishers, 1994.

———. *Sheer Joy.* San Francisco: HarperCollins Publishers; 1992.

Frankel, Victor. *Man's Search for Meaning.* Boston: Washington Square Press, 1984.

Frazier, Craig. "Managing Oneself." *Harvard Business Review.* March/April 1999, 65–74.

Fuller, Buckminster. *Critical Path.* New York: St. Martin's Press, 1982. Gabor, Andrea.

Gabor, Andrea. *The Man Who Discovered Quality: How W. Edwards Deming Brought the Quality Revolution to America—The Stories of Ford, Xerox, and Ford.* New York: Times Books/Random House, 1990.

Gallwey, W. Timothy. *The Inner Game of Work*. New York: Random House, 2000.

Gerber, Michael. *The E Myth: Why Most Small Businesses Don't Work and What to Do About It*. Cambridge, Mass.: Ballinger Press, 1985.

Goldratt, Eliyahu, and Jeff Cox. *The Goal: A Process of Ongoing Improvement*. New York: North River Press, 1987.

Gouillart, Francis J. and James N. Kelly. *Transforming the Organization*. New York McGraw-Hill, 1995.

Harkness, Helen. *Don't Stop the Career Clock*. Palo Alto-Davies-Black, 1999.

Holmes, Ernest. *The Science of Mind*. New York: G. P. Putnam's Sons, 1988.

Howard, Jennifer M., and Lawrence M. Miller. *Team Management: Creating Systems and Skills for a Team-Based Organization*. N.p.: Miller How, 1994.

Hutchins, Greg. *ISO 9000: A Comprehensive Guide to Registration, Audit Guidelines, and Successful Certification*. New York: Wiley, 1997.

————. *Taking Care of Business: Quality Lessons from the Corner Office to the Factory Floor*. Somerset, N.J.: John Wiley and Sons, 1994.

Jensen, Bill. *Simplicity: The New Competitive Advantage in a World of More, Better, Faster*. Cambridge, Mass.: Perseus Books, 2000.

Johnson, Robert. *Ecstasy: Understanding the Psychology of Joy*. New York: Harper and Row, 1987.

Kahn, Jeffrey P., M.D. *Mental Health in the Workplace*. New York: Van Norstrad Reinhold, 1993.

Kantner, Rob. *The ISO 9000 Answer Book*. 1993.

Keyes Jr., Ken, and Penny Keyes. *Handbook to Higher Consciousness: The Workbook*. Coos Ore.: Love Line Books, 1989.

Kondrasuk, Jack, Mary Riley, and Walt Hall. "If We Want to Pay for Performance, How Do We Judge Performance?" *Journal of Compensation and Benefits*. 15, no. 2 (September/October 1999): 35–40.

The Koran. Translated by N. J. Dawood. New York: Penguin Books, 1990.

The Koran. Translated by J. M. Rodwell. London, 1968.

Kotter, John P., and James Heskett. *Corporate Culture and Performance*. New York: Free Press, 1992.

Kotter, John P. *The New Rules*. New York: Free Press, 1995.

Kuhn, Thomas. *Structure of Scientific Revolutions*. Chicago: University of Chicago Press, 1962.

Lama, Dalai. *Ethics for the New Millennium*. New York: Penguin Putnam, 1999.

Lawton, Robin. *Creating a Customer-Centered Culture: Leadership in Quality, Innovation, and Speed*. Milwaukee: Quality Press, 1993.

Lee, Blaine. *The Power Principle*. New York: Simon and Schuster, 1997.

Levering, Robert. *A Great Place to Work*. New York: Random House, 1998.

Levine, Stuart R., and Michael A. Crom. *The Leader in You*. New York: Simon and Schuster, 1993.

Lichtenberg, Ronna. *Work Would Be Great If It Weren't for the People*. New York: Hyperion, 1998.

Maccoby, Michael. *Harvard Business Review*. "Narcissistic Leaders: the Incredible Pros, the Inevitable Cons." (January/February 2000). 68–77.

Manin-Morrissey, Mary. *Building Your Field of Dreams*. New York: Bantam Books, 1996.

Mondavi, Robert. *Harvests of Joy*. San Diego: Harcourt Brace, 1998.

Morgan, John Brooke. *How to Keep a Sound Mind*. New York: Macmillan, 1939.

Naisbitt, John. *High Tech High Touch: Technology and Our Search for Meaning*. New York: Broadway Books, 1999.

Nanus, Burt. *Visionary Leadership*. San Francisco: Jossey-Bass, 1992.

Naranjo, Claudio. *Enneatypes in Psychotherapy*. Prescott, Ariz.: Hohm Press, 1995.

O'Brien, Michael J., and Larry Shook. *Profit from Experience*. Austin: Bard and Stephen, 1995.

Pasquale, Richard, Mark Milleman, and Linda Gioja. *Surfing the Edge of Chaos*. New York: Crown Business, 2000.

Peck, M. Scott. *A Different Drum*. New York: Simon and Schuster, 1987.

———. *A World Waiting to Be Born*. New York: Bantam Books, 1993.

Pepa, Barbara Kate. *Employees' Rights in the Workplace*. Berkeley: Nolo Press, 1999.

Peters, Tom. *Liberation Management*. New York: Knopf, 1992.

———. *The Pursuit of WOW*. New York: Random House, 1994.

———. *Thriving on Chaos*. New York: Harper Perennial, 1987.

Radhakrishnan, S. *The Bagavadgita*. N.p.: South Asia Books, 1993.

Riley, Mary. *Corporate Healing: Solutions to the Impact of the Addictive Personality in the Workplace*. Deerfield Beach, FL.: Health Communications, 1990.

Rockefeller, John D. *Big Business: Economic Power in a Free Society*. New York: Doubleday, Page, 1908.

Rosen, Robert H. *The Healthy Company: Eight Strategies to Develop People, Productivity, and Profits*. Los Angeles: Jeremy P. Tarcher, 1991.

———. *Leading People: The Eight Proven Principles for Success in Business*. New York: Penguin Books, 1996.

Ruiz, Don Miguel. *The Four Agreements*. San Rafael, Calif.: Amber-Allen Publishing, 1997.

Ryan, Kathleen, and Daniel Oestreich. *Driving Fear Out of the Workplace*. San Francisco: Jossey-Bass, 1991.

Sheindlin, Judge Judy. *Beauty Fades, Dumb Is Forever*. New York: HarperCollins, 1999.

Senge, Peter. *The Fifth Discipline: The Art and Practice of the Learning Organization*. New York: Doubleday/Currency, 1990.

Senge, Peter et al., *The Fifth Discipline Fieldbook: Strategies and Tools for Building a Learning Organization*. New York: Doubleday/Currency, 1994.

Stephanopoulos, George. *All Too Human: A Political Lesson*. New York: Little, Brown, 1999.

Tannen, Deborah. *The Argument Culture: Stopping America's War of Words*. New York: Ballantine Books, 1998.

Templeton, John Marks "Worldwide Laws of Life: 200 Eternal Spiritual Principles Templeton Foundation Press London 1997.

Tichy, Noel M., and Stratford Sherman. *Control Your Destiny or Someone Else Will*. New York: Doubleday, 1993.

Ury, William. *Getting Past No: Negotiating Your Way from Confrontation to Cooperation*. New York: Bantam Books, 1991.

Walsch, Neale Donald. *Conversations with God*. New York: Putnam and Sons, 1995.

————. *Friendship with God*. New York: Putnam and Sons, 1999.

Williamson, Marianne. *The Healing of the Soul of America*. New York: Simon and Schuster, 1997.

————. *A Return to Love*. New York: HarperCollins Publishers, 1992.

Wikland, Patricia. *Taking Charge When You're Not in Control*. New York: Ballantine Books, 2000.

Wilson, Thomas B. *Innovative Reward Systems for the Changing Workplace*. New York: McGraw Hill, 1995.

————."*You Don't have to Be CEO Anymore to Want to Rule the Internet.*" Fortune 141, no.3, February 7, 2000.

Zuckerman, Army. *ISO 9000 Made Easy: A Cost-Saving Guide to Documentation and Registration*. New York: AMACON, 1995.

Index

Page numbers in *italics* indicate figures; those in **bold** indicate tables.

Abrasive (light gray) behavior, **95, 286**
Abusive (dark gray) behavior, **95, 286**
Adult children and agreements, 179
Advanced Fiber Communications, 71
Against all odds, 179–80
Agreements creation, 181–202
  Alignment Agreement, *182–83*
  Alignment Agreement Follow-up, 181, *183–84,*
    185–86, *189,* 248
  Alignment auditors, 185, 187, 190
  conflict resolution, 201–2
  Conscious Communication, 201, 202
  Eight-Step Checklist for Effective Listening,
    193–201, 202
  family and listening, 199–201
  follow-up results, 187–93
  over-committing caution, 193
  resetting unkept agreements, 186–87
  "shadow side" and, 185
  See also Power of agreements; Rule 3: Keep
    Agreements
Albom, Mitch, 269–70
Alignment Agreement, *144–45, 176–77, 182–83*
Alignment Agreement Follow-up, 181, *183–84,*
  185–86, *189,* 248
Alignment auditors, 185, 187, 190
Alignment Meeting (Step 4), *244–45, 246,*
  246–49
Alignment Tool, *89–91, 89–92,* 94
All Too Human (Stephanopoulos), 214
American Journal of Compensation and Benefits, 238
Americans with Disabilities Act, 109
Aquinas, Thomas, 50
Argument Culture, The (Tannen), 96
Aristotle, 271
Armstrong, Karen, 289–90

Balanced contribution, 62–63
Baron, Robert, 281
Barrington, Michael, 109
Behavior and mid-managers, 280–87
Bethune, Gordon, 63
Big Business (Rockefeller), 22
Blaming, 21–22
Blanchard, Ken, 119, 270
Borderline personalities, 107–9, 111–12
Bradford, David, 135
Breaking Free of the Shame Trap (Evans), 60
Broken agreements, insight from, 175–78
Brooks, Sidney, 152
Buber, Martin, 290
Burns, George, 280
Business Hall of Fame, 288, 289
Business plan, 17–18
Business Week, 225, 279
Buy-in to Rules, 222–36
  input versus buy-in, 225–27
  Management by Objectives (MBO), 222, 224–25,
    226, 227
  Management by Two-Way Objectives
    (MBTWO), 227–34
  Management by Unstated or Unclear Objectives
    (MBUO), 223–25
  Rule 1: Everyone Contributes, 222–34
  Rule 2: No Put-downs, 234–36
  Rule 3: Keep Agreements, 222–34

Capacity to carry out agreements, 171–73
Careers from jobs, 44, 52–54
Carlson, Richard, 28
Carnegie, Andrew, 110
Carnegie, Dale, 28
Center for Non-Violent Communication, 286

CEO (Creative Entrepreneurial Opportunist), 1–15
  clean management, 3–4
  contributing to workplace, 3–4
  defining, 2–3
  employee effectiveness, 14
  financial and emotional health, 4–6
  implementing The Three Rules, 13
  intangibles, 4–5, 6
  Internet Revolution and, 1, 2, 69
  introspection for, 6
  leading oneself, 14–15
  manager effectiveness, 14
  responsibility-based leaders, 2
  Rule 1: Everyone Contributes, 5, 6–8
  Rule 2: No Put-downs, 5, 8–11, 10
  Rule 3: Keep Agreements, 5, 11–12
  Three Rules, 5–6
Certification/accreditation procedures, 121–24
Chambers, John, 1, 69
Chaos creation, 23–24
Charismatic consensus, 217–18
Charles Schwab, 282–83
Churchill, Winston, 181
Clarifying contributions, 69–70
Clark, Margaret, 205
Clean management, 3–4
Commitments that hold up, 173–75
Complaints as customer input, 120
Conflict resolution, 201–2
Conscious Communication, 101–2, 135–46, 137,
  137–43, 144–45, 201, 202
Consensus building, 214–19
Constructive discontent, 115
Contagiousness of contribution, 56–58
Contribution, 50–66
  balanced contribution, 62–63
  careers from jobs, 52–54
  clarifying, 60–62
  contagiousness of, 56–58
  delegation skills for, 55–56
  determining, 54–59
  goals for, 32, 42–44, 63–66
  misaligned contributions, 58–59
  mission communication, 62
  mutual contribution, 50–51
  nonmaterial rewards, 65–66
  procedures for implementing, 51–52
  raises from, 59–62
  shame trap and raises, 60
  short-term contributions, 54
  See also Mutual contribution; Rule 1: Everyone
    Contributes
Controlled consensus building, 214–15

Conversations with God (Walsch), 287
Cooper, Robert R., 136, 155, 203, 238
Corporate Healing: Solutions to the Impact of the
  Addictive Personality in the Workplace (Riley),
  287
Corrections (Merrill), 73
Cost-benefit analysis, 29–30
Covey, Stephen, 28, 73, 78, 216, 273, 288, 292
Creative Entrepreneurial Opportunist. See CEO
Criticism without hope, 95–97

Dabefko, Dave, 288–89
Dalai Lama, 97, 260
Dark gray (abusive) behavior, 95, 286
Delegation skills, 55–56
Deming, Edward, 234, 287
Destructive employees, 112–14
Detachment for introducing Three Rules, 219–20
Dialogue consensus building, 216–18
Direct orders, 204–7
Direct request, 207–9
Disabled employees, 45–49
Distorted contributions, 35–39
Dole, Rod, 45–46
Don't Sweat the Small Stuff at Work (Carlson), 28
Door slammers, 33–34
Driving Fear Out of the Workplace (Ryan and
  Oestreich), 95
Drucker, Peter F.
  on Management by Objectives (MBO), 222, 224,
    226
  on managing one-self, 14–15
  on morale, 67
  on Personal Contribution Analysis, 70–71
  on quality, 34
  on responsibility-based leaders, 1, 2
  on strengths, building from, 129, 204, 252

Edison, Thomas, 110
Ego versus Second Opinion, 255–56
Egypt Air Flight 990 crash, 274–76
Ehrhart, Werner, 140
Eight-Step Checklist for Effective Listening,
  100–101, 193–201, 202
Einstein, Albert, 269
Ellisan, Larry, 110
Emerson, Ralph Waldo, 237
Empire building, 26
Employee requests of mid-managers, 41
Entropy in workplace, 16–30
  blaming, 21–22
  business plan, 17–18
  chaos creation, 23–24

cost-benefit analysis, 29–30
defined, 16–17
empire building, 26
gossiping, 22
PricewaterhouseCoopers (PwC) cost-benefit analysis, 29–30
procrastinating, 23
sabotage prevention, 18–28
self-sabotage, 20–21
simplicity of Three Rules, 28–29
stealing, 24–25
substance abuse, 25
subtle sabotage, 19
withholding information, 27–28
See also Rule 1: Everyone Contributes
Ethics for the New Millennium (Dalai Lama), 97
Evans, Christine, 60
Executive contribution principles, 31–32
Executive EQ: Emotional Intelligence in Leadership and Organizations (Cooper and Sawaf), 155, 203, 238

Families
listening and, 199–201
Rule 1: Everyone Contributes, 47–49
Rule 3: Keep Agreements, 162–67, 178
Farrell, Mary, 47
Feelings Chart, 103, 137
Fifth Discipline: The Art and Practice of A Learning Organization, The (Senge), 16
Financial and emotional health, 4–6
Fiorina, Carly, 215
"Five Key Ways Executives Advise on Building Consensus among Managers" (Stettner), 215
Flex Products, Inc., 71–72, 173, 174
Follow-up results, 187–93
Ford, Henry, 110
Four Agreements, The (Ruiz), 151
Fox, Matthew, 270
Frese, Bridget, 289
Frese, Fred, 289
Freud, Sigmund, 110
Friendship with God (Walsch), 256
Funnel/Gap Analysis, 126–27, *128*
Funnel Tool, 81–88, *83, 87–88*, 92–93, 243–44, *245, 247*

Galvin, Bob, 31, 81
Gap analysis, 126–27, *128*
Gates, Bill, 110
Generations: The History of America's Future: 1584-2069 (Howe), 293
Gittins, Bill, 250

Globalization impact on workplace, 274–79
Global profit from contributions, 44–45
Global view of agreements, 152–53
Goals for contributions, 32, 42–44, 63–66
Goman, Carol, 254
Gossiping, 22
Graves, Steve, 154
Green, Don, 71
Gregorsky, Frank, 293
Group input for Three Rules, 211–13
Group setting and Second Opinion, 269–70
Gulick, Luther, 222

Handbook to Higher Consciousness (Keyes), 288
Hardy, Mike, 216, 217
Harris v. Oregon Health Services, 109
Harvard Business Review, 109
Harvest of Joy (Mondavi), 217, 219
Haskvitz, Sylvia, 286
Head, Don, 227–31
Headman, Keith, 282–83
Healing of the Soul of America 1997, The (Williamson), 256
Henning, Paul, 173
High Tech High Touch (Naisbitt), 45, 46, 248, 279
Hope from criticism, 116–17
Hostility management, 138–46, *144–45*
Howe, Neil, 293
How to Keep a Sound Mind (Morgan), 271
Hua, Wang, 237–38
Human Resources (HR) and Professional Growth Plan (PGP), 238
Humble Approach, The (Templeton), 255

"If We Want to Pay for Performance, How Do We Judge Performance?" (Kondrasuk and Wang), 238
Impasses, 84–92
Implied agreements, **156–61**, 156–62
Incivility in workplace, 280–87
Inner Solution. *See* Second Opinion
Input versus buy-in, 225–27
"Instant consciousness doubler," 288–89
Intangibles, 4–5, 6
International Standards Organization (ISO), 121
Internet Revolution, 1, 2, 69
Introducing Three Rules, 203–21
charismatic consensus, 217–18
consensus building, 214–19
controlled consensus building, 214–15
detachment for, 219–20
dialogue consensus building, 216–18
direct orders for, 204–7

Introducing Three Rules (*continued*)
  direct request for, 207–9
  foundation laying for, 220–21
  group input for, 211–13
  manipulated consensus building, 215–16
  matter-of-fact style of direct order, 206–7
  military style of direct order, 204–5
  playful style of direct order, 205–6
  policies for, 146–49, *149–50*, 209–11, *210–11*
  political consensus building, 214
  self-awareness for, 203–4
  structure to carry out rules, 213
  synergy consensus building, 216–18
  win-win style for, 209–11
Introspection, 6
Investors Business Daily, 215
ISO (International Standards Organization), 121
ITS (Irritation, Time, Strength), *130–32,* 130–35,
  134

Jetronics Company, *210–11*
Jobs, Steven, 110
Jordan, David, 16

Kao, John, 95
Keyes, Ken, 288
Kimper, Reverend Frank, 255
Knight-Rider Newspaper, 19
Kondrasuk, Jack, 237–38
Kotter, John, 274

Lawly, Susan, 179, 180
Leader in You: How to Win Friends and Influence People,
  The (Carnegie), 28
Leadership. *See* Buy-in to Rules; CEO (Creative
  Entrepreneurial Opportunist); Entropy in
  workplace; Introducing Three Rules; Mid-
  managers and Three Rules; Professional
  Growth Plan (PGP); Rule 1: Everyone
  Contributes; Rule 2: No Put-Downs; Rule 3:
  Keep Agreements; Second Opinion (Inner
  Solution)
Leadership by the Book (Blanchard), 270
Leading oneself, 14–15
Levin, Jack, 281
Lichtenberg, Ronna, 215–16
Light gray (abrasive) behavior, **95, 286**
Listening, Eight-Step Checklist for Effective,
  100–101, 193–201, 202
Love Those Millennials (Gregorsky), 293

Maccoby, Michael, 109–10
Mahatma Gandhi, 155, 238

Majerowicz, Vincent, 45–46
Management by Objectives (MBO), 222, 224–25,
  226, 227
Management by Two-Way Objectives (MBTWO),
  227–34
Management by Unstated or Unclear Objectives
  (MBUO), 223–25
Management Challenges for the 21st Century (Drucker),
  14, 129
Management versus union, 169–71
Manager effectiveness, 14
Manin-Morrissey, Mary, 76
Manipulated consensus building, 215–16
Matter-of-fact style of direct order, 206–7
MBO (Management by Objectives), 222, 224–25,
  226, 227
MBTWO (Management by Two-Way Objectives),
  227–34
MBUO (Management by Unstated or Unclear
  Objectives), 223–25
Measuring contribution, 35
Merrill, Roger, 73
Mid-managers and Three Rules, 274–94
  behavior and, 280–87
  dark gray (abusive) behavior, **286**
  Egypt Air Flight 990 crash, 274–76
  globalization impact, 274–79
  incivility in workplace, 280–87
  "instant consciousness doubler," 288–89
  juggling, 39–45, **40–41**
  light gray (abrasive) behavior, **286**
  millennials (new generation), 292–93
  private or public displays, 290–92
  private spiritual growth, 292
  public conflict resolution, 288–89
  religion versus spirituality, 289–90
  spirituality in workplace, 289–90
  technology impact, 279–80
  Three Rules and, 274
  values and, 291–92
  violence in workplace, 281–85
Military style of direct order, 204–5
Millennials (new generation), 292–93
Milosz, Czeslaw, 185
Misaligned contributions, 58–59
Mission statements, 32, 62, 67–73, *68–71*
Mitroff, Jan, 290
Mondavi, Cesare, 153
Mondavi, Robert, 72, 153, 217, 219
Morgan, Burton, 205
Morgan, Jack, 153
Morgan, John Brooke, 271–73
Mother Teresa, 53–54, 204

Mutual contribution, 50–51, 67–94
  Alignment Tool, *89–91, 89–92,* 94
  clarifying contributions, *69–70*
  Funnel Tool, 81–88, *83, 87–88,* 92–93
  impasses, 84–92
  Internet Revolution and, 1, 2, 69
  mission statements, 32, 62, 67–73, *68–71*
  Personal Contribution Analysis, 70–71, *70–71*
  personal mission statements, *73–76*
  requests and positive outcomes, 92–93
  truth to power, 81, 89
  values in mission statements, 71–72
  visualization for, 78–80
  See also Contribution; Rule 1: Everyone
    Contributes

Naisbitt, John, 45, 248, 279
Narcissistic bosses, 109–11
"Narcissistic Leaders: The Incredible Pros, the
    Inevitable Cons" (Maccoby), 109
Nastke, Jason, 293
New generation (millennials), 292–93
New Year's Eve/Day 2000, 278–79
New York Times, 92, 106, 185
Noland, Rich, 237
Nonmaterial rewards, 65–66
Number One Request Identification (Step 3),
    243–44, *245*

Oestreich, Daniel, 95
Office Automation and Administration, 179
Opportunities from agreement keeping, 153–54
Orfalea, Paul, 205
Otté, Father Joseph, 233
Out of Crisis (Deming), 287
Over-committing agreements, 193

Participation versus contribution, 32–33
Peck, M. Scott, 135, 280–81
Penny counters, 34
Perceived put-downs, 120–21
Performance review. *See* Professional Growth Plan
    (PGP)
Personal Contribution Analysis, 70–71, *70–71*
Personality disorders, 106–9
Personal mission statements, *73–76*
PGP. *See* Professional Growth Plan
Plant Services, 250
Playful style of direct order, 205–6
Policies for Three Rules, 146–49, *149–50,* 209–11,
    210–11
Political consensus building, 214
Positive requests from put-downs, 98–99, 111–12,

115–19, 124–26
Power of agreements, 169–80
  adult children and, 179
  Alignment Agreement, *176–77*
  against all odds, 179–80
  broken agreements, insight, 175–78
  capacity to carry out, 171–73
  commitments that hold up, 173–75
  families and, 178
  management versus union, 169–71
  See also Agreements creation; Rule 3: Keep
    Agreements
Power of No Put-downs, 115–28
  certification/accreditation procedures and,
    121–24
  complaints as customer input, 120
  constructive discontent, 115
  Funnel/Gap Analysis, 126–27, *128*
  gap analysis, 126–27, *128*
  hope from criticism, 116–17
  perceived put-downs, 120–21
  positive requests from put-downs, 98–99,
    111–12, 115–19, 124–26
  safety from zero tolerance, 118–19
  zero tolerance for put-downs, 118–19
  See also Responsible communications; Rule 2: No
    Put-downs
Pre-Review (Steps 1 & 2), *240–42, 243*
PricewaterhouseCoopers (PwC), 29–30
Private or public displays, 290–92
Private spiritual growth, 292
Procrastinating, 23
Professional Growth Plan (PGP), 237–53
  Alignment Follow-up, 248
  Alignment Meeting (Step 4), 244–45, *246,*
    246–49
  benefits of, 249
  example, 249–51
  Funnel Tool, 243–44, *245, 247*
  Human Resources (HR) and, 238
  Number One Request Identification (Step 3),
    243–44, *245*
  objectives of, 239
  Pre-Review (Steps 1 & 2), *240–42, 243*
  tailoring, 252–53
  Three Rules and, 239
Public conflict resolution, 288–89
Put-downs. *See* Rule 2: No Put-downs
PwC (PricewaterhouseCoopers), 29–30

Raises from contributions, 59–62
Realigning goals, 42–44
Religion versus spirituality, 289–90

Requests
  positive from put-downs, 98–99, 111–12,
    115–19, 124–26
  positive outcomes from, 92–93
  put-downs versus, 96
Resentment removal from put-downs, 99–105
Resetting unkept agreements, 186–87
Responsibility-based leaders, 2
Responsible communications, 129–50
  Alignment Agreement, *144–45*
  Conscious Communication, 135–46, 137,
    137–43, 144–45
  Feelings Chart, 103, 137
  hostility management, 138–46, *144–45*
  ITS (Irritation, Time, Strength), *130–32,*
    130–35, *134*
  policies for, 146–49, *149–50, 209–11, 210–11*
  See also Power of No Put-downs; Rule 2: No
    Put-downs
Rockefeller, John D., 3, 22, 62, 110, 256
Roddick, Anita, 31, 44–45
Roosevelt, Eleanor, 115, 284
Rotary International, 277–78
Ruiz, Don Miguel, 151, 169
Rukeyser, Louis, 47
Rule 1: Everyone Contributes, 31–49
  buy-in generation for, 222–34
  careers from jobs, 44
  disabled employees and, 45–49
  distorted contributions, 35–39
  door slammers versus, 33–34
  employee requests of mid-managers, 41
  executive contribution principles, 31–32
  family application of, 47–49
  global profit from, 44–45
  goals for, 32, 42–44, 63–66
  measuring contribution, 35
  mid-managers juggling, 39–45, 40–41
  overview, 5, 6–8
  participation versus, 32–33
  penny counters versus, 34
  realigning goals, 42–44
  top management requests of staff, 40
  See also Contribution; Mutual contribution
Rule 2: No Put-downs, 95–115
  borderlines and, 107–9, 111–12
  buy-in generation for, 234–36
  Conscious Communication, *101–2*
  criticism without hope, 95–97
  dark gray (abusive) behavior, 95
  destructive employees and, 112–14
  Eight-Step Checklist for Effective Listening,
    100–101

Feelings Chart, 103, 137
  light gray (abrasive) behavior, 95
  narcissistic bosses and, 109–11
  overview, 5, 8–11, 10
  personality disorders exposure, 106–9
  positive requests underneath put-downs, 98–99,
    111–12, 115–19, 124–26
  requests versus put-downs, 96
  resentment removal from, 99–105
  sabotage from put-downs, 97–98
  self-empowerment for, 111–12
  spiritual practices for managing, 105–6
  truth to power, 99
  See also Power of No Put-downs; Responsible
    communications
Rule 3: Keep Agreements, 151–68
  buy-in generation for, 222–34
  family and, 162–67
  global view of, 152–53
  implied agreements, 156–61, 156–62
  meaning of, 151–52
  opportunities from, 153–54
  overview, 5, 11–12
  self-empowerment from, 154–56
  "shadow side" and, 154–56
  trust building from, 152–54
  See also Agreements creation; Power of agreements
Ryan, Kathleen, 95

Sabotage
  prevention, 18–28
  put-downs and, 97–98
Safety from no put-downs, 118–19
Sargent, Tom, 237
Second Opinion (Inner Solution), 254–73
  case studies, 260–69
  conclusion from, 271–73
  ego versus, 255–56
  group setting and, 269–70
  obtaining, 257–60
  self-empowerment, 254–57
  spiritual incest, 270
  stress and careers, 254
Self-awareness for introducing Three Rules, 203–4
Self-empowerment, 111–12, 154–56, 254–57
Self-sabotage, 20–21
Senge, Peter, 16–17
Serenity Prayer, 67
Seven Habits of Highly Effective People, The (Covey),
    28, 73, 78, 216, 288, 292
"Shadow side," 154–56, 185
Shame trap and raises, 60
Shoft, Jerry, 215

Short-term contributions, 54
Simplicity of Three Rules, 28–29
Singapore, world city, 276–77
Snyder, Paul, 215
Sovos, George, 110
Spiritual
incest, 270
management of put-downs, 105–6
Spiritual Audit of Corporate America, A (Mitroff), 290
Spirituality in workplace, 289–90
Stealing, 24–25
Stephanopoulos, George, 214
Stettner, Morey, 215
Stress and careers, 254
Structure to carry out rules, 213
Substance abuse, 25
Subtle sabotage, 19
Sullivan, Michael, 71–72, 173–75
Sawaf, Ayman, 136, 155, 203, 238
Synergy consensus building, 216–18
Systemix Performance Appraisal, 239

Taking Charge When You're Not in Control (Wiklund), 1
Tannen, Deborah, 96–97
Technology impact on workplace, 279–80
Teller, Edward, 77
Templeton, Sir John, 1, 78, 255, 256
Thoreau, Henry David, 254
Three Rules, The. *See* Rule 1: Everyone Contributes; Rule 2: No Put-downs; Rule 3: Keep Agreements
Three Rules and Professional Growth Plan (PGP), 239
Top management requests of staff, 40
Total Quality Management (TQM), 231, 234

Toyota's 2000 Echo, 276
Trust building, 152–54
Truth to power, 81, 89, 99
Tuesdays with Morrie (Albom), 269–70

USA Today, 289

Values
mid-managers and, 291–92
mission statements and, 71–72
Vaught, George, 204–5, 214
Violence in workplace, 281–85
Visualization, 78–80

Wall Street Journal, 30
Wall Street Week, 47
Walsch, Neale Donald, 256, 287
Watson, Thomas, Sr. and Jr., 20
Weil, Andrew, 46
Welch, Jack, 110
Wendell, Lesley Mallow, 215
Wiklund, Patricia, 1
Wilkinson, Laura, 78
Williamson, Marianne, 255
Win-win style, 209–11
Withholding information, 27–28
Work Would Be Great If It Weren't for the People (Lichtenberg), 215
World Waiting to Be Born, A (Peck), 135, 280

Xerox Learning Systems (XLS), 22, 79, 118, 239

You Just Don't Understand Me (Tannen), 96

Zero tolerance for put-downs, 118–19
Zimmer, George, 8, 95